TR's Last War

ALSO BY DAVID PIETRUSZA

1932: The Rise of Hitler and FDR—Two Tales of Politics, Betrayal, and Unlikely Destiny

1948: Harry Truman's Improbable Victory and the Year That Transformed America

1960: LBJ vs. JFK vs. Nixon: The Epic Campaign That Forged Three Presidencies

1920: The Year of the Six Presidents

Rothstein: The Life, Times, and Murder of the Criminal Genius Who Fixed the 1919 World Series

Judge and Jury: The Life and Times of Judge Kenesaw Mountain Landis

Silent Cal's Almanack: The Homespun Wit and Wisdom of Vermont's Calvin Coolidge

Calvin Coolidge: A Documentary Biography

Calvin Coolidge on the Founders: Reflections on the American Revolution & the Founding Fathers

TR's Last War
Theodore Roosevelt, the Great War, and
a Journey of Triumph and Tragedy

David Pietrusza

Guilford, Connecticut

An imprint of Globe Pequot

Distributed by NATIONAL BOOK NETWORK

British Library Cataloguing in Publication Information available

Library of Congress Cataloging-in-Publication Data Available

ISBN 9781493028870 (cloth : alk. paper)
ISBN 9781493028887 (electronic)

♾™ The paper used in this publication meets the minimum requirements of American National Standard for Information Sciences—Permanence of Paper for Printed Library Materials, ANSI/ NISO Z39.48-1992.

Printed in the United States of America

Contents

Cast of Characters vii

"We must not weep" 1
"Murder on the High Seas" 7
"A noise like 10,000 babies" 17
"A true logothete, a real sophist" 33
"Pretty boys who know all of the latest tango steps" 53
"The most educational drama I have ever witnessed" 73
"Go home to Germany" 81
"The country is not in a heroic mood" 87
"Rules is rules here" 107
"When a weasel sucks eggs" 113
"One colossal figure of American manhood" 127
"The cowardly stab" 143
"Black blood crusted round their mouths" 159
"I'm only asking to be allowed to die" 181
"I wish I could get my hands on him!" 201
"Everybody works, but father" 217
"I would not have it otherwise" 231
"I have kept my promise" 247

Epilogue: "Death was the only relief" 287
Acknowledgments 297
Notes 299
Bibliography 345
Index 365
About the Author 383

Cast of Characters

James Edward Amos (1879–1954): TR's black valet and bodyguard.

Robert Bacon (1860–1919): TR's Harvard classmate and friend. Briefly his secretary of state. President of the pro-Preparedness National Security League. 1916 U.S. Senate candidate.

Newton Diehl Baker Jr. (1871–1937): Diminutive former progressive Democratic mayor of Cleveland. Woodrow Wilson's surprise choice as secretary of the army. Avowed pacifist.

Alexander W. Bannwart (1881–1959): Swiss-born, Boston-based pacifist. Henry Cabot Lodge's unlikely sparring partner.

William F. "Billy" Barnes Jr. (1866–1930): Albany-based Republican boss of New York State. No fan of TR or Charles Evans Hughes. Sued TR for libel in 1915.

Commodore James Stuart Blackton (1875–1941): English-born Vitagraph film executive. TR's Oyster Bay neighbor. Producer of 1915's pro-Preparedness epic *The Battle Cry of Peace*.

Charles Joseph Bonaparte (1851–1921): TR's secretary of the navy and later his attorney general. Active Progressive.

Senator William Edgar Borah (1865–1940): Idaho Republican US senator. A progressive but not a third-party Progressive.

John Gutzon de la Mothe Borglum (1867–1941): Prominent American sculptor. Progressive Party activist.

William Jennings "The Great Commoner" Bryan (1860–1925): Legendary voice of agrarian-based populism. Thrice-defeated Democratic presidential nominee. In 1915, the pacifist Bryan resigned as Wilson's secretary of state.

Dr. Nicholas Murray "Nicholas Miraculous" Butler (1862–1947): Columbia University president. A key player at 1916's GOP convention.

Joseph Hodges "Joe" Choate (1832–1917): Prominent Republican attorney. TR's first political mentor and his first ambassador to Britain.

Russell Jordan Coles (1865–1928): Noted marine hunter and naturalist. TR's host for his successful 1917 devilfish expedition.

Anna Roosevelt "Bye" Cowles (1855–1931): TR's older sister and trusted confidant.

Senator Albert Baird Cummins (1850–1926): Progressive Iowa U.S. senator. Dark horse candidate for 1916's GOP nomination.

Josephus Daniels (1862–1948): North Carolina populist Democrat newspaper publisher. Wilson's secretary of the navy. FDR's boss.

Ethel Carow Roosevelt Derby (1891–1977): TR's younger daughter. A nurse in France alongside her husband, Dr. Richard Derby.

Dr. Richard "Dick" Derby (1881–1963): Manhattan surgeon. TR's son-in-law. Winner of the Croix de Guerre with the American Medical Corps.

Charles Warren Fairbanks (1852–1918): TR's conservative former vice president. A dark horse for president in 1916 but was nominated again for vice president.

Senator Albert Bacon Fall (1861–1944): Senator from New Mexico. He nominated TR at 1916's GOP convention.

Charles Marron Fickert (1873–1937): San Francisco district attorney. TR forcefully opposed his recall.

Henry Ford (1863–1947): Creator of the Model "T" and the five-dollar workday. Much-ridiculed peace activist. 1918 Senate candidate.

Representative Augustus Peabody "Gussie" Gardner (1865–1918): North Shore Massachusetts GOP congressman. Henry Cabot Lodge's son-in-law. Pro-Preparedness.

James Rudolph Garfield (1865–1950): Son of President James A. Garfield. TR's secretary of the interior. Active Progressive.

Hannibal Hamlin "Hamlin" Garland (1860–1940): Popular novelist. TR's friend.

Lindley Miller Garrison (1864–1932): Wilson's first secretary of war. Resigned over Wilson's failure to support a four-hundred-thousand-man "continental army."

Samuel Gompers (1850–1924): British-born leader of the American Federation of Labor. Sparred with TR over 1917's bloody East St. Louis race riots.

John Campbell "Jack" Greenway (1872–1926): Rough Rider. Arizona mining executive. Prominent in 1917's Bisbee Industrial Workers of the World deportations.

Senator Warren Gamaliel Harding (1865–1923): Small-town Ohio newspaper editor, Republican politician, and philanderer. Republican National Convention chairman and keynoter in 1916.

William Harrison "Will" Hays Sr. (1879–1954): Republican National Committee chairman.

William Randolph Hearst (1863–1951): Controversial American press baron. Antiwar and anti-Wilson. A Democrat.

Colonel Edward Mandell House (1858–1938): Texas-born Democratic political operative. Wilson's powerful and cunning éminence grise.

Charles Evans Hughes (1862–1948): Progressive, reform governor of New York. Associate Supreme Court justice. Privately derided by TR as a "bearded icicle," the famously aloof Hughes reluctantly departed the high court to head 1916's Republican ticket.

Harold LeClair Ickes (1874–1952): Chicago attorney. Progressive Party activist.

Hiram Warren Johnson (1866–1945): TR's 1912 Progressive Party running mate. California governor. Ran for U.S. senator in 1916.

John T. King (1875–1926): Irish-Catholic GOP boss of Bridgeport, Connecticut. Backed TR for 1920.

Philander Chase Knox (1853–1921): TR's first attorney general. William Howard Taft's secretary of state. U.S. senator from Pennsylvania.

Senator Robert Marion "Fighting Bob" La Follette Sr. (1855–1925): Veteran Wisconsin progressive who danced to his own—and not TR's—tune. Antiwar.

Robert "Duke" Lansing (1864–1928): Wilson's pro-British second secretary of state.

John J. "Jack" Leary Jr. (1874–1944): *New York Tribune* correspondent. Member of Roosevelt's "newspaper cabinet."

Arthur Hamilton Lee, First Viscount Lee of Fareham (1868–1947): Aristocratic British Conservative Party politician. Honorary Rough Rider.

Walter Lippmann (1889–1974): *New Republic* editor. For TR in 1912, Wilson in 1916.

Senator Henry Cabot Lodge (1850–1924): Patrician Republican Massachusetts U.S. senator. TR's longtime friend and staunch ally on Preparedness. TR vainly pitched Lodge to Progressives as their 1916 nominee.

Alice Lee Roosevelt "Princess Alice" Longworth (1884–1980): TR's glamorous and intractable oldest child. Wife of Ohio GOP congressman Nicholas Longworth.

Representative Nicholas "Nick" Longworth III (1869–1931): TR's son-in-law. Ohio GOP congressman. For Taft in 1912.

Thomas Riley Marshall (1854–1925): Former governor of Indiana. Wilson's vice president.

Senator Joseph Medill "Medill" McCormick (1877–1925): "Brilliant but unstable" Progressive Party vice chairman. Elected to the U.S. Senate from Illinois in 1918.

John William "Mac" McGrath (1890–1924): Newfoundland-born Montreal hockey player. Secretary to TR and the faltering Progressive Party.

George von Lengerke Meyer (1858–1918): TR's postmaster general. Taft's secretary of the navy. Head of 1916's "Roosevelt Republican Committee."

Mayor John Purroy "The Boy Mayor" Mitchel (1879–1918): New York City "Fusion" reform mayor. Avidly pro-Preparedness. Doomed volunteer for the Army Air Corps.

Representative Victor Murdock (1871–1945): Kansas congressman and newspaperman. 1914 Progressive senatorial candidate.

George Albert Newett Sr. (1856–1928): Publisher of the *Ishpeming (MI) Iron Ore*. TR appointed him postmaster in 1906; sued him for libel in 1912.

John Callan "Cal" O'Laughlin (1873–1949): *Chicago Tribune* Washington correspondent.

Fremont Older (1856–1935): *San Francisco Bulletin* editor. Tussled with TR over District Attorney Charles Fickert's recall.

John Milliken Parker Sr. (1863–1939): Louisiana Progressive; the party's 1916 gubernatorial and vice presidential nominee.

Senator Boies "Big Grizzly" Penrose (1860–1921): Pennsylvania GOP boss. A formidably pro-tariff standpatter. Anti-TR in 1912.

George Walbridge Perkins (1862–1920): J. P. Morgan partner. Prominent Progressive Party official and financial angel, widely distrusted by its antibusiness wing but supported by TR.

Brigadier General John Joseph "Black Jack" Pershing (1860–1948): Commander in chief of American expeditionary forces in both Mexico and France.

Caroline "Carrie" Fulton Phillips (1873–1960): Vexatious, pro-German mistress of Ohio senator Warren Harding.

Amos Richards Eno Pinchot (1873–1944): Progressive Party stalwart. Gifford Pinchot's younger brother. Booted from the party for opposing wealthy TR backer George W. Perkins.

Gifford Pinchot (1865–1946): Ardent conservationist. Flashpoint of the TR-Taft rift. 1914 Pennsylvania Progressive gubernatorial candidate.

Dr. John Harold Richards (1881–1958): TR's English-born general practitioner.

Raymond Robins (1873–1954): Christian social worker. Chairman of 1916's Progressive National Convention.

Corinne Roosevelt "Pussie" Robinson (1861–1933): TR's gregarious younger sister. Edith Roosevelt's best friend. A published poet.

Douglas Robinson Jr. (1855–1918): Wealthy New York realtor. Corinne Roosevelt's husband.

Theodore Douglas Robinson (1883–1934): Douglas and Corinne Robinson's son. Progressive Republican New York state senator.

Anna Eleanor Roosevelt (1884–1962): Daughter of TR's younger brother, Elliott. Franklin Roosevelt's wife.

Captain Archibald Bulloch "Archie" Roosevelt (1894–1979): TR's second-youngest son. Badly wounded by enemy shrapnel in the knee and upper left arm in France.

Belle Wyatt Willard Roosevelt (1892–1968): Daughter of America's ambassador to Spain. Wed in Madrid, in June 1914, to Kermit Roosevelt.

Edith Kermit Carow "Edie" Roosevelt (1861–1948): TR's childhood sweetheart and second wife, mother of five of his children, stepmother to Alice Roosevelt. Her mercurial husband's emotional anchor.

Eleanor Butler Alexander Roosevelt (1889–1960): Married in 1910 to Theodore Roosevelt Jr. With her husband fighting at the front, and already the mother of his three children, she traveled to Paris to assist the YMCA.

Franklin Delano Roosevelt (1882–1945): Woodrow Wilson's assistant secretary of the navy. TR's fifth cousin. Married to TR's niece Eleanor. Covert TR ally in the battle for Preparedness.

Grace Stackpole Lockwood Roosevelt (1893–1971): Boston socialite. Married Archie Roosevelt in April 1917 as he prepared to depart for France.

Captain Kermit Roosevelt (1889–1943): TR's moody, alcoholic second-born son. His companion in exploring Africa and the Amazon. An officer with the British in Mesopotamia and the American Expeditionary Force in France.

Nicholas Roosevelt (1893–1982): TR's first cousin once removed.

First Lieutenant Quentin Roosevelt (1897–1918): TR's youngest, most promising—and best-loved—child. Shot down and killed northeast of Château-Thierry.

Colonel Theodore Roosevelt (1858–1919): Spanish-American War "Rough Rider." Former president. Failed 1912 Progressive presidential candidate. Opposed to "hyphenated-Americanism." Ardently pro-Preparedness. Virulently anti-Wilson.

Colonel Theodore "Ted Jr." Roosevelt III (1887–1944): TR's oldest son. Gassed and wounded in the summer of 1918.

William Emlen Roosevelt (1857–1930): TR's first cousin, close friend, personal financial adviser, and summertime next-door neighbor. Prominent New York banker. President of Roosevelt Hospital.

Elihu Root (1845–1937): Former GOP secretary of state and of war. U.S. senator from New York. Nobel Peace Prize winner. A respected—but septuagenarian—1916 presidential possibility.

Judge Samuel Seabury (1873–1958): New York State Court of Appeals justice; 1916 Democrat-Progressive gubernatorial candidate.

Sir Cecil Arthur "Springy" Spring-Rice (1859–1918): British ambassador to the United States. The best man at TR's second wedding.

Henry Lewis "Harry" Stimson (1867–1950): TR's U.S. attorney for the Southern District of New York. Taft's secretary of war. For Root in 1916.

Henry Luther Stoddard (1861–1947): Editor of the *New York Evening Mail*. TR's friend and fellow Progressive.

Oscar Solomon Straus (1850–1926): TR's German-Jewish-born secretary of commerce and labor. Bull Moose candidate for New York governor.

Josephine M. Stricker (1877–1944): TR's loyal German-Irish-descended private stenographer.

William Ashley "Billy" Sunday (1862–1935): Flamboyant barnstorming revivalist. Ardent TR enthusiast.

William Howard "Big Bill" Taft (1857–1930): TR's erstwhile protégé. Defeated for reelection by Wilson in 1912—and by TR's splitting of the GOP.

George Sylvester Viereck (1884–1962): Avant-garde poet and relentless German-American propagandist. Publisher of *The Fatherland* magazine. Reputed illegitimate grandson of Kaiser Wilhelm I. Onetime TR ally— then his impassioned foe.

Francisco "Pancho" Villa (né José Doroteo Arango Arámbula) (1878–1923): North Mexican rebel leader. Longtime *bandolero*.

Senator John Wingate Weeks (1860–1926): Massachusetts GOP U.S. senator. A 1916 favorite son.

Edith Newbold Jones Wharton (1862–1937): Expatriate American novelist. Friend of TR.

William Allen White (1868–1944): Nationally renowned editor of Kansas's *Emporia Gazette*. A passionate TR Progressive.

Governor Charles Seymour Whitman (1868–1947): Republican-Progressive governor of New York. For Hughes in 1916. In 1917, TR rejected Whitman's plan to place him in uniform.

Flora Payne "Foufie" Whitney (1897–1986): Quentin Roosevelt's slender, dark-haired socialite fiancée. TR disapproved of her fabulously wealthy (and Democratic) family—and vice versa.

Wilhelm II, Kaiser of Germany (Friedrich Wilhelm Viktor Albrecht von Preußen) (1859–1941): Bombastic, insecure, and widely hated kaiser of Germany.

Horace Simpson Wilkinson (1889–1937): Syracuse-based steel and steamship magnate. TR's Progressive Party ally and host during 1915's *Barnes v. Roosevelt* libel trial.

Edith Bolling Galt Wilson (1872–1961): The Washington, DC, jeweler's widow who became Woodrow Wilson's second wife.

Thomas Woodrow Wilson (1856–1924): President of Princeton. Reform Democratic governor of New Jersey. Elected president in 1912, trouncing TR and Taft. A progressive.

Owen "Dan" Wister (1860–1938): Author of the classic Western novel *The Virginian* (dedicated to TR). Roosevelt's close friend from Harvard days.

Major General Leonard Wood (1860–1927): TR's Spanish-American War comrade and staunch ally on the Preparedness issue—despite pushback from his civilian superiors in the Wilson administration.

"We must not weep"

THEODORE ROOSEVELT'S HEART LAY BROKEN NEAR CHÂTEAU-THIERRY amid a biplane's twisted wreckage.

Beside the lifeless body of a beloved son.

This early morning—Monday, September 30, 1918—Colonel Roosevelt neared Columbus, Ohio.

Barely four months previously, First Lieutenant Quentin Roosevelt had soared skyward on only his second combat mission. Two German bullets pierced his skull, and he was dead before he hit the ground.[1]

The Colonel's three older sons remained in France.

In March, red-hot shrapnel hideously ripped through Captain Archibald Roosevelt's flesh, severing the main nerve of his left arm and damaging his left knee. For fourteen hours, Archie lay wounded in the muck of no-man's-land. Doctors debated about amputating his mutilated leg. It survived. His arm remained crippled.[2]

At Cantigny, TR's oldest son, Major Theodore Roosevelt Jr., was gassed in the eyes and lungs. At Ploisy, southwest of Soissons, "Ted" charged helmetless against a machine-gun nest. A German bullet caught him above his own left knee.[3] A fourth son, Captain Kermit Roosevelt, fresh from duty with the British in Mesopotamia, was now assigned to an American artillery unit on the Meuse-Argonne.[4] TR's son-in-law, Dr. Richard Derby, also served in France—none the worse for wear for being sent skyward by an exploding German shell.[5]

TR craved to fight alongside them. He could not. But stateside he could still wield words as weapons.

Like Jolson and Chaplin, Pickford and Fairbanks, he pitched war bonds. The nation's Fourth Liberty Loan Drive tendered a full $6 billion at 4.25 percent interest, redeemable in thirty years upon the full faith and credit of the United States in gold.[6]

War costs a great deal—in treasure and in blood.

TR peddled more than bonds. He sold "Preparedness"—with a capital *P*. He demanded Preparedness in the fitful lead-up to war. He argued for it now—and for increased armaments and training in the peace to follow. Two days previously, he had spoken at a Baltimore ballpark, arguing for a permanent peacetime "universal service"—for men and women alike. "The man who will not render this service has no right to vote," he thundered, and possesses "no place in a republic like ours and should be expelled from it."[7]

Some at Columbus feared TR might excoriate President Woodrow Wilson. To TR, the vacillating Wilson was "the worst President we have had since Buchanan, an even worse President than Taft"[8]—a chief executive responsible for the deaths of too many neutral Americans on the high seas and, yes, of brave fighting men like Quentin Roosevelt.

TR arrived in Columbus at 7:00 a.m. sharp, facing another grueling day. Meetings and rallies, bands and dignitaries. Aeroplanes overhead. Ceremonies commemorating the local war dead. Even a photographic portrait sitting[9] and a hasty, unscheduled out-of-town detour to visit a bedridden Spanish-American War comrade.[10] "How I loathe it!"[11] he would complain of the tour upon its completion.

At Columbus, however, good tidings greeted him. German might was crumbling. Allied armies advanced along the western front. Berlin's exhausted ally Bulgaria had surrendered. The Ottoman and Austro-Hungarian empires neared capitulation. Germany might soon follow.

At Columbus, TR learned that a serviceman wished to speak with him. In France, Lieutenant Christian Holmes had received a Distinguished Service Cross from Major Theodore Roosevelt Jr. and visited Quentin's makeshift grave, now liberated by advancing American troops. TR jumped at the chance to dine with him that night—but his host committee vetoed the idea. Seventeen guests were invited, and that was that.

"Tell the chairman that I want . . . the commandant at Camp Sherman and Lieutenant Christian Holmes to dinner at 6:30 p.m.," snapped TR.

Lieutenant Holmes dined with Roosevelt.[12]

At lunch, TR addressed a thousand Liberty Loan volunteers.[13] "Good old Columbus town," proclaimed the city's Democratic mayor, George Karb, "is signally honored by the presence here of this real patriotic, red-blooded American, the most successful and effective piece of fighting machinery ever born of woman. He is willing and ready to do his full share in putting the Kaiser and the whole Hohenzollern outfit so far under the ground they will never be heard of again."[14]

"In my youth, Mr. Mayor," TR responded, "I used to be quite fond of glove fighting and . . . was taught that when you've got a man groggy, put him out. I have more than once seen a fight lost . . . because the man that got his opponent groggy, held back and did not finish him. . . . If we oversubscribe the Liberty loan now it will dishearten every German, every man and every country of the Central allies. Let there be no letting up for a moment."[15]

As TR exited, the Colonel's longtime black valet and bodyguard, James Amos, recalled,

> *He passed a group of gold star mothers, and doubtless they were stirred by his address, coming from . . . a fellow sufferer. . . . [T]hey were weeping, and as he went by the sobbing became audible. He clenched his teeth, stopped, and turning to them, raised his hand to silence them so he could be heard and said:*
>
> *"We must not weep. Though I too have lost a dear one, I think only of victory. We must carry on no matter what the cost."*
>
> *But he had to swallow in order to talk.[16]*

This, Amos recalled, was "the nearest I saw him come to breaking down."

Quentin's ghost haunted TR. Urged to tour Columbus's "Khaki Club," a USO-like haven for visiting servicemen, he protested that he had time only to pop in and sign the guest register. But once inside, he met three doughboys who had attended services at Quentin's grave. He grasped their hands, unable to let go. "Take back with you to France," he begged them, "the appreciation of Quentin's mother and myself."[17]

Thousands thronged downtown. Rain fell off and on, building to occasional downpours. But by 4:30, twenty thousand persons awaited him. The parents of Columbus's war dead sat before TR. Wearier than he admitted, he balanced himself between his podium and an adjacent support stanchion. In staccato fashion, he unleashed a litany of patriotic talking points:

- "The man who loves America and some other country also is like a man who loves his wife, but other women more."
- "If America had been prepared the war would have been over ninety days after this country entered it."
- "We are paying the price of unpreparedness. What we want to do is to remain prepared so no nation will dare look cross-eyed at us."[18]

"But with the end of war in sight, we must prepare for peace," he urged. "We must see to it that the red flag of Anarchy has as little place in America as the black flag of German socialism. This creed ruined Russia and made it a byword for all the other nations of the world. We have got to be on our guard against the Romanoffs of the industrial world. Our business is to set our house in order with a better and wiser industrial system in the future."[19]

Ohio had decreed that as "Taps" sounded among U.S. troops in France, it would simultaneously play at every county courthouse—and at the state capitol itself.

As TR now implored "those at home to show a little of the idealism of their boys who have gone abroad," a bugler sounded the call's first note.

Roosevelt halted, standing silently transfixed. The crowd hushed, not only spellbound by the bugling but also taken by the sight of the black mourning band upon TR's sleeve. "Men bared their heads," a reporter noted. "In front of Col. Roosevelt in seats of honor sat the mothers and fathers of the dead. . . . Women wept unrestrainedly and men wiped their eyes. . . . Col. Roosevelt stood erect and silent, facing the bugler, until the call ended."[20]

Roosevelt finally resumed speaking, his voice now muted.

Friends, that is a very beautiful and significant ceremony. The bugle is sounding taps, because at this hour in France the day's work is done— not for those who are fighting, but for those behind the first line, for those who did their day's work yesterday and will do it tomorrow. And it is significant, because at this hour the day's work is done forever for not a few of the gallant souls, the best of our young men, on the other side.

That should serve as an appeal to us.[21]

The crowd wept. The anguished TR did not.
A real man never wept in public.
Nor might Theodore Roosevelt.

"Murder on the High Seas"

THEODORE ROOSEVELT STOOD TRIAL.

He was many things. Author. Editor. Soldier. Peacemaker. Conservationist. Explorer. Cowboy. Ornithologist. Governor. Police commissioner. Etc., etc., etc. He was also among our more litigious chief executives.

As plaintiff—and as defendant.

In October 1908, Joseph Pulitzer's *New York World* reported on possible profiteering from construction of the new Panama Canal—most significantly by Roosevelt's brother-in-law, the wealthy New York realtor Douglas Robinson Jr. TR instructed U.S. Attorney for the Southern District Henry L. Stimson to indict the blind and aged Pulitzer for criminal libel of the federal government. The U.S. Supreme Court unanimously threw the case out.[1]

TR was no stranger to controversy. William McKinley's chief adviser, Mark Hanna, famously considered him a "madman."[2] His October 1901 invitation of black educator Booker T. Washington to dine at the White House triggered a huge southern blowback, with Mississippi populist James K. Vardaman deriding TR as a "coon-flavored miscegenist."[3] During 1907's perilous financial crisis, critics accused him of insanity, drunkenness, and morphine addiction.[4] His erstwhile protégé and successor, William Howard Taft, damned him as a "demagogue," a "dangerous egotist," a "honeyfugler," and a "flatterer of the people."[5]

In May 1912, Cornell University "Professor of Mental Diseases" Dr. Allan McLane Hamilton penned a *New York Times* article, "The Perils of a Progressive Administration."[6] Hamilton warned of "the very great danger of electing Presidential candidates about whose sanity there was any doubt." The implication was obvious. "The querulent lunatic who may quarrel or find fault with everything and everybody," Hamilton (a grandson of *that* Hamilton) concluded, "is really a psychopathic individual, and should be looked upon with pity, or properly protected."[7]

In October 1912, George A. Newett, publisher of *The Iron Ore*, a newspaper in remote Upper Peninsula Ishpheming, Michigan, editorialized, "Roosevelt lies and curses in a most disgusting way; he gets drunk, too, and that not infrequently, and all his intimates know about it."[8] Rumors of drunkenness had long dogged TR, as he would later say, being "almost as widespread as the belief in my existence."[9] Meeting him, even admirers, like the young Chicago attorney Harold Ickes, checked to verify them.[10] They weren't true. Roosevelt rarely drank. As Henry Adams observed, the man was "drunk with himself and not with rum."[11]

By early 1912, Roosevelt was casting about to sue for "the heaviest kind of damages"[12] and finally put the rumors to rest.

He sued Newett (appointed by TR to a local mastership in 1906) for a hefty $10,000. At their May 1913 trial, TR summoned a spectacular array of character witnesses to verify his abstemious character: muckraker Jacob Riis, Spanish-American War hero and admiral of the navy George Dewey, the social gospel–preaching Reverend Lyman Abbott, and his old Rough Rider comrade, former army chief of staff General Leonard Wood.[13]

Newett's hopes rested on a single witness. In 1904, Newark newspaperman J. Martin Miller had edited an adulatory Roosevelt campaign tome, *The Triumphant Life of Theodore Roosevelt*. He later served as TR's consul at Rheims. But Miller now planned to testify about TR's imbibing at House Speaker Joseph "Uncle Joe" Cannon's May 1906 seventieth birthday party. TR branded Miller's allegation a "pure lie."[14]

When Manhattan authorities indicted Miller for passing a $100 bad check, he fled to Winnipeg, sinking Newett's defense.[15] When Newett contritely apologized, TR magnanimously requested that the jury award him only minimum damages. It did—six cents.[16]

However, a more perilous lawsuit loomed.

In 1914, Old Guard New York Republicans rallied behind crusading Manhattan district attorney Charles Seymour Whitman for governor.[17] TR—still technically a Progressive—endorsed former Binghamton state senator Harvey D. Hinman. His endorsement included a blast at state Republican chairman William F. "Billy" Barnes: "The State government is rotten throughout in almost all of its departments directly due to the dominance in politics of Mr. [Charles Francis] Murphy [of Tammany Hall] and his sub-bosses . . . aided and abetted when necessary by Mr. Barnes."[18]

Mr. Barnes sued Mr. Roosevelt for $50,000.[19]

For twenty years Barnes ("The Boy Boss") had ruled Albany County with an iron hand. He now controlled the entire state GOP and had his eye on a U.S. Senate seat. The typical political boss sprang from the backroom of a saloon. *Albany Evening Journal* publisher Barnes was the grandson of Thurlow Weed, a prominent founder of the Republican Party. Like TR, he sprang from Harvard. He graduated magna cum laude, just missing Phi Beta Kappa. He edited the *Harvard Crimson* and made the Hasty Pudding Club. Barnes was tough, and he was smart— "the most clear thinking of the conservative bosses,"[20] as Charles Evans Hughes conceded. Henry Stimson saw in him "more of principle and less of unadulterated bossism than many critics saw."[21]

"The [socialist/progressive] sea of experiment," Barnes argued that April, "offers no possibility of return. It is not within the power of the human mind having secured largesse—something for nothing—not to develop further demands for acquisition without performance. . . . The certain destination . . . will not be the attainment of the socialistic ideal but the tyrannous autocratic state."[22]

Barnes claimed to hate the word *progress* "because in its political sense progress means nothing good and may be synonymous with evils unless it is in the right direction, and most frequently, under the promptings of ill-considered popular demands and the reaction to these of cowardly men in public office, it is not."[23]

TR may not have been cowardly. But he was progressive. By suing Roosevelt, Barnes could salvage his own reputation and scuttle the damnably radical TR's—a boon service, in Barnes's view, to party, nation, and mankind.

Barnes and Roosevelt had once been uneasy allies, TR being a master politician, adept at dealing with his less virtuous counterparts whenever necessary. By 1910, however, not only had Barnes and Roosevelt tussled over a contentious direct primary bill, but TR had also bested Barnes to deliver the GOP gubernatorial nod to Henry Stimson. Two years later, Barnes delivered the votes that sank Theodore at 1912's fractious Republican National Convention.[24] A fact TR never forgot.

Four years earlier, Barnes and his brilliant counsel, William N. Ivins Sr., had successfully repulsed similar accusations of corruption, and Ivins now boasted to TR's ex–secretary of war Elihu Root that he would "nail Roosevelt's hide to the fence." Root, high on TR's list of enemies, sadly retorted, "I know Roosevelt, and you want to be very sure that it is Roosevelt's hide that you get on to the fence."[25]

Barnes was no pushover. But he was slipping. In June 1911, his older son, Thurlow Weed Barnes II, had suffered severe burns at the family's Nantucket boathouse. His drinking accelerated. "His naturally florid complexion is more than florid," observed the *Saturday Evening Post*. "He likes to eat and likes to drink, and he does a little more of each than is entirely good for him."[26]

By 1914, as one associate noted, Billy Barnes "had more wrath than judgment."[27]

He wanted his case tried in Albany County, where he controlled the courts. TR secured a change of venue to more progressive Syracuse. TR's Harvard classmate New York Supreme Court justice William Shankland Andrews presided.

The trial commenced on the rainy Monday morning of April 19, 1915.[28] Outside, admirers cheered the brown-suited, black-fedoraed TR. Curiosity seekers, well-wishers, and reporters jammed the 150-seat courtroom.

Barnes's witnesses included multimillionaire August Belmont and a rising Tammany officeholder, assembly minority leader Alfred Emanuel Smith. TR's most notable witness was a former upstate backbench state senator: his remote cousin Franklin Delano Roosevelt.

FDR was a Democrat; TR (on his more restrained days) was a Republican. Both were small *p* progressives and, more important, large *R* Roosevelts. In 1914, the precociously ambitious Franklin (now Woodrow Wilson's assistant secretary of the navy) pondered a gubernatorial race.

He drew back, fearing that TR himself might also run. "I will not run against him," said Franklin. "You know blood is thicker than water."[29]

In Syracuse, FDR introduced himself as "fifth cousin by blood [to the defendant] and nephew by law!"[30] He was not bad at all on the stand, though his appearance proved largely inconclusive. When FDR had entered the state senate in 1911, Democrats stood poised to appoint the state's next U.S. senator. Tammany proposed Wall Street lawyer William "Blue-Eyed Billy" Sheehan. FDR, leader of the Democratic reformers opposing Sheehan, had entreated Barnes for support. Barnes refused. Both Roosevelts considered that evidence of a long-standing Barnes-Tammany axis of corruption.

But witnesses meant little in Syracuse. How Barnes and TR comported themselves counted for everything. Barnes, grumpy and ill at ease, testified for parts of four days. TR testified for portions of nine days. He unleashed the whole of his charm, dazzling all with his amazing photographic memory, directly addressing the jurymen as if they were old friends. His chief counsel, New York City attorney John M. Bowers, meticulously presented evidence of Barnes's suspiciously lucrative state printing contracts.[31]

Yet TR had his concerns—some related to the case, some purely personal. A week before the trial opened, his second wife, Edith Kermit Roosevelt, entered Manhattan's Roosevelt Hospital for a "serious operation," most likely a hysterectomy. The news from war-torn Europe was not much better.

Distant Europe's quarrels were not our quarrels. But not far distant was the Atlantic Ocean. Desperately struggling for every advantage, both warring camps fought to control sea traffic, to starve their foes into submission, to choke off armaments and supplies. London's immense fleet imposed a near-impenetrable surface blockade. Berlin retaliated in less "gentlemanly" fashion. German U-boats proved their deadly worth. In September 1914, the U-9 sank three British cruisers within the space of a single hour, killing 1,459 crewmen.[32] In April 1915, the SM UB-4 torpedoed Britain's *Harpalyce*, America-bound to fetch relief supplies for Belgium. Flying a white flag, the *Harpalyce* bore huge white letters reading "Commission for Belgian Relief" on both bows. Fifteen of its forty-four crewmen died.[33]

An American mining engineer was among a hundred dead when the U-28 struck the British liner *Falaba* off the southern Irish coast on March 28. On April 28, a German airplane dropped three bombs on the American steamer USS *Cushing* as it approached Antwerp. On May 1, the U-30 torpedoed the U.S. oil tank steamer *Gulflight* bound for Rouen, costing three lives.[34]

TR damned the *Gulflight's* sinking as "piracy pure and simple."[35] But worse news soon arrived from the *Chicago Tribune's* Washington correspondent, John Callan "Cal" O'Laughlin. O'Laughlin was also TR's longtime friend, his former first assistant secretary of state, and a delegate to 1912's Progressive Party convention. In May 1913, he was among many journalists testifying for him against George Newett.

O'Laughlin had recently conferred with a German official just returned from Berlin. U-boats stood ready to sink the British Cunard Line's luxury passenger ship RMS *Lusitania* "without a moment's hesitation." Germany, O'Laughlin reported, believed that British leaders had "loudly proclaimed their intention to starve our peaceful people, women and children, so we need not bother about theirs being drowned incidentally."

"If I did not keep a grip on myself," Roosevelt fumed, "[it] would make me favor instant war with Germany."

"Lord," he exclaimed, "how I would like to be President in view of . . . the . . . possible sinking of the *Lusitania*. . . . [I]f any of our people were sunk on the *Lusitania* I would confiscate all the German interned ships." Regarding any German efforts to rally German- and Irish-Americans to the U.S. cause if war came, TR vowed to "hang any man [who] raised his little finger [to] put the union to a serious test."[36]

Two weeks earlier, the imperial German embassy had warned of the dangers of transatlantic travel. For months to come, the following ad ran in American newspapers:

NOTICE!

TRAVELLERS intending to embark on the Atlantic voyage are reminded that a state of war exists between Germany and her allies and Great Britain and her allies; that the zone of war includes the

waters adjacent to the British Isles; that, in accordance with formal notice given by the Imperial German Government, vessels flying the flag of Great Britain, or any of her allies, are liable to destruction in those waters and that travelers sailing in the war zone on the ships of Great Britain or her allies do so at their own risk.
IMPERIAL GERMAN EMBASSY
Washington, D.C. 22 April 1915[37]

At 2:08 p.m. on Friday afternoon, May 7, 1915, the RMS *Lusitania*, bound for Liverpool, lay eleven miles off the coast of southern Ireland. Well inside Germany's "zone of war" and flying an Allied flag, it was fair game for German "destruction."

Below the waves, thirty-year-old Kapitänleutnant Walther Schwieger maneuvered U-boat U-20. He shouted, "Fire!" and three hundred pounds of explosives ripped through the *Lusitania*'s starboard bow. Moments later, a second explosion rocked the wounded vessel. Some said it resulted from contraband munitions; New York's collector of customs reported that "180 cases of military goods; 1,271 cases of ammunition and . . . 4,200 cases of cartridges" had been on board.[38]

The torpedoing claimed 1,198 lives; 63 of the dead were infants and children. Composer Jerome Kern had booked passage but overslept. Novelist Elbert Hubbard and theatrical producer Charles Frohman ("Why fear death? It is the most beautiful adventure that life gives us"[39]) weren't so lucky. The fabulously wealthy playboy Alfred Gwynne Vanderbilt died a hero's death, giving his own lifejacket to a young mother and her infant child. Just 726 passengers and crew, just 4 of 30 babies, just 11 of 139 American citizens survived.[40]

In Syracuse, TR received a telegram: the *Lusitania* had been sunk. No details accompanied the missive, not even the number of dead. He boiled with rage.

Justice Andrews adjourned the day's proceedings. TR hiked back to the opulent mansion of steel and steamship magnate and Progressive Party activist Horace S. Wilkinson, where he lodged throughout the five-week trial ("the Wilkinsons were simply trumps"[41]). That night, the *Lusitania* and not *Barnes v. Roosevelt* preyed upon his mind.

His trial neared completion. His acquittal seemed assured. But two or three members of the jury were German-Americans. Alienating them—as his earlier comments denouncing German aggression had already angered other German-Americans—might yet yield a Barnes' victory. "Well, it doesn't make any difference," TR concluded. "It is more important that I be right than to win this suit. I've got to be right in this matter."[42]

He retired early, reading in bed, as was his practice. Around midnight, an Associated Press reporter called, seeking a statement on the *Lusitania*. TR demanded to know the death toll. "That's murder!" he exclaimed. "Will I make a statement? Yes, yes. I'll make it now. Just take this."[43] He declared, "This represents not merely piracy, but piracy on a vaster scale of murder than old-time pirates ever practised. . . . It is warfare against innocent men, women and children, traveling on the ocean, and our own fellow-countrymen and country-women, who are among the sufferers. It seems inconceivable that we can refrain from taking action in this matter, for we owe it not only to humanity but to our own self-respect."[44]

Newspapers broadcast his words nationwide. At the courthouse, TR apologized to his defense team: "Gentlemen, I am afraid that I have made the winning of this case impossible. . . . [W]e have two German-American jurors, whose sympathies I have likely alienated . . . but I cannot help it if we lose the case. There is a principle . . . far more vital to the American people than my personal welfare."[45]

That evening, Henry J. Whigham, the Scottish-born editor of *Metropolitan Magazine* ("The Magazine Col. Roosevelt Writes For"),[46] phoned. He wanted an article that would really sell: TR's thoughts on the *Lusitania*.

TR asked, "Has [Wilson] seized the ships?"[47] No, Wilson had not retaliated by seizing whatever German ships remained in American harbors. Enraged, TR dashed off his response. The result—"Murder on the High Seas"—could not, however, run before *Metropolitan Magazine*'s June edition. Whigham proposed releasing Roosevelt's white-hot sentiments to the press the following day. TR agreed.[48]

"Murder on the High Seas" read in part,

*In Queenstown [Ireland] there lay by the score the bodies of women
and children, some of the dead women still clasping the bodies of the
little children they held in their arms when death overwhelmed them.
. . . The action of the German submarines in the cases cited can be
justified only by a plea which would likewise justify the wholesale
poisoning of wells in the path of a hostile army, or the shipping of
infected rags into the cities of a hostile country: a plea which would
justify the torture of prisoners and the reduction of captured women
to the slavery of concubinage. . . .*

*[W]e earn as a nation measureless scorn and contempt if we fol-
low the lead of those who exalt peace above righteousness, if we heed
the voice of those feeble folk who bleat to high Heaven for peace when
there is no peace. For many months our Government has preserved
between right and wrong a neutrality which would have excited the
emulous admiration of Pontius Pilate—the arch-typical neutral of all
time. . . . Unless we act with immediate decision and vigor we shall
have failed in the duty demanded by humanity at large and demanded
even more clearly by the self-respect of the American Republic.*[49]

On Monday morning, a local reporter approached TR. Germany had
dispatched its regrets over the *Lusitania*'s sinking—though also protesting that the liner had carried war supplies.

A scowling TR muttered, "That is no excuse," before vowing silence
on the matter.

The reporter told him of the *New York Herald*'s headline in that
morning's edition: "WHAT A PITY THEODORE ROOSEVELT IS
NOT PRESIDENT!"[50] TR burst out laughing. "Isn't that singular!" he
roared. "Isn't that funny?"

A barrage of telegrams from New York newspaper editors begged
him for comment. "The colonel was visibly moved by [them]," the *Syracuse Journal* observed. "Several times a flush overspread his face and it
appeared as if he was having difficulty in restraining his true feelings on
the matter."[51]

But he wouldn't budge.

He and Barnes had different ways of dealing with the stress of the trial. Barnes doodled away, constantly drawing flocks of sheep.[52] That Friday, TR had commenced reading a rare volume of Aristophanes's *The Anarchians*, provided by Barnes's counsel Ivins.[53] Today, however, he could not concentrate on it at all.[54]

Later that Monday, he broke his silence. In Philadelphia, Wilson proclaimed to four thousand naturalized citizens, many German-born,[55] "There is such a thing as a man being too proud to fight. There is such a thing as a nation being so right that it does not need to convince others by force that it is right."[56]

TR despised barbarity, but he despised spinelessness more. To him, no nation embodied wretched, cowardly feebleness than supine and defenseless China, a once-proud empire now unworthy of nationhood. And so, he fumed,

> *China is entitled to draw all the comfort she can from [Wilson's Philadelphia] statement, and it would be well . . . to ponder seriously what the effect upon China has been of managing her affairs during the past fifteen years on the theory thus enunciated.*
>
> *If the United States is satisfied with occupying some time in the future the precise international position that China now occupies, then the United States can afford to act on this theory.*
>
> *I do not believe the assertion of our rights means war, but we will do well to remember there are things worse than war. Let us, as a nation, understand that peace is worthy only when it is the handmaiden of international righteousness and of national self-respect.*[57]

TR had declared war—on Woodrow Wilson.

"A noise like 10,000 babies"

THE *LUSITANIA* SANK.

And so did Billy Barnes.

His capsizing required two nights, forty-two and a half hours of jury deliberations, forty ballots, and a single holdout juror, a Republican streetcar motorman named Edward Burns,[1] who insisted that both parties split the $65 court costs.[2] In the end, TR won his case, posed for pictures with the jury—and invited all, including Burns, to Sagamore Hill.[3]

Barnes had sued for $50,000. To avoid paying him (and, more important, to avoid confessing error), TR expended somewhere between $42,000[4] and $52,000.[5] He recovered just $1,443.[6]

But it was worth it. The case resuscitated his battered reputation as a slayer of bosses and special interests, the white knight of American politics. It positioned him exactly where he had to be when the *Lusitania* went under: amid an adoring gaggle of news-hungry reporters.

Indeed, Theodore Roosevelt had been dead and buried in a grave of his making, the headstone pointedly engraved "1912."

But not anymore.

TR was a wildly successful president. Abroad, he resolved disputes involving German and French interests in Morocco and German and British conflicts over Venezuelan debts. He concluded the Russo-Japanese War and reached a face-saving "gentlemen's agreement" with Tokyo. Speaking softly but carrying a big stick, he dispatched our Great White Fleet around the world. If the Caribbean was not already "an American lake" when he assumed office, it was when he departed. He dispatched troops to quell a revolt in Cuba's infant republic and strong-armed the recalcitrant Republic of Colombia to secure Panamanian independence—in both instances without congressional authorization. "I took the Canal Zone, and let Congress debate," he bragged, "and while the debate goes on, the Canal does also!"[7] Americans loved him for it.

At home, he busted trusts and enacted pure-food legislation. He settled a potentially calamitous coal strike. A pioneering conservationist, he created the National Forest Service and designated 150 national forests. For good measure, he established five national parks, eighteen national monuments, four game preserves, and fifty-one bird reserves. All the while, he reduced the national debt by $90 million. Peace, it seems, is cheaper than war.

And he inspired people. Indeed, he transfixed and mesmerized them—particularly reporters. "Theodore Roosevelt did more to corrupt the press than anyone else," concluded Oswald Garrison Villard, editor of both *The Nation* and the *New York Evening Post*. "By that I meant that he warped and twisted, consciously and unconsciously, by his fascinating personality, the judgements of the best of the reporters and correspondents and many of the editors."[8]

TR once presented two documents to the waiting press corps. "Here is a story," he instructed them, "and here is the denial you will print the next day."[9]

They did.

Reporters, Villard explained, "adored [Roosevelt] for himself, because he created so much news, because he was so stimulating, so vital, and so athletic. Moreover, he took a deep interest in them, their lives, their interests, and their hobbies. He would talk birds with one until two A.M., horses with another, boats with a third, and one was especially welcome because his grandfather rode in the Charge of the Light Brigade."[10]

He was good copy, and he was good company.

The nationally influential editor of Kansas's *Emporia Gazette*, William Allen White, described his own infatuation: "I put his heel on my neck and I became his man. . . . [H]e became my lifetime liege and I became his yeoman in his service."[11]

Corinne Roosevelt Robinson, TR's poetess younger sister, composed the following:

THEODORE ROOSEVELT
A WOMAN SPEAKS TO HIS SISTER

I NEVER clasped his hand,
He never knew my name,
And yet at his command,
I followed like a flame.

I pressed amid the crowd
To touch his garment's hem,
As one of old once touched
The Man of Bethlehem.

I was of those who toil,
Whose bread is wet with tears,
A daughter of the soil,
And bent, though not with years.

His words would lift the veil
That blurred my tired eyes,
They seemed to strengthen me
To serve and sacrifice.

And all the values lost,
When life was cold and grim,
Were clear and true again
Interpreted by him.

Our leader and our friend,
He knew what we must bear,
And to the gallant end
He bade us do and dare.

Clad in an armored truth
And by high purpose shod,
He gave us back our youth,
Our country, and our God![12]

I think one gets the picture.

In 1908, Roosevelt quit while he was ahead, eschewing a second elected term. Nearly effortlessly, he bequeathed power to his friend and secretary of war, William Howard Taft.

His problem was not the quitting. It was the un-quitting. He was just fifty when he voluntarily abandoned the White House. His cousin Franklin would be fifty-one when he *entered* it.

TR vacated not merely the White House but also the entire Western Hemisphere, embarking on a nearly year-long expedition to sub-Saharan Africa, collecting nearly 11,400 specimens (i.e., carcasses)—and, for good measure, a Nobel Prize in Oslo. He returned to a Republican Party in turmoil. Taft had promised to retain all of TR's cabinet; he retained just two members. Out the door went such Roosevelt favorites as Secretary of War Luke Wright, Attorney General Charles J. Bonaparte (grandnephew of Napoléon I), Commerce and Labor Secretary Oscar S. Straus, Navy Secretary Truman H. Newberry, Treasury Secretary George B. Cortelyou, and Interior Secretary James R. Garfield (yes, the son of *that* Garfield).

It was downhill all the way for "Big Bill" Taft. "Protectionism" had long cemented Grand Old Party unity. "Thank God I am not a free trader," said TR. "Pernicious indulgence in the doctrine of free trade seems inevitably to produce fatty degeneration of moral fibre."[13] But not every Republican supported every tariff measure. Few relished the ugly logrolling and vote buying often accompanying new tariff schedules. The savvy TR never risked initiating an overall tariff revision. Taft did. And 1909's Payne-Aldrich Tariff infuriated not only every Democrat but also at least half of the GOP.

Taft busted more trusts than TR. But TR hated how he busted them—or which Taft busted. When Taft's Justice Department moved against the United States Steel Corporation in October 1911, TR only saw the move as a gibe at his coziness with the company during the Panic of 1907.[14]

Further, Taft allied himself too closely with Congress's Old Guard elements, particularly House Speaker "Uncle Joe" Cannon and senators such as Rhode Island's Nelson Aldrich and Pennsylvania's Boies Penrose. Insurgent Iowa senator Jonathan P. Dolliver pungently assessed Taft as a "ponderous and amiable man completely surrounded by men who know exactly what they want."[15]

Taft defended the independence of strict-constructionist courts. He infuriated the GOP's conservationist wing. Regarding issues of mineral and hydroelectric development of western public lands, he sided with his interior secretary, Richard Ballinger, over Forest Service chief Gifford Pinchot, a particular TR favorite. When Pinchot went public, Taft fired him.

Precious little remained of the Taft-Roosevelt friendship.

Perhaps a break was inevitable. Two days before Taft's inauguration, *Collier's Weekly* correspondent Mark Sullivan inquired of Roosevelt, "How do you really think Taft will make out?"

"He's all right. He means well and he'll do his best," TR answered. "But he's weak."[16]

TR hesitated to challenge Taft. Wisconsin progressive Republican senator Robert La Follette didn't. In February 1912, however, the high-strung "Fighting Bob" suffered a spectacular mental crackup while addressing a gathering of magazine and newspaper publishers. His candidacy largely evaporated.

Progressives—"like iron filings mobilizing to the pull of a revitalized magnet"[17]—trooped to Oyster Bay to cajole their hero into yet another race. He needed little urging. Soon he was manipulating the entire "Draft Roosevelt" movement. When eight GOP governors publicly entreated him to yield to "popular demand" and run again, they did so at his behest.[18]

His most ardent Progressive followers fairly worshipped him, admitting no fault in their idol. Some kept their wits about them, recognizing their champion's less admirable characteristics. In February 1911, federal district judge Learned Hand, a fervent TR supporter, observed to the influential Progressive theorist Herbert Croly, "No one . . . has anything like the real breadth of vision that [TR] has; no one the foresight; granting his violence, and his lying, his personal untrustworthiness, he is today the best patriot we have. It seems to me incredible that in the situation which the next ten years will bring us, he should not again come to the front. I believe he will, provided he lives and does not go crazy."[19]

The mildly progressive "Square Deal" of Roosevelt's White House days no longer interested him. He touted a "New Nationalism," an energetic combination of electoral reform, labor legislation, income and estate taxes, and government (especially federal) regulation of wealth and industry. "We grudge no man a fortune in civil life if it is honorably obtained and well used," he proclaimed at Osawatomie, Kansas, in August 1910. "It is not even enough that it should have been gained without doing damage to the community. We should permit it to be gained only so long as the gaining represents benefit to the community."[20]

He decried socialism and communism, but his "New Nationalism" placed the collective above the individual, the federal over the state and local, and scorned the traditional American system of checks and balances. "The New Nationalism puts the national need before sectional or personal advantage," he explained. "It is impatient of the utter confusion that results from local legislatures attempting to treat national issues as local issues. It is still more impatient of the impotence which springs from over-division of governmental powers."[21]

But how much of his evolution was genuine? How much an infatuation with the spirit of the times? What percentage sheer opportunism?

John Chamberlain, an early chronicler of the Progressive movement, theorized,

> *By stepping out of his social context, Roosevelt was forced to make a game of life. His background of inherited wealth, with its assumed*

concomitant of noblesse oblige, engendered . . . a certain feeling of responsibility; but it was never whole-souled. Since he was making a gift of his life to the commonweal, since he was playing a game, there were privileges he might assume, laurels he might demand for the victory he was making a career; the career should make him.

And so, at crucial moments, consistency, proclaimed philosophical principle, the assumptions he made at beginning points and in his books on ideas, went casually by the board.[22]

"He is essentially a fighter and when he gets into a fight he is completely dominated by the desire to destroy his adversary," concluded his former trusted cabinet secretary Elihu Root (now loyal to Taft). "He instinctively lays hold of every weapon which can be used for that end. Accordingly he is saying a lot of things and taking a lot of positions which are inspired by the desire to win. I have no doubt he thinks he believes what he says, but he doesn't. He has merely picked up certain popular ideas which were at hand as one might pick up a poker or chair with which to strike."[23]

America had never elected a chief executive to a third term. Early in his second term, TR had famously ruled out another run. Some backtracking was now in order. In Boston, in February 1912, Roosevelt argued, "My position . . . is perfectly simple. I stated it as clearly as I could. . . . I said I would not accept a nomination for a third term under any circumstances, meaning, of course, a third consecutive term."[24]

The *New York Times* sarcastically titled its subsequent editorial "Of Course."[25]

Coincidentally, at that very same Boston event, Colonel Roosevelt also found himself asked, "Do you intend to support the Republican nominee, whoever he may be?"

To which he naturally answered, "Of course."[26]

But, of course, he didn't.

William Howard Taft was hardly amused by the new Roosevelt. "Such extremists," Taft warned, "would hurry us into a condition which would find no parallel except in the French revolution or in that bubbling anarchy that once characterized the South American republics.

Such extremists are not Progressives, they are political emotionalists or neurotics."[27]

Taft denied painting TR as neurotic. But, neurotic or not, TR soon announced, "My hat is in the ring,"[28] and "The fight is on and I am stripped to the buff."[29]

Taft raised the specter of a permanent Roosevelt presidency, of limitless federal power. TR, said Taft,

> *is convinced that the American people think that he is the only one to do the job. . . . We are left to infer, therefore, that the job which Mr. Roosevelt is to perform is one that may take a long time, perhaps the rest of his natural life. There's not the slightest reason why, if he secures a third term . . . he should not have as many terms as his natural life will permit.*
>
> *If he is necessary now to the Government, why not later? One who so lightly regards constitutional principles, and especially the independence of the judiciary, one who is so naturally impatient of legal restraints, and who has so misunderstood what liberty regulated by law is, could not be intrusted with successive Presidential terms.*[30]

TR berated Taft as a "puzzlewit" and a "fathead."[31] Taft denounced his old pal as a "honeyfugler," "demagogue," and "hypocrite."[32] Taft found himself literally reduced to tears as he pondered an old friendship so brutally and publicly sundered. Roosevelt, however, as his acolyte William Allen White once observed, "was not the weeping sort. When he decided to cut a throat, he generally justified it and rarely regretted it."[33]

TR dominated the primaries, capturing 281 delegates to Taft's 71. Taft sputtered, "Even a rat in a corner will fight,"[34] and he did. He controlled federal patronage, the state conventions, and the various rotten-borough southern delegations and made 1912's GOP convention no settled matter. Passions ran so high that Taft's people ringed the dais with barbed wire. Dozens of contested delegates were awarded to Taft, triggering loud Roosevelt protests. "If you didn't know where you were," chuckled William Jennings Bryan, "you might think you were in a Democratic convention."[35]

Or a religious revival. On Monday evening, June 17, TR addressed five thousand impassioned supporters at Chicago's Auditorium Theatre: "We fight in honorable fashion for the good of mankind; fearless of the future; unheeding of our individual fates; with unflinching hearts, and undimmed eyes; we stand at Armageddon, and we battle for the Lord!"[36]

It was TR or nothing—TR or bust. The Old Guard proved less wedded to the unpopular Taft. At one point, Billy Barnes offered the nomination to progressive, pro-TR Idaho senator William E. Borah. Borah turned it down. Party bosses also tendered the nod to TR's floor manager, Missouri governor Herbert S. Hadley. Edith Roosevelt advised her husband to agree to the Hadley move. He wouldn't.[37]

Taft barely won, garnering 561 votes to 107 for TR, 41 for La Follette, 19 scattered, and 7 absent. A whopping 348 disgruntled delegates refused to cast any ballot at all. Roosevelt's crowd disgustedly refused even to place him in nomination.[38]

Less than a month later, two thousand boisterous TR supporters reconvened at Chicago's Orchestra Hall to launch a new Progressive Party. The *New York Times* damned the gathering as "a convention of fanatics" before reconsidering: "It was not a convention at all. It was an assemblage of religious enthusiasts. It was such a convention as Peter the Hermit held. It was a Methodist camp following[,] done over into political terms."[39]

Even TR had to admit that the new party came "into this world making a noise like 10,000 babies."[40]

TR flung himself into the contest. After he exclaimed that he felt "like a bull moose!"[41] his party became the "Bull Moose Party." Its platform demanded income and inheritance taxes, the direct election of U.S. senators, women's suffrage, a ban on child labor, a minimum wage for women, and tariff reform. Bitterly reacting to the recent GOP convention, the Progressives banned federal officeholders from serving as convention delegates.

But TR was not as popular as he imagined. "Vote for Taft," Connecticut's *Waterbury Republican* soon advised, "pray for Roosevelt, and bet on Wilson."[42] Within six weeks, the bloom was so far off the Bull Moose rose as to generate this tragic story:

Bull Moose Causes Suicide.

New York, Aug. 20. Fear that he could not raise money enough to launch a dancing bull moose novelty he had invented was the only reason his friends could give for the suicide of Albert Funk. The [forty-five-year-old] man was found dead in bed at his lodgings today with the end of a gas tube between his teeth. About the room were several models of his invention and sheets of paper covered with figures, indicating that Funk had spent his last hours calculating the cost of manufacturing the toy. Funk came here three weeks ago from Cincinnati.[43]

Teddycide—or at least attempted Teddycide—soon followed suicide in the personage of a thirty-six-year-old Bavarian immigrant and former New York saloonkeeper named John Flammang Schrank. Schrank insanely blamed Roosevelt for William McKinley's assassination. He trailed TR to Milwaukee and shot him point-blank. A .38-caliber slug lodged in the Colonel's chest. Blood drenched his starched white shirt. But he insisted on traveling on to Milwaukee Auditorium. There he reassured the shocked ten-thousand-person audience, "Friends, I have to ask you to be as quiet as possible. I know you fully understand that I have just been shot, but it takes more than that to kill a Bull Moose."[44] He spoke for more than an hour before heading for a hospital.[45]

Roosevelt survived. His candidacy didn't. Regarding TR and Taft, New York's ancient former U.S. senator Chauncey Depew gibed, "It is only a question now which corpse gets the most flowers."[46]

TR and Taft sank. Woodrow Wilson rose.

Roosevelt was never as close to Wilson as he was to Taft. On many levels the Rough Rider and the "Professor in Politics" were very different. TR, so visceral, the gregarious man of action, the war hero and explorer. Wilson, the intellectual academic, the bloodless exemplar of pure reason.

They were, however, surprisingly similar. Both were children of the Civil War. TR's southern-born mother had moved north, whereas Wilson's northern parents had moved south. At age eight, Wilson witnessed Union soldiers dragging a captive Jefferson Davis through the streets of Augusta. Four-year-old TR peered from the second-story window of his grandfather's three-story New York mansion as the martyred Abraham Lincoln's funeral cortege processed down Broadway.

Each was blind in his left eye: Wilson from a May 1906 stroke, Roosevelt from a 1908 White House boxing match. Both suffered the loss of a first wife from Bright's disease. Alice Hathaway Lee Roosevelt died following childbirth on Valentine's Day 1884. Ellen Axson Wilson died in August 1914. Both men took second wives named Edith. Both sired daughters who married prominently (if not permanently happily) to substantially older husbands: Alice Roosevelt wed future Speaker of the House Nicholas Longworth; Eleanor Randolph Wilson married Treasury Secretary William Gibbs McAdoo.

Both were conservatives turned progressive with many a confusing stop along the way. William Jennings Bryan left both aghast in 1896. Both embodied certain nineteenth-century attitudes of race and empire (more racial in the southern Wilson's case, more imperial in Roosevelt's). Despite TR's Dutch roots and Wilson's Scotch-Irish antecedents, both were proud Anglophiles. Both served a single term as governor, installed via the machinations of their respective party bosses. Both were decidedly Ivy League. Both swayed audiences with their oratorical skills (the prissy-looking Wilson possessed a sonorously rich, manly voice; the virile TR's vocal chords emitted shrill chirps). Both were formidably intellectual and prolific, best-selling authors.

And both desired power—very, very great power.

Invariably, they discarded old allies. TR jettisoned William Howard Taft and Elihu Root. But by then, that was his habit. In 1896, he had turned his back on his earliest political mentor and benefactor, Joseph H. "Joe" Choate, stabbing the liberal patrician reformer in the back in favor of Thomas "The Easy Boss" Platt in the course of their contest for the U.S. Senate.[47] Two years later, he abandoned his supporters in the state's good-government "Independent Party"[48] as Platt, Billy Barnes, and Manhattan GOP boss Lemuel Quigg maneuvered him into the governorship. It was said that "not one of [the Independents] ever had any faith in the moral integrity of Roosevelt thereafter."[49]

Reform could wait. The governorship couldn't. After all, TR would soon be thirty-eight.

He may not have needed (or wanted) the Independents' help that year. But he needed all the help he could muster at the GOP's statewide nominating convention in Saratoga Springs. Aided by their friends at Tammany Hall, the forces of embattled GOP governor Frank Black produced Assistant Secretary of the Navy Roosevelt's sworn March 1898 affidavit, affirming, "I have been and am now a resident of Washington."⁵⁰

Designed to dodge local taxes, TR's letter rendered him ineligible for the governorship ("this doubtless was stupid on my part"⁵¹). Tom Platt's allies employed a smart New York attorney to convince the convention that TR's words did not—could not possibly—mean what they said.

That lawyer's name was Elihu Root ("I mixed my argument with a lot of ballyhoo and it went over with a bang"⁵²), later TR's secretary of state and of war. Regarding Root, in February 1910, Theodore gushed to Andrew Carnegie,

> *He was the man of my cabinet, the man on whom I most relied, to whom I owed the most, the greatest Secretary of State we have ever had, as great a cabinet officer as we have ever had, save Alexander Hamilton alone. He is as sane and cool-headed as he is high-minded; he neither lets facts blind him to ideals, nor ideals to fact; he is the wisest and safest of advisers, and staunchly loyal alike to friends and causes—and all I say I mean, and it is said with full remembrance that on certain points he and I would hardly agree.*⁵³

By 1912, Theodore Roosevelt would despise Elihu Root.

Wilson, meanwhile, turned on nearly everyone who assisted his rise from professor to Princeton University president to New Jersey governor to U.S. president. As Princeton's president, he turned on his old friend Professor John Grier Hibben when the two clashed regarding Wilson's English-style "quad" plan for undergraduate residency. In 1910, New Jersey Democratic Boss Jim Smith desired a respectable name atop his state ticket. None was more respectable than Wilson's. Smith pushed Wilson into the governor's chair. But when Smith demanded Wilson's support to return to his old U.S. Senate seat, Wilson refused. Smith felt betrayed.

In 1911, Smith's nephew, state Democratic chairman James R. Nugent, publicly blasted his uncle's unappreciative protégé in a mock toast: "To the Governor of New Jersey, the commander-in-chief of the Militia, an ingrate and a liar. I mean Woodrow Wilson. I repeat, he's an ingrate and a liar."[54]

Even before reaching the governorship, Wilson had captivated *Harper's Weekly* publisher Colonel George Harvey. Harvey became obsessed with the idea of a Wilson presidency. Each issue of *Harper's Weekly* assaulted readers with the banner headline "FOR PRESIDENT—WOODROW WILSON."

By 1912, Wilson—lurching leftward—had dumped the conservative Harvey for a new mentor: the wealthy Texan Colonel Edward Mandell House. "He is my independent self," gushed Wilson. "His thoughts and mine are one."[55] Two years later, House, departing for Europe, wrote Wilson, "You are the bravest wisest leader, the gentlest and most gallant gentleman and the truest friend in all the world."[56] Such a relationship burning so brightly could not but soon dim.

America was then both a larger and a smaller place. Distance and primitive communication separated people. But fewer persons existed to bond with, and certainly fewer accomplished persons. Thus, TR and Wilson had met as early as November 1890.[57] In March 1896, before a three- to four-thousand-person Baltimore Music Hall crowd, the thirty-eight-year-old Police Commissioner Roosevelt and the forty-year-old Professor Wilson addressed a "Monster Non-Partisan Assemblage" supporting municipal reform.[58] Roosevelt called for centralizing all appointive power. Wilson drew raves as "an eloquent talker"[59] but took his success modestly, commenting, "I suddenly found that I had become an authority on municipal government, simply because I got in the position of agreeing with the best people in town."[60]

A year later, they dined at Princeton.[61] That same January, Wilson interceded with newly appointed Assistant Secretary of the Navy Roosevelt to retain his former Atlanta law partner, Edward I. Renick, as chief clerk of William McKinley's State Department.[62]

As governor of New York, TR ("There is much I should like to talk over with you"[63]) invited Wilson to visit Albany. Wilson never got there.[64] In 1900, Wilson consulted Theodore on a Princeton faculty appointment,[65] and when TR wrote back, Wilson passed his letter on to his wife, Ellen, "because I think it will interest you as showing a side,—a very sane, *academic side* of him,—not known by everybody so much as to exist, but constituting his hope of real and lasting eminence."[66]

Most remarkably, when, in September 1901, TR raced down from the Adirondacks to McKinley's deathbed, quite by coincidence, among the first persons he received as the nation's new president was Wilson, en route home from several weeks of vacationing in rustic Ontario.[67]

Wilson wasn't exactly sure what to make of this rising dynamo. He may have admired him (even spending part of a weekend at Sagamore Hill while TR served as vice president[68]). He was certainly amused by him and perhaps just looked down upon his boisterous, decidedly non-academic ways. In any case, TR's sudden elevation to the White House alarmed him. "What will happen to the country," he puzzled, "with that mountebank as president?"[69]

Barely a month later, their paths crossed at Yale's bicentennial celebrations. TR became an honorary doctor of laws; Wilson and Mark Twain garnered honorary doctor of letters degrees.[70] Soon Wilson was considering the new president a "larger" man than Americans knew, "a very interesting and strong man."[71] In 1902, however, he joked with alumni that on the recent Groundhog Day, the rodent in question had quickly scurried back underground—fearful that TR would otherwise invite a "coon" in.[72]

In June 1902, Princeton's trustees unanimously selected Wilson as the university's thirteenth president. TR wrote him, "As an American interested in that kind of productive scholarship which tends to statesmanship, I hail your election . . . and I count myself fortunate in having the chance to . . . witness your inauguration."[73]

Flattery (of perhaps varying sincerity) peppered TR's voluminous correspondence. But Theodore also effusively praised Wilson's appointment to others. "Woodrow Wilson is a perfect trump," he wrote to a mutual friend. "I am overjoyed at his election."[74] To Grover Cleveland (a

Princeton trustee and local resident), he commended Wilson's "constructive statesmanship and administrative ability; and I am very glad from every standpoint."[75]

In September 1902, at Pittsfield, Massachusetts, a speeding electric trolley car rammed TR's horse-drawn presidential carriage, killing one Secret Service agent and seriously injuring another. His frock coat ripped, his top hat ruffled, TR shook his fist at the motorman, shouting, "This is the most damnable outrage I ever knew."[76] Two weeks later, an infected abscess required surgery. Hobbled for weeks, he missed Wilson's swearing-in.[77]

Nevertheless, he devoured Wilson's inaugural address, "Princeton for the Nation's Service." Calling it "really notable," he congratulated Wilson: "As a decent American I want to thank you for it."[78]

But then the relationship went sour, at least from Wilson's perspective. To faculty, Wilson castigated the administration.[79] By 1905, he had determined that his old acquaintance was "not quite a statesman."[80]

That December, for the only time in Army-Navy Game history, West Point and Annapolis competed at Princeton. Beforehand, Theodore, his oldest (and still unmarried) daughter Alice, his brother-in-law Douglas Robinson, Secretary of War Taft, Attorney General Bonaparte, and the remainder of the presidential party lunched at Wilson's elegant official residence, "Prospect."

Ellen Wilson queried her neighbor, Mrs. Grover Cleveland, regarding proper protocol. Requiring female attendees, Ellen invited her maiden twenty-four-year-old sister, Margaret Axson, to lunch with the Roosevelt entourage. Margaret had not far to travel. She lived there.

Everyone dined at one long table. Margaret sat halfway down from TR, beside fifty-one-year-old Douglas Robinson. They quickly struck up a conversation. "Miss Axson," roared TR, "stop making eyes at that man on your left. He's a gray-headed old grandfather. Devote yourself to the chap on your right. He's a rich bachelor."

"I felt," she recalled, "myself turning tomato-red up to the roots of my hair, and that apparently was just what Mr. Roosevelt wanted. He shouted with delight and pounded the table until the plates all down its length danced a crazy jig."

"Mr. President," Robinson shouted, "I'll have you know that I'm only a grandfather by marriage."

TR was hardly finished. Periodically, he'd bellow "Miss Axson!" each time banging his fist upon the table.

Miss Axson's lunch from hell finally concluded. A Secret Service agent, waiting outside, inquired, "What in heaven's name has been going on in there? Never have I heard such sounds issuing from a respectable dining room!"

"That was just the President of the United States engaged in mild banter," she snapped, "and if that's the way Presidents behave, I hope to the Lord I never meet another!"

At dinner she bristled, "Why should he deliberately set himself to make me conspicuous and uncomfortable? Who on earth would ever want to be President?"

"I should!" Wilson rejoined. "I know a whale about the Constitution of this country and I'd like to watch the wheels go round."[81]

They knew he was joking.

As TR might say, "Of course."

"A true logothete, a real sophist"

WOODROW WILSON SOON TURNED HIS ATTENTION FROM ACADEMIA TO Democratic politics. Just as quickly, he turned on Roosevelt. "We hurry and rush and live a strenuous life," he gibed in March 1906, "and at the end of it we see many things done, but nothing finished."[1]

In November 1907, he sniffed to the *New York Times*, "Mr. Roosevelt seems to be set on that idea [of government regulation of business], but I see no solution of the predatory conditions in such a method. It would merely mean taking the power away from the people and putting it into the hands of political discontent. I have not seen much of Mr. Roosevelt since he became President, but I am told that he no sooner thinks than he talks, which is a miracle not wholly in accord with the educated theory of forming an opinion."[2] For good measure, he concluded by mocking TR's crusade for simplified spelling.

Ideas have consequences. So do words. Within a year, the Colonel complained to his friend Lyman Abbott of being "rather impatient with [Wilson's] recent attitude on certain matters, notably the effort to control corporations."[3] Professor Wilson may not have known (or cared), but he had wounded his old friend grievously, for on one very basic level TR was made of far less stern stuff than he appeared. "No man that I have known liked personal approval more than Roosevelt," Abbott's son, Lawrence F. Abbott (like his father, TR's editor at *The Outlook*), later observed. "He had a kind of childlike responsiveness to commendation and praise. He did not wear his heart on his sleeve, but I think he was really hurt when those to whom he was attached were displeased with him. There are people who thought he was thick-skinned. On the contrary, he was highly sensitive."[4]

33

He remained sensitive for a very long time concerning Thomas Woodrow Wilson.

—◦—

Thanks to William Howard Taft and Theodore Roosevelt, Wilson ("God save us from of another four years of [TR] now in his present insane distemper of egotism!"[5]) indeed got to watch the wheels go round.

With the GOP vote split wide open, he triumphed with an abysmal 41.8 percent of the popular vote—a worse tally than three-time loser William Jennings Bryan's most abysmal outing. Nonetheless, he was president, and he proved remarkably aggressive and resourceful in pushing his progressive "New Freedom" through a Senate dominated by Democrats and insurgent Republicans and through a hugely Democratic (291–134) House. In a rush came the Federal Reserve Act, the Clayton Antitrust Act, workers' compensation for federal employees, a federal income tax, the Newlands Labor Act (creating a railroad Board of Mediation and Conciliation), federal highway matching grants, banking regulations, aid to agriculture, and on and on.

Wilson's "New Freedom" and TR's "New Nationalism" diverged primarily on "protection" (the Democrats' Underwood Tariff slashed rates) and whether to dismantle or merely control monopolies, but at day's end Wilson more than swiped TR's progressive thunder. TR talked a good game. Wilson played a better one.

But all the above involved domestic matters.

Historically, Democrats—Wilson among them—had displayed scant interest in foreign policy. "It would be an irony of fate," he remarked just prior to assuming office, "if my administration had to deal chiefly with foreign affairs."[6]

His cabinet reflected that indifference. Secretary of the Navy Josephus Daniels, a North Carolina newspaper editor, not only possessed infinitesimal (if any) background in that field but also was an avowed pacifist. New Jersey judge Lindley M. Garrison's appointment as secretary of war was almost pure afterthought. And as for prairie populist William Jennings Bryan's selection as secretary of state, well, that was pure politics.

Treasury Secretary William Gibbs McAdoo deemed Bryan "one of the shrewdest men I have ever known. In him, unsophistication and sagacity were strangely blended."[7] But few—well, actually, no—Republicans possessed much use for "The Great Commoner." Numerous Democrats—particularly high-toned eastern reformers like Woodrow Wilson, but also practical men like those who staffed Tammany Hall's numerous clubhouses—pretty much agreed. Wilson himself termed him "that strange man" and said that he "suffers from a singular sort of moral blindness and is as passionate in error as in the right causes he has taken."[8]

Bryan lacked foreign policy experience (and stuffed the diplomatic service with dubiously qualified "deserving Democrats"[9]). More, he lacked gravitas—TR derided him as "our own special prize idiot"[10] and "a professional yodeler, a human trombone."[11] Never a rich man, he augmented his $12,000 State Department salary by delivering paid speeches on the popular Chautauqua circuit. "He's goin' to change his act nex' year," jeered the Irish-dialect humorist Finley Peter Dunne ("Mr. Dooley"), "an' play his lecture on a piccolo while suspinded from a thrapeze. Th' British Minister called on him th' other day an' discovered him practicin' a handspring."[12]

Bryan's Chautauqua activities did little to improve official Washington's already negligible opinion of the man. Neither did his refusal to serve any alcoholic beverages at official department soirees.

For his part, TR might overlook Bryan's speechifying or his Prohibitionist sympathies but not his ardent pacifism.

TR might merely have politely applauded Wilson's handling of domestic policy. He might have swallowed hard and even ignored Daniels and Bryan. But for one matter.

Panama.

Of TR's many accomplishments, the Panama Canal ranked among his favorites. The canal conquered topography and vanquished disease. It furthered commerce and naval flexibility. And it was even a family enterprise of sorts. In 1889, Franklin Roosevelt's father, James, had served as president of the House of Morgan–backed (and federally chartered and, more important, guaranteed) Maritime Canal Corporation of Nicaragua.[13] And, of course, TR's brother-in-law Douglas Robinson had been accused of profiting from the canal's acquisition.

In April 1914, Wilson and Bryan concluded the Treaty of Bogotá, which not only provided Colombia with a $25 million indemnity for its former Panamanian territory but also expressed "sincere regret" for American (i.e., TR's) actions. TR fumed that the treaty represented a "crime against the United States, an attack upon the honor of the United States,"[14] and he demanded to testify personally before the Senate Foreign Relations Committee.

That August, as the canal formally opened, the administration heaped insult upon insult, inviting neither TR nor Taft to attend.[15] Beyond that, Wilson also reneged on his own party platform, stripping American merchantmen of the right to toll-free canal passage. Some saw Wilson's move as principled and courageous. Others viewed it as "a great economic blunder" and a surrender to British influence.[16]

August 1914 was a terrible month. Ellen Axson Wilson, just fifty-four, died of Bright's disease on the sixth,[17] leaving her husband distraught and inconsolable. "I thought at that time," recalled his adviser, Colonel Edward M. House, "and on several other occasions afterward, that the President wanted to die."[18] FDR feared a Wilson "breakdown."[19]

Far worse, in the days preceding Ellen's death, Europe bolted toward war. America had long pursued a policy of official neutrality regarding European conflicts, honoring George Washington's warnings against "foreign alliances." The nation, Wilson proclaimed, "must be neutral in fact as well as in name" and "impartial in thought as well as in action."[20]

It couldn't. Not when German armies violated neutral little Belgium. Not when so many Americans proudly boasted Anglo-Saxon, French, Celtic, or Teutonic ancestry.

TR wasn't neutral about either Europe or Wilson. He excoriated Wilson's failures to fortify the Canal Zone or upgrade the U.S. battleship fleet. He rebuked Wilson and Bryan's ultimately fruitless web of thirty arbitration treaties. That TR and Taft negotiated (but could not secure ratification for) a host of similar treaties entered not at all into his thought process.[21]

Belgium obsessed him. Within a week of Germany's invasion of that nation, a German nobleman (most likely military attaché Franz von Papen) arrived at TR's Progressive Party headquarters. He bore personal greetings from Kaiser Wilhelm II, who hoped that TR would recall the hospitality extended to him in Berlin in 1910. And, more so, might display a "sympathetic understanding" of German actions.

TR bowed to his visitor before responding: "Pray, thank His Imperial Majesty from me for his very courteous words; and assure him I am very deeply conscious of the honors done me in Germany . . . [and of] the way in which His Majesty King Albert received me in Brussels."[22]

"He looked me straight in the eye," TR recalled, "without changing countenance, clicked his heels together, bowed—whereat I bowed in return—and left the room without speaking another word; nor did I speak another word."[23]

His low opinion of Wilhelm predated Belgium. On his 1910 visit to Berlin, Theodore remarked to Edith that the kaiser was "too strong to allow himself to appear weak, and too weak to be strong in a really crucial decision. I'm tremendously disturbed."[24] "In international affairs [Wilhelm] at times acts as a bully," TR observed in October 1911, "and moreover as a bully who bluffs and then backs down; I would not regard him nor Germany as a pleasant national neighbor."[25]

Yet TR's initial public response to 1914's great crisis remained atypically muted. In early August of that year, Theodore's former Progressive supporter, the renowned German-American poet George Sylvester Viereck, apprised him of plans for a pro-German weekly magazine, *The Fatherland*. On Saturday, August 8, TR blandly responded, "Dear Viereck:—I am very glad to hear from you and to know what your plans are. But, of course, as you say, my desire is at present to avoid in any way saying anything that would tend to exaggerate and inflame the war spirit on either side and to be impartial; I simply do not know the facts. It is a melancholy thing to see such a war."[26]

In a rambling, interminable article in *The Outlook*'s August 22, 1914, issue, Roosevelt vowed to "stand by not only the public servants in control of the Administration at Washington, but also all other public servants, no matter of what party" during this crisis.[27] "I am not now taking sides one way or the other as concerns the violation [of Belgium]," he added. "When giants are engaged in a death wrestle, as they reel to and fro they are certain to trample on whomever gets in the way of either of the huge straining combatants."[28]

A month later, he reiterated, "We . . . must stand ready loyally to support the Administration."[29] He defended the "necessity" of German actions in Belgium, claiming, "Disaster would surely have attended her arms had she not followed the course she actually did follow."[30]

"We can maintain our neutrality," he continued, employing strangely Wilsonian tones, "only by refusal to do anything to aid unoffending weak powers which are dragged into the gulf of bloodshed and misery through no fault of their own. I am sure the sympathy is compatible with full knowledge of the unwisdom of uttering a single word of official protest unless we are prepared to make that protest effective; and only the clearest and most urgent National duty would ever justify us in deviating from our rule of neutrality and non-interference."[31]

"America," he further reminded readers, "has no claim whatever to superior virtue in this matter. We have shown an appalling recklessness in making treaties."[32]

Thus, TR formulated a policy of calculated inaction. "It would be folly to jump into the gulf ourselves to no good purpose," he wrote in a syndicated column in early September, "and very probably nothing that we could have done would have helped Belgium. We have not the smallest responsibility for what has befallen her . . . and only the clearest and most urgent national duty would ever justify us in deviating from our rule of neutrality and non-interference."[33]

He noted a week later,

To paint the Kaiser as a devil merely bent on gratifying a wicked thirst for bloodshed, is . . . worse than an absurdity. . . . [H]istory will declare the Kaiser acted in conformity with the feelings of the German people and as he sincerely believed the interests of his people demanded; and, as so often before in his personal and family life, he and his family have given honorable proof that they possess the qualities that are characteristic of the German people. Every one of his sons went to the war, not nominally, but to face every danger and hardship. Two of his sons hastily married [their] betrothed and immediately afterward left for the front.[34]

For now, Roosevelt remained calmer regarding events than, say, his close friend, Massachusetts senator Henry Cabot Lodge, who in May 1915 threatened Herbert Hoover, chair of the Commission for Relief in Belgium, with Logan Act prosecution for his efforts to feed starving Belgians. Hoover returned stateside to quiet such talk, confronting Lodge in Boston. The next day, TR invited "The Great Humanitarian" to lunch at Sagamore Hill, where (perhaps recalling Hoover's 1912 campaign contributions to him) he promised to "go at 'em" if any Democrats caused the philanthropist trouble. He "laughed uproariously" at Hoover's account of his meeting with Lodge and derided Lodge's obsession with seeing European "involvements" under every bed. For good measure, he vowed to "hold [Lodge's] hand," if necessary, to contain his wrath.[35]

More privately, the Colonel seethed. He could not hate Wilson more or favor Germany less. He would just take his time about letting his true feelings slip publicly. With his many British friends, discretion proved impossible. In late August, he wrote to former British military attaché (and honorary Rough Rider) Arthur Hamilton Lee, "I thought England behaved exactly as she ought to behave [regarding Belgium], and with very great dignity. It was a fine thing."[36]

To British ambassador Cecil Spring-Rice (his longtime friend and the best man at his second wedding), TR privately confided in early October 1914, "I believe that you will put the war through. I am glad the opinion of our country is on your side. . . . At any rate there is no question as to where the interests of civilization lie at this moment." The only thing preventing his speaking out was a nagging suspicion that "the majority are now following Wilson. Only a limited number of people could or ought to be expected to make up their minds for themselves in a crisis like this; and they tend, and ought to tend, to support the President in such a crisis. It would be worse than folly for me to clamor now about what ought to be done or ought to have been done, when it would be mere clamor and nothing else."

"The above is only for yourself," he admonished Spring-Rice. "It is a freer expression of opinion than I have permitted myself in any letter hitherto."[37]

In August 1914, British foreign secretary Sir Edward Grey dissolved in tears before U.S. Ambassador Walter Hines Page as he contemplated with a "stunned sense . . . the impending ruin of half the world."[38] The year 1915 proved him prescient. Zeppelins attacked Paris and London. Flamethrowers and poison gas degraded conditions on the already hellish western front. Russia threatened to knock Austria-Hungary out of the war, and Berlin returned the favor with Moscow. Italy betrayed its treaty obligations to the Central Powers and entered the fray as an Ally. The conflict spread to Asia. Ottoman Turks massacred Armenians, attacked the Suez Canal, and invaded Aden. Britain invaded Mesopotamia and launched an amphibious invasion at Gallipoli. Colonial forces skirmished throughout Africa.

The Royal Navy blockaded German ports, hoping to starve Berlin out of the war. German submarines graduated from sinking Britain's warships to attacking its merchantmen and passenger liners and then targeted American vessels.

When the U-20 sank the *Lusitania* on May 7, Woodrow Wilson cancelled his golf game. Later he composed a love letter to his new lady friend, Mrs. Edith Bolling Galt.[39] Only past nightfall did he fully grasp the immensity of events. Three days later, speaking in Philadelphia, he uttered not a word regarding the *Lusitania*, save only that America—or perhaps he—was "too proud to fight."

It was a grievous political mistake, infuriating not only TR but also millions of other outraged, sickened, and vengeful Americans. The *New York Herald* headlined "WHAT A PITY THEODORE ROOSEVELT IS NOT PRESIDENT!" and asked, "What is President Wilson going to do about it?"[40]

Twenty-nine-year-old army second lieutenant George S. Patton Jr. knew what *he* would do about it. The Pattons were Democrats. Patton Sr. would soon emerge as his party's nominee for U.S. Senate from California. But his son (no shrinking violet even then) quickly advised him, "We ought to declare war. . . . If Wilson had as much blood in him as the liver of a louse is commonly thought to contain he would do this."[41] Wilson, bristled Lieutenant Patton, "has not the soul of a louse nor the mind of a worm. Or the backbone of a jellyfish."[42]

Even William Randolph Hearst's papers, never pro-Ally, denounced the sinking of the *Lusitania* as "wholesale murder."[43]

Wilson furiously backtracked the day following his Philadelphia comments. Being "too proud to fight" had nothing to do with the U-20 or the *Lusitania*, he alibied to reporters. "I was expressing a personal attitude, that was all. . . . I did not regard that as a proper occasion to give any intimation of policy on any special matter."[44]

The special matter on Woodrow Wilson's mind that day was his beloved Edith Bolling Galt. Less than a week before, they had dined at the White House, and afterward, alone on the south portico, he confessed his love to her and plotted how best to discreetly arrange their courtship.[45]

That evening, Mrs. Galt resisted his professorial ardor, but soon she pledged to him "all that is best in me—to help, to sustain, to comfort. . . . [I]nto that space that separates us, I send my spirit to seek yours."[46]

The day before the *Lusitania* sank, the lovesick Wilson responded, "Here stands your friend, a longing man, in the midst of world affairs—a world that knows nothing of the heart he has shown you . . . but which he cannot face with his full strength or with the fullest of keen endeavors unless you come into that heart and take possession, not because it is exposed but because, simply and only because, you love him. Can you love him?"[47]

They rendezvoused at the White House just before he departed for Philadelphia. Their tryst obviously affected his remarks. At seven the next morning, he wrote her, "I do not know just what I said in Philadelphia (as I rode along the streets in dusk I found myself a little confused as to whether I was in Philadelphia or New York!) because my heart was in such a whirl from that wonderful interview of yesterday and the poignant appeal and sweetness of the little note you left me with . . . but many other things have grown clear in my mind. . . . I am waiting and am already your own."[48]

Not everyone was so distracted. Inside Woodrow Wilson's administration, the fight was on. Colonel House (who had recently traveled to Europe via the *Lusitania*) telegraphed Wilson that an "immediate demand should be made upon Germany for assurance that this shall not happen again.... America has come to the parting of the ways, when she must determine whether she stands for civilized or uncivilized warfare. We can no longer remain neutral spectators."[49] At a London dinner party, he predicted to U.S. Ambassador Walter Hines Page, "We shall be at war within a month."[50] The pro-British Page cabled Wilson, "The United States must declare war or forfeit European respect."[51]

House calculated that he would return to an America ready for war—until he saw newspapers blaring Wilson's "too proud to fight" comments. He was not pleased.[52]

William Jennings Bryan counseled caution. If the *Lusitania* really did transport contraband, "The Great Commoner" argued, that "puts a different phase on the whole matter!"[53]

Through Bryan, Wilson dispatched an objection to Berlin's "present method of attack" on enemy trade, disregarding "rules of fairness, reason, justice, and humanity, which all modern opinion regards as imperative."[54]

Germany's tepid response caused House to regard war as "inevitable."[55] Secretary of War Garrison urged toughness, a virtual ultimatum. Bryan (having posited to his wife, Mary, that "England has been using our citizens to protect her ammunition"[56]) accused his colleagues of being "not neutral. You are taking sides."[57] Wilson slapped him down. A new note was drafted. Bryan privately warned Wilson that it would lead to war—then he resigned. "You are the most real Christian that I know,"[58] Interior Secretary Franklin K. Lane consoled Bryan. But the vast majority of the press—of all editorial persuasions—regarded Bryan's action with contempt. The pro-Wilson *New York World* damned him for "unspeakable treachery, not only to the President but to the nation."[59] The Republican *Hartford Courant* gibed that those saying "Mr. Bryan was in bad taste made a slight mistake. He is a bad taste."[60]

"Hurrah! Old Bryan is out!" cheered Edith Galt, already evolved from mere presidential helpmate to policy adviser.[61]

Bryan considered Wilson's second *Lusitania* note ominously warlike. TR did not. Later that month, he confided to his friend and former Harvard chum, popular novelist Owen "Dan" Wister,

Wilson is considerably more dangerous . . . than Bryan. . . . Bryan is not attractive to the average college bred man; but [those] who claim to represent all that is highest and most cultivated . . . are all ultra-supporters of Wilson, are all much damaged by him, and join with him to inculcate flabbiness of moral fiber among the very men, and especially the young men, who should stand for what is best in American life. . . . I feel particularly bitter toward him . . . because when Bryan left I supposed that meant that Wilson really had decided to be a man and I prepared myself to stand wholeheartedly by him. But in reality the point at issue between them was merely as to the proper point of dilution of tepid milk and water.[62]

The world focused on Wilson's "too proud to fight" dictum. TR most likely focused on another sentiment from that same address, one aimed squarely at him. "I am sorry," Wilson informed his audience, "for the man who seeks to make personal capital out of the passions of his fellow-men. He has lost the touch and ideal of America. . . . [T]he man who seeks to divide man from man, group from group, interest from interest in this great Union is striking at its very heart."[63]

"Nothing is more sickening than the continual praise of Wilson's English, of Wilson's style," TR also wrote to Wister. "He is a true logothete, a real sophist; and he firmly believes . . . that elocution is an admirable substitute for and improvement on action."[64]

Or, as Roosevelt previously informed Britain's Arthur Hamilton Lee, "In international affairs Wilson is almost as much of a prize jackass as Bryan."[65]

A high standard indeed.

At lunch in New York in early 1915, *Chicago Tribune* publisher Joseph Medill Patterson inquired of TR, "Why are you so sympathetic with the Allies? You even seem to want to get us into war on the Allied side. Is it just Belgium, or do you feel that America itself is menaced?"

Patterson was clearly onto something. Roosevelt cared for Belgium, but he cared for America more. TR responded, his voice slowly rising in pitch,

If Germany won the war, she would probably not attack us at once but she would begin to meddle in the Caribbean, to effect landings in Cuba, and to threaten the Panama Canal. In this way we would be thrown into hostilities with Germany sooner or later and with far less chance of success than if we joined with the powers which are now fighting her. . . . [I]f Germany and the United States were engaged in a duel, the other European powers, which had already suffered from Germany's aggression—which we had not helped them to check— would be—shall we say?—extremely philosophical about the evil things happening to us.[66]

That Germany might traverse an ocean to attack Panama, let alone U.S. shores (and let alone the nation's interior), seems fanciful. By 1915, German naval power had been swept from the seas. In March of that year, off Chilean waters, British warships sank the *Dresden*, the last German light cruiser left at sea. A month later, the converted German merchant cruiser *Prinz Eitel Friedrich* ingloriously sought refuge in Newport News, Virginia. The bulk of the imperial German fleet lay hiding at Kiel, fearful of battle with its British counterpart. Its vaunted submarines might sink the occasional British warship or passenger liner or American merchantman but proved unable to effectively blockade the British islands, let alone transport hundreds of thousands of troops for a transatlantic invasion. Further, the Allies' disaster at Gallipoli demonstrated the difficulty of anyone (let alone land-bound Germany) mounting a successful large-scale amphibious invasion.

His fears, however, did possess some (though not much) rationale, largely based on Germany's previous hemispheric adventures dating back to Berlin's 1902–1903 threatened Venezuelan intervention. In 1905, the crew of the German gunboat SMS *Panther* invaded the Brazilian port of Itajaí, searching for a deserting seaman. Germany was long involved in Haitian affairs. Its warships muscled their way into Port-au-Prince harbor during crises in 1872, 1887, and 1911. In 1902, the *Panther* even sank the pride of the four-vessel Haitian fleet, the armed cruiser *Crête-à-Pierrot*.[67]

In Mexico, Germany enjoyed substantial commercial interests under longtime strongman Porfirio Díaz. Its fleet ostentatiously visited Mexican waters in the century's first decade. In 1903, Berlin even investigated establishing a naval base in Baja California (the year before, it similarly toyed with purchasing Venezuela's Margarita Island).[68] In 1906, Díaz initiated discussions with Berlin regarding its possible training of Mexico's army. That went nowhere, but soon Berlin was initiating talk of training Díaz's navy.

But Venezuela, Haiti, and Mexico were not the United States of America. It would take more than a stray gunboat for imperial Germany to advance upon American shores. It would require tens of thousands of men—tens of thousands of men whom others besides Theodore Roosevelt believed threatened us. Fanciful thoughts of an invaded, violated, prostrate America filled the air. Gotham seemed particularly vulnerable to Germanic despoilment, as if Wilhelm II were some great Teutonic Kaiser Kong poised to vault an ocean and surmount the Woolworth Building.

In the December 12, 1914, issue of *Harper's Weekly*, Henry Stimson (also Taft's onetime secretary of war) raised the idea of an unspecified enemy's landing 150,000 troops near New London, Connecticut's submarine base before capturing New York.[69] Henry Cabot Lodge's son-in-law, Massachusetts congressman Augustus P. "Gussie" Gardner, warned of German fifteen-inch battleship guns demolishing lower Manhattan.[70] In August 1915, the *North American Review* fretted that "a great European military empire, getting control of the sea with a superior fleet, could throw an expeditionary force of 250,000 men upon our shores."[71] That December, General Leonard Wood cited "the amazing efficiency shown by the Australian forces in reaching Gallipoli" (!) to illustrate the danger of invasion.[72] The Hearst newspapers warned of German hordes seizing a swath of territory stretching from Erie, Pennsylvania (a point of no known strategic importance) to Washington, DC. Kansas's William Allen White possessed a more mid-American paranoia, fearing a German invasion at Galveston and a march "cross country to the Missouri

Valley"[73] (presumably coming for him). Franklin Roosevelt warned Congress of a strike in the south, launched via the West Indies.[74]

German-Americans constructed their own scenarios, featuring, of course, other villains. George Sylvester Viereck's *The Fatherland* serialized a novel titled *The War of 1920*, chronicling a joint British-French-Japanese and Mexican invasion of the continental United States. Chapter 9 ("Hyphenated-Americans Turn the Tide") depicted the "Allied atrocities in this war: the burning of homes and cities, the cruel fate of thousands of women and girls, the savage repression of the patriots of California, the hideous negro uprising, and all the nameless cruelties inflicted on a white people by other whites and their Japanese, Mexican, Hindu and Senegalese mercenaries, to further the plots of the gang of English politicians for whom humanity blushes!"[75]

Meanwhile, Wilson struggled to maintain American neutrality, both publicly and privately. A story circulated about one of Wilson's three daughters having impulsively expressed some inconsequential admiration for the French people before sheepishly inquiring, "Oh dear! Was that unneutral?"[76]

Neutrality—or, rather, public neutrality—reigned within Wilson's household, even regarding Theodore Roosevelt. TR might fuss and fume and sputter regarding his successor, but the thin-skinned Wilson maintained remarkable composure regarding his attacks. "The only way to treat an adversary like Roosevelt," he once remarked, "is to gaze at the stars over his head."[77]

Wilson, however, hardly minded if others acted otherwise. In the July 3, 1915, issue of *Harper's Weekly*, journalist George Creel mercilessly pilloried nearly every facet of the Roosevelt record, from tax evasion to trust busting to Panama to women's suffrage to judicial recall—including, of course, Preparedness and Woodrow Wilson:

Nothing is more plain than that Mr. Roosevelt has deliberately chosen Red Blood as a campaign cry. Undoubtedly convinced that President Wilson will be able to hold America back from the abyss that has engulfed Europe, he feels it safe to trade upon the irritations that are inevitably engendered by any policy of non-activity. . . .

More than any other man in public life, he has the gift of making people thrill rather than think. He is to statesmanship what the "movies" are to the drama. He gives a picture but never a thought. Like a kaleidoscope, his incessant play of color forces forgetfulness of form. . . .

He blazes across the mediocrity of everyday existence like a meteor, and dull slaves of routine, chained to the treadmill, find a certain vicarious pleasure, a definite satisfaction of romance, in watching his sweep. The strength of Theodore Roosevelt is that he makes his rivals seem colorless and shabby.

It takes time and patience to make people think. The boom of a gun, the roar of fustian, a piece of claptrap sentiment, will make them feel.

Such a man is always dangerous, and doubly so when he appeals to primitive instincts and ancient, wanton lusts. . . .

It is not meant to charge Mr. Roosevelt with premeditated insincerity. It is simply the case that he lacks deep-seated convictions and runs his race without regard to other than purely personal goals. He lives by impressions and works through impressions, and by virtue of a hugely developed egoism he is able to transmute his daily vagary into an eternal verity.[78]

Woodrow Wilson was actually neutral about neither Roosevelt nor the war, privately favoring the Allies (and particularly the British). But he was not about to go anywhere near war. The American people might loathe the kaiser but not sufficiently to send their boys "over there" to battle him—at least not yet. "These are indeed deep waters," he confessed to Josephus Daniels. "In one breath the people demand that I keep the country out of war. In the next breath they demand I do not surrender our rights. . . . They talk of me as though I was a God. Any little German lieutenant can put us into war at any time by some calculated outrage."[79]

But some little German lieutenant just about had, and for TR that was enough to charge off to the trenches.

In the wake of the *Lusitania* tragedy, while the *Barnes v. Roosevelt* trial still progressed, Theodore ruminated to his most interventionist son, Archie,

There is a chance of our going to war; but I don't think it is very much of a chance. Wilson and Bryan are cordially supported by all the hyphenated Americans, by the solid flubdub and pacifist vote. Every soft creature, every coward and weakling, every man who can't look more than six inches ahead, every man whose god is money, or pleasure, or ease . . . is enthusiastically in favor of Wilson; and at present the good citizens, as a whole, are puzzled and don't understand the situation, and so a majority of them also tend to be with him. . . . He and Bryan . . . are both of them abject creatures and they won't go to war unless they are kicked into it, and they will consider nothing whatever but their own personal advantage in the matter.[80]

Third-party efforts are invariably one-ring circuses. Their presidential candidates take center ring, with star-quality acts seldom in tow. The Colonel's 1912 Bull Moose effort was decidedly different. He attracted such celebrity followers as sculptor Gutzon Borglum and Chicago social worker Jane Addams. High-profile journalists such as the *Chicago Tribune*'s Medill McCormick, the *Philadelphia North American*'s E. A. Van Valkenburg, the *New York Evening Mail*'s Henry L. Stoddard, the *Kansas City Star*'s W. R. Nelson, the *Pittsburgh Leader*'s Alexander Moore, the *Wichita Beacon*'s Henry J. Allen, the *Emporia Gazette*'s William Allen White, the *Manchester Leader*'s Frank Knox, and the *Fresno Morning Republican*'s Chester H. Rowell enlisted in his cause. So did rising progressive theorists Herbert Croly and Walter Lippmann. Money poured in, primarily from J. P. Morgan partner George W. Perkins and magazine and newspaper publisher Frank A. Munsey, a major investor in U.S. Steel.[81] Other deep-pocketed financial angels included Crucible Steel's Horace Wilkinson, Bon Ami cleaning powder magnate William Hamlin Childs, Chicago furniture magnate Alexander Hamilton Revell, and even the highly controversial stock manipulator Thomas W. Lawson.[82] Mining industry magnate Herbert Hoover dispatched a contribution from London.[83] Actor William Gillette and actress Lillian Russell (Alexander Moore's new bride; she was fifty-one, he forty-four) endorsed him. So did Charles Edison.[84]

Sitting GOP senators such as Iowa's Albert Cummins, Montana's Joseph M. Dixon, and Kansas's George L. Bristow supported him, as did New Hampshire governor Robert P. Bass. Missouri appeals court judge Albert D. Nortoni ran as the Bull Moose gubernatorial candidate. California governor Hiram Johnson, just hitting his stride as a national figure, served as his running mate.

TR's bruising 1912 defeat hardly dented his supporters' fervor. "I have been thinking," Borglum soon gushed to the *New York Herald*, "of attempting what should be the masterpiece of my life. I am planning a heroic statue of Theodore Roosevelt. When that work shall be completed, I will be willing to let posterity assign my rank as a sculptor. . . . What an inspiration the life of Roosevelt offers me! To put into stone a great man—a typical American! My attention will certainly be satisfied when I have executed in the 'imperishable' the features and figure of the greatest man of his time!"[85]

Borglum's medium may have been imperishable. TR's wasn't. Frank Munsey contributed $229,255 to the Progressives in 1912. In January 1913, he abandoned ship, loudly urging the "amalgamation" of the Republican and Progressive parties into a new "Liberal Party." By 1914 Munsey was again a Republican.[86] The Progressive Party shattered like cheap porcelain in November 1914, forfeiting three of its already minuscule nine House seats. Of thirty-two Senate seats in play, Progressives contested only eighteen. They won none, though their candidates included such luminaries as Gifford Pinchot in Pennsylvania (TR mailed out more than a million postcards on his behalf[87]), former senator Albert Beveridge in Indiana, former San Francisco prosecutor Francis J. Heney in California, national party chairman Raymond Robins in Illinois, Representative Victor Murdock in Kansas, the brilliant Manhattan attorney Bainbridge Colby in New York, and former representative Ole Hanson in Washington State. In only ten of those races did a Bull Mooser register more than 10 percent. Arizona's Progressive hopeful trailed both his Socialist and his Prohibitionist rivals.

Progressive ranks in New York's state legislature skidded from one senator and nineteen assemblymen to a single assemblyman: Putnam County's Hamilton "Ham" Fish Jr. Fish barely survived—and then only thanks to a Democratic cross-endorsement.[88] In Illinois, the party's "brilliant but unstable"[89] national party vice chairman, Medill McCormick, remained as his state legislature's last surviving Progressive—before promptly and ingloriously deserting to the Republicans.[90]

Bull Moose gubernatorial candidates fared even worse. TR's former interior secretary, James R. Garfield, lost handily in Ohio, barely ahead of a nonentity Socialist. TR carried Pennsylvania in 1912. Two years later, William Draper Lewis resigned his University of Pennsylvania Law School deanship to run for governor. He polled 0.59 percent of the vote. New York's Frederick Davenport garnered a third of a million votes fewer than Progressive Oscar Straus collected in 1912. More depressingly, he trailed three other third-party tickets. "The Bull Moose party," mourned William Allen White, "was a group of leaders without followers."[91]

TR fumed to Kermit that voters simply didn't give a whit about "civic morality or industrial justice or anything else," that they were "sick and tired of hearing us exhort them to be virtuous and they wished to relieve their feelings by voting for every corrupt scoundrel in sight. Accordingly they did so!"[92]

Two months later, he wrote Kermit,

> *My immediate and acute trouble is over. The Progressive Party cannot in all probability make another fight as a national party; and, if it does, there will be no expectation that I will have to lead. . . .*
>
> *There is just one element of relief to me in the smash that came to the Progressive party. We did not have many practical men with us. Under such circumstances the reformers tended to go into sheer lunacy. I now can preach the doctrines of labor and capital just as I did when I was President, without being hampered by the well-meant extravagances of so many among my Progressive friends.*[93]

The election of 1914 produced no real victor. Progressives were decimated. Democrats took a drubbing. Republicans gained sixty-nine seats in the House and three in the Senate but failed to win control of either body, as what remained of the Bull Moose vote cost them thirty-nine House and four Senate seats.[94]

In Indiana, Republican billboards teasingly asking prodigal Progressives, "Eventually, why not now?"[95]

It was a question TR had already asked himself.

TR's popularity stayed on the bubble. Retaining an intensely loyal core of followers, he remained anathema to both Democrats and regular Republicans. His strident salvos against Wilhelm and Wilson and Berlin and Bryan failed to sway the bulk of voters, who, while not necessarily too proud to fight, were nonetheless hardly eager to die for causes not their own.

Antiwar songs were the craze, commencing in 1914 with Irving Berlin's "Stay Down Here Where You Belong" and W. W. Williams's "We Stand for Peace While Others War" ("But Uncle Sam's a neutral power / And we must stand by him"[96]). The following year, Alfred Bryan's "I Didn't Raise My Boy to Be a Soldier" sold a phenomenal seven hundred thousand copies of sheet music as well as countless phonograph records. Across America, vaudeville audiences could not get enough of it.

> I didn't raise my boy to be a soldier
> I brought him up to be my pride and joy.
> Who dares to place a musket on his shoulder
> To shoot some other mother's darling boy?[97]

TR retorted that the song "ought always to be sung with a companion piece entitled 'I Didn't Raise My Girl to Be a Mother' as the two stand on precisely the same moral level."[98] In San Francisco, he snapped, "A mother who is not willing to raise her boy to be a citizen is not fit for citizenship."[99]

Not all mothers, or all citizens, supported such jingoism—or him. In late May 1915, he confessed misgivings along these lines to a British journalist:

> *My feeling is that harm and not good would come if I should again be a candidate. . . .*

I have been like an engine bucking a snow-drift . . . and finally I accumulated so much snow that I came to a halt and could not get through. . . .

I believe that there are a far larger number of men who would at once sink every other purpose, no matter what their convictions might be, for the purpose of smashing me once and for all. . . . I believe that the bulk of our people would accept my candidacy as a proof of greedy personal ambition on my part, and would be bitterly hostile to me in consequence, and bitterly hostile therefore to the cause for which I stood. . . .

I think the people have made up their minds that they have had all they want of me.[100]

TR, 1906's Nobel Peace Prize winner, now longed for one last Rough Rider charge—if not up San Juan Hill, then to a mud-and-blood, artillery-wracked French no-man's-land. That June, he confided to Britain's Arthur Hamilton Lee, "I only wish I and my boys were beside you in the trenches. I am already planning to raise a division of mounted riflemen such as our old regiment. (It will fight in the trenches or anywhere else.) I have the brigade commanders and regimental commanders picked; but I do not believe Wilson can be kicked into war."[101]

But if America could not be kicked into war, it might be kicked into Preparedness.

"Pretty boys who know all
of the latest tango steps"

TO RAISE ANY DIVISION OF "MOUNTED RIFLEMEN," TR FACED INNUMER-
able obstacles. How might they coordinate with British or French
contingents? How might he cajole a decidedly uninterested Woodrow
Wilson to grant his request? And last but, practically, not least, how
would Theodore Roosevelt stay on his horse?

The battered fifty-six-year-old Bull Moose of 1915 was not the
jaunty Rough Rider of 1898. The years—and a foolhardy expedition into
the Amazon jungle—had inflicted their toll. In May 1915, his children
Ethel and Archie presented him with a new horse in honor of his splendid victory in the *Barnes v. Roosevelt* libel trial.[1] On Monday morning,
May 27, it threw to him to the ground, breaking two of his ribs.[2]

"I am practically over the effects of the accident," he ruefully wrote
Arthur Hamilton Lee in mid-June. "Of course, they were a little painful
for two or three weeks. The simple fact is that I tried to ride a horse that
was too good for me. I might just as well admit that I am old and stiff;
and while I can sit on a horse fairly well, I cannot mount him if he mis-
behaves. This horse threw me before I got my right foot into the stirrup,
and I struck the ground a good deal as if I had been a walrus."[3]

If some of his dreams seemed too personal and fanciful for his own
good, others did not.

Prior to assuming the presidency, or even the vice presidency, TR had
regularly employed the old West African proverb "Speak softly and carry
a big stick."[4] By 1915, he hadn't spoken softly for a long time, but he still
deemed "a big stick" necessary to national defense.

He also believed that had he held office in August 1914, war might never have erupted. Certainly, Wilson, distracted by a recent widower's grief, was not at his best. Even Colonel House took note of that, daring to write to the invariably thin-skinned Wilson on August 3, 1914, "Our people are deeply shocked at the enormity of the general European war, and I see here and there regret that you did not use your good offices in behalf of peace."[5]

True, TR would have brandished the gleaming sword of military might to secure that end, but it might have worked. The cheap sheen of Wilson's beatific weakness had not.

In the summer of 1915, Wilson chanced upon a little newspaper filler article indicating that "the General Staff is preparing a plan in the event of war with Germany."

Such news unhinged Wilson. With Secretary of War Lindley M. Garrison out of town, he summoned Garrison's assistant secretary, Henry Breckinridge. When Breckinridge pled ignorance, Wilson ordered him to get to the bottom of the matter—and, if the report was true, to immediately fire every member of the General Staff *and* order them all out of Washington.

Breckinridge contacted Acting Army Chief of Staff Tasker Bliss. Bliss recalled,

> *I told [Breckinridge] the law creating the General Staff made it its duty "to prepare plans for the national defense"; that I was President of the War College when the General Staff was organized in 1903; that from that time till then the College had studied over and over again plans for war with Germany, England, France, Italy, Japan, Mexico, etc. I said that if the President took the action threatened, it would only make patent to everybody what pretty much everybody already knew and would create a great political row, and, finally, it would be absurd.*
>
> *I think the President realized this in a cooler moment. Nothing further was said to him, about the matter, nor did he again mention it. But Mr. Breckinridge directed me to caution the War College to camouflage its work. It resulted in practically no further official studies.*[6]

A year or two later, Wilson had replaced Garrison with former Cleveland mayor Newton D. Baker. To Baker, he complained that the General Staff was still formulating contingency plans. Baker, new to his job and a confirmed pacifist, had no problem with that. "Mr. President," he calmly explained, "they have made war at the War College with every country in the world. The way they do it is to propose a problem. For example, suppose we had a war with France. Then a war is fought with France on paper, and the paper folded up and put away." Wilson pondered that. "That seems to me a very dangerous occupation," he commanded Baker. "I think you had better stop it."[7]

There was to be no planning—nor, for a long while, much Preparedness. "If this country needed a million men," William Jennings Bryan famously remarked in December 1914, "and needed them in a day, the call would go out at sunrise and the sun would go down on a million men under arms."[8] TR claimed to have heard a "Bryanite" senator do "The Great Commoner" one better, maintaining that "ten million freemen would spring to arms, the equals of any regular soldiers in the world."[9] TR countered that those ten million instant soldiers would possess "at the outside four hundred thousand modern rifles to which to spring. Perhaps six hundred thousand more could spring to squirrel pieces and fairly good shotguns. The remaining nine million would have to 'spring' to axes, scythes, handsaws, gimlets and similar arms."[10]

The country *was* unprepared for war. In early 1915, its army boasted a mobile force of only twenty-four thousand men—just twice the manpower of New York City's Police Department. It possessed barely enough ammunition for a day and a half of combat.[11] Army expenditures dropped by $6 million from June 30, 1914, to June 30, 1915, and by another $17 million in the following twelve months.[12]

Bryan, Baker, Secretary of the Navy Josephus Daniels—pacifists all. This was a very strange cast of characters for an administration teetering on war's edge. Yet not all of Wilson's men harbored such feelings. Colonel House's diary for July 1915 contained this entry: "If we had gone actively to work . . . to build up a war machine commensurate with our standing among the nations, we would be in a position to-day to enforce peace. If war comes with Germany because of this submarine controversy it will be because we are totally unprepared and Germany feels we are impotent."[13] A few days later, he warned Wilson directly of the "terrible gamble" that a policy of unpreparedness entailed.[14]

Wilson's first secretary of war, Lindley Garrison, favored a get-tough policy with Mexico, and when in early 1916 Wilson finally did proclaim his public support for Preparedness, Garrison advocated a "Continental Army Plan," a 140,000-man army augmented by 400,000 volunteer reservists.

Outstripping Garrison's enthusiasm for Preparedness was Franklin Roosevelt's.

From war's very onset Franklin grasped the magnitude of the responsibility—and the opportunity—to come. "A complete smash up is inevitable," he wrote to Eleanor on August 1, 1914, as Germany declared war on Russia. "These are history-making days. It will be the greatest war in the world's history"[15]—a war that would place him at odds not only with his superior, Josephus Daniels ("Mr. D. totally fails to grasp the situation"[16]), but also with much of the Wilson administration.

Franklin wrote to Eleanor the next day:

Mr. Daniels [was] feeling chiefly very sad that his faith in human nature and civilization and similar idealistic nonsense was receiving such a rude shock. So I started in alone to get things ready and prepare plans for what ought to be done by the Navy end of things. . . . Some fine day the State Department will want the moral backing of a "fleet in being" and it won't be there. All this sounds like borrowing trouble I know but it is my duty to keep the Navy in a position where no chances, even the most remote, are taken. Today we are taking chances and I nearly boil over when I see the cheery "manana" way of doing business.[17]

"I just know," he confided (or perhaps boasted) to Eleanor in April 1915, "I shall do some awful unneutral thing before I get through!"[18]

Unneutral not only in foreign matters but also in those of a domestic nature. With remarkably little respect for Josephus Daniels, Franklin was not above surreptitiously reaching across the political aisle to pro-military

Republicans. In October 1914, with Daniels out of town, FDR took it upon himself to release a memo supporting allegations of naval unpreparedness levied by Henry Cabot Lodge's son-in-law, Massachusetts Representative Augustus Gardner.[19] Two months later, at a public debate at Times Square's Hotel Astor, FDR advocated universal military training as "just plain common sense."

"An able-bodied boy," argued Franklin, "is better from every standpoint than a wretched runt, including the standpoint of the man at war."[20] Three days later, Woodrow Wilson essentially opposed universal military training in his annual address to Congress.[21]

Franklin tread on hostile territory even among his own friends. Theodore, however, recognized the perils that his cousin faced and further recognized how he might only aggravate them. In October 1914, as TR campaigned across New York State for his faltering Progressive Party, Franklin's mother, Sara Delano "Sally" Roosevelt, invited him to stop off at their Hyde Park estate. TR's son Ted accepted the invitation, and Franklin himself seemed overjoyed by the prospect. "I am perfectly delighted to hear . . . you . . . will spend the night of October 5 here," he advised his uncle. "*Nothing* could give me greater pleasure and I am counting on seeing you."[22]

When he was not being warlike, TR could be intensely diplomatic. This occasion demanded TR's best behavior—and he provided it. He gently advised Sara,

I am more than pleased at your letter. It was the first notice I had that we were to stay with you. Now, Sara, I am very doubtful, from Franklin's standpoint, whether it is wise that we were to stay with you and I have communicated with [Ted Jr.] to this effect. I shall be in the middle of a tour in which I am attacking the Administration, and I think it might well be an error, from Franklin's standpoint, if we stayed with you. If it were not during the campaign there is literally no place where I would rather go. And, of course, if the matter has been made public, it may be fine to go anyhow.

I hope you understand, dear Sally, that it is the exact truth to say that I am only thinking of Franklin's interest.[23]

Sara rescinded her invitation, advised her son of events, and continued on with a bit of political observation: "Of course, it is very kind of him, but why he should go on a tour deliberately to attack the Administration, is what I cannot see the wisdom of. I think no one gains by pulling others down. It is not a noble or high-minded viewpoint."[24]

TR's concerns regarding Franklin's safety were grounded in a more fearsome reality than either Sara or Franklin knew. As he toured upstate in October 1914, TR still concentrated on excoriating Billy Barnes's GOP machine, but with Primary Day past, he turned his fire on Washington, on Democrats—and on Franklin Roosevelt's Navy Department.

"During the last twenty months," he charged later that month in a *New York Times* article titled "The Navy as Peacemaker," "there has been in our Navy a great falling off relative to other nations. . . . The President who entrusts the departments of State and the Navy to gentlemen like Messrs. Bryan and Daniels deliberately invites disaster in the event of serious complications with a formidable foreign opponent."[25]

Wilson did not appreciate criticism, either of himself or of loyal subordinates—particularly not of Josephus Daniels. At a January 1916 luncheon, he was advised of a new rumor besmirching his navy secretary. "Daniels is surrounded by a network of conspiracy and of lies," he roared, pounding his fist upon the table. "His enemies are determined to ruin him. I can't be sure who they are yet, but when I do get them—God help them."[26]

If Wilson had ever fully realized FDR's attitudes regarding his chief, Franklin might also have needed God's help.

For his part, TR thought Wilson needed divine intervention regarding his seemingly unending transmittal of stern but ultimately toothless notes protesting German U-boat policy. Discussing Wilson's latest diplomatic note with his daughter Alice, he asked, his voice dripping with sarcasm, "Did you notice what its serial number was? I fear I have lost track myself; but I am inclined to think it is No 11,785, Series B."[27]

Theodore Roosevelt was always the manly sort and advocated similar manliness in his four sons.

His standards had their price. At age eleven, his oldest son Ted suffered blinding headaches—perhaps a nervous breakdown.[28] He recovered, overcoming his own diminutive frame, to emerge as quite the physical bruiser at Groton and a battered but undaunted 126-pound football player at Harvard. An academic suspension and an altercation with a Boston police officer further marked his undergraduate career. "I would rather one of [my sons] should die," TR said even after Ted's breakdown, "than have them grow up weaklings."[29]

One Sunday at Oyster Bay, the Colonel asked his friend and adviser, the *New York Tribune*'s labor correspondent John J. "Jack" Leary, how his own son was getting along. "All right," Leary answered, "only a little too much foot-ball and swimming and not enough school-work—almost too much boy." TR reassured him,

> *That's all right. Don't let that worry you. Do you know you are fortunate in having a real boy? Some of the most splendid fellows I know have boys that if they were mine I'd want to choke them—pretty boys who know all of the latest tango steps and the small talk, and the latest things in socks and ties—tame cats, mollycoddles, and their fathers real men, and their mothers most excellent women! Throw-backs, I suppose. I'd feel disgraced beyond redemption had I such boys.*
>
> *Mine, thank God, have been good boys, a bit mischievous at times, all of them, but every boy is. Honestly, if I had to take my choice, I'd rather have a boy that I'd have to go to the police station and bail out for beating a cab driver or a policeman, than one of the mollycoddle type. He might worry me, but he wouldn't disgrace me.[30]*

TR believed that all boys—and young men and some older men too—required training in the manly art of . . . war.

Nearly two months before the *Lusitania* tragedy, TR (thanks to Leonard Wood[31]) endorsed an organization called the American Legion, designed to provide a database of a quarter million experienced reservists poised to serve at the outbreak of hostilities. "Line" members were former military. "Specials" were those men (and occasionally women) possessing special skills needed by the military, everyone from nurses to steam fitters, mule packers to radio operators, hunters and trappers to photographers and pharmacists. Dues were set at twenty cents a year. Membership was limited to actual citizens between the ages of eighteen and fifty-five. Eschewing "militarism," cofounder Dr. John E. Hausmann, editor of *Adventure Magazine*, nonetheless freely admitted that the idea originally sprang from a prewar concept of "a legion of adventurers."

Among the Legion's founding cadre at New York's Adventurers Club was Theodore Roosevelt Jr. "I and my four sons will gladly become members," TR informed the Legion in late February. "I especially hope and pray that there will be no war; but the surest way to avert war is to be prepared for it."[32]

He was not always so pacific. In 1889, when German and American warships challenged each other in Samoa, he had confided to Cecil Spring-Rice, "Frankly, I don't know that I should be sorry to see a bit of a spar with Germany; the burning of New York and a few other seacoast cities would be a good object lesson on the need of an adequate system of coastal defences."[33]

During 1895's British-Venezuelan border spat, TR wrote Cabot Lodge, "I don't care whether our sea coast cities are bombarded or not. We would take Canada. . . . Personally, I rather hope that the fight will come soon. The clamor of the peace faction has convinced me this country needs a war."[34] He shifted gears, to war with Spain, not long afterward, confessing to his older sister, Anna Roosevelt "Bye" Cowles, "If it wasn't wrong I would say personally I would rather welcome a foreign war!"[35]

At the Naval War College in June 1897, he had thundered, "All the great masterful races have been fighting races; and the minute that a race loses the hard-fighting virtues, then . . . it has lost its proud right to stand as the equal of the best. . . . No triumph of peace is quite so great as the supreme triumphs of war."[36]

There lay within him a sheer bloodlust. In December 1892, he informed *The Cosmopolitan*'s readers, "Every man who has in him any real power of joy in battle knows that he feels it when the wolf begins to rise in his heart; *he does not shrink from blood and sweat*, or deem that they mar the fight; *he revels in them*, and the toll, the pain and the danger, as but setting off the triumph"[37] (emphasis added).

Why such a martial strain?

The boy is father to the man, and the sickly asthmatic boy who built himself up into a cowboy and a Rough Rider provides a partial answer to the riddle.

But Theodore repeatedly averred that he considered his own father "the best man I ever knew."[38] Perhaps he was. Or perhaps TR protested too much, for there remained a singular blot on the escutcheon of Theodore "Thee" Roosevelt Sr.

The man was a draft dodger.

A *legal* draft dodger but nonetheless one who paid a substitute a then princely $1,000 to take his place in the Civil War.

"Thee" Roosevelt was never proud of his decision.

And though he never mentioned it, his son likely wasn't either.[39]

Nor would he ever wish to emulate it.

In his early Washington years, TR acquired a lifelong friend and ally: "a playmate who fairly walked me off my legs; a Massachusetts man moreover, an army surgeon named Wood."[40]

Leonard Wood had battled Geronimo in the 1880s. He attended both Grover Cleveland and William McKinley as personal physician. He served alongside Theodore in Cuba and later as military governor of Santiago, Cuba, where he faced charges of improperly accepted gifts from Havana jai alai interests.[41] In the Philippines, he commanded anti-insurgent troops. In December 1909—partially to please TR—William Howard Taft designated him army chief of staff, an unprecedented appointment for a physician. He had climbed the rungs of power—and not entirely by accident. "His zeal for the public service always went hand in hand with his zeal for his own advancement," reflected journalist Oswald Garrison Villard. "Of all the men I have known and studied, [he] seems to me to have been the most blindly ambitious. . . . [H]e would have been the ideal fascist leader."[42]

Wilson replaced Wood as chief of staff in 1914, but he remained on active duty, loudly echoing TR's Preparedness worldview. When the *Lusitania* sank, Wood confided to his diary, "Rotten spirit in the *Lusitania* matter. Yellow spirit everywhere."[43] To Wood, William Jennings Bryan was "an ass of the first class."[44] His public remarks were little better guarded. In December 1914, he informed Manhattan's New York Merchants Association, "A government is the murderer of its people which sends them to the field uninformed and untaught."[45] Woodrow Wilson was not amused.[46] Two secretaries of war eventually deemed Wood sufficiently insubordinate to merit court-martial—though neither dared to grant him public martyr status.[47] As a later historian observed, Wood was "a fine soldier but a poor subordinate."[48]

To ensure a trained officer cadre if war came, in 1913 Wood established two summer camps, at Gettysburg, Pennsylvania, and Monterey, California. Middle- and upper-class males rallied to the idea the following summer at camps in Michigan, North Carolina, and Vermont. By 1915, fifteen young patriots (twenty-seven-year-old Theodore Roosevelt Jr. and TR's thirty-four-year-old son-in-law Dr. Richard Derby among them) gathered at New York's Harvard Club to petition Wood to institute a "Businessmen's Camp" at Plattsburgh, New York. A thousand men attended that summer's first session. Even more attended in 1916. Full-page advertisements in *Collier's Weekly*, the *Saturday Evening Post*, and the *New Outlook* exhorted recruits, "Give your vacation to your country and still have the best vacation you ever had."[49]

To American Federation of Labor president Samuel Gompers, Wood described his Plattsburgh recruits as "a very typical American group."[50] Almost exclusively upper-class, they were anything but. Celebrity "rookies" included New York mayor John Purroy Mitchel, Mitchel's police commissioner Arthur Woods, *Vanity Fair* publisher Frank Crowninshield, legendary war correspondent Richard Harding Davis, TR's former secretary of state Robert Bacon, Harvard football coach Percy Duncan Haughton, Rhode Island Episcopal bishop James

DeWolf Perry, and New York assemblyman Hamilton Fish Jr.—as well as three Roosevelt offspring: Ted, twenty-five-year-old Kermit, and twenty-one-year-old Archie.[51] An emergency appendectomy shelved Franklin Roosevelt's plans to attend in 1915[52] but not his enthusiasm for the idea. In 1916, he instituted its naval version.[53]

"You feel yourself to be nothing—merely a cog in a powerful machine that is marching irresistibly on," Derby (a better surgeon than shot) wrote his wife, Ethel. "And then the tramp of 250 [marching] feet on the hard macadam road thrills you with a sensation entirely new. You are part of it, and you are glad and proud that you are, and are ever alert to make the whole as perfect as is in your power."[54]

Woodrow Wilson endorsed this "Plattsburgh Idea," but, like Gompers, Garrison, Taft, and Elihu Root, he categorically refused Wood's invitation to view its facilities. TR did not. On Tuesday night, August 24, 1915, he arrived not only to tour the site but also to address its recruits. Wood vetted his remarks—but not nearly enough.

The next morning, TR, attired in a tan suit, military-style campaign hat, and leather breeches, reviewed battalion exercises. He took midday "chow" with the men. He observed the camp's cavalry, engineering, and artillery units in action. All fourteen hundred trainees passed in review. After supper, with two thousand civilians crowding behind them, they assembled on the camp's drill plain to hear TR not merely flay the dangers of complacency and a soft life but also—at a federal military base—openly lacerate the Wilson administration.

> *For thirteen months America has played an ignoble part among the nations. We have tamely submitted to seeing the weak, whom we have covenanted to protect, wronged. We have seen our men, women, and children murdered on the high seas without protest. We have used elocution as a substitute for action.*
>
> *During this time our government has not taken the smallest step in the way of preparedness to defend our own rights. . . . Reliance upon high sounding words, unbacked by deeds, is proof of a mind that dwells only in the realm of shadow and of sham.*

It is not a lofty thing, on the contrary, it is an evil thing, to practise a timid and selfish neutrality between right and wrong. It is wrong for an individual. It is still more wrong for a nation.[55]

As he spoke, a little wire-haired Airedale terrier wandered by, seeking its master. Bewildered by the huge gathering, it raced back and forth. Bumping into TR, it lay flat on its back, paws pointed upward as the crowd convulsed with laughter. "That's a fine dog. I like him," TR exclaimed. "His present attitude is strictly one of neutrality."[56]

Wood ordered his friend's text softened before its distribution to the press. Instead, one of TR's aides circulated his unexpurgated remarks.

Later that night, TR poured more gasoline on the fire, informing reporters,

I wish to make one comment on the statement so frequently made that we must stand by the President. I heartily subscribe to this on condition, and only on condition, that it is followed by the statement "so long as the President stands by the country."

It is defensible to state that we stand by the country, right or wrong; it is not defensible for any free man in a free republic to state that he will stand by any official right or wrong, or by any ex-official. . . .

Presidents differ, just like other folks. No man could effectively stand by President Lincoln unless he had stood against President Buchanan. If, after the firing on Sumter, President Lincoln had in a public speech announced that the believers in the Union were too proud to fight, and if instead of action there had been three months of admirable elocutionary correspondence with Jefferson Davis, by midsummer the friends of the Union would have followed Horace Greeley's advice, to let the erring sisters go in peace—for peace at that date was put above righteousness by some mistaken souls, just as it is at the present day.

The man who believes in peace at any price or in substituting all-inclusive arbitration treaties for an army and navy should instantly move to China. If he stays here, then more manly people will

have to defend him, and he is not worth defending. Let him get out of
the country as quickly as possible.[57]

At 5:00 the next morning, Assistant Secretary of War Henry Breckinridge learned of TR's Plattsburgh adventures. Hostile to General Wood to begin with, he raced to Lindley Garrison's home, determined to goad him into action. An enraged Garrison (who implausibly denied discussing the matter with Wilson) noted,

> *It is difficult to conceive of anything which could have a more det-*
> *rimental effect upon the real value of this experiment than such an*
> *incident. . . .*
>   *There must not be any opportunity given at Plattsburgh or any*
> *other similar camp for any such unfortunate consequences.*[58]

The Colonel's words shocked even many Preparedness advocates. Willard Straight, publisher of the recently founded *New Republic* (once rumored to be wed to Ethel Roosevelt[59]), complained of Roosevelt's "unfortunate habit of deterring a great many people from supporting a perfectly good cause."[60] The *Chicago Tribune* pronounced his speech in "bad taste or worse. . . . [It] has hurt the movement of national defense a little. It has hurt Mr. Roosevelt more."[61]

Wood's Plattsburgh volunteers stood solidly behind him. "There was not a dissenting voice in the matter,"[62] noted the *New York Herald*, but still General Wood had to swallow hard, salute, and agree with Lindley Garrison.[63] Colonel Roosevelt didn't, firing yet another salvo toward the Potomac: "If the Administration had displayed one-tenth the spirit and energy in holding Germany and Mexico to account for the murder of men, women, and children that it is now displaying . . . to prevent our people from being taught the need of preparation to prevent the repetition of such murders in the future, it would be rendering a service to the people of the country."[64]

Secretary Garrison tried heaping ridicule upon TR. Roosevelt derided Garrison's "buffoonery."[65] Moreover, he claimed that *he* was the man of peace in this great debate:

I challenge [Garrison] to show where I have ever advocated going to war with any nation because of our preparedness.

During my service . . . as president not one shot was fired by any American soldier or sailor against a foreign foe nor was any American sailor or soldier killed by a foreign foe.

But while President Wilson was waging peace a score or two of American sailors and soldiers or Marines have been killed or wounded at Veracruz and on our own soil along the Mexican border and in Haiti. If we had acted properly in Mexico in all probability there never would have been an American ship sunk nor a single American murdered on the high seas by Germany.[66]

Haiti.

Haiti was another of those decrepit republics-in-name-only located to our south that managed their internal affairs badly and their external financial matters not at all. In both 1897 and 1902, Germany had seriously interfered in Haitian internal affairs (in 1897 demanding an apology for the arrest of a German national in the form of a twenty-one-gun salute to the German flag). January 1914 saw German, British, and American troops land to protect order. The following year, outraged Haitians invaded the French embassy in pursuit of their latest repressive president. They tossed his corpse over the embassy fence before tearing it to pieces and parading the remains through town. A horrified Wilson dispatched 330 Marines and declared a virtual American protectorate over the essentially failed state.

"What is being done for Hayti . . . is to lift her out of the hands of her thieves," observed *Life* magazine. "It can be done for her, because her need . . . is so conspicuous, and because she is so small. It needs, apparently, to be done for Mexico also, but Mexico is bigger, her neighbors are more sensitive, her population averages several shades lighter in complexion, and her capacity for self-help, though not imposing, undoubtedly beats Hayti's."[67]

Mexico.

"Lord, I am feeling warlike with this Administration!"[68] TR wrote Cabot Lodge in February 1915, in part because of Mexico.

Mexican strongman Porfirio Díaz had provided decades of stability and economic growth to his nation. But his administration had also parceled out the nation's landholdings to his supporters. By early 1911, his increasingly unpopular regime offered scant resistance to a wide variety of revolutionary forces. From exile in America, wealthy ranch owner Francisco Madero provided an intellectual rationale for resistance. Regional insurgents Francisco "Pancho" Villa, Pascual Orozco, and Venustiano Carranza flourished in the north. Emiliano Zapata led a peasant revolt further south. In October 1911, the ineffectual Madero emerged as Mexico's new president but was soon overthrown and brutally murdered ("while attempting to escape"[69]) by General Victoriano Huerta. Huerta's May 1913 coup (and most likely Madero's murder) had been abetted by Taft's ambassador to Mexico, Henry Lane Wilson.

Mexico descended into revolution and murder. Woodrow Wilson assisted its fall into absolute chaos. Deeply offended by Madero's killing, he sacked Ambassador Wilson, took the largely unprecedented step of refusing to recognize Huerta,[70] and "earnestly urge[d] all Americans to leave Mexico at once."[71]

In March 1912, Taft had embargoed all American arms and munitions from reaching Mexico. In February 1913, Wilson exempted Carranza—but not the embattled Huerta—from the ban. Even Madero's foreign affairs secretary, Manuel Calero y Sierra, observed, "Huerta was a usurper. But did it belong to the President of the United States to drive him from the place usurped? This was a matter that concerned exclusively the Mexican people."[72] And if Mexicans did not already resent Woodrow Wilson's campaign to make Mexico safe for democracy, they soon would.

"This was intervention," Roosevelt seethed, "and nothing else; it was such intervention as if in 1877 some European government had declined to recognize Hayes as President, and insisted upon the seating of Tilden."[73]

In April 1914, nine sailors from the U.S. Navy gunboat USS *Dolphin* went ashore at the Huerta-controlled oil and port city of Tampico to secure gasoline. Confused Huertista forces briefly arrested them. Though they were released within minutes, American naval forces demanded a full apology and a twenty-one-gun salute to the U.S. flag. Huerta agreed to apologize but refused to salute the U.S. flag on Mexican soil.

Huerta agreed to arbitration. Wilson refused.[74] He demanded congressional authorization for "the employment of armed forces" against Mexico ("but not to make war on" her) to secure "unequivocal amends" for unspecified "affronts and indignities." The House acceded 337–37. The Senate followed suit 72–13, all opposed being Republicans, including senators Lodge, Root, and La Follette.[75]

New sparks flew at Veracruz when the German tank steamer SS *Ypiranga* arrived bearing arms and munitions for Huerta. Wilson ordered the city seized. Mexicans rioted. More U.S. warships—including the battleships *Utah*, *Florida*, and *New Hampshire*—arrived. Soon 19 dead and 70 wounded Americans littered Veracruz's streets; 126 Mexicans perished, with another 250 injured.

With U.S. forces occupying Veracruz through November 1914, anti-American feeling erupted throughout Mexico. Thousands of American citizens fled back across the U.S. border. Venustiano Carranza might be battling Huerta, who might be battling Wilson, but Carranza still had no use for American Marines shooting up Mexican streets. A move designed to portray America as a friend to Mexican democracy and reform thus only accelerated the growing anti-Yankee backlash.

At home, Bryan alienated Americans protesting the seizure of their land and property. "You seem," he pooh-poohed their concerns, "to be afraid that one of your steers will be killed and eaten by the Mexicans."[76] Joseph Tumulty curtly informed one American owner of Mexican property that "the President could not see every gink who came from Mexico. . . . I suppose you are another fellow who has lost a cow."[77]

TR held his tongue during 1914's midterms but scalded Wilson and Bryan in a December 6, 1914, *New York Times Magazine* article. Deriding claims that Wilson had "kept us out of war with Mexico," TR asserted, "Thanks to President Wilson's action . . . this country has become partially (and guiltily) responsible for some of the worst acts ever committed even in the civil wars of Mexico."[78]

Devoting much space to anti-Catholic outrages in war-ravaged Mexico, TR charged,

Messrs. Wilson and Bryan . . . have assumed a certain undoubted responsibility for the behavior of the victorious faction in Mexico which has just taken the kind of stand . . . hostile to every principle of real religious liberty. . . . Catholic schools almost everywhere in Mexico have been closed, institutions of learning sacked and libraries and astronomical and other machinery destroyed, the priests and nuns expelled by hundreds and some of the priests killed and some of the nuns outraged. . . . [C]hurches have been profaned by soldiers entering them on horseback, breaking statues, trampling on relics and scattering on the floor the Sacred Hosts and even throwing them into the horses' feed; . . . in some churches the revolutionaries have offered mock masses and have in other ways, some of them too repulsive and loathsome to mention, behaved precisely as the Red Terrorists of the French Revolution behaved in the churches of Paris.[79]

In a March 1915 *Metropolitan Magazine* article, "Uncle Sam and the Rest of the World," TR denied any sympathy for Huerta but derided any "endeavor to replace him with a polygamous bandit" like Pancho Villa. He decried Wilson's habit of condemning Huerta's actions while "ignoring" Villa's "far worse misdeeds" before shifting U.S. support from Villa to Carranza, "who was responsible for exactly the same kind of hideous outrages."

"Murder and torture, rape and robbery; the death of women by outrage and children by starvation; the shooting of men by the thousand in cold blood—Mr. Wilson takes note of these facts only to defend the right of vicious and disorderly Mexicans to 'spill' as much as they please of the blood of their fellow-citizens and of law-abiding foreigners."[80]

In newspapers across America, from New York to Boston to Atlanta to Emporia, *Metropolitan Magazine* purchased two-column display ads touting TR's article:

Stop the Murders in Mexico
—Col. Roosevelt

In Mexico men like you, Americans, brothers to you by the same blood, have been murdered. American women like your wife and sisters have

been outraged. American homes like your home, hallowed with the
same dear associations, have been pillaged and burned.
    Read Colonel Roosevelt's indictment of a government that has
done nothing. Learn the menace that present-day Mexico is to our
peace with the world.[81]

Yet, in one very real (albeit short-term) sense, Wilson's policy of
Mexican "watchful waiting" had succeeded. Surrounded on all sides and
without funds or materiel to wage war, Huerta fled the country in July
1914, first to Jamaica, then to Spain and the United Kingdom, and finally
(and most ironically) to the United States. Fulfilling Wilson's hopes, Carranza replaced Huerta. Yet Carranza's rise could not prevent his nation's
further fall. In revolutionary Mexico the game was simple: change partners and kill. Within weeks, Zapata, hungering for speedier and more
ambitious land reform, turned on Carranza. By September 1914, so had
Pancho Villa.

Influential Americans fell over themselves to flatter Villa. "His soldiers idolize him," gushed Bryan, "and he seems to have no ambition
whatsoever except to see [land] reforms carried out."[82] Colonel House
saw Villa as "the only man of force now in Mexico."[83]

Hearst proclaimed,

The one man in [Mexico] who has appeared to tower above all others
in personal power and capacity, in the magnetism to lead, the mastery
to command, and the ability to execute, is Francisco Villa.
    If Villa is made president he will . . . establish a stable and
reliable government. If another man is made president by foreign
interference he will have to reckon with Villa and with the masses
who believe in Villa.[84]

Despite Hearst's warm words, as Villa and Carranza battled in
Chihuahua Province in December 1915, two thousand Villistas invaded
Hearst's 1,625,000-acre Barbicora ranch. Before Diaz's fall, Barbicora
boasted seventy-five thousand head of cattle, six thousand sheep, and two
thousand horses. By 1915, it had deteriorated sharply. But it remained a

tempting target for any starving army to loot—and the Villistas did. Over a fourteen-month period, Hearst lost somewhere between twenty-five and sixty thousand head of cattle—plus a thousand horses and mules. Villistas confiscated thirty-five thousand bushels of corn and beans and burned an equal amount. For good measure, they kidnapped four Hearst employees and killed the hacienda's bookkeeper.[85]

Some might have gloated that Hearst deserved whatever befell him. Not, however, because he exploited the Mexican economy or because he was fabulously wealthy or because his papers sometimes sensationalized the truth (or simply ignored it). No, it was because of Hearst's positions on war and peace, on Teutons and on Allies.

TR might have been one of those lacking sympathy for "The Chief," as Hearst's minions called him. For the Colonel regarded William Randolph Hearst as "the most sinister pro-German traitor in the country and much the ablest and most dangerous."[86]

To Theodore Roosevelt, there were far too many sharing Hearst's brand of treason.

He called them "hyphenated-Americans."

"The most educational drama
I have ever witnessed"

WILLIAM RANDOLPH HEARST DIDN'T JUST OWN A STRING OF DAILIES IN such cities as New York, Chicago, Atlanta, Boston, Detroit, and Los Angeles, as well as several major magazines; he also produced films.

In 1916, he issued an action-packed, fifteen-episode silent-film serial featuring a rough-and-ready heroine: *Patria*, which chronicled "Preparedness heiress" Patria Channing's battle against invading Japanese and Mexican armies. "Evidence in support of Japan's designs against our peace are not lacking," read one of *Patria*'s title cards. "The presence of her armies in Mexico, a hotbed of revolution, is known to the administration in Washington, if not the people."[1] Irene Castle, the distaff half of the immensely popular Vernon and Irene Castle ballroom dance team,[2] played Patria. Swedish-born Werner Oland (not yet ready for his close-up as Charlie Chan) portrayed the villainous Baron Huroki. The plot: Patria inherits a $100 million fortune, outfits and commands an entire army, and gives the evil Huroki what's coming to him.

Except by the time Episode 11 reached theaters, Baron Huroki (still played by Oland) had become Manuel Morales, as America had by then entered the war allied with formerly nefarious Japan. When Woodrow Wilson (an enthusiastic film and vaudeville fan) happened to catch *Patria* at Washington's National Theater, he personally intervened to soften (i.e., censor) its anti-Japanese message.

The infant film industry had lost no time in becoming politicized.

Crudely faked accounts of the battles of the Spanish-American War's Manila Bay and Santiago Bay or of France's Dreyfus Affair thrilled unwary early audiences. D. W. Griffith's *The Birth of a Nation* shattered box office records with politics of a different sort. His three-and-a-half-hour 1916 follow-up effort, *Intolerance*, featured vaguely pacifist themes, while Thomas Ince's million-dollar blockbuster *Civilization: An Epic of Humanity* pulled out all the antiwar stops: aerial combat, a doomed passenger liner, cavalry charges, a conscience-stricken submarine commander, the pleas of a grieving mother—and direct (though silent) cautions issued by Jesus Christ. That same year, Broadway's exotic Crimean-born Alla Nazimova starred in Lewis J. Selznick's *War Brides*, a distinctly feminist antiwar melodrama exhorting women against bearing a new generation of soldiers for slaughter, ending with Nazimova's character publicly killing herself and her unborn child. The film netted an immense $300,000 profit.

The year 1916 also witnessed a slew of offerings designed to exploit hysteria, the most elaborate emanating from D. W. Griffith's erstwhile *The Birth of a Nation* muse, Thomas Dixon Jr. Dixon's elaborate *The Fall of a Nation* featured not only the usual hubbub over a decidedly Germanic-looking foreign invasion but also an original score by Victor Herbert.

A quartet of sensational serials augmented Dixon's pro-Preparedness theme. The fifteen-part *The Secret of the Submarine* promised not merely to strike "the keynote of real Americanism"[3] but also to somehow produce "a powerful bearing on the presidential campaigns."[4] *The Yellow Menace* ("SIXTEEN EPISODES EACH OF WHICH LEAVES YOUR AUDIENCE WONDERING—WHAT NEXT?"[5]) highlighted a suspiciously Caucasian-looking "Mongolian Demon" (with an oddly Indian-sounding name, Ali Singh) bent on invading "a Helpless United States"[6] following passage of restrictionist immigration legislation. The film sounded "a trumpet call of preparedness against the danger from across the Pacific, against which Ex-President Roosevelt has warned the country."[7] Pearl White, of *The Perils of Pauline* fame, battled the black-masked "Silent Menace" to preserve the secret plans for defending the Panama Canal in Astra Studio's fifteen-episode *Pearl of the Army*. A Philadelphia theater owner reported that it "created a remarkable sensation," noting, "As the various notable men of our national life were introduced, including Lincoln, Roosevelt and President Wilson, the enthusiasm of the spectators waxed, and as the alert orchestra leader swung into the strains of 'The Star Spangled Banner,' the audience joined lustily in the chorus. The picture was shown at the end of the regular vaudeville program, yet scarcely a person left a seat until it was ended."[8] Not to be outdone (save, perchance, in quality), Carl Laemmle's Universal Studios churned out the five-episode *Behind the Lines*[9] as well as the twenty-part *Liberty*, both dealing with plucky heroines along and beyond the Mexican border.[10]

Even before those films came to a movie theater near you (or, rather, your great-grandparents), Theodore Roosevelt assisted in producing the most powerful pro-Preparedness film of all.

In early 1915, Hearst's International Library Co. published inventor Hudson Maxim's *Defenseless America*, a detailed study of American military weakness—periodically punctuated by gibes against domestic pacifist thought. Suffice it to say, Maxim was no pacifist. He had invented smokeless gunpowder, losing his left hand in the process. His older brother developed the Maxim machine gun. His nephew perfected the Maxim Silencer.[11] Despite a hefty $2.00 price tag, *Defenseless America* quickly achieved best-seller status.

Nearly next-door to TR's Sagamore Hill lay Harbourwood, the magnificent, sixty-one-acre estate of Yorkshire-born Vitagraph film studios executive Commodore (the title reflected his New York Yacht Club status) J. Stuart Blackton, perpetrator of 1898's staged (i.e., faked) documentary films *Battle of Manila Bay* and *Battle of Santiago Bay*. The two neighbors had known and admired each other since their Spanish-American War days, when Blackton may—or may not (accounts differ)—have filmed TR's assault on San Juan Hill.[12]

In 1915, Blackton aimed to convert Maxim's data-driven, plotless, characterless *Defenseless America* into a rip-roaring pro-Preparedness melodrama—the rough equivalent of translating *On the Origin of Species* into *Jurassic Park*. In April 1915, he approached TR.

"Mr. Roosevelt," he pled, "I intend to make a motion picture showing what would happen if this country was invaded by an enemy army. I'm going to put the facts before the American public and try to arouse them to . . . their danger. If I succeed in this I believe we will see action. I believe that we will arm and be ready to fight . . . if we must. What do you think of the idea?"

TR banged his fist and proclaimed (what else?), "Bully!"

"Then," asked Blackton, "are you willing to give me your support, to help me then reach the men who are needed to give this thing substance and authority?"

"Blackton," TR responded, "get a bang-up story for your movie and bring it here Sunday. I'll have the men you want alright, and I'll give you a theme for that story."

"Here it is," TR quickly continued. "Ezekiel chapter 33, verse 4, 'Then whosoever heareth the sound of the trumpet and take it not warning, if the sword come and take him away, his blood shall be upon his head.'"

The Commodore lit up a cigarette. "Blackton," the Colonel admonished him, shoving a box of cigars at him, "you look like a fool with that thing in your mouth. Here, have a man's smoke!"

Blackton never smoked another cigarette in his life.

A week later, Blackton pitched his outline not only to TR but also to Leonard Wood, New York City mayor John Purroy Mitchel, the Reverend Lyman Abbott, Cornelius "Neily" Vanderbilt III (yet another Yacht Club commodore—and soon to see service in Mexico), and even seventy-seven-year-old Admiral of the Navy George Dewey.

With TR's prodding, Wood soon supplied hordes of troops to serve as *Defenseless America* extras. Secretary of War Lindley Garrison provided his assistance, and twenty-five thousand National Guardsmen ultimately appeared in Blackton's epic.

That August, Blackton previewed his nine-reel epic for the press, promising similar previews at military camps, for various unnamed officials in Washington and the Army and Navy League, and even upon the White

House lawn. He vowed that an incredible 75 million people would view the film within six months. Furthermore, a novelization of the film debuted "simultaneously with the release of the film, thus for the first time linking . . . a work thru two different media—literature and the motion picture."[13]

The Battle Cry of Peace debuted at Times Square's nine-hundred-seat Vitagraph Theatre on Thursday, September 9, 1915, amid an avalanche of what *Variety* lauded as a "whirlwind publicity." "Every bit of [publicity] copy," *Variety* gushed, "has been on a high class, dignified and convincing plane."[14] A twenty-five-piece orchestra afforded proper accompaniment, while khaki-clad usherettes ("girl soldiers"[15]) escorted patrons to their seats. Capacity crowds literally snaked around Broadway to 44th Street.

The *New York Dramatic Mirror* described the film itself:

> *While the peace advocates are holding a monster meeting, the shells of an invading fleet burst just as the doves of peace encircle the meeting hall. The shells were apparently the only warning or declaration of war that is needed in modern international affairs. As a picture, "The Battle Cry of Peace" now reaches its strongest moments. The brilliant White Way and gay pleasure-seekers that we had seen a few moments before are replaced by shell-torn buildings and terror-stricken inhabitants fleeing inland. Big guns roar, aeroplanes whirl over the city with death-dealing bombs. Our coast guns are out-ranged and the capture of the city is naturally not long delayed. There are more battles in store—vivid scenes they are—before the American army, unequipped and outnumbered, surrenders.*[16]

Embracing even more didactic "propaganda," the film also featured lengthy commentary ("The Remedy") from Maxim and (with TR's assistance) appearances by Leonard Wood, Henry Stimson, and Admiral Dewey. Democrats Lindley Garrison, TR's 1904 opponent Alton B. Parker, and William Jennings Bryan's more warlike and pro-British replacement as secretary of state, Robert Lansing, delivered similar on-screen encouragement—as did William Howard Taft.

TR demurred, arguing that he did not wish to be seen as politicizing the film.[17] Also not appearing was Leon Trotsky, though a legend eventually developed that, as "Leber Bronstein," he toiled among Blackton's eight thousand extras.[18] Perhaps he, too, did not wish to politicize the motion picture.

The Canadian army employed the film as a recruiting tool.[19] Los Angeles theaters exhibiting it doubled as recruiting stations.[20] The show-business weekly the *New York Clipper* mused, "Fifty years from now 'The Battle Cry of Peace' may be considered in the present light of 'Uncle Tom's Cabin.'"[21]

The *Clipper* loved it. The *New York Times* didn't: "Mr. Blackton deals roughly with the pacifists and generally advances his argument by bludgeon strokes. There is nothing in the least bit subtle about 'The Battle Cry for Peace.' None of it will go over the head of even the 75th million. And it is designed to make many a person in each audience resolve to join the National Guard, the American Legion, the National Security League, and the Navy League, forthwith, and to write to his congressman by the next mail."[22]

TR—who rarely attended anything cinematic or theatrical[23]—neglected to actually view the film until a late October matinee. "I wish I had it in my power," he told the press, "to make a law compelling every man, woman and child in the United States to see 'The Battle Cry of Peace,' particularly the young pacifists. It is the primer, the public school and the college of preparedness. 'The Battle Cry of Peace' preaches the text, not of 'America for Americans,' but of 'The Americans for America.' It is the most educational drama I have ever witnessed. I did not think that motion pictures were so capable of impressing the human mind."[24]

The *Boston Globe* thought the film rivaled *The Birth of a Nation*.[25] But just as Boston had unsuccessfully debated banning Griffith's epic, outraged Bay State German-Americans now clamored to censor *The Battle Cry of Peace*. Alerted to this development by the manager of Boston's Majestic Theater, TR responded,

> *These Germans and German sympathizers are hostile . . . because it advocates American preparedness. It shows that they wish to keep America unprepared and therefore liable to fall a victim exactly as*

Belgium fell a victim. Such action . . . is absolutely incompatible with their being really loyal citizens of the United States.

Now, as to their allegation that the play is calculated to excite animosity to Germany. This allegation on their part can only come from guilty consciences. There is not an allusion to Germany in the play. Mr. Blackton . . . told me that he was exceedingly careful, even in such matters as the uniform of the invaders not to give a scene which would indicate one foreign nation more than another. . . .

Every good American should be grateful to Mr. Blackton. . . . Every uninformed but well-meaning American should attend the exhibition and profit by it. The men who oppose it . . . are thoroughly bad Americans and are engaged in an action hostile to the vital interests of the United States.[26]

TR argued that *The Battle Cry of Peace*'s spike-helmeted invaders were not German. But, as the *Times* observed, "they are certainly not Portuguese."[27] Or, as Blackton admitted to his daughter, "I think I'll call them Ruritanians, but I'll make them look like Germans."[28]

From Boston, *The Battle Cry of Peace* moved west. That December Vitagraph airplanes bombarded Detroit passersby with leaflets touting the film. Outraged Detroiter Henry Ford counterattacked with full-page advertisements in 250 newspapers nationwide, including the *Washington Post*, the *Brooklyn Eagle*, the *Los Angeles Herald*, and New York's *Times*, *Evening Post*, *Evening Telegram*, *World*, and *Herald*. "Mr. Maxim," Ford's ads asserted, "was merely advertising his wares and playing on your fears to make a market for his goods. Mr. Maxim has something to sell—war munitions."[29]

Resenting such imputations (and, more important, a potential loss of business), Vitagraph, in August 1916, sued Ford for $1 million. Legal motion followed legal motion before Vitagraph's case died of natural causes, but not before *The Battle Cry of Peace* returned a handsome profit.[30]

"From all this," chortled Blackton, "the deduction is plain. Mr. Ford shouldn't have built a Peace Ship, he shouldn't have put up placards, he shouldn't have called names. He should have made a motion picture!"[31]

"Go home to Germany"

BLOCKBUSTER FILMS WERE FAIRLY NOVEL. TR'S VIEW OF AMERICANISM was hardly new. In April 1890, in prefacing his *A History of New York City*, he declared, "Our citizens should act as Americans; not as Americans with a prefix and qualification;—not as Irish-Americans, German-Americans, Native Americans,—but as Americans pure and simple."[1] In the April 1894 issue of *The Forum* magazine, he proclaimed,

> *We welcome the German or the Irishman who becomes an American. We have no use for the German or Irish-man who remains such. . . . [W]e want only Americans, and, provided they are such, we do not care whether they are of native or of Irish or of German ancestry. We have no room in any healthy American community for a German-American vote or an Irish-American vote, and it is contemptible demagogy to put planks into any party platform [to catch] such a vote. We have no room for any people who do not act and vote simply as Americans and nothing else.*[2]

German and Irish (or Italian or Swedish, etc.) Americans might find it far less easy than TR imagined to abandon all affections and sympathies for their native lands. Even J. Stuart Blackton, who had immigrated from England at age ten, never sought citizenship until commencing production on *The Battle Cry of Peace* in the summer of 1915.[3]

Blackton retained a natural sympathy for his fatherland. So did German-born George Sylvester Viereck.

Viereck's father, journalist Louis Viereck, had served as a Socialist Workers' Party Reichstag deputy. More interestingly, he was reputedly the illegitimate son of Germany's first kaiser, Wilhelm I, by the royal court actress Edwina Viereck. In October 1889, both Louis and his ten-year-old son George Sylvester relocated to New York. Barely a decade later, critics acclaimed George as one of America's great young poets. Alice Roosevelt Longworth shared his 1907 effort "Ninevah" with her father,[4] who deemed it "a bully poem."[5] Others were less enthusiastic. The "incredible egotism" of Viereck's poems, thought *The Dial*'s William Morton Payne, "is very amusing when we realize upon how slight a foundation of achievement it is based. For the author is a very minor poet, distinguished chiefly by an erotic mania and a predilection for toying with unclean themes."[6]

Father and son Viereck were political progressives and TR supporters. TR found Louis Viereck's endorsement helpful in securing German-American votes. Thus, when in 1910 George solicited funds for a new German-language magazine, *Rundschau Zweier Welten* (*Review of Two Worlds*), TR rallied to his cause ("I feel that in America there is especial need of keeping alive a thorough knowledge of German"[7]) at a Manhattan fund-raising luncheon. When Theodore ("the only candidate in the race with German blood, who has received part of his education in Germany and who refuses to tie this country to the apron strings of Great Britain"[8]) bolted the GOP in 1912, Viereck galloped along with him. His dramatic poem "The Hymn of Armageddon" gushingly memorialized TR's campaign ("The hope of twenty centuries has found a voice in him"[9]). And not only was George Sylvester to be found among TR's forty-five New York State Progressive Party electors,[10] but the party's hollow, square symbol appeared borrowed from Viereck père's old Socialist Workers' Party campaigns.[11]

George Sylvester was hardly Rough Rider material. A bemused observer of the January 1913 annual dinner of the Poetry Society of America (Viereck proposed TR's gregarious younger sister Corinne for membership[12]) labeled him an "eccentric Narcissus" and "a German edition of the late Oscar Wilde"—a "young boy, with curly blond hair, handkerchief ostentatiously peeping from his cuff, a snakelike ribbon hanging from his eyeglasses, a gray necktie of the fashion of 1845 wound round his neck, white socks and large velvet pumps."[13]

When war erupted in 1914, Viereck instantly hastened to Berlin's aid. With German funds, he launched a weekly magazine, *The Fatherland: Fair Play for Germany and Austria-Hungary*. Extolling everything Teutonic, it soon reached a circulation of one hundred thousand.[14]

Befitting Viereck's boast of collecting the violets strewn upon Oscar Wilde's Parisian grave,[15] *The Fatherland*'s staff included such notorious bohemians as the Satanist Aleister Crowley and the libertine Frank Harris.[16] For Viereck's monthly sister publication, *The International*, Crowley authored an insane screed ("The Crime of Edith Cavell") against the German-executed English nurse. Dismissing her as "vermin," Crowley flippantly argued,

I do not think she was morally responsible. Women, with rare exceptions, are not. They are not soul, but only sex; they have no morals, only moves. . . .

It is this consideration and only this, which prevents our ranking the actions of Edith Cavell as constitutionally one of the most loathsome and abominable crimes in the history of the planet.[17]

Shortly after European hostilities commenced, Viereck brokered a meeting at Sagamore Hill between TR and Dr. Bernhard Dernberg, a former German cabinet secretary for colonial affairs, hoping that the brilliant Dernberg (half-Jewish and a political liberal by Wilhelmine standards) might nudge TR toward a more pro-Berlin path. Dernberg and Roosevelt debated into the night. Neither budged an inch. A lively correspondence followed. Again, to no effect—except, perchance, to convert the lumpen coal of their conflict into hardened diamond.

Viereck and Roosevelt met again. "Germany," TR insisted, "is a nation without a sense of international morality."[18] His public statements only emphasized that point. "I was beginning to hate Theodore Roosevelt," Viereck recorded. "Yet, strange to say, this hatred in no way diminished my love for him. In fact, my love intensified my recoil."[19]

In February 1915, Viereck fired off an intemperate letter to Oyster Bay. "I think you have lost every German-American friend you had," he snapped, "with the exception of myself. . . . Now Germany no longer needs apologists nor sympathizers. Her sword has won the war. But I do not think that the Germans will forget the attitude of their fair-weather friends on either side of the ocean."[20]

TR's private secretary, a Newfoundland-born former Montreal hockey player by the name of John W. "Mac" McGrath, dispatched this terse response: "My Dear Sir:—Mr. Roosevelt directs me to say that the tone of your letter, and especially of the last paragraphs, is such that he does not desire to answer it."[21]

That may have been the first time Theodore had declined to respond to anything.

In early March 1915, Viereck tried again:

I received a note from your secretary which somewhat surprised me. In view of all that I have done for you in the past, giving unstintingly of my enthusiasm, my personality, it seems that I have earned the right to speak frankly to you. . . .

My Progressive training has made it impossible for me to see wrong and remain silent. For that reason I must speak out even at the loss of your friendship, which, as you know, is very dear to me.[22]

TR scathingly replied,

In view of your second letter, I think it probable that your first letter was not intentionally offensive and that your sending it was due to mental and not moral shortcomings: therefore I answer your present letter. . . .

No man can retain his self-respect if he ostensibly remains as an American citizen while he is really doing everything he can to subordinate the interests and duty of the United States to the interests of a foreign land. You made it evident that your whole heart is with . . . Germany, and not with the country of your adoption, the United States. Under such circumstances you are not a good citizen here. But neither are you a good citizen of Germany. You should go home to Germany at once; abandon your American citizenship, if, as I understand, you possess it; and serve in the army, if you are able, or, if not, in any other position in which you can be useful. As far as I am concerned, I admit no divided allegiance in United States citizenship; and my views of hyphenated-Americans are those which were once expressed by the Emperor himself . . . that he understood what Germans were; and he understood what Americans were; but he had neither understanding of nor patience with those who called themselves German-Americans.[23]

An attempt at reconciliation occurred when TR's longtime friend, Danzig-born Harvard professor of experimental psychology Hugo Münsterberg, arranged a conference between Viereck and Roosevelt at Oyster Bay. It did not go well. "The Kaiser," TR asserted, "is plotting against the United States."

When Viereck demanded proof of the allegations, TR rummaged furiously through his papers, shouting, "I have the evidence. I told no other German-American why I am against Germany. I shall tell you because you have been my friend. I hold here a copy of the plan of the German General Staff for the invasion of the United States. If Germany wins, America will be the next objective of her aggression."[24]

Viereck dismissed any thought of a cross-ocean invasion as an absurdity. But TR wouldn't budge, and Viereck departed convinced that TR's documents were outright forgeries.

Before long, Treasury Department authorities were investigating Viereck's activities. On the sweltering afternoon of Saturday, July 24, 1915, federal agents shadowed him to the lower Broadway offices of Germany's Hamburg-Amerika Line, where he conferred with Berlin's dueling-scarred commercial attaché Dr. Heinrich Albert, the official responsible for disbursing $30 million for pro–Central Powers propaganda efforts. Following their meeting, Viereck and Albert caught an uptown Sixth Avenue line elevated train. Viereck detrained at West 23rd Street. Albert remained on board, still surveilled by Treasury agent Frank Burke. The drowsy Albert exited at West 50th Street, leaving behind his bulging, brown briefcase. Before he could rush back to retrieve it, Burke had already made off with it. The briefcase contained a treasure trove of details exposing German activities, including efforts to hamstring American armament and chemical-weapons-related shipments to the Allies, foment labor unrest, and disburse payments to such sympathetic media allies as Viereck. With Woodrow Wilson's authorization, William Gibbs McAdoo, Edward Mandell House, and newly installed Secretary of State Robert Lansing leaked the incriminating material to the pro-administration *New York World*.[25]

Whatever flickering hope George Sylvester Viereck retained of regaining TR's trust and friendship was now as lost as a briefcase on a Sixth Avenue El.

"The country is not in a heroic mood"

WOODROW WILSON STILL SCORNED PREPAREDNESS. TOO PROUD TO fight, he was also too proud to prepare to fight.

The Fall of a Nation's Thomas Dixon Jr. had been Woodrow Wilson's classmate at Johns Hopkins University. In February 1915, Dixon arranged a screening of D. W. Griffith's *The Birth of a Nation* at Wilson's White House.

"I didn't dare allow the president to know the real big purpose of my film," Dixon confided to Wilson's trusted secretary Joe Tumulty, "which was to revolutionize Northern sentiments by a presentation that would transform every man in the audience into a good Democrat! And make no mistake about it . . . we are doing just that thing."[1]

Whether the Virginia-born and Georgia- and South Carolina–bred Wilson grasped Dixon's partisan motivations or not, he loved *The Birth of a Nation*. "It is like writing history with Lightning," he supposedly gushed, "and my only regret is that it is terribly true."[2]

He was not enamored of Dixon's next project. "I must frankly say to you," he lectured Dixon in September 1915, "that I am sorry after reading the synopsis of your new enterprise, because I think the thing a great mistake. There is no need to stir the nation up in favor of national defense. It is already soberly and earnestly aware of its possible perils and of its duty, and I should deeply regret seeing any sort of excitement stirred in so grave a matter."[3]

In February 1916, Secretary of War Lindley Garrison had finally had enough and resigned over Wilson's opposition to his "Continental Army" plan.[4]

Franklin Roosevelt, fleetingly mentioned as Garrison's successor, was never actually considered.[5] Instead, Wilson continued his painful zigzag course. Having replaced the ultra-neutral William Jennings Bryan with the pro-British Robert Lansing, he now supplanted pro-Preparedness Garrison with pacifist Newton D. Baker. "I am an innocent," Baker soon confessed to Army Chief of Staff Major General Hugh L. Scott. "I do not know anything about this job. You must treat me as a father would his son."[6]

Baker was a quick study and had to be. In October 1915, Wilson embargoed arms sales to Mexico, exempting Venustiano Carranza's forces but not Pancho Villa's band of Chihuahua-based guerillas.[7] That November, Wilson intervened further, allowing five thousand Carranzistas onto American railroads to shortcut from Mexico, through New Mexico and Arizona, and then back home to Mexico to ambush Villa's already beleaguered forces.[8] The result: Villa's crushing defeat at Agua Prieta on the Sonora-Arizona border.

Villa lashed out at Americans. Near Santa Isabel, Chihuahua, in January 1916, Villistas stopped Train 41, ordered the passengers out, and brutally massacred eighteen American mining personnel.[9] That February, Wilson submitted a grim account to Congress. In the previous three years, seventy-six Americans were killed on Mexican soil—plus another twenty civilians and sixteen soldiers slain by Mexicans on U.S. territory.[10]

The following month, Villa attacked the Mormon settlement at Chihuahua's Cave Valley, capturing four Americans. At Boca Grande, he executed three Americans attached to the Palomas Land and Cattle Company.[11]

Then *it* happened.

Past midnight on the morning of Saturday, March 9, 1916, Villa personally led five hundred raiders across the Chihuahua–New Mexico border. His target: the tiny mining town of Columbus (population three hundred). Burning part of it down, he killed nine civilians. Stationed at Columbus were seven officers and 341 troopers of the U.S. 13th Cavalry on alert that Villa might try something—if not there, then nearby. They quickly chased him back into Mexico.[12] They lost 8 men; Villa, an estimated 190.[13]

Baker had arrived at the War Department just two days earlier. Within a week, he dispatched ten thousand troops under General John J. "Black Jack" Pershing across the border to pursue Villa. Among them was Pershing's aide-de-camp, Second Lieutenant George S. Patton.[14] In mid-May, a Patton-led patrol party of fourteen battled Villistas at the San Miguelito Ranch in southern Chihuahua. America's first motorized military action led to the death of Villa's second in command and head of his personal bodyguard, Captain Julio Cardenas, along with two other Mexicans. Patton brought their carcasses back, strapped to the hoods of his vehicles.

Which may have been the high point of Pershing's nearly yearlong Mexican goose chase.

More Americans now shared TR's suspicions of Woodrow Wilson's schizophrenic foreign policy: neutral toward Europe and incessantly (and often counterproductively) meddlesome within the Americas. On Tuesday evening, February 15, 1916, Elihu Root (at the behest of Billy Barnes[15]) addressed a packed Carnegie Hall convention of New York State Republicans. He flayed Wilson's foreign policies as "weak, vacillating, and stultifying,"[16] arguing that Wilson commanded America to be "neutral between right and wrong, between justice and injustice, between humanity and cruelty, between liberty and oppression."[17]

"We have been blindly stumbling along the road that, continued, will lead to inevitable war," Root argued. "Our diplomacy has dealt with symptoms and ignored causes . . . our peace depends [on] whether the rule of action applied to Belgium is to be tolerated. If it is tolerated by the civilized world this nation will have to fight for its life. There will be no escape. This is the critical point of defense for the peace of America."[18]

"With the occupation of Vera Cruz the moral power of the United States in Mexico ended," he concluded. "We were then and we are now hated for what we did to Mexico, and we were then and we are now despised for our feeble and irresolute failure to protect the lives and rights of our citizens. No flag is so dishonored and no citizenship so little worth the claiming in Mexico as ours. And that is why we have failed in Mexico."[19]

Word buzzed regarding a Root presidential candidacy. In early April, seventy-four prominent Republicans (including Henry Stimson,

Chauncey Depew, Joe Choate, U.S. Senator James Wadsworth Jr., and Columbia University president Nicholas Murray Butler) affirmed, "Root is the ablest living American."[20]

But many regarded Root as too conservative for progressive times, too much the "corporate lawyer" to ever secure popular election to anything (he won his Senate seat by legislative, not popular, vote). Yet there was more to Root than Wall Street balance sheets and a conservatism now rapidly being abandoned by Progressive era America. He was, noted journalist Mark Sullivan, "humane, tender, almost emotional, essentially more benevolently sympathetic to the average man than some who made political capital out of self-asserted spokesmanship for democracy."[21]

Yet worse than Root's conservatism was the center-stage role he had played in what TR regarded as the wholesale "theft" of delegates at 1912's GOP convention.

No, TR would not support Elihu Root.

Nor would the Republican Party—or the American nation—support TR.

Such was the opinion of Berlin's Washington ambassador Johann Heinrich von Bernstorff. In February 1916, he wrote Chancellor Theobald von Bethmann-Hollweg that TR's "fanaticism no longer knows any bounds. The question now is whether Mr. Roosevelt can still be considered sane. Madness appears to have enveloped his mind. . . . If Roosevelt continues to go on in this manner he will provide the Republican party with defeat for a second time."[22]

TR may not have agreed with Bernstorff's assessment of his sanity, but he certainly concurred concerning his popularity.

It wasn't so much that Americans were effete mollycoddles; rather, they were prosperous mollycoddles. A dip in the economy in 1913 and 1914 sent unemployment to 7.9 percent.[23] But the ill wind that blew Europe asunder in August 1914 blew stacks of dollars into American pockets. American exports soared from $691 million in 1913 to $4.333 billion for the twelve months ending in June 1916, the vast bulk being dispatched to Allied ports.[24]

"Wartime industries paid the highest wages ever," noted historian John Dos Passos. "Cotton prices were good. Wheat was high. The stock market was optimistic. Shipping, meatpacking, steel flourished. Gold imports for 1915 reached an all-time crest of four hundred and eleven million dollars. The favorable trade balance was estimated at nineteen billions as against eleven billions in 1914. The risks of wartime trade were great, but so were the profits. New York was eclipsing London as the center of world finance."[25]

Many influential Americans deduced that the nation's economy could not survive an Allied defeat or even a setback. The United States might intervene against Germany but never against Britain—though London played as fast and loose with naval law as had Berlin, perhaps more so. Britain's North Sea blockade not only starved German armies (and women and children) but also eviscerated Wilson's cherished "freedom of the seas" concept. Beyond that, British commercial vessels took their own liberties with the rules of the game. When Colonel Edward Mandell House traveled to Europe aboard the *Lusitania* in February 1915, its captain illegally hoisted the American flag for protection.[26] On August 19, 1915, not only did the armed merchant ship HMS *Baralong*, using American colors as a decoy, sink the German submarine U-27, but its crew also shot the U-27's survivors.[27]

Earlier that day, the U-24 had torpedoed the British White Star liner SS *Arabic*, killing forty-four, including three Americans. When Wilson threatened to sever diplomatic relations, Berlin responded by sacking Grand Admiral Alfred von Terpitz and naval chief of staff Gustav Bachman and by issuing the "*Arabic* Pledge": "Liners will not be sunk by our submarines without warning and without safety of the lives of noncombatants provided that the liners do not try to escape or offer resistance."[28] Ironically, this was already secret German U-boat policy (the U-24's captain claimed the *Arabic* tried ramming his craft—and there was considerable debate regarding disciplining him).

The incident translated into a diplomatic coup for Wilson.[29]

Its glow soon faded. In late February 1916, Germany's war hawks, inflamed by the open arming of merchant ships, the use of false flags by British merchantmen, and London's use of Q-ships (armed decoy ships), reinstituted unrestricted submarine warfare. That March, U-29 captain Herbert Postkuchen either did or did not mistake the French cross-channel passenger ferry *Sussex* for a minelayer. Fifty passengers and crew died, including the famed Spanish composer Enrique Granados. Several Americans were injured (none perished), and Wilson again vowed to sever relations. Berlin responded with the so-called *Sussex* Pledge: all passenger vessels were to be left unmolested; merchant ships would be searched prior to sinking. Berlin, however, appended several conditions to its response regarding British blockade, mine-laying, and contraband practices. Wilson ignored them.[30]

As far as TR was concerned, Wilson achieved nothing. "American ships were sunk and torpedoed before and afterward; other American lives were lost; and the President wrote other notes upon the subject," TR wrote in the January 1916 *Metropolitan Magazine*. "Even the . . . *Arabic* [Pledge] came only when the last possibility of profit to Germany by killings that extended to neutrals had vanished. President Wilson had done nothing beyond uttering prettily phrased platitudes about abstract morality without any relation to action."[31]

Wilson hedged his bets regarding the Preparedness issue. People might not be marching off to war—or even to Plattsburgh—but suddenly they were in the streets, noisily demanding Preparedness. In May, 125,683 people streamed for a full twelve hours down New York's Fifth Avenue past Leonard Wood and Mayor John Purroy Mitchel.[32] Amid the clatter of two hundred bands, Ted Jr.'s wife Eleanor organized a "battalion" of twelve hundred female marchers behind a gold-lettered banner reading, "INDEPENDENT PATRIOTIC WOMEN OF AMERICA." Marching with them was her mother-in-law, Edith Kermit Roosevelt.[33]

Robert Bacon's 155-chapter National Security League organized pro-Preparedness parades in ten more U.S. cities. On June 3, 350,000 patriots marched, including 130,000 in Chicago.

As Eleanor and Edith marched in Manhattan, Theodore hosted his very own Sagamore Hill Preparedness event, featuring Boy Scouts and a Methodist Bible study group. "Mrs. Roosevelt felt that she must go in and march," he declared to reporters and newsreel men, "because we both regard it as a prime duty that this country at this moment prepare. . . . [T]he significance of 160,000 men [*sic*] marching to-day means that the nation is waking to understand that a weakling never earns anything but contempt."[34]

TR glad-handed old adversaries while stiff-arming old friends. TR's 1912 coalition—marshaled in frenzied anti-Taft haste and the serenity of world peace—quickly disintegrated. Northeasterners—like Henry Cabot Lodge, Gussie Gardner, and John Purroy Mitchel—emulated his Preparedness posture. But even in the anglophile Northeast, not everyone hungered for war. "While I am pro-ally in my sympathies," averred William Howard Taft in April 1916, "I am utterly opposed to the view that we now have a responsibility . . . that should carry us into this war. . . . I am utterly out of patience with any such view. . . . I sympathize with [Wilson's] desire to avoid war."[35]

In 1912, many midwestern and western progressives overlooked TR's jingoism—then a nonissue compared to antitrust battles, conservation, and ballot reform. By 1915, GOP progressives like Robert La Follette and Hiram Johnson, Nebraska's George Norris, Idaho's William E. Borah, Iowa's William S. Kenyon, Minnesota's Moses Clapp, and North Dakota's Asle Gronna found themselves in the isolationist camp—as did Gifford Pinchot's younger brother Amos, formerly a key TR aide. Another staunch acolyte, Indiana's Albert Beveridge, exhibited unmistakable German sympathies.[36] "Many Progressives," William Allen White later admitted, "heard Roosevelt's war drum with distaste and uneasiness."[37] Or, as Harold Ickes observed decades later, the Colonel "believed in a 'righteous' war but he also believed, and doubtless sincerely, that any war was a 'righteous' war in which he might have an opportunity to fight."[38]

Chicago reformer Jane Addams, long ardently anti-imperialist, had placed TR's name in nomination at 1912's Progressive National Convention. By January 1915, however, she served as president of the newly minted Women's Peace Party. A disgusted TR quickly complained to his friend Cecil Spring-Rice of "Jane Addams inspired idiots."[39] Soon he would be decrying "poor bleeding Jane"[40] and her "shrieking sisterhood."[41]

"As for Jane Addams," he gibed, "and the other well-meaning women who plead for peace without daring even to protest against the infamous wrongs, the infamies worse than death which their sisters in France and Belgium have suffered, I lack patience to speak of them."[42]

But that was mild compared to his reaction when Herbert Croly's infant *New Republic* termed his critique of Wilson's Mexican policy "the kind of fighting which has turned so many of his natural admirers into bitter enemies."[43] Two years earlier, TR had offered Croly a position with the Progressive Party. Now, he tartly severed all relations with him. Privately TR derided the *New Republic's* management as "three anemic Gentiles and three international Jews."[44]

Two of the "international Jews" were Nathaniel Weyl and Walter Lippmann. Nobody was quite sure who the third was. Lippmann had counted himself TR's "unqualified hero-worshipper"[45] since first meeting the returning Rough Rider as an eight-year-old in Saratoga Springs in summer 1898. In November 1914, Lippmann, Weyl, and Croly visited Sagamore Hill, there to be charmed by the great man. "I spent the night at Oyster Bay with Roosevelt," Lippmann gushed to a friend, "and loved him more than ever."[46]

By January 1916, Lippmann loved him far less. That month, he wrote attorney Felix Frankfurter, "I had long talks will all sorts of people [in the Midwest], ranging from Jane Addams to the Roosevelt-at-any-price people, and I am pretty well convinced Roosevelt will not do.... The kind of people who are turning out to support him are a crowd that I do not wish to see in power in the United States. . . . After all, you and I have been banking on a theoretical Roosevelt, a potential Roosevelt, but not a Roosevelt who at this moment is actually at work."[47] That June, he confessed to the British Foreign Office's Lord Eustace Perry, "TR gets on my nerves so much these days that I shall become a typical anti-Roosevelt maniac if I do not look out."[48]

In July 1915, TR and Edith, accompanied by his secretary John "Mac" McGrath, embarked for San Francisco to attend the Panama-Pacific Exposition's "Theodore Roosevelt Day." En route, Roosevelt declared to

Spanish-American War veterans at Portland, Oregon, "It does me a lot of good to see some real men when mollycoddles seem to be so much to the fore. The only human being that I think as little of as I do of a mollycoddle is a crook. To my mind there is no one so degraded as a crook, and a mollycoddle is little better than a crook." Asked to define a "mollycoddle," he snapped, "Nothing but a grown-up sissy, a grown-up sissy of either sex."[49]

That same day, the *New York Times* reported on how a growing number of edgy transatlantic passengers were convinced of seeing U-boats where none existed. That morning, three police detectives hauled a barefoot and screaming ("Help! Murder, Police!") Newark Republican congressman R. Wayne Parker to the New Jersey State Hospital for the Insane. Parker raved that Secretary of State Robert Lansing would "scuttle the ship" and that he, Parker, had to rush to Washington, seize control of the State Department, and confer with German ambassador Bernstorff. He also babbled about visiting Germany—adding for some reason (or none at all) that four horses would accompany his voyage. Voters reelected him the following year.[50]

Two afternoons later, TR reached San Francisco. A cavalry detachment escorted him to the exposition's "Court of the Universe," where sixty thousand admirers had begun gathering four full hours previously. "No nation ever amounted to anything if its population was composed of pacifists and poltroons,"[51] he warned. "The professional Pacifists, the peace-at-any-price, non-resistance, universal arbitration people are now seeking to Chinafy this country."[52]

"He spoke from notes," an observer remembered, "but with great vehemence, and as he reached the end of a sheet he would crumble it in his hand and throw it angrily to the floor, as though he therewith flung from him every loathed Chinaficationist and mollycoddle in the country."[53]

Mac McGrath accompanied him to a California Exposition Commission banquet in his honor. Afterward, in the foyer, McGrath conversed with commission executive secretary Harry H. Cosgriff, expounding that "Roosevelt and [Hiram] Johnson are the two greatest men in the United States today." A prominent San Francisco attorney, club man, and golfer (once playing 125 holes in a single day[54]), Gaillard "Gailly" Stoney, passed by.

Stoney was an ardent Democrat and Wilson admirer. His wife would eventually present Wilson with a petition signed by three hundred thousand California schoolchildren entreating his attendance at the exposition. She would also bestow upon the president a quantity of gold to hopefully craft his fiancée's wedding ring.[55]

"Of course, gentlemen," Stoney now remarked, "every man is entitled to his opinion. I believe that Wilson is the greatest man in the United States today."

The twenty-six-year-old McGrath struck the much taller, but forty-seven-year-old, Stoney on the cheek. Stoney, evidently too proud to fight, sneered, "If you were not so small, I'd throw you out of the building, but I prefer to confine my pugilistic activities to some one of more mature growth."

McGrath smacked him again before being hauled outside.[56]

McGrath played rough with Democrats. His boss played rough with pacifists ("persons of indeterminate sex"[57]), particularly pacifist journalists. He especially detested his longtime critic, the *New York Evening Post*'s Oswald Garrison Villard. "He is the kind of crawling thing we step on," he fulminated in November 1916, "provided the resulting crunch won't leave too large a stain on the floor."[58]

Conversely, he mended fences with some old enemies. The lion might not lie down with pacifist lambs, but a formerly trust-busting Bull Moose might indeed sup with trust-controlling bulls and bears.

On Friday evening, December 14, 1915, he dined at the Fifth Avenue townhouse of Judge Elbert H. Gary, president and board chairman of the United States Steel Corporation. Gary's other guests included a veritable who's who of New York finance, controlling an estimated $12 billion in assets.[59]

It was all hush-hush. No one revealed what was said or even how the dinner came about. An unnamed source informed the *New York Times*,

The financial side of the Republican party was well-represented, and if the financial side has decided to cast its lot with Colonel Roosevelt again the politicians will be brought into line.

Whatever else it does the dinner will exert a tremendous influence on the . . . Republican and the Progressive Parties, and it undoubtedly shows that men of the first importance politically are considering a fight under Colonel Roosevelt's leadership.[60]

That so many bankers attended—and remained so silent—spoke loudly to the session's true purposes.

Some attendees, like Medill McCormick and George W. Perkins, were Bull Moose true believers. Perkins donated $263,000 to the cause in 1912[61] and continued pouring money into it thereafter. Prominent progressives such as both Pinchot brothers, Hiram Johnson, William Allen White, Raymond Robins, Harold Ickes, Gutzon Borglum, Chester H. Rowell, and even McCormick all manifestly distrusted Perkins—a Morgan partner allied with such entities as U.S. Steel, the New York Life Insurance Company, and International Harvester. They resented his shameless self-promotion.[62] They feared his troubling sway over their supposedly trust-busting hero. Thanks in part to Perkins, their party's 1912 platform unceremoniously jettisoned its antitrust plank to instead declare, "The corporation is an essential part of modern business. *The concentration of business*, in some degree, is both inevitable and necessary for *national business efficiency*" (emphasis added).[63]

William Howard Taft jeered that "letting the people rule when reduced to its lowest terms, it seems, is letting the Steel Trust rule."[64] By May 1914, Amos Pinchot was publicly upbraiding Perkins: "To talk against monopoly, to place the words 'Social and Industrial Justice' on our banner, and then to hand over this banner to a man who has been monopoly's ardent supporter and one of the most distinguished opponents of social and industrial justice . . . is, in my opinion, a handicap to the party, and a fraud on the public."[65] The Colonel quickly shunted Pinchot—not Perkins—onto the scrap heap of history previously reserved for the likes of Taft, Barnes, and Root.

To others, TR castigated Amos's ilk as those who would turn his party "into an aid to the [Industrial Workers of the World] or a kind of parlor anarchist association."[66]

George Perkins soldiered on. "Pinchot," gibed the Democratic *New York World*, "can keep on battling for the Lord, and Perkins can keep on signing the checks."[67]

To many banking houses (particularly the House of Morgan) fearing that if Britain and France fell, their portfolios and country estates would fall with them, in 1916 TR looked less like the wild-eyed radical of 1912 and more like the guardian of Western European civilization.

"Roosevelt," argued fervently antiwar Amos Pinchot, "could be relied on [by such men] in every way. He was fiercely pro-British and pro-Ally, so that if he were elected the Morgan group [might] feel that its loans to the Allied governments would have whatever security came from the support of the White House."[68] Pinchot further excoriated TR's long-standing ties to Morgan and to U.S. Steel—to men like Elbert Gary, Henry Clay Frick, J. P. Morgan, and U.S. Steel corporate attorneys like Root, Stimson, and Philander Knox. Trust-busting TR had even appointed Morgan's son-in-law Herbert Livingston Satterlee as assistant secretary of the Navy. In 1916, Satterlee returned the favor by organizing a "businessmen for Roosevelt" movement.[69]

"When [TR] left office," Pinchot further explained, "his first two choices for his successor were Elihu Root and Philander Knox. When the Steel Corporation was indicted in 1911, he issued a violent protest denouncing Taft for permitting such a crime against common sense. . . . He had allowed Perkins and Frank Munsey, both allies of Gary, to finance his 1912 campaign, and the former to turn Progressive headquarters into a propaganda bureau for the Steel and [International] Harvester trusts."[70]

Such suspicions were by no means restricted to radicals like Pinchot, as witnessed by this testimony from 1915's *Barnes v. Roosevelt* trial:

WILLIAM N. IVINS: Did you ever cause the Attorney General of the United States to take any action whatsoever against the Steel Corporation?

Roosevelt: I did not.

Ivins: Mr. Frick was a contributor to your campaign fund in 1904?

Roosevelt: He was.

Ivins: Mr. Gary was a contributor?

Roosevelt: He was.

Ivins: Mr. Perkins was a contributor?

Roosevelt: He was.

Ivins: These gentlemen were connected with the Steel Corporation?

Roosevelt: They were.

Ivins: Did you ever instruct the Attorney General to proceed in any manner whatsoever against the Harvester Company?

Roosevelt: I did not.

Ivins: Was Mr. Perkins a contributor to your campaign in 1904?

Roosevelt: He was.

Ivins: Did you ever instruct the Attorney General to take any action whatsoever against the American Powder Company?

Roosevelt: I did not.

Ivins: Mr. T. Coleman du Pont was a contributor, was he not?

Roosevelt: He was.[71]

Theodore Roosevelt, who spoke at Milwaukee Auditorium for eighty minutes with a .38-calibre slug lodged in his chest, thus employed a mere twenty-one words to answer nine questions—and not very reassuring words either.

In December 1915, the *Literary Digest* polled 751 Republican newspaper editors, senators, and congressmen. A solid plurality of 251 backed Elihu Root. But Root remained a highly problematic favorite.[72] "The ablest living American"[73] was hardly the ablest presidential candidate. He was old—seventy-one by Election Day 1916—and not that well. Two years previously, his doctor virtually ordered him to abandon his Senate seat. He himself worried that another term might deliver a "break down."[74]

Progressives saw him as far too conservative; TR recalled and still resented his role as a "receiver of stolen goods"[75] at 1912's GOP convention. Beyond that, Root simply didn't want the job that much—if at all. For as he confided in June 1914, "A large part of the fights that are going on fail to interest me. Things which I thought great fun thirty or forty years ago are rather a bore now."[76]

Trailing Root in the *Literary Digest* poll was U.S. Supreme Court associate justice Charles Evans Hughes—another reluctant possibility. Hughes refrained from challenging William Howard Taft in 1908 and later refused Taft's offer (made with TR's approval[77]) of the vice presidency. Many saw him as a compromise candidate in 1912.[78] With 1916 approaching, he protested to Root, "The Supreme Court must be kept out of politics. . . . [I]f nominated, I should decline."[79]

Taft averred he would be "very much gratified" by a Hughes nomination. "Roosevelt could not afford to oppose him," he reasoned in January 1916. "He would merely put himself in a ridiculous position, and no one appreciates that more than" TR himself. Moreover, Taft predicted, Roosevelt would "jump into the campaign and call names and seek to make himself the leader of it—a situation which will make Hughes, with his judicial temperament, nervous and impatient, to a point where he will call out 'save me from my friends.'"[80]

Beyond Root and Hughes lay a gaggle of more enthusiastic but even less electable also-rans: Old Guard Illinois senator Lawrence Yates Sherman (144 votes in the *Literary Digest* sampling), Idaho senator William E. Borah (108 votes), progressive Iowa senator Albert Cummins (77), TR's conservative former vice president Charles W. Fairbanks (68), first-term Massachusetts senator John W. Weeks (53), and, then, Taft himself (51).

Literary Digest's sampling forecast a nearly impossible hurdle for any new TR candidacy. Boasting a woeful forty-seven votes, Roosevelt outpaced only his irascible 1916 Bull Moose running mate Hiram Johnson (with sixteen).[81]

But what if party majordomos did throw caution (and principles) to the wind to board a TR bandwagon? Rumors swirled of such a startling development following a bombshell three-hour March 31, 1916, luncheon at the One Park Avenue home of Robert Bacon.

Bacon had long numbered among Roosevelt's "chief friends."[82] At Harvard they had been boxing partners, and TR pronounced him "as pleasant as he is handsome."[83] Bacon, not TR, had been the big man on campus, but, despite earning a J. P. Morgan partnership, he quickly lagged behind Roosevelt. Fretting over his "weakness, a lack of preeminent attributes of the masculine anima,"[84] Bacon suffered a nervous breakdown in 1902.[85] TR put him to work under Secretary of State Root and later briefly designated him as Root's successor. When TR bolted the GOP in 1912, Bacon departed with him.

Now presiding over the National Security League, Bacon was, as one historian assessed him, the "linchpin of the whole civilian preparedness movement."[86]

Four men attended his luncheon: TR, Leonard Wood (a cofounder of Bacon's National Security League, though even he found Bacon's eagerness for overseas combat "almost pathetic"[87]), Elihu Root, and Henry Cabot Lodge.

If not exactly a historic rapprochement, it was, at least, a historic truce, with TR and Root reportedly shaking hands.[88] "Roosevelt and Root seemed to be glad to be together again, really so," Wood's diary recorded. "Roosevelt cussed out Wilson as did Root and Lodge. Opinion that the country never so low in standing before."[89]

They ostensibly discussed Preparedness. Few dared believe that was all they discussed.

Lunch concluded, and TR scurried a few blocks northward to George Perkins's 76 Park Avenue abode to confer with a dozen top Progressive allies—including Medill McCormick, Syracuse's Horace Wilkinson, *New York Evening Mail* editor Henry L. Stoddard, and "radical" *Wichita Beacon* editor Henry J. Allen.[90] As Roosevelt departed, he revealed to waiting reporters his earlier session with Wood, Lodge, and Root, grinning, "I may anticipate your next question—we had not discussed politics at all."[91] Root issued similar denials, though he privately chortled that the group had mightily "cussed"[92] Wilson. Wood—savoring his own ambitions—recalled that TR confided to all present that "he would be for me in case things went right, a quiet way of letting what he would do be known."[93]

The *New York Times* pronounced the luncheon "the most significant happening of the political campaign. His friends said that Colonel Roosevelt's chances of capturing the Republican nomination had jumped 100 per cent."[94]

When old enemies break bread, new common enemies have usually arisen—in this case, the aforementioned Justice Hughes. The *New York Herald* speculated,

> *The Roosevelt boom is certain to [explode] within a very short time. And the reason, therefore, is as important as it is interesting. The Hughes boom . . . has somewhat staggered the old-line Republicans. It has flabbergasted the Roosevelt men.*
>
> *It is no secret . . . that the Hughes boom was pushed merrily along by the Roosevelt and machine Republicans because [all believed] that the Supreme Court Justice would not accept the nomination. They had hoped to urge it along so that . . . the "bosses" would have a lot of uninstructed delegates on their hands with whom, presumably, they could do pretty much as they pleased.*
>
> *The prospect satisfied the Roosevelt boomers because the best they hoped for was a general mix-up at Chicago [offering] the greatest opportunity for a Roosevelt stampede.*
>
> *But the swift spread of the Hughes movement and the growing belief that he fully expects, if nominated, to resign . . . and make the run, has knocked the supports from under all the little dream structures reared by the regular politicians.*[95]

Many regular GOP leaders actually preferred Roosevelt to Hughes. Once so nonchalantly partners with the likes of bosses Thomas Platt, Lemuel Quigg, and Billy Barnes, TR ("In politics, we have to do a great many things we ought not to do"[96]) might once more demonstrate such practicality. "In the vernacular of the politicians," concluded the *Herald*, "Mr. Roosevelt will pay off a political obligation, and Justice Hughes would not even assume one."[97]

And so TR gingerly prepared to depart from Elba.

For all his outward swagger and manic enthusiasms, he remained calculating and realistic regarding his political odds. His old party still despised him. His new party lay in tatters. The nation enjoyed prosperity and feared war. German- and Irish-Americans had little interest in shedding blood—or even tears—for Britain, Belgium, or American passengers reckless enough to travel on British vessels.

Which made another TR run problematic—and he knew it.

TR estimated his support to be in short supply. In August 1915, he wearily grumbled, "I am sick at heart about Wilson, and therefore about the American people. The only thing to say in defense of the people is that a bad colonel always makes a bad regiment. . . . I have done everything I can to rouse them."[98] Nor was his own party as gung ho for action as he might wish. In February 1916, a majority of House Republicans supported a resolution banning American travel on belligerent vessels.[99] In May, the House overwhelmingly rejected plans for a 250,000-man army.[100]

As his political fortunes waned, his contempt waxed for voters' intelligence and acumen. "You know at least as well as I do that the public cannot take in an etching," he theorized to Cabot Lodge in early February 1916. "They want something along the lines of a circus poster. They do not wish fine details, and it is really not to be expected that they should see them. They want the broad strokes of the brush."[101]

But the public was not even buying his circus poster.

To James R. Garfield, TR wrote in January 1916, "No other public man has ventured to tell the truth of Germany, of the pacifists, of the German-Americans, of Wilson. I have told it and shall tell it as strongly as I know how and without regard to its effect upon me. . . . I have followed this course, believing that it would in all probability render it out of the question to nominate me. . . . It would be quite impossible to nominate and elect me unless this nation were in heroic mood. . . . I see no signs of such possibility."[102]

"Heroic mood."

He savored the phrase, repeating it in correspondence with his older sister "Bye,"[103] before unleashing it via a celebrated March 9, 1916, interview with the *Evening Mail's* Henry Stoddard.

On the snowy, bitterly cold morning of Friday, February 11, Theodore and Edith sailed from New York aboard the British steamer *Guiana* for a five-week western Caribbean tour.

A month before, Mac McGrath explained that the Roosevelts' trip resulted from "Mrs. Roosevelt's health. You know she had an operation some time ago, and it is thought she will recuperate faster if she is taken to a warmer climate."[104] Edith *had* undergone surgery, which her husband had pronounced "rather serious" and "absolutely necessary."[105] Most likely, it was a hysterectomy.[106] But that was fourteen months previously. And TR had since confided that Edith was "better than she has been for a longtime [*sic*]."[107] Most likely, the trip involved ducking what Edith termed the "boiling political cauldron" and the chaotic emerging situation with which both she and Theodore found themselves "wholly out of sympathy."[108]

The Roosevelts island-hopped from Saint Thomas to Saint Croix to Saint Kitts. At Antigua, "the populace strewed flowers in his pathway and likened him [to] Queen Victoria."[109] Guadeloupe, Dominica, "never was so stirred except by volcanic eruption."[110] In Fort-de-France, Martinique, he was greeted "at 7 o'clock in the morning by a committee made up mostly of negroes wearing full evening dress."[111] Barbados and British Guiana were next.[112]

In Trinidad, Theodore descended into a mysterious guano-encrusted cavern in search of nesting oilbird (guacharos) chicks. He spent the night in the crude hut of a dusky local coconut farmer. Returning to town, the Colonel received a wire from Henry Stoddard advising him of moves to place him on Massachusetts's April 25 primary ballot.[113]

TR had continued to follow political events as obsessively as if he remained stateside. Rumors concerning Elihu Root's potential candidacy triggered a flurry of telegrams from Stoddard to Roosevelt. TR now suggested that Stoddard "catch up with him in Trinidad."[114] Braving submarine-infested waters, he (accompanied by his wife) left the next day.

His mission: "to keep [Roosevelt] from declaring himself irrevocably out of presidential talk."[115]

For two days, TR wrestled with developing a proper public statement. His measured pace hardly surprised Stoddard, for, as he would observe, Roosevelt, for all his frantic bluster, "never made a decision of consequence without thoughtful consideration."[116]

More annoying to Stoddard, however, was "the slow processes of the English censor in satisfying himself that no secret conspiracy in behalf of Germany lay concealed in Roosevelt's words! . . . I sat by the cable operator's side until the last word had gone, so as to be ready for any new objection from the censor."[117]

TR launched a triple-headed salvo: a lukewarm declination of his own candidacy, a lack of interest in anyone else's, and, most significantly, a full-throated challenge to the nation to turn to him—but only if it dared: "I will not enter into any fight for the nomination, and I will not permit any factional fight to be made in my behalf. Indeed, I will go further and say that it would be a mistake to nominate me unless the country has in its mood something of the heroic, unless it feels not only like devoting itself to ideals, but to the purpose measurably to realize those ideals in action."[118]

To supporters, his words marked greatness. Others remained unmoved. The headline in the *Brooklyn Eagle* declared,

"I WON'T RUN," SAYS T.R.,
BUT HE MIGHT AFTER ALL[119]

An editorial cartoon in the pro-Wilson *New York World* lampooned a flag-draped, sword-in-hand Roosevelt, depicting him as boasting,

WILSON IS <u>NOT</u> HEROIC
HUGHES IS <u>NOT</u> HEROIC
ROOT IS <u>NOT</u> HEROIC
I AM HEROIC
(PERKINS IS HEROIC TOO)[120]

"Rules is rules here"

THE *NEW YORK WORLD* PONDERED TR'S HEROISM.

Not long before, others had asked, *Was his private secretary John McGrath heroic?*

Or a thug?

In June 1915, TR toured Louisiana's Breton Island, admiring the swarms of black skimmers, laughing gulls, terns, and brown pelicans inhabiting the Gulf Coast island's woods and sandy beaches. "To watch the terns flashing in a shifting maze above the beach," he pronounced, "or to see a file of pelicans winning their way homeward across the afterglow of sunset, is like a gallery of Old Masters—their loss would be like the loss of artists for all time."[1]

To TR, nature consisted of far more than beauty or artistry. There existed a pitiless, grinding Darwinism. "Nature is ruthless," he added, "and where her sway is uncontested there is no peace save the peace of death; and the fecund stream of life, especially of life on the lower levels, flows like an immense torrent out of non-existence for but the briefest moment before the enormous majority of beings composing it are engulfed in the jaws of death, and again go out into the shadow."[2]

John McGrath accompanied him neither to the Caribbean nor to Breton Island.

He should have.

Left to his own devices, on Friday evening, June 11, 1915, the then twenty-five-year-old McGrath visited his twenty-year-old cousin William Powers, a steamship company mechanic engineer who resided near the Long Island Railroad's Flatbush Avenue, Brooklyn, terminal. McGrath missed the 9:10 p.m. train to Oyster Bay, where he, his wife, and his two children lived in a cottage at Sagamore Hill. From a nearby saloon he phoned to tell his wife of his delay before joining Mr. and Mrs. Powers for beer. Sitting nearby was a thirty-six-year-old bottler of mineral waters, Charles Lighte Jr., and his thirty-five-year-old wife, Emma.

A savage brawl erupted. Police hustled to the scene, hauling Lighte to nearby Swedish Hospital. His leg broken, Lighte spent ten weeks homebound recuperating and filed third-degree assault charges against both McGrath and Powers.

The case silently dragged on until late March 1916. McGrath informed authorities that he worked as a stenographer at the Progressive Party's national headquarters. Only on the morning of March 28, 1916, did a prosecutor finally ask whether McGrath had any other employers.

The Bull Moose was out of the bag.

The case itself was a clear instance of diametrically contradictory tales of pristine virtue threatened by unprovoked aggression. As the *New York Herald* duly reported,

After they had had "two dark beers," Mr. Lighte said, his wife suggested that they go home and get a bite of cold supper.

"McGrath heard her," Mr. Lighte said, "and called out:—'That's right, kid; stick up for your eats.' I asked him what he was butting in for, and he said I was like a barber's cat [a loud braggart] and asked:—'Who's the skirt with you? She looks like a street girl.' The fight started and in the struggle I was knocked and beaten unconscious. When I recovered my senses I was in the Swedish Hospital. My leg was broken and I was covered with cuts and bruises."

Mrs. Lighte testified that Mr. McGrath and Mr. Powers had knocked her husband down and had repeatedly kicked him and jumped on him with their feet, one of them several times, crying, "Kick him in the face! Jump on him!" Both accused men denied there had been any insult offered to Mrs. Lighte or her husband. Mr. McGrath testified that Mr. Lighte and his wife began to misbehave, kissing and hugging each other in a disgusting manner, and that Mrs. Powers became greatly embarrassed.

*"I did not wish Mrs. Powers to see such a disgraceful perfor-
mance," said Mr. McGrath, "and I went over to their table, told them
there were ladies in the restaurant and they would have to stop that.*

*"Then both Lighte and his wife attacked me, and I think she was
the stronger fighter. She went after me with a bottle from the table
and then a chair. Powers came to my aid, and after Lighte fell we held
Mrs. Lighte until Mrs. Powers could get out. Then we released her
and left the restaurant."[3]*

The *New York Sun* offered further details:

*[Mrs. Lighte] said that Powers struck her while McGrath sat in the
chair using bad language and saying he was going to get a policeman.
When her husband fell she chased Powers into the street, where, she
said, he kicked her in the face and rolled her into the gutter. She got up
and a boy helped her run after Powers until a policeman grabbed the
quarry. McGrath made no attempt to get away. . . .*

*McGrath testified that Mr. and Mrs. Lighte were quarreling
when they entered the cafe. He said the Lightes spoke to his party and
started the trouble. He insisted that Mrs. Lighte slapped Powers' face
and tore his collar off, whereupon Powers told Lighte to keep Mrs.
Lighte away. Lighte, said McGrath, refused to interfere, and then
struck Powers. Thereupon Powers went after Lighte and knocked him
over the chair and table. McGrath did not deny that he used his fists,
but he said he did not get into the fight until Mrs. Lighte threatened
Mrs. Powers. He denied that he struck Mrs. Lighte.[4]*

Now, it must be admitted that the round-faced McGrath, though
short of height and pudgy of build, was nonetheless the physical type.
The son of a Newfoundland cod fisherman turned Liberal Party politician, McGrath had played a fine game of hockey for Montreal's crack
outfit, the Wanderers, before starring for a similarly named New York
amateur outfit. Before joining TR in May 1913, he had similarly served
George Perkins.[5] When TR was shot in Milwaukee in 1912, McGrath

was with him. As a blood-drenched TR had valiantly delivered his eighty-minute speech, McGrath sat behind him, recording every word.[6]

In July 1914, at Oyster Bay, McGrath crashed a motorcycle Perkins had bestowed on him to facilitate his daily Manhattan–Sagamore Hill commute.[7] A year later, McGrath had, of course, punched out San Francisco's Gaillard Stoney. But Mac was popular enough with Progressive Party loyalists and with reporters (having served as one in Toronto)—and TR relied on him nearly completely. "He has always been a hard worker and a shrewd diagnostician of political affairs, so wise beyond his years," noted the *New York Sun*, "that Col. Roosevelt was struck by his efficiency and immediately insisted upon having him as his own private secretary."[8]

Thus, when the Roosevelts returned from Trinidad, aside from journalists, no one save Mac McGrath greeted them dockside. Queried regarding his future plans, TR merely responded, "I shan't know until I've talked with Mac."[9]

It was not until McGrath actually departed Sagamore Hill for his trial that he finally disclosed to his employer the criminal charge dangling over his fine Irish head. "Mr. McGrath," TR informed reporters later that day, "told me this morning he had been in a restaurant, but had nothing to do with the assault except to try to save a woman from being hurt."[10]

Expecting acquittal, Mac also advised TR that he would return from Brooklyn at roughly two in the afternoon.[11]

McGrath and Powers's trial was brief, their optimism misplaced. Found guilty, they spent the night in Brooklyn's miserable Raymond Street Jail, facing thirty days more at Blackwell's Island's city workhouse. It was all very embarrassing, particularly since McGrath's late father had once overseen Newfoundland's provincial penitentiary.

The news stunned workers at Progressive Party headquarters. At Oyster Bay, TR conferred with Perkins and remained loyal:

He has been associated with me now for nearly four years in the closest relations, and I have felt I could not only have absolute confidence in his energy and ability, but in his straightforward integrity.

He will continue in my employ exactly as if this had not happened, with entirely undiminished trust and regard on my part.[12]

TR swung into action. He contacted Mrs. McGrath. He engaged counsel to represent her husband.[13] He phoned McGrath. A jailer informed the Colonel,

"It is against the rules to permit any one to speak with a convicted prisoner."

"But this is Mr. Roosevelt—Theodore Roosevelt—and he is my secretary."

"I can't help who you are. Rules is rules here."[14]

And so they were.

It was not looking good for McGrath—no matter whom he knew.

Yet one had to wonder about the Lighte family.

In January 1904, a former coachman successfully sued Lighte's father for $10,000 for alienation of affection.[15] In 1912, a carbonic gas tank exploded at the Charles Lighte & Son bottling works. Flying metal shards killed a workman's fifteen-year-old son. The tank's dial was broken. The factory itself had recently been barred from use "for any purpose except the stabling of horses." Authorities arrested Lighte Jr.[16] In October 1915, Emma Lighte sued a Yellow Taxicab driver for $6,000, alleging assault and false arrest following a "tango tea" that she and a friend had attended two years earlier at the Waldorf-Astoria.[17]

McGrath and Powers appealed their convictions, contending they had been denied a jury trial and deprived of the right to question their accusers' character—a crucial point, as their convictions rested largely upon the Lightes' testimony. Specifically excluded was Emma Lighte's 1915 Yellow Taxicab imbroglio. Also excluded was any mention of a subsequent altercation, when men entered a Brooklyn restaurant—"and encouraged by Mrs. Lighte and using a cane lent by Mr. Lighte, gave Mr. Powers a beating."[18]

Rumors flew of TR's testifying as McGrath's character witness.[19] He didn't have to. McGrath and Powers won release and the right to a new trial.[20]

Mac McGrath's legal battles temporarily abated. Theodore Roosevelt's latest battle for the White House commenced.

"When a weasel sucks eggs"

If observers couldn't peg the likelihood of another TR candidacy, well . . . neither could he.

He wanted the presidency, craved vindication, fairly lusted for a chance to crush Woodrow Wilson and all his old enemies. But he knew that for all his heroism, he lacked public support, and that fatal defect preyed upon him. Chicago Progressive Harold Ickes found him "deep down into the doldrums."[1] Progressive Party functionary Oscar King "O. K." Davis considered early 1916 "about the blackest period of [TR's] life. He felt . . . all his efforts had been well nigh useless. Still, he did not give up."[2]

The Colonel might well have folded his tent following his party's utter collapse in November 1914. A January 1916 nationwide poll of *Chicago Herald* correspondents found just 30 percent of respondents reporting increased sentiment for TR's Republican nomination, 56 percent indicating no change, and 14 percent evincing decreasing enthusiasm.[3] Few regular Republicans, it seemed, savored any TR-dominated version of "hyphenated Republicanism."[4]

Even many Progressives saw his mantle passing elsewhere. Progressive Republican Iowa senator Albert Cummins hoped to snag Theodore's midwestern supporters. Robert "Fighting Bob" La Follette, as always, awaited a cue that never came. Some entreated the western firebrands Hiram Johnson and William E. Borah to run. Neither exhibited much interest. Connecticut's Bull Moose leader, the renowned sculptor Gutzon Borglum, importuned TR to retire to private life so as to "automatically become the center of world arbitration . . . a great unprejudiced force, and in readiness to wait upon the world." Borglum wanted Roosevelt to endorse Leonard Wood, promising TR that Wood would, of course, "include you [TR] in his privatest councils."[5]

The decidedly sluggish Republican delegate-selection process commenced. TR's former vice president, the conservative Charles W. Fairbanks, secured delegates in his home state of Indiana.[6] New Hampshire provided Massachusetts's favorite son, Senator John W. Weeks, with a plurality of votes but none of its unpledged delegates.[7] La Follette captured North Dakota.[8] Cummins took Minnesota.

In April, La Follette barely won Wisconsin.[9] In Michigan, Henry Ford bested the state's U.S. senator, William Alden Smith.[10] Later that month, Ford seemingly upended Cummins and Charles Evans Hughes in Nebraska.[11] "Ford's victory," reported the *New York Times*, "was entirely unexpected. His petition was filed last Fall as a joke."[12] A recount narrowly awarded Cummins a narrow victory.[13] Illinois senator Lawrence Sherman (praised by George Sylvester Viereck as possessing "a strict American, as distinguished from a pro-British attitude"[14]) won his state's primary,[15] while Cummins captured Montana and Iowa. Former senator Theodore Burton won his home state of Ohio.

Back east, prominent New York Reform rabbi Stephen Wise boosted Ford as a third-party antiwar candidate.[16] TR took 73.7 percent of New Jersey's vote—a decline from his 1912 total. In Massachusetts, Representative Augustus "Gussie" Gardner's TR slate fell to former U.S. senator W. Murray Crane's anti-TR coalition—"the final death knell of Roosevelt's hopes,"[17] as Columbia University's Nicholas Murray Butler saw it. In Vermont, TR lost again—this time easily falling to Hughes, with Elihu Root, Ford, and Weeks even further in the rear.[18]

The Grand Old Party thus remained a Great Big Mess, tempting TR all the more to keep bluffing in a game in which he held few cards.

In early April 1916, he reassured *Boston Journal* publisher Matthew Hale, chair of Massachusetts's Progressive Party and its national committeeman, that he meant

> *every word of my Trinidad statement. Not only [is] no kind of faction fight [to] be made to secure my nomination but . . . it would be worse than worthless to have the nomination unless it comes of their*

own accord from the Republicans, because they feel they need me, and because they feel that the country is ripe for the kind of campaign . . . I would consent to make. After Lincoln became President the question of retaining the Union was of such absorbing consequence that for the next eighteen months he declined to consider even such a tremendous question as Slavery. He subordinated everything else to the question of the Union. There are certain tremendous national questions affecting our attitude as regards the primary duties of a nation, affecting . . . whether we are to continue as a nation, which transcend infinitely in importance any [other] question. . . .

My sole usefulness at present [is] to preach nationally [what] I have been preaching for the last eighteen months. [In 1914] . . . I fought in every kind of locality . . . for Progressive principles. I not only did no good but I am not at all certain that I did not do damage. . . .

If this nation is to be helped in the least by me, it is to be helped by my teachings in national and international matters. If the nation gets the slightest idea that I am acquiescing in faction fights in my own interests, there is the end of my accomplishing anything whatever.[19]

Hale was an intractable bitter-ender, the sort to hoist his tattered battle flag as his craft lay rusting upon the ocean floor. By now, TR grasped when to charge up San Juan Hill and when to tiptoe around it. By early 1916, a TR-GOP rapprochement had been inching forward for some time. Accordingly, on the very day TR tossed cold water on the Progressive Hale's enthusiasm, George Perkins revealed to William Allen White that TR was indeed meeting with Republican leaders. "We are ready and willing to do our part," Perkins revealed, "to sink past differences [with the GOP] and make . . . some arrangements next June by which all of the opponents to the Wilson Democracy could unite . . . to win next November's elections."[20]

Two days later, the nation learned of TR's strategizing at Oyster Bay with three unnamed GOP notables.[21] "You know, Colonel," said a congressman slated to serve as a GOP convention delegate, "that I may make up my mind that I will have to nominate you."

"Let me give you one piece of advice," TR countered, banging his fist on the table. "If you have any doubt on the subject do not nominate me. Get it perfectly clear in your head that if you nominate me it mustn't be because you think it is in my interest, but because you think it is in your interest and the interest of the Republican party, and because you think it to the interest of the United States to do so."[22]

Over and over again, TR insisted, "*Do not* nominate me," "Do not nominate me *unless* . . ." fairly whispering "do not" and thundering "unless." Even the densest observer might grasp his meaning: TR was running, though determined not to embarrass himself in the process. He would run, all the way decrying "pussyfooting." But he would pussyfoot mightily regarding his own intentions and strategies. Was he a candidate? Was he a Progressive candidate? A Republican candidate? A fusion nominee uniting what he had so recently sundered? Or a kingmaker, dictating to both parties whom they could—or, more likely, could not—nominate.

One thing he would not be—could never again be—was a spoiler, delivering yet another victory to such unworthy creatures as Wilson and Bryan, Daniels and Baker. In 1912, he had hated Taft more than he hated Wilson. By 1916, he hated Wilson more than he had ever hated anyone.

Republicans hated Wilson too. Or at least they hated being out of office, hated being shut out from all the cabinet posts, ambassadorships, judgeships, and postmasterships. The GOP might not be heroic, but it could be practical, and practicality suggested an alliance, as uneasy and awkward as any alliance might be with the apostate Rough Rider. What, after all, was party politics but a system of enforced practicality? Of embarrassing alliances and awkward embraces? Democrats had learned that lesson well. Their coalition of Wall Street Bourbons, prairie populists, southern conservatives, western radicals, and big-city crooks might not make any sense to students in Professor Wilson's political science classes, but it nonetheless placed said professor in the White House. It might very well keep him there for another four years.

No, the Republican Party, the party of intensely practical men, required even greater practicality. The impractical dreamers idolizing TR needed to learn it.

And TR had to relearn it.

In early February 1916, Cabot Lodge apprised the skeptical TR of "a very steady drift of Republicans (I am not speaking of Progressives) toward you"[23]—at least on issues of Preparedness. In April, Taft's former secretary of the navy, George von L. Meyer, and Senator John W. Weeks's campaign manager, Charles G. Washburn, visited Oyster Bay. Meyer publicly predicted that TR "will be the psychological candidate and that popular sentiment is rolling up in that direction."[24] A poll of Connecticut GOP committeemen revealed a newfound appreciation of Roosevelt's nomination.[25]

In mid-April, the Republican *New York Tribune* issued this endorsement: "We are for Colonel Roosevelt in spite of the fact that we were against him four years ago. No one fought him harder than we. No one will fight harder for him. It has not been easy to put aside our pride, our sense of resentment at what occurred in 1912, and the hundred other things that tend to keep alive divisions. But we have put them aside, and are putting them aside because we feel that they have no place in a crisis like this. We come out for Colonel Roosevelt as a Republican newspaper, intending to remain Republican."[26] More significantly, Senator Boies Penrose, king of the standpatters, initiated negotiations with Roosevelt regarding Pennsylvania's upcoming primary. Penrose had little use for TR, but facing his first popular primary and embroiled in a series of state intraparty disputes, he respectfully conferred with him.

Such news alarmed W. Murray Crane, who dispatched Nicholas Murray Butler to investigate. Butler located the six-foot-four, 350-pound Penrose ("so gigantic that he could balance a glass on the fold of his stomach"[27]) lounging in a "comfortable chair" at the Waldorf-Astoria. "My dear boy," the wily Penrose reassured him, "you people must remember that the Progressives carried Pennsylvania in 1912, and that they are very strong there now. I am going to have a hard fight in the primaries next Tuesday, so I have entered into partnership with the Roosevelt men, which partnership will be dissolved on Tuesday afternoon at six o'clock. I shall have all the assets and they will get all the liabilities."[28]

Yet Penrose saw some virtue in TR. "I don't want Hughes," he confided to Perkins. "I cannot do business with Hughes; I can do business with Roosevelt."[29] He certainly could. During 1916's conventions, TR tempted him thusly: "Supposing that matters come about so that I am nominated ... you will be the leader in the Senate at that time."[30] Yes, given the circumstances, one could indeed do business with Theodore Roosevelt.

George Perkins boosted Roosevelt with both cash and high-powered advertising. To counter fears of TR as a jingoistic warmonger itching to plunge America into war, he organized the Roosevelt Non-Partisan League: A Union of Patriotic Citizens of All Parties. Four-page ads in the *Saturday Evening Post, Collier's Weekly, Leslie's,* and *The Outlook*[31] argued as to "why Roosevelt would be our best guarantee of Peace," pointing to his presidential record and contending that he was the tried, experienced leader necessary in a time of international crisis. Each ad included a coupon soliciting support. Twelve hundred readers responded; seven hundred dispatched donations totaling a measly $3,089.36.[32]

But Perkins continued strategizing, and Roosevelt continued receiving GOP "gentleman callers" and providing conflicting messages to friends near and far. Resistance to him within Republican ranks persisted. In some cases, it intensified. In April 1916, the now eighty-five-year-old Joe Choate, in publicly endorsing Elihu Root, appended a barbed shot at TR: "Mr. Roosevelt is not a 'tried Republican,' or rather he was 'tried' in 1912 and found wanting. He then deliberately attempted to destroy the party, bolted from it, and set up his Progressive machine for the sole purpose of defeating Mr. Taft and gratifying his own selfish aims. . . . It is inconceivable that the same party should so soon forget and forgive as to give him a re-nomination now as a reward for what he did then."[33]

Such insults merely strengthened Roosevelt's resolve. Two weeks later, he hinted that if the GOP was foolish enough to nominate Root, he would again be fool enough to run as a third-party candidate.[34]

In early May, New York City banker and philanthropist Guy Emerson, secretary of Perkins's Roosevelt Non-Partisan League, wrote TR that his organization believed

Americanism is the great issue before the country to-day. . . . We believe that you are the only man now available who can carry that platform into effect, and at the same time has any chance of being elected.[35]

TR responded, "I am glad and proud, as an American, that you are fearlessly and efficiently backing these ideals."[36] Observers saw this as an endorsement of league efforts to draft him for both the GOP and the Bull Moose nominations.

The game was on.

Roosevelt Non-Partisan League efforts exploded from New York to Syracuse to Chicago to Boston to Philadelphia,[37] attracting well-heeled endorsers such Albert R. Erskine, president of Studebaker Motors (a Democrat), meatpacking king J. Ogden Armour, Alfred I. du Pont, and Thomas Alva Edison.[38] Charles Mackay—Irving Berlin's future father-in-law—supplied free office space at his Postal Telegraph and Cable Corporation headquarters.[39]

A Roosevelt Republican Committee also emerged, though observers questioned both its effectiveness and its membership's actual loyalty to the Grand Old Party.

"We are here," announced George von L. Meyer in presenting twenty-four fellow Roosevelt Republicans to the Colonel, "to notify you of our organization and to inform you that we intend to do what we properly can to bring about your nomination in the Republican convention." As innocent as a snow-white bull moose, TR listened, as the *Sun* noted, "as intently as if he had never heard of the Roosevelt Republican Committee before."[40]

Roosevelt headed into the Midwest, heart of a hyphenated, noninterventionist America. First stop: Detroit, home not only to such "Roosevelt Republicans" as former navy secretary Truman H. Newberry and two auto company presidents, Packard's Henry B. Joy and Chalmers's Hugh Chalmers, but also to pacifist Henry Ford. That January, when Ford had invited TR to tour his own motor works, TR sharply responded,

I trust you have not extended this invitation in ignorance of the position I have publicly taken about your . . . pacifism. If you did not know my attitude when you wrote, I shall of course understand absolutely if you withdraw the invitation, for, as I supposed you knew, I am emphatically out of sympathy with you (just as I am radically out of sympathy with my friend Miss Addams). . . . If you do know my attitude and have sent the invitation knowing it, I wish you would give me the chance . . . to make a very earnest appeal to you to use your good influence, not on behalf of a peace that will not bring righteousness, but on behalf of righteousness; for if that is obtained the peace worth having comes with it.[41]

Shunning Ford, TR delivered three addresses in Detroit. At a massive rally at the city's opera house, he demanded a standing army of a quarter million men, universal military training, creation of a navy second only to Britain's, and a government-regulated industrial "mobilization" of the nation's businesses and railways. He asserted,

There is no use in saying that we will fit ourselves to defend ourselves a little, but not much. Such a position is equivalent to announcing that, if necessary, we shall hit, but we shall only hit soft. The only right principle is to prepare thoroughly or not at all. The only right principle is to avoid hitting if it is possible to do so, but never under any circumstances to hit soft. To go to war a little, but not much, is the one absolutely certain way to ensure disaster. To prepare a little but not much, stands on a par with a city developing a fire department which after a fire occurs, can put it out a little, but not much.[42]

Throngs packed city streets. Crowds loved not only him but also his message. Eight days later, twenty-five hundred enthusiastic Roosevelt Non-Partisan League members descended on Sagamore Hill,[43] nearly collapsing its porch. To the tune of "Glory, Glory Hallelujah," they sang,

> We'll vote for Theodore Roosevelt
> Because we know that he'll be true,
> He loves our starry banner—
> Our own red, white, blue;
> We know that he'll defend it
> From the enemy in view, as we go marching on.[44]

TR swayed crowds. He hypnotized individuals even more. Russian-born Sonya Levien (his "little miss anarchist"[45]) edited his *Metropolitan*

Magazine articles and marveled at the spell cast not only upon her but also upon the immense number of visitors he received. "I used to watch them," she recalled, "as he crowded them into the waiting elevator with the last handshake; their faces had that trance-like expression, as if living over again within themselves some dramatic moment just passed; some smiling at nothing in particular; others, excited and muttering to themselves, all showing some signs of having passed through a tidal moment in their lives."[46]

TR headed for Kansas City. Fifty thousand devotees hailed his Union Station arrival.[47] TR stood standing and waving from his car. Mac McGrath rode immediately before him. Within the immense crowd, a tall man in a straw hat (police thought him a random drunk) flung a small jackknife toward TR. He missed. Handle first, it struck McGrath just below the elbow.

Most Kansas Citians were friendlier (if not necessarily soberer) than TR's assailant. TR passed "through crowds so anxious to shake hands that they near tore his clothes."[48] Their frenzy proved so great that TR remained ignorant of the jackknife incident for a full three hours afterward.[49]

Everything was indeed up to date in Kansas City. Wilson had recently visited, though TR's throngs were larger and more enthusiastic. So too had William Jennings Bryan and sawdust-circuit evangelist Billy Sunday. Sunday and his staff of forty remained in town for seven weeks, eventually packing 1.356 million persons into his temporary twelve-thousand-seat Billy Sunday Tabernacle.

At TR's Hotel Muehlebach suite, Sunday (original family name Sonntag) conferred privately with Roosevelt for a full half hour. At the banquet downstairs, he sat to TR's right. At the Kansas City Coliseum, Sunday ensconced himself in the front row, lustily cheering TR—and literally flag waving. "I don't know what those delegates in Chicago are going to do," he assured the Colonel. "But I can tell you this, the plain people are with you to a man, and if you run this fall, they are going to give you the biggest majority ever piled up by an American candidate."[50]

TR warned of an inevitable Germanic invasion: "When this war is over it is possible that some one of the combatants, being fully armed, will assail us because we offer ourselves as a rich and helpless prize."[51]

The following day in St Louis, a hotbed of pro-German sentiment, he denounced the 2.5-million-member "German-American Alliance" as the "anti-American alliance."[52]

"No one had dared to talk out like that before," observed a local Republican, "and no one but Roosevelt would dare do it. It was the most magnificent exhibition of nerve I have ever known."[53]

Talk he did, eviscerating Wilson:

The President said that he was for universal voluntary training. . . . Now, universal voluntary training is an expression precisely similar to . . . a truant law for the schools . . . for every child that did not wish to stay away.

. . . One of our defects as a nation is . . . to use what have been called "weasel words." When a weasel sucks eggs the meat is sucked out of the egg. If you use a "weasel word" after another there is nothing left of the other. Now, you can have universal training, or you can have voluntary training, but when you use the word "voluntary" to qualify the word "universal" you are using a "weasel word"; it has sucked all the meaning out of "universal."[54]

But TR aimed rhetorical artillery at the wrong target, fighting the last (and perchance the next) electoral skirmish but not the one immediately before him: a battle involving the Honorable Charles Evans Hughes.

The Republican Party possessed a surfeit of options in 1916—virtually all horrendously bad. Nominating a conservative like Elihu Root would only spark a second Bull Moose suicide run, guaranteeing Wilson's reelection. Conversely, a TR-led GOP ticket appeared similarly unfeasible. True to principle (or at least to pique and/or ambition), the Colonel had demolished his party in 1912—and an elephant never forgets, certainly not in a mere four years. Aside from TR or Root, the GOP field—a bowl of porridge, either too hot or too cold—was unquestionably too bland to appeal to Republican delegates, let alone to the nation at large.

And then there was Justice Hughes.

Hughes was neither too hot nor too cold—neither an overly wild progressive nor a hidebound standpatter. Ensconced on the Supreme Court since 1910, he, unlike every other prominent Republican, assumed no role in 1912's fratricide.

Hughes was, in his own methodical, lawyerly way, a marvelous reformer. Virtually single-handedly, he cleansed New York's insurance industry. As governor, he instituted a host of other reforms. His personal and political rectitude lay beyond reproach. If you craved a GOP candidate who had tussled with bosses like Billy Barnes and *not* bolted the party in 1912, Justice Hughes, and not Colonel Roosevelt, was your man.

But not TR's.

For Theodore Roosevelt hated Charles Evans Hughes.

In part, he logically feared anointing someone, as he had with Taft, only to suffer grievous disappointment. Or, as he now grumbled, to "have merely swapped Wilson for another Wilson with whiskers."[55]

Policies matter. So do personalities, and fire and ice do not mix. TR was blazing fire, often generating more heat than light. Hughes personified purest ice. The "bearded iceberg,"[56] TR termed him, and he was hardly alone.

Beyond that, TR may have been jealous of a rising younger reform figure clouding his own glory.

And Hughes may have simply been too honest for the often flexible TR.

During Hughes's 1905 insurance industry investigation, he had stumbled upon a mysteriously unexplained $48,702.50 expenditure by George W. Perkins's New York Life Insurance Company.[57]

During a luncheon recess, Perkins privately warned Hughes, "You're handling dynamite. That $48,000 was a contribution to President Roosevelt's campaign fund. You want to think very carefully before you put that in evidence. You can't tell what may come of it."

"After lunch," Hughes coolly responded, "I'm going to ask you what was done with that $48,000, and I expect a candid answer."[58]

Nonetheless, TR had supported Hughes's 1906 gubernatorial bid, praising him as "fighting the battle of civilization. If you were an ordinary time-serving politician, if you had the slightest taint of subserviency to the great monied interests, I would not give a rap for your success. But you are an honest fearless square man, a good citizen and a good American first and a good Republican also. . . . If I were not president I'd be stumping New York from one end to the other for you."[59]

Such harmony proved illusory. TR and Hughes soon sparred over the state GOP's slate of judicial candidates. Hughes argued for qualifications. TR played the practical political angle.[60] Greater acrimony followed.

In 1907, newly elected Governor Hughes required legislative approval to replace an ineffective nonentity named Otto Kelsey as New York State's insurance commissioner. It was suggested to TR (though not by Hughes) that pressure placed upon Rochester collector of internal revenue Archie Sanders (a federal employee) might in turn entice two Rochester assemblymen to support Kelsey's ouster. TR thus demanded Sanders's resignation.

Complications ensued when Oswald Garrison Villard's *New York Evening Post* reported Hughes's denial of having instigated Sanders's firing—and hinted strongly that Hughes resented Roosevelt's intervention. The *Evening Post* also charged that Sanders's dismissal was actually unrelated to either Hughes or Kelsey, instead stemming from Roosevelt's ongoing vendetta against Sanders's mentor, former western New York congressman James W. Wadsworth Sr. (the father of Barnes-backed future U.S. senator James W. Wadsworth Jr.).[61]

Hughes had nothing to do with these reports. But from that moment on, the Colonel detested him. As Henry Stoddard recollected, Hughes was "almost the last candidate [TR] cared to see nominated as his successor."[62]

In January 1908, TR sabotaged Hughes's potential presidential candidacy. To jump-start his White House bid, Hughes, on Friday evening, January 31, 1908, addressed eleven hundred members of the New York Republican Club. That very day, TR dispatched an incendiary special message to Congress, blasting business and the courts in unprecedentedly vitriolic terms, utterly obliterating the news value of Hughes's talk and permanently short-circuiting his campaign.[63]

"If Hughes is going to play the game," TR chortled to his friend, journalist Mark Sullivan, "he must learn the tricks."[64]

Hughes hardly helped matters when Roosevelt requested his testimony as a character witness in 1915's *Barnes v. Roosevelt* trial. Citing judicial propriety, Hughes declined, further infuriating TR.[65] "Hughes," TR privately fumed to the *New York Tribune*'s Jack Leary, "is grateful to nobody but Almighty God, and I am not sure he is overgrateful to him."[66]

Grateful or not, by early 1916, Hughes had emerged as the logical—yet morbidly reluctant—GOP candidate. "I do not want the work that is before the next president," he confided to Henry Stoddard. "He may wear a crown, but it will be a crown of thorns." When Hughes's wife urged him to enter the race, he replied, "When you see me in my coffin, remember that I did not want to take this burden on myself."[67]

Others eagerly worked to place it upon him. New York governor Charles Whitman prominently touted him as the one Republican capable of defeating Wilson.[68] So did Woodrow Wilson's old mentor Colonel George Harvey ("Nobody wants Hughes—; Nobody but the People!").[69] And without Hughes's authorization—indeed, to his annoyance—William Howard Taft's former postmaster general, Frank Hitchcock (among the party's more skilled political operatives), scurried about the country recruiting Hughes delegates.[70] By early April, the *Brooklyn Eagle* headlined, "SENTIMENT STRONGEST FOR HUGHES IN RACE FOR G.O.P. NOMINATION," and projected a solid delegate lead for him.[71]

Republicans from New York to Oregon prized Hughes's electability. Democrats feared it.

The Wilson administration calculated that the best way to keep Hughes out of the race was to keep him on the bench—indeed, on the highest bench of all.

Wilson's interior secretary, Franklin K. Lane, sidled up to Hughes at a dinner party, hinting that if Hughes remained on the High Court, a chief justiceship lay in the cards.

Hughes dismissed Lane's message as mere idle chatter. Soon he received a far more direct one. "Before you decide on what course you will take," Chief Justice Edward D. White, a Louisiana Democrat, informed him, "I feel that you should know that I am going to retire and that if you do not resign you will succeed me."

"Why," Hughes protested, "President Wilson would never appoint me Chief Justice!"

"Well, he wouldn't appoint anyone else, as I happen to know."[72]

Anyone else might have taken that deal. But not Charles Evans Hughes.

Not long afterward, while leaving the White House, Henry Stoddard chanced to meet Samuel Untermyer, a prominent New York attorney active in Democratic circles and close to President Wilson.

"What are you fellows going to do in Chicago, Roosevelt or Hughes?" Untermyer asked.

"Roosevelt," Stoddard answered, partly to gauge Untermyer's reaction.

"Well, that will suit the man in there exactly," Untermyer retorted, nodding back toward the White House. "He can lick Roosevelt on the war issue, and he wants to do it. If Wilson could name your candidate he would name Teddy."[73]

Stoddard relayed the conversation back to TR.

"I refuse to believe that the people out there are pacifists," TR fussed, suddenly reversing his invariably pessimistic assessment of public sentiment, "or that they will indorse Wilson's flabby policy."

"But, Colonel," said Stoddard, "Wilson's people have studied the situation carefully and really believe it. They believe it so much that they would rather have had you nominated. They feel certain they could defeat you."

"That would be the keenest humiliation I could suffer," Theodore pronounced, "but Wilson would have a fight on his hands before he licked me."[74]

TR returned to Oyster Bay. Mac McGrath did not. He had other business—mercifully, not in a Brooklyn courtroom.

"I am going to Chicago," he announced, "to co-operate with the friends of Mr. Roosevelt in whatever party they may be."[75]

The awkward courtship dance of Bull Moose and Elephant was about to begin.

"One colossal figure of American manhood"

THE WINDY CITY APPROACHED HISTORIC WINDINESS.

Not one but two national political conventions convened roughly eight blocks apart—Republicans at their usual Coliseum (soon to be dubbed the "Mausoleum"[1]) stomping grounds, Progressives at the four-thousand-seat Auditorium Theatre. Bull Moosers hoped that the Republicans would come to their senses and nominate a Progressive (most likely named Roosevelt), and Republicans calculated that Progressives would recoup their sanity and nominate a Republican (hopefully *never* named Roosevelt).

Republicans damn near always convened in Chicago. They nominated Lincoln and Grant there, Garfield and Blaine and Harrison, TR and Taft—Taft being the only presidential candidate twice nominated in Chicago. TR also received two nominations there. Only the first was the GOP's; the second had been bestowed by renegade, infuriated Progressives just four years previously.

The Progressive gathering of 1912 followed that year's fractious GOP affair. In January 1916, however, the 150-member Progressive National Committee agreed to convene its upcoming June convention concurrently with the Republicans' Chicago Coliseum confab. Progressives also proclaimed a willingness to confer jointly with their GOP counterparts "to secure for our country the required leadership . . . by having, if possible, both . . . Parties choose the same standard-bearer and the same principles."[2]

Or, as one columnist observed, "the progressive party advertised that it would be on a certain corner at a certain time, wearing a red carnation, and that its intentions were matrimonial."[3]

Which, of course, is a far easier proposition when one has not abandoned the bride at the altar four years previously.

Brides—even Republican brides—tend to recall such matters.

By late spring 1916, the odds of TR capturing the GOP nod remained at 5:1. By Thursday, June 1, Chicago and St. Louis gamblers declared him even money.[4] The following day, at New York's Hotel Vanderbilt, one adventuresome soul wagered $10,000 on those odds.[5] Chicago Stock Yards gambling kingpin James Patrick O'Leary reported $25,000 in Roosevelt wagers, "a majority . . . not inspired by partisan feeling."[6] Odds on dark horses such as John W. Weeks, Theodore Burton, Charles W. Fairbanks, and the like, ranged from 40:1 to 100:1.[7]

Politicians are often more accomplished than gamblers at hedging their bets. If TR would not or could not run . . . well, the most acceptable alternative remained Charles Evans Hughes.[8]

A thought TR did not relish.

Republicans convened on Wednesday morning, June 7; Progressives a day later. So very much hinged on timing. "Radical" Progressives demanded quick action. Their plan: to nominate TR before the GOP anointed a Hughes, an Elihu Root, or anyone else—and to compel Republicans to choose between TR and another suicidal three-way race. More moderate Progressives, led by George W. Perkins, counseled a waiting game. Let the GOP act first, and either unite or bolt only then. Many Progressives feared a sellout. Gifford Pinchot warned Perkins, "Nothing ought to be said which would put the Progressive Party in a position of wearing a sign 'Price 99 cents' on its chest."[9]

Old Guard Republicans, while opposing any Roosevelt restoration, recognized that accommodations were in order—though not many. "Republicans," observed *New Republic* editor Walter Lippmann, "were polite to [Progressives], but not profoundly interested in them. They were regarded as a small collection of spoilt children who had no important influence and were neither to be feared nor insulted."[10]

No, they were not to be insulted.

Accordingly, Resolutions Committee chair Henry Cabot Lodge conferred directly with his Progressive counterpart, William Draper Lewis, in crafting nearly identical GOP and Bull Moose platforms, particularly regarding Preparedness and foreign policy.

On domestic policy, the GOP lurched sharply leftward, endorsing "the rigid supervision and strict regulation of the transportation [industry] and of the great corporations of the country. . . . The entire transportation system of the country has become essentially national. We, therefore, favor such action by legislation, or, if necessary, through an amendment to the Constitution . . . placing it under complete Federal control."[11]

To the assembled convention, Lodge declaimed his draft in a clear, firm voice, his elocution aided by the listless crowd's eerie silence. The *New York Times* reported that as Lodge (no friend of suffrage)

> *came to the woman suffrage plank the Suffragists present got a premature thrill. He read the words declaring in favor of suffrage, and the . . . Suffragists . . . began to cheer. Alice Roosevelt "Princess Alice" Longworth, turning to two friends of hers who were active suffrage workers, with a mischievous twinkle in her bright eyes, said "Get up. Get up and show yourselves and cheer. It's your moment of victory."*
>
> *So they arose and cheered, and just then, Lodge's clear voice again emerged above the noise with a loud and explosive "but." The cheering subsided in a scared sort of way, and he read the concluding and modifying clause, whereby the platform said it "recognized the right of each State to settle the question for itself." Mrs. Longworth laughed herself into convulsions as her suffrage friends hurriedly sat down, applauded till her hands were sore, and hurled gay taunts at them.[12]*

Princess Alice might giggle and guffaw regarding suffrage. Her father did not. As the convention neared, Mrs. Carrie Chapman Catt, president of the National American Woman Suffrage Association, solicited his stance. TR, a late (and generally unimpressed) convert[13] to the cause, caustically responded,

My dear Mrs. Catt:

It is a little difficult for me to give a statement to any person, male or female, who won't take the trouble to read what I have publicly said. You might just as well write me to know whether I believe in Americanism or in Preparedness, or in the U.S. Army, or in the U.S. Navy, as ask the questions you write me about. Write to Miss [Alice] Carpenter [president of the Women's Roosevelt League] if you are in ignorance of what I have said. I have explicitly, within a few weeks, made a statement as to what the exact amendment to the Federal Constitution should be. Of course, I have spoken [about] . . . woman suffrage again and again and again, and in a speech on the subject before your own society. . . . Take that speech and take my public statements, which Miss Carpenter will furnish you, and you will find they will explicitly and minutely answer the questions you raise. And if you will look at them, my dear Mrs. Catt, you will save your association from the absurdity of questions the answers to which every human being in the United States knows.

Sincerely yours[14]

Indeed.

Platforms define a convention. So do keynote addresses. The GOP keynoter in 1916 was Ohio's rising freshman senator, Warren Gamaliel Harding ("an estimable gentleman who looks like McKinley and talks like the year 1876"[15]). Preconvention observers confidently expected Harding's oration to ignite a dark horse candidacy on his behalf,[16] though such buzz ignited speculation that TR would "not be averse to a third ticket if the Republicans nominate . . . Harding or any other dark horse [he] considers a reactionary."[17]

TR need not have fretted. History recalls the standpat Harding as an abysmal speaker. In truth, he wasn't that bad. He even derived a good portion of his income from lecturing on the Chautauqua circuit. Nonetheless, Harding's Wednesday, June 7, 1916, keynote proved simply abysmal and totally vacuous. *New York Tribune* columnist Heywood Broun termed it a "cheap"[18] effort. The *New York Times* concurred. Recalling TR's recent blast at Woodrow Wilson's "weasel words," it gibed that "Harding's address is overrun with those graceful little quadrupeds."[19] Worse, it editorialized that "nobody could stampede this convention, and Harding could not stampede any convention.... His full name is Warren G. Harding and he is a Senator ... from Ohio; but it is not necessary to burden one's memory with these statistics if one is merely trying to remember the names of persons likely to be nominated for President."[20]

Critics dismissed Harding as a noncontroversial boor. Progressives recalled a far different Harding, white-hot with fervor, employing words not as soporific salve but as napalm.

Harding had loyally delivered Taft's 1912 renominating address ("Taft is the greatest *progressive* of the age"[21]). His small-town newspaper, the *Marion Star*, lacerated TR at every level, from his connections to Perkins and U.S. Steel to his friendship with boxer John L. Sullivan; it even gave an unflattering account of events at San Juan Hill. Harding likened TR to Aaron Burr ("the same overbearing disposition and ungovernable temper [as Burr], the same ruthlessness ... the same tendency to bully and browbeat").[22] He damned Roosevelt as "utterly without conscience and regard for truth, the greatest fakir of all times[23] ... selfish, intolerant, unstable, violently headstrong, vain and unstably ambitious of power."[24]

Most relevant in 1916, in September 1912 he rated TR "a bully by nature and a lover of war, not to be trusted with control of the army and navy and our relations with our neighbors."[25] Following Wilson's election, he jeered, "Well, the mad Roosevelt has a new achievement to his credit. He succeeded in defeating the party that furnished him a job for nearly all of his manhood days ...The eminent fakir can now turn to raising hell, his specialty, along other lines."[26]

Thus, neither Roosevelt nor his acolytes gazed fondly upon Harding. He was "a handsome dog," recounted William Allen White, with "the harlot's voice of the old-time political orator. . . . I distrusted him, and into my distrust came something unpleasantly near to hate."[27]

Speaking of harlots ...

Not long before the unhappily married Harding had rendezvoused with his paramour, his equally married Marion neighbor, Carrie Fulton

Phillips. Mrs. Phillips, literally a jealous mistress, had long disdained her lover's political career. She absolutely detested the possibility of his dark horse nomination (his "mad pursuit of honors")—and at a clandestine meeting in Baltimore, she firmly let him know it. Thus, Harding may have deliberately sabotaged his convention star turn—and any longshot candidacy—to calm his agitated lady love.[28]

His profoundly boring keynote address set the tone for one of the most enervated, unenthusiastic gatherings in American convention history. Meanwhile, at Chicago's Auditorium Theatre, enthusiasm reigned—at least among Progressive delegates, alternates, and hangers-on. Behind the scenes, it was all the same, as men like Perkins and Mac McGrath pulled the strings, and TR tugged the longest string of all, all the way from Sagamore Hill.

Republicans grasped such facts of political life. Progressive delegates—starstruck romantics at best, idol-worshipping fanatics at worst—didn't.

Back at the Coliseum, on Friday, June 9, Governor Charles Whitman nominated Justice Hughes ("the American spirit incarnate").[29] An eight-minute demonstration resulted, followed by some additional noise-making.[30] Calculation more than fervor drove Hughes's support. "No one wanted Hughes," it was said, "but everyone was for him."[31]

"There is," TR's man George von L. Meyer lamented, "the feeling that [Hughes] is the easiest man to win with."[32] Billy Barnes disagreed. "We're going to nominate Hughes," he dissented on convention eve. "We're going to be strongest on nomination day and weakest on election day."[33]

Barnes's statewide influence lay in tatters. In April, Whitman bested him for control of the state committee.[34] Within days of the convention's opening, he'd lose his national committee slot.[35] But he remained aboard Elihu Root's capsizing ship and cajoled Nicholas Murray Butler into nominating him.[36] A distinctly unconservative, un-Rootian reaction followed Butler's address. Above the dais, a bespectacled yet distinctly good-looking young woman arose, emitting the most fearsome of noises—bloodcurdling, insane shrieks, really. "It took the crowd a couple of minutes," observed the *Brooklyn Eagle*, "to discover that she was not being murdered but was enjoying herself."[37] Endeavoring to rouse the crowd for Root, she triggered the opposite effect. Dumbstruck by her performance, those cheering Root silently halted to behold her caterwauling. "The shrill screaming is painfully like that of an insane patient," noted Arthur Brisbane of Hearst's *Washington Herald.* "Root's lady friend now has a flag in each hand. She stands stiff, with her mouth wide open, screaming as long as she can endure the strain, then sat down to rest for a few seconds."[38] Eighty-two-year-old Chauncey Depew stood upon a chair, yowling back at her.[39] He soon gave up—and for a while so did she.

Convention chair Harding vainly shouted into his megaphone, attempting to restart the nomination process. But she resumed. A Tennessee delegate "then started an imitation of the fair yeller, and he and she divided attention, the delegates being unable to decide which yell was the most blood-curdling."[40]

At 5:00 p.m., New Mexico senator Albert B. Fall mounted the podium to nominate Colonel Roosevelt ("one colossal figure of American manhood"[41]). But when Fall first dared utter Roosevelt's name ("Starving mothers in Mexico . . . will put their hope in one great American and one alone—and that one is Theodore Roosevelt"[42]), a volley of hisses stopped him in his tracks.

Harding intervened:

Gentlemen of the convention, no Republican in any Republican convention has a hiss for a Republican delegate in the convention. . . .

The Chair knows that the delegate body of this convention will listen with courtesy and respect, and if the galleries do not, they may listen from the street outside.[43]

Fall resumed, although, as the *Chicago Tribune's* Percy Hammond noted, the New Mexican—like every speaker preceding him—somehow "lacked the precarious fascinations of eloquence."[44]

Roosevelt's adoring partisans nonetheless cheered for thirty-six minutes,[45] the longest for any candidate. Princess Alice lustily led them in "My Country, 'Tis of Thee." Sears, Roebuck president Julius Rosenwald (for Taft in 1912; for TR now) ripped red-white-and-blue decorations from his box to wave about his head. A dozen reporters chanted, "We want Teddy!"[46]

Events, however, at the GOP convention paled beside those at the Auditorium Theatre, where Progressives stomped, whistled, and cheered their Teddy for a record ninety-three minutes, easily surpassing 1908's eighty-minute ovation for William Jennings Bryan.[47]

"The convention wanted to run away," noted the Tribune's Heywood Broun.

> Only with difficulty was it restrained from nominating Theodore Roosevelt by acclamation. "You want Teddy!" shouted [former Kansas congressman] Victor Murdock, with blazing eye and hair. "Well, the way to get him is to go ahead and nominate him right now." A little later [former representative William J.] McDonald, of Michigan, in response to the harmony plea of a preceding speaker, declared that "the only message to send to the Republican party is to tell it to go to hell.". . .
>
> Several gentlemen had suggested . . . conferring with the Republican party and waiting action upon the issue of that conference. And then Murdock came down the aisle. "I'm for harmony," he said, "but I want a little harmony on both sides." There was a shout throughout the big theatre. It startled us, for we had been lulled by two sessions of the Republican convention. "Are you going to get down on your knees to the Republican party?" asked Murdock. This is a rhetorical question and in a Republican convention it requires no answer, but a broadside of "noes" came booming back at the speaker.[48]

Not every Progressive burned every bridge. Thus Progressives did authorize a five-man committee (Perkins; Hiram Johnson; Charles J. Bonaparte; TR's old Syracuse host, industrialist Horace Wilkinson; and recent Louisiana gubernatorial candidate Captain John M. Parker) to negotiate with Republicans.[49]

The Progressive Party was at war with itself, the chasm between its leadership and rank and file as deep and jagged as that dividing Republicans in 1912. Victor Murdock and Gifford Pinchot, Harold Ickes and William Allen White distrusted Perkins as a tool of Wall Street, a sinister force playing to TR's more Machiavellian instincts. To them, plutocrats like Perkins and Frank Munsey, as much as Belgium and the *Lusitania*, had caused TR to shift focus from domestic progressivism to international preparedness. "[Men like Amos] Pinchot can keep on battling for the Lord," gibed the *New York World*, "and Perkins can keep on signing the checks."[50]

William Allen White represented many of the fissures wracking TR's Progressive legions. Though still worshipping Roosevelt (and heartily favoring yet another TR candidacy), he shared neither the Colonel's absolute loathing of Woodrow Wilson nor his contempt for Robert La Follette, nor any great desire for war.

In Chicago in 1916, Perkins's eastern crowd triggered White's immense unease—"what jarred and angered me and made me mad was that the [bulk of Bull Moose] delegates . . . from the East were big businessmen, who had come at Perkins' beck and call. . . . [A] great steel master was one of them. A group of Wall Street brokers and bankers of some renown sat with New York when the convention opened."[51]

The same crowd, indeed, that White's bête noire Warren Harding had railed against in 1912.

However, 1916 was not 1912, and at Perkins's behest, Progressive Party executive secretary O. K. Davis informed Harding of their party's selections for a joint Bull Moose–GOP "peace" committee. Harding instantly designated their Republican counterparts: William E. Borah (for Hughes[52] after originally backing Albert Cummins[53]), representing the party's remaining "small-*p*" progressive elements; Utah senator Reed Smoot (also a Hughes man[54]); W. Murray Crane (officially backing his fellow Bay Stater Weeks; in reality, for Hughes[55]); Nicholas Murray Butler (for Root); and former one-term conservative Ohio congressman Adna R. Johnson. Even back then, nobody was quite sure who Adna R. Johnson was.[56]

Maryland's former U.S. senator William P. "Young Bill" Jackson— not even a delegate—ignited a stir by unilaterally inviting Theodore Roosevelt to address the GOP.[57] TR, connected to events in Chicago via an expensive ($9,000 for ten days[58]) long-distance telephone wire, begged off. Yes, he might attend later if formally invited, and, yes, all concerned concurred that Wilson had rendered "the most evil service that can be rendered to a great democracy by its chosen leader."[59]

"Can we not," purred TR, "forgetting past differences, now join, for the safety and honor of our country, to enforce the policies of genuine Americanism and genuine preparedness?"[60]

Ominous roars—and threats—still accompanied the lion's purr. "The professional German-Americans are seeking to terrorize your convention," he warned, "for they wish to elect . . . a man who shall not be in good faith an American President, but the viceroy of a foreign government. It is for your convention in emphatic fashion to repudiate them."[61] It was an unmistakable jab at Hughes, for the Republicans and Progressives were not the only ones to convene in Chicago; so had the German-American Newspaper Publishers Association ("They may be hyphenated Americans, but their Americanism is unhyphenated"[62]). On May 28 and 29, German-American publishers from twenty-eight states gathered at Chicago's Hotel Kaiserhof. Demanding a true (i.e., not anti-German) foreign policy, they deplored "utterances, voiced by officials, ex-officials, and others designed to create a division along racial lines"[63]—obvious barbs aimed at Woodrow Wilson and particularly TR ("demagogs who trade upon national antipathies and seek to extol their own loyalty by impugning that of others"[64]). The organization's Illinois chapter declared, "Alle gegen Roosevelt und Wilson" ("All against Roosevelt and Wilson").[65]

Late in the evening on Monday, May 29, a delegation from the Republican National Committee advised outgoing chairman Charles D. Hilles that while TR and Root remained verboten, Hughes, Fairbanks, Lawrence Sherman, "or any favorite son" would prove acceptable.[66]

Acceptable to them, but a "viceroy of a foreign government" to TR. "In other words," as the *New York Tribune* explained, "a third ticket looms more . . . than it has at any previous time."[67]

Reports from Oyster Bay were maddeningly contradictory. TR was traveling to Chicago—rooms had even been reserved for him at the Hotel LaSalle.[68] TR was not traveling to Chicago. He would support Root but not Hughes. Hughes but not Root. He would run third-party. He was joining with the GOP to vanquish Wilson.

Or might he support Leonard Wood? The day following the famous TR-Wood-Root-Bacon luncheon, TR conferred with Cabot Lodge and his son-in-law Representative Augustus "Gussie" Gardner, one of whom fed a story to the *Chicago Tribune's* Washington correspondent, Arthur Sears Henning. TR would not formally authorize his entry into any state primary. He would instead support "a man younger than himself who has indomitable courage, who believes fervently in the ideals of Americanism, who interprets America in forms of nationalism, and who believes that in a democracy every citizen owes his first duty to the state, and that it is necessary in the best interests and greatest happiness of the whole people that individual liberty shall at times be subservient to the greater cause of national liberty."[69]

Leonard Wood, not two years younger than TR, took that to mean himself, particularly when TR dispatched his twenty-two-year-old first cousin once removed, Nicholas Roosevelt, to Wood's headquarters at Governor's Island to discuss a Wood candidacy and to posit that the time was ripe for defense hard-liners like Root or Lodge to publicly boost Wood's candidacy.[70]

In mid-April, General and Mrs. Wood visited Oyster Bay, and TR assured Louisa Wood, "If things get out of hand at Chicago, I want you to know that I shall give my support to Leonard."[71]

And upon the Woods' departure, TR portentously informed Edith, "The shadow of the White House rests heavily upon him."[72]

It may not have been a compliment.

Trusting such omens, Gutzon Borglum traveled to Chicago to engineer Wood's nomination.[73] "We will take any man the Colonel will name," former House Speaker "Uncle Joe" Cannon assured Borglum, "provided the Colonel will go with the man."[74] A frustrated Borglum waited and waited and waited for that moment.

Evidently neither Wood nor Borglum pondered the remainder of Henning's *Tribune* article, wherein the Colonel pronounced it "imbecilic" to think he did not want the nomination or that he would decline its offer. At Chicago (or, rather, via long-distance wire from Oyster Bay), Theodore kept his options open, his options including hanging Wood and Borglum out to dry.

Tuesday, June 6, press reports revealed a potential new subplot in Roosevelt's convoluted convention saga: not only was TR running, but he had also selected his running mate, the man in question being not Wood but General John J. Pershing, still engaged in chasing Pancho Villa through Mexican mountains and sagebrush.[75]

The *New York Times* derided the Pershing scenario (though TR and Pershing were, in fact, cordially corresponding just prior to the convention).[76] Two days later, Treasury Secretary William Gibbs McAdoo received word from El Paso collector of customs Zack Lamar Cobb: "Most Confidential. State Department red code. Just informed that . . . Roosevelt had telephoned Pershing in effect asking him to be his running mate."[77]

Whether the Pershing rumors were true or fanciful, Gutzon Borglum would soon bitterly complain that Wood would have emerged as the nominee "if that back slider and self-centered individual who makes his habitat in Oyster Bay had not utterly deserted his best friend at the crucial moment. I would not enlist under Roosevelt to charge a strawberry patch, or anything else. I have lost every bit of confidence I ever had in the man, and I say that with genuine regret."[78]

While Borglum jeered Roosevelt privately, others openly taunted him. William Randolph Hearst mockingly implored TR, "Come to Chicago. Come quickly. Come courageously. There is nothing inspiring in your present attitude. It savors too much of 'watchful waiting.' It suggests the possibility that you also are 'too proud to fight.'"[79]

Everyone was wobbling, unsure of what to do and what fallback position to employ. Cabot Lodge placed his Senate colleague John W. Weeks in nomination—but in decidedly terse and vague fashion. In reality, he kept his options wide open—much to Gussie Gardner's disgust. Informed that Lodge now favored Hughes, the pro-TR Gardner fumed, "Yes, and I have been advised also that he would name Col. Roosevelt. The fact is that the esteemed Senator is for Roosevelt Mondays, Tuesdays, and Wednesdays, and Hughes Thursdays, Fridays, and Saturdays."[80]

TR wasn't even sure about Mondays, Tuesdays, and Wednesdays. Lodge was the ultimate intraparty game player. "Cabot's belief," TR complained to George von L. Meyer in early May, "that the way to pick a winner is to pick a man who has no record on the vital questions of the day, and whose views on these vital questions are not known, may be politically sagacious. If so, the American people occupy a pretty poor attitude."[81]

Conversely, Lodge harbored his own suspicions regarding his old chum TR—or at least said he did, to excuse his support for Hughes. As late as April 1915, he confided to historian Brooks Adams (brother of Henry) that the GOP "would nominate Roosevelt in a moment if he said that the time had come for us all to get together. . . . The trouble is that I think Theodore is bent on the destruction of the Republican party." Adams dissented, arguing that TR had mellowed since 1912. "He felt that a great wrong had been done him at Chicago," Lodge answered Adams in early May 1916, "and his uppermost desire was to sweep away the Republican party."[82]

Lodge wavered. TR's people did not. For his Progressive enthusiasts, the convention was a religious camp meeting disguised as a political convention, a convocation of city folk attorneys and social workers exhibiting the unwashed faith of backwoods snake handlers. And, sometimes, worse manners. The *Washington Times*'s Judson Welliver observed "amateur mobs" of "Rooseveltians" that "burst into cafes, hotel parlors, corridors, and lobbies, and shouted, campaign doggerel in raucous voices through megaphones at the guests."[83]

"More than at any other time," recalled William Allen White, "Roosevelt was a little tin god to his idolaters. Not at any time in 1912, not even when he escaped an assassin's bullet, was he so vividly lifted in the hearts of his followers as the hero-god of their hopes."[84]

Walter Lippmann witnessed much the same thing. Loyalty to progressivism's leader replaced loyalty to the Bull Moose cause. The leader had become the cause. Lippmann concluded of the Colonel's blinded followers, "They clung to him as a woman without occupation or external interest will cling to her husband. They clung so hard that they embarrassed him with their infatuation. They loved too much. They loved without self-respect and without privacy. They adored him as no man in a democracy deserves to be adored."[85]

The ten-man Progressive-Republican peace commission met peacefully and amicably but not at all productively. Progressives went first—for two and a half hours—with John M. Parker (in Butler's recollection) "harp[ing] upon the old and tuneless string of carrying the solid South for Republican principles" and Hiram Johnson for once exhibiting "his very best side. He wholly lacked the violence, the temper and the bad manners which marked his appearance in the Convention of 1912."[86] Each Bull Mooser urged a Roosevelt candidacy. Butler tersely retorted that "under no circumstances whatever"[87] would the GOP nominate Roosevelt. He asked his Progressive counterparts to name their second choice.

They had none.

Perkins asked Republicans their choice. With a dozen names still before their convention, they respectfully declined.

Tick . . . tick . . . tick . . . The clock was ticking. Ticking on whether Perkins could further delay a TR nomination. Or on whether the Hughes boomlet was real or as ephemeral as any of the dark horses'.

It was indeed real.

On Friday, June 9, Republicans balloted. For the first time since 1888, they failed to achieve a first-ballot nomination. Hughes led the pack.

Candidate	Votes
Charles Evans Hughes	253.5
John W. Weeks	105
Elihu Root	103
Theodore Roosevelt	85
Theodore E. Burton	77.5
Charles W. Fairbanks	74.5
Lawrence Y. Sherman	66
Albert B. Cummins	65
Philander C. Knox	36
Henry Ford	32
Martin G. Brumbaugh	29
Robert M. La Follette	25
William Howard Taft	14
T. Coleman du Pont	12
Frank B. Willis	4
William E. Borah	2
Samuel W. McCall	1
Absent	2.5[88]

Hughes fell 220.5 votes short of the 494 votes needed to win—but well ahead of anyone else. TR lay mired in a weak fourth place, barely ahead of such midwestern fantasies as Burton, Fairbanks, Sherman, or Cummins.

A second ballot saw no one save Hughes progress. TR fluttered downward, from eighty-five to eighty-one votes, from fourth to fifth place, now trailing even Fairbanks and Cummins.

Candidate	Votes
Charles Evans Hughes	328.5
Elihu Root	98.5
Charles W. Fairbanks	88.5
Albert B. Cummins	85
Theodore Roosevelt	81
John W. Weeks	79
Theodore E. Burton	76.5
Lawrence Y. Sherman	65
Philander C. Knox	36
Robert M. La Follette	25
T. Coleman du Pont	13
John Wanamaker	5
Frank B. Willis	1
Warren G. Harding	1
Samuel W. McCall	1
Leonard Wood	1
Absent	2[89]

Only Hughes seemed capable of garnering 494 delegates, let alone 266 electoral votes in November. The GOP adjourned at 9:50 p.m.

Perkins barely held his own convention in check. Bull Moose delegates demanded Roosevelt. They wanted him now and didn't particularly care whom the despised GOP nominated. Had they not detoured into debating (though not adopting) a Prohibition plank, they might have galloped into nominating their leader.

The ten-member Republican-Progressive conference committee reconvened at 11:00 that evening to vastly different circumstances than had previously greeted them. GOP conferees now designated Hughes as their man, for "he [would] soon command the support of a majority"[90] of their delegates.[91] Still, they remained unsure of his stand on any issue— or even if he would leave the bench. Butler, Borah, and Adna Johnson remained wary of his virtues. But he had the votes, and that was enough for them.

It was hardly sufficient for Progressive conferees or delegates—or, most significantly, for the foremost Bull Moose of them all.

"The cowardly stab"

THE WIRES TO OYSTER BAY KEPT BUZZING.

George Perkins carried news to TR that convention chairman Raymond Robins intended to proceed with his nomination. "The other fellows have all the crooks," groused TR, "and we have all the cranks."[1]

At approximately 9:00 p.m., when Gifford Pinchot took the line, TR's pussyfooting only accelerated as he suggested that Pinchot "look around and see who else would run" and advanced Hiram Johnson as a possibility.

"Your refusal to run," countered Pinchot, "would kill the Progressive party entirely."

Roosevelt refused to commit to running—or to anything else ("My will [made] known to the managers? I am not going to dictate to that convention as if I were a Tammany chieftain"[2]). And certainly not to supporting Charles Evans Hughes while ignorant of his positions on the issues.

"May I quote you as to that?" Pinchot asked regarding the latter point.

"Yes, but you must not quote me to the newspapers."

"Well, then, whom can I quote you to?"

"What do you mean? Do you mean to say that you think you can quote me to the newspapers? Of course you cannot. Quote me to Hiram Johnson, to William Allen White, to Henry Allen, to George Perkins."[3]

And so, TR, who would not commit to Hughes unless Hughes publicly commented on the issues, now refused to publicly comment upon Hughes not commenting publicly.

And the night was just beginning.

At 10:30 p.m., George B. Cortelyou, TR's old White House secretary and triple cabinet appointee (Commerce and Labor, Post Office, and Treasury), took the receiver, worrying that if Hughes were "killed off," the GOP would turn to Elihu Root. "We had much better have it Hughes," TR answered, "than Root."[4]

Barely a week previously, Mac McGrath had blandly announced, "Of course [Roosevelt] is a candidate. I thought that every one understood that and so does the colonel, [and] you may say that I am authorized to speak for him and that *he will accept the Republican nomination if it is tendered to him*"[5] (emphasis added).

McGrath tendered no such rejoinder regarding a Progressive nomination. And so, on this night, TR blandly and cynically answered Cortelyou regarding any third-party nod, "But, my dear boy, *I do not intend to accept.*"[6]

Yes, a bad colonel does make a bad regiment, and on this evening Colonel Roosevelt, exploiting his Progressive foot soldiers in a game bereft of any consistent morals, strategy, or goals, was the very worst colonel of all.

All ten party conferees, Moose and Elephant alike, knew that they were wasting their time—time fast expiring. Republicans would soon nominate Hughes, and Progressives would retaliate with TR. Was another three-way race and guaranteed Wilson victory in the cards? Neither TR nor his Old Guard Republican rivals relished that possibility. But sometimes even the most rational plans go awry.

And they seemed to have gone awry by 3:00 a.m. that morning, as the second GOP-Progressive conference ingloriously adjourned, and George Perkins inquired as to whether Nicholas Murray Butler wanted to speak directly to TR via his private phone line.

GOP conferees authorized Butler to suggest three names to TR for possible support: Root, Pennsylvania senator Philander Knox (TR's first attorney general), and former vice president Charles W. Fairbanks—precisely in that order.

Butler shared a rocky history with TR. They had once been friends, but when Butler dared privately question Roosevelt's inflammatory January 31, 1908, message to Congress, TR essentially read him out of the human race.[7] As late as November 1916, he privately derided Butler as "the silliest and most vicious of those reactionaries who are really reactionaries, and not merely grafters."[8]

Yet their conversation this night proceeded amicably enough, sharing, as they did, pro-Allied sympathies and anti-Hughes animus. Butler alleged that "all the pussyfooters and pro-Germans in Chicago are for" Hughes and that it would be "impossible to elect him, no matter who endorses him. I regard [a Hughes nomination] as assuring four more years of this awful Wilson."[9] Butler had TR's attention, but not his support for Root, Knox, or Fairbanks. TR wouldn't even discuss Root (though he was dispatching drafts of his speeches to Root for review[10]). He blamed Knox, as William Howard Taft's "Dollar Diplomacy" secretary of state, for helping create the Mexican disaster. He professed "a real liking" for his former vice president, Fairbanks, but instantly dismissed his chances at either convention as "impossible."

Which put Butler and Roosevelt back to exactly . . . nowhere.

"Would there be any chance of taking up an entirely new man?" inquired TR, having vetoed anyone the GOP might realistically propose.

"I think it possible," Butler answered, "although it might surprise them very much."

"Would there be a chance of taking up Leonard Wood?"

Butler thought not. "As a military man, the General would be unacceptable in the Middle West."

"He wouldn't have to do as Brother Hughes will have to do—improvise," Roosevelt protested, though that was as far as his protest went. Quickly, he shifted gears. "Would there be any possibility of putting Lodge across?"

Lodge! Not only was Lodge anathema to Progressives, but he was barely palatable to anyone else. It was not merely a question of ideology; it was also a question of personality. Lodge, as TR's cousin Nicholas Roosevelt recalled, suffered from "the aristocrat's indifference to the impression that he made on people. He could be supercilious with ease—and often with intent—and in the main seemed to have little interest in his fellows. From my own contacts with him I retain a clear picture of a highly intelligent, cultivated gentleman, rather small in stature, gracious to his friends, but self-centered, narrow, and unyielding."[11]

This was the man TR proposed to unite two vitriolically sundered parties, two fractious conventions. Progressives found the Boston Brahmin Lodge too conservative. And if TR and Root remained far too bellicose for midwestern and German-American tastes, so did the hyper-pro-Preparedness, hyper-imperialist Lodge.

Butler despised Lodge. Gingerly, he pointed out that fissures within the Massachusetts delegation worked against Lodge (Murray Crane, for example, also detested him). Still, Lodge might prove feasible, Butler mused, before he caught himself with "I don't know what vote-getting qualities Lodge has."

"I don't myself," Roosevelt conceded, "but he has the political habit and these men would get on with him," which was as far as he dared proceed before shifting gears to suggest an alternative of markedly dissimilar geography, background, and ideology.

"Now," continued TR ingenuously, "I am speaking of a man I don't even know myself; what do you think of Borah?"

William E. Borah was progressive (though not Progressive; he reluctantly remained with the GOP in 1912), a man of the Wild West, and eventually acclaimed as the Senate's foremost orator—the renowned "Lion of the Senate."

Theodore's suggestion stupefied Butler—as, perhaps, TR knew it would. "The trouble with Borah (which I would not like even you to mention to anyone)," Butler responded, "is his personal habits in Washington. You can infer the rest. He has troubles in Washington of a very personal nature; personal habits that are objectionable."

"Apparently only Wilson can get away with anything of that sort," the properly Victorian TR snorted.

Somehow it always came back to Wilson.

Some of Borah's personal habits were admirable: he neither smoked nor drank. Others, less so. As it turned out, the "Lion of the Senate" was also the "Stallion of the Senate." An unplanned pregnancy had caused the young bachelor's hasty 1890 migration from Kansas to Boise, where he reputedly spent each night in one or another of the town's twenty-eight brothels—though, perhaps, not every evening. His April 1895 marriage to Governor William J. McConnell's daughter was whispered to have been of the shotgun variety. Also likely was an abortion ending said alleged pregnancy, leaving the bride sterile and the groom unreformed.[12]

Butler, wanting nothing to do with Borah, now spoke privately with Perkins concerning TR's bizarre Lodge gambit. Perkins, viewing a Lodge candidacy as "ridiculous," abandoned his long-standing opposition to Progressives' nominating TR before Republicans moved to nominate anyone, wanting it understood "that it was we who saved them (from Hughes) and that you are not going to hold it up against us for nominating our man first."[13]

That conversation concluded, Perkins phoned TR. He conceded Lodge's "mastery of foreign relations" but complained that he was "sorry you mentioned Lodge."

TR cut him off: "I know Lodge's record like a book. There has never been anything against it at any time, except of course, George, that he does not have as advanced views as you and I." Replete with bad ideas, TR asked whether he should again confer with Hiram Johnson.

"Not on your life," Perkins retorted, "not for an hour or two."

"Then I won't say a word," Roosevelt agreed. "I want to add this, if you will, George. Keep Hiram Johnson in touch with me so he won't fly off the handle and think I am neglecting him."[14]

Dawn broke. News of his "anointing" startled the pajama-clad Lodge—and just about everyone. TR's letter to Progressive conferees read,

> *Gentlemen:*
>
> *I understand that this morning you are to have your last conference with the conferees of the Republican National Convention, [and] that they have repeatedly asked you to present . . . a second choice. . . .*
>
> *For months I have thought of this matter, and for the last few weeks it has been the chief thing of which I have thought, as I feel with all my heart that it is the imperative duty of all of us [to] come together if by any possibility we can find a common standing ground. . . .*

In view of the conditions existing, I suggest . . . Senator Lodge. . . . He is a man of the highest integrity, of the broadest national spirit and of the keenest devotion to the public good. . . . I, therefore, urge upon you favorably to consider his name and report on it to the [Republican] Conferees . . . and if you do not agree with me in this respect nevertheless to . . . request them to place it before their Convention, at the same time yourself laying the telegram before the Progressive Convention.

Let me again quote from my telegram . . . to Senator Jackson, of Maryland: "The differences that have divided, not merely Republicans and Progressives, but good Americans of all shades . . . sink into nothing when compared with the issues now demanding decision[:] . . . the issues of a unified Americanism and of National Preparedness."

. . . The nomination of Senator Lodge will meet these vital needs. I earnestly ask that what you can do to bring about that nomination in the name of our common Americanism be done.

THEODORE ROOSEVELT.[15]

Such fantasies nauseated Hiram Johnson and John M. Parker. Both boycotted that morning's final interparty confab, leaving it to Perkins, Horace S. Wilkinson, and Charles J. Bonaparte to offer Lodge's name to their GOP counterparts. They presented it as TR's idea—not theirs.[16]

TR remained on the phone: with William Allen White, James R. Garfield, and former New Hampshire governor Robert P. Bass. Each favored his nomination. He insisted on Lodge—or at least said he did.[17]

At 11:00 a.m., Warren Harding gaveled Republicans to order, recognizing Utah's Reed Smoot. Smoot, observed *St. Louis Post-Dispatch* columnist Clark McAdams, had been "a great power in the convention. . . . He looks the Mormon churchman all over. A tall, dark man, with graying temples, he stands forth in Brigham Young black. . . . It is amazing that the 'Old Guard' has not before this featured Smoot. He is the very embodiment of its desert of ideas, its seclusion from the world, and its political priesthood."[18]

To Smoot fell the unhappy task of revealing TR's communiqué anointing Lodge. "The extreme stillness [as] Smoot read the Colonel's last word," noted McAdams, "was the most sound proof thing that ever rested human ears. When the Colonel nominated Senator Lodge the delegates began to admire the decorations on the roof. He would just as well have said Santa Claus."[19]

Republicans eventually cheered—but not for Lodge. They cheered Roosevelt's capitulation—the ludicrous end of his candidacy—if, in reality, it ever possessed a true beginning. What had been his game? Certainly not to run third party again—not that he ever revealed that to his loyal Bull Moose acolytes. The heroic figure who excoriated "pussy-footing" and "weasel words" had in fact callously employed both to lure his disciples into one last noisy, doomed political camp meeting.

What was his goal? Had he aimed to secure both nominations, using a prospective Progressive nomination as a gun to the head of the GOP to secure its nomination? He might have succeeded but in fact held out little private hope of achieving both nominations. Was his strategy merely to obtain an acceptably progressive, reasonably pro-Preparedness GOP candidate to vanquish the hated Wilson, who had so effortlessly enacted so much of the progressive program—*his* program?

The Progressive Party of 1916 was a pawn in a particularly cynical game of political chess—the most cynical move of all being the abortive crowning of Henry Cabot Lodge.

At the Republican convention, TR's letter had no effect—surely none generating any votes for Lodge. If anything, it accelerated a stampede to Hughes. Earlier that morning, Theodore E. Burton, Albert B. Cummins, and Robert M. La Follette had called it quits, tossing their support to Hughes.[20] So did Pennsylvania's fractious seventy-six-vote delegation. John W. Weeks and Lawrence Sherman withdrew. Medill McCormick—informed by TR only two evenings previously that Hughes was "a good deal of a skunk"[21]—now abandoned TR for him. McCormick's pale face betrayed his anguish.[22] From the platform, Mac McGrath stared down, "angry and disappointed."[23]

Warren Harding ordered a vote, and a tired but relieved convention nominated Hughes by near acclamation.

Candidate	Votes
Charles Evans Hughes	949.5
Theodore Roosevelt	18.5
Henry Cabot Lodge	7
T. Coleman du Pont	5
John W. Weeks	3
Robert M. La Follette	3
Absent	1[24]

The Republicans had more or less wrapped up their work. There remained, of course, the question of whether their candidate really was a candidate or merely an associate justice of the Supreme Court. But compared to the angst bedeviling their Bull Moose counterparts, this was nothing.

Progressives reconvened late Saturday, still frothing to nominate their hero. Sick of Perkins's delays, and with Hughes nearing nomination, they now possessed sad proof that Perkins's stratagems had failed abysmally. Another TR candidacy could only deliver another Wilson term. But they'd run their man anyway.

The most tumultuous roller coaster in convention history now careened off the tracks.

Ominous signs abounded. The band, previously awash in "Teddy music," suddenly shifted to more candidate-neutral, classical fare. A dozen uniformed police ringed the podium, shielding party leaders from their own delegates.[25]

And there was the crowd itself. "The noise that rose from . . . the auditorium," noted the *New York Times*, "and was rolled back echo like from the stage had none of the light singing and rough laughter of yesterday in it; it was a combination of voices that together formed a stormy and angry brawl. Everyone felt it."[26]

When convention chairman Raymond Robins ("He seemed worried. His brows were contracted and his jaw set"[27]) summoned delegates to order at 10:45 a.m., an anti-Perkins aura resonated throughout—even in Robins's opening remarks.

"There will be no parliamentary delay, no confusion," Robins reassured delegates. "The will of the convention is to prevail this morning." The crowd erupted, chanting, "Robins, Robins!" Shaking his head to silence the outburst, he plowed onward. "This is no time for speaking. This is a time for action. We are going to do just what we came to Chicago to do."[28]

But first George Perkins would do his best to prevent—or at least delay—that outcome.

Perkins was rarely the most vocal of public speakers. Normally energetic, he seldom exhibited much weariness, but on this day, impossibly long hours, hostile delegates, and vanishing options had taken their toll. His voice was weaker still. Had his audience of thirty-five hundred restless men and women more easily heard him, they might have soundly booed him. But, straining to understand him, they remained respectfully silent as he summarized his fruitless negotiations with the GOP ("I have been under much criticism. It was no easy task"[29]) before introducing O. K. Davis to read TR's telegram endorsing Lodge. Delegates *could* hear Davis. Booing and catcalls buffeted his conclusion.

"Suddenly the crowd surged from astonishment to anger," noted Amos Pinchot, present merely as an observer. "It felt that in naming Lodge, Roosevelt had done something not merely fantastic but grossly insulting. They were taken by surprise. They had been kept in the dark, treated like children—pawns in a game . . . of which they had had no inkling. I saw men and women sitting as if stunned, like unjustly punished children, with tears streaming down their cheeks."[30]

Perkins entreated Bull Moosers to await further GOP balloting. Perhaps Lodge might pull it off after all. But they could not have cared less about Henry Cabot Lodge—or, for that matter, much about George Walbridge Perkins, no matter how much cash he might provide their party. "Lodge, Lodge," snorted Hiram Johnson to an ally seated nearby, "why not Penrose and be done with it? I came here as a Progressive."[31]

John M. Parker sprinted ("in three jumps") to the dais.

Captain Parker, TR's old Louisiana bear-hunting buddy, was perhaps the worst possible Progressive ambassador to either African-Americans or northern ethnics. In March 1891, he had participated in the lynching, shooting, and/or clubbing to death of eleven Italian immigrant mafiosi in New Orleans. He never regretted or apologized for his actions.

Coincidentally or not, Henry Cabot Lodge ("such acts . . . do not spring from nothing without reason or provocation") had quickly excused the violence as "a kind of wild justice."[32] Nonetheless, Parker was not about to return the favor and endorse Lodge or any other Republican save Roosevelt. "We come here for a deliberate purpose," he announced, "with the solemn assurance of our leader of four years ago that this is a permanent party."[33]

Shouts of "We want Teddy!" "Roosevelt!" "Parker!" and "Now, nominate now!" interrupted him.

At 12:10 p.m., Robins—desperate to nominate TR before Republicans tapped Hughes—recognized New York's Bainbridge Colby, who exclaimed,

> *Once more, thank God, we are a militant army. I know the name with which your hearts are throbbing and which is quivering on your lips. For four days you have been held in check, crushing down the impulses of your heart.*
>
> *There has never been a crisis which has not furnished a man adequate for that crisis. There was Lincoln and Washington, and we have a man who embodies every impulse and feeling with which this nation is, surging. . . .*
>
> *This is the only convention in session through which the people . . . can speak. In the name of the nation that is waiting I present the name of that man who embodies the issues and spirit of the hour— that man we delight to honor, Theodore Roosevelt.*[34]

Amos Pinchot detected "a touch of irony"[35] in Colby's deliberate words. But whether motivated by sincerity or sarcasm, Colby had delivered the only ninety-second nominating address in convention history.[36]

Delegates expected a seconding address. Instead, Perkins frantically provided news from the Coliseum. His audience grew raucous. Robins threatened to expel any disruptive voices.

Perkins droned on: Weeks had dropped out, as had Sherman. McCormick had abandoned TR for Hughes. The crowd seethed.

A delegate shouted, "What do we care what they do?"[37]

What indeed?

Hiram Johnson no longer cared—if indeed he ever did.

Nervous energy possessed him. His booming voice engulfed the hall, its sheer volume enhanced by his whirlwind delivery. His eyes fairly popping with fervor, he roared,

There comes a time in every man's life when he goes up against the guns. You are going up against the guns now.

There is just one way, and that is put up the man who never shirked responsibility in his life. Make the nomination without loss of another minute.

Engulfed by cheers, he continued: "I don't know whether he will accept or not, but I suggest we nominate him, and within two hours, we should have word from him, and he and this convention will be face to face. I second the nomination of Theodore Roosevelt and make it before the landslide begins in the other convention."[38]

The assembly nominated Theodore Roosevelt not so much by a vote as by an avalanche at 12:33 p.m. on Saturday, June 10, 1916.

But would he run?

Johnson, Parker, and (for some reason) Maine's Progressive committeeman Halbert P. Gardner rushed to Perkins's Blackstone Hotel suite to confer once more with TR.[39]

Back at the Auditorium Theatre, Victor Murdock commended his party for its alacrity in nominating TR, mistakenly boasting that it had bested the GOP's Hughes nod by thirty-nine seconds. "To have nominated Roosevelt in the beginning," he continued, excoriating the Perkins strategy, "without waiting for any delay or dickering would have been the only way to make the Republicans know that we are in earnest."[40]

But was TR in earnest? Murdock merely piously announced, "We are expecting a message from Theodore Roosevelt, I hope to God it will read, 'I am your candidate now without qualification.'"[41]

Tears streamed down his cheeks. Choking with emotion, he bemoaned "the tremendous force against us, power money, everything."[42]

Scrutinizing this pandemonium from the press box was none other than William Jennings Bryan, paid a reputed $1,000 per day[43] by William Randolph Hearst's International News Service[44] to cover both Chicago conventions. Murdock noted his presence, praising his "sincerity," adding that he "should like to see him running on a ticket [with] Henry Ford on a platform of pacifism and prohibition."[45]

"The Great Commoner" laughed heartily.

"Mr. Bryan," Murdock continued, "is a straightforward pacifist. He is going to have a militarist plank rammed down his throat at [the upcoming] St. Louis [Democratic Convention] and he won't stand it."

"Mr. Bryan has stood by his convictions," continued Murdock.

Progressives cheered and laughed ("He has, he has!"). They knew exactly where Murdock was going. He postulated,

This will give us a four-cornered fight. There will be Wilson and [Vice President Thomas R.] Marshall; there will be that tribute to the arctic circle, that Hughes-Fairbanks ticket; there will be Bryan and Ford.

And there will be that ticket with two men on it—one from the North and one from the South [Murdock anticipated Parker's nomination for vice president]—who stand for peace and preparedness and for bringing this country to the level God Almighty meant that it should occupy.[46]

Murdock's audience cheered even more. Even they grasped that only in a four-way field might their hero triumph. A five-way field wouldn't hurt either.

Calls erupted for Bryan to address the convention. "Roosevelt is going to refuse this nomination in a few minutes," a friend sitting nearby advised him. "He hasn't the courage to run. Why don't you lead this crowd? You would get 5,000,000 votes."[47] Bryan kept smiling, enjoying the irony of it all.

Bryan ignored his chance to raise hell. Chairman Robins raised cash while simultaneously skewering his party's most charitable—yet distrusted—benefactor: "This radical party needs money for a campaign as all parties do and it does not intend to rely on one or two or three men for its contributions or have any man say that he owns the party."[48] Perkins smiled blandly.

Progressive delegates were not just impassioned; they were also well-to-do and uncommonly generous. Within minutes, Robins had amassed $100,000 in pledges. Gifford Pinchot kicked in $5,000—by no means the largest offering.[49] His brother Amos, loath to kick in anything to a party that had essentially kicked him out, theorized that his former colleagues' beneficence was "partially . . . a means of rebuking Roosevelt and showing they were ready to fight."[50]

Hours passed without news from Oyster Bay. At 3:00 p.m., Robins announced that word would be arriving soon from TR, and he solicited nominations for vice president, receiving John M. Parker's, Hiram Johnson's, and his own name in response. Robins and Johnson quickly bowed out. Hallucinating about shattering the Solid South (and absent any other volunteers), delegates anointed Parker.[51]

Meanwhile, on Perkins's private line, no one save Parker had actually asked TR to run—and Parker did so only obliquely. For his part, TR congratulated Perkins for having "done everything exactly right"[52]—whatever that meant. The Progressive Party, launched in earnestness, now capsized in a sea of insincerity.

Matters advanced more smoothly on the GOP side. Warren Harding broke precedent by immediately telegraphing Charles Evans Hughes news of his nomination. Hughes, in turn, instantly resigned from the Supreme Court and accepted the nod.

Charles W. Fairbanks didn't want to be vice president again and telegraphed the convention to that effect. But before receiving his wire, delegates nominated him 863–108 over someone who did want the job: former Nebraska senator Elmer E. Burkett ("he may not be heroic but he is safe . . . progressively conservative and conservatively progressive").[53] Fairbanks unhappily accepted his fate, providing the twentieth century with its sole all-bearded ticket.

TR remained maddeningly coy. That afternoon, in yet another telephone conversation, son Ted Jr. advised, "I think we want to be particularly careful, if we are going to support Hughes, as we probably will, that we say nothing that will reflect on him in our statements here. The statement reads as if you did not approve of Hughes. You don't of course."

"Of course I will support him," TR cavalierly responded, "but I will not be responsible for him."[54]

Just after 3:00 p.m., Theodore conferred with a strangely low-key Hiram Johnson. "How is the Honorable Hiram?" Roosevelt bantered, knowing all too well that Johnson was not well—or currently well disposed—at all.

"When I can do anything that concerns you in any way, I am all right," Johnson replied disingenuously. TR confided, equally dubiously, that he planned "to go fishing" during the upcoming Wilson-Hughes contest.

"It would," Johnson answered, "be a crime to ask you to run unless there is some great national thing that demands it."[55]

TR's declination soon reached Progressive delegates—his words not what they wanted but what they feared.

> *To the Progressive Convention:*
>
> *I am very grateful for the honor you confer upon me by nominating me as President. I cannot accept it at this time. I do not know the attitude of the candidate of the Republican party toward the vital questions of the day. Therefore, if you desire an immediate decision, I must decline the nomination. But if you prefer it I suggest that my conditional refusal to run be placed in the hands of the Progressive National Committee. If Mr. Hughes' statements when he makes them shall satisfy the committee that it is for the interest of the country that he be elected, they can act accordingly and treat my refusal as definitely accepted. If they are not satisfied they can so notify the Progressive party and at the same time they can confer with me and then determine on whatever action we may severally deem appropriate to meet the needs of the country.*
>
> *THEODORE ROOSEVELT.[56]*

Such a message, as the *Chicago Examiner* noted, was

a fairly short and utterly dismal throwing overboard of sincere devoted friends. . . . In dead, dismal silence the message is heard in depressed spirits and in silence the crowd moves out. A sad disappointing bitter ending to a week of hard work by a sincere gathering of men and women. Theodore Roosevelt has tossed aside a following of which any man might be proud. He has treated contemptuously proofs of devotion and loyalty that should have filled him with gratitude. They say that Roosevelt is a good politician. It will take more than good politics to undo this injury to his reputation and to his influence.[57]

That was the Hearst press speaking, and it was glad of the outcome. Loyal Progressives weren't. "[It] fell upon [delegates] like a curse," wrote William Allen White. "For a moment there was silence. Then there was a roar of rage. It was the cry of a broken heart such as no convention ever had uttered in this land before. Standing there in the box I had tears in my eyes, I am told. I saw hundreds of men tear the Roosevelt picture or the Roosevelt badge from their coats, and throw it on the floor."[58]

That evening, Amos Pinchot entered the crowded lobby of the Auditorium Hotel filled with "wild-eyed," angry Progressives. Entering the hotel café, he was asked, "How are you on your history?"

"Pretty weak," he responded. "Why?"

"Well, we have run out of adjectives to use on the Colonel, and we are searching history for the names of traitors. Can you help?"[59]

Pinchot, long ago burned by Roosevelt, possessed little sympathy for their plight. "I think the majority of them," he would later reflect, "got exactly what was coming to them."[60]

Yet, in their naivety, in their loyalty, in their principles, whether right or wrong, rank-and-file Progressives comported themselves with far greater honor than their leaders.

The pioneering muckraking journalist Ida Tarbell ("I wabble terribly whenever I see him face to face"[61]) had once swooned over Roosevelt.

But not today.

She said of the expiring Progressive gathering,

It was a fighting crowd, prepared at every moment to struggle for its will—and it was a crowd which from start to finish, through all its wild cheering, its fits of suspicion, its rage . . . —its bursting desire to nominate its Teddy—never for one moment so lost control of itself that it could not in 30 seconds bring itself to order if it saw the necessity.

It was a steamroller of a convention, able to check itself at the very moment it seemed about to destroy itself by its mad momentum. It controlled itself over delays. . . . It controlled itself even [at] Col. Roosevelt's amazing suggestion of Lodge. . . . It was a great and noble-hearted body, and its tremendous fight deserved a better end than the cowardly stab that its leader gave it in the message which its chairman mercifully and wisely withheld until almost the moment of adjournment.[62]

A betrayed multitude departed. The band kept playing, but Progressives had no reason for song. "They stalked out buzzing like angry bees," recalled William Allen White, "and I followed them."[63] He didn't sing but still managed to sadly whistle the recent Broadway hit "Good-Bye, Girls, I'm Through"[64] as he disappeared out the door.

He retreated to his room to dictate the day's column, dripping with sarcasm aimed at his beloved khaki-clad chieftain: "So, we have the picture of the dear, tender-hearted colonel cutting off the tail of the dog an inch at a time, to save the feelings of the dog. The colonel is blameless; he is doing all that he can do, and when the next inch of the dog's tail comes off, it will be taken off in all gentleness and with all consideration for the good of the dog."[65]

Elsewhere in the hall, White's colleagues grumbled that their hero was about "to run out on them."[66] Prominent Progressives pronounced their grand enterprise finished. A hardly surprised Amos Pinchot and a "vastly chagrined" Hiram Johnson slowly trudged out together.

At 6:00 p.m., still at Sagamore Hill, Theodore Roosevelt trudged downstairs.

"Black blood crusted round their mouths"

TR reassured George Perkins that he had "done everything exactly right."[1]

Little *seemed* right—not near to Lake Michigan, or near to Long Island Sound.

Theodore had barricaded himself in his third-floor gun room for days—and, worse, for too many nights—in constant communication with whomever he deemed it useful to converse. Occasionally, he ventured downstairs to speak with the gaggle of reporters who decamped at Sagamore Hill to discern the great man's thoughts—or at least to file sufficient copy to mollify impatient editors.

Awake until 5:00 a.m. that Saturday, June 10, at 9:30 that morning he announced his unavailability to the press until further notice. At noon, he materialized briefly to reveal his suggestion of Lodge. Not until 6:00 p.m. did he reemerge, khaki-clad and smiling as ever. His cousin, close friend, and financial (but not political) adviser, fifty-nine-year-old New York banker W. Emlen Roosevelt, accompanied him, as did Emlen's much more political twenty-four-year-old son, Philip, and TR's recently hired thirty-two-year-old military secretary, Walter J. Hayes.[2] Suddenly TR ordered Hayes back upstairs to surveil his private wire for new developments.

The Colonel's eyes, noted the *New York Sun*, were "red from lack of sleep and his bronzed face wrinkled from the strain he has undergone. . . . He [retained none] of his old-time buoyancy and cheeriness, none of his impetuous spirit."[3]

"What have I got to say?" he grinned wanly. "Nothing at all; nothing."

Even that smile quickly vanished. Awkward silence followed.

Having vowed to keep mum, he spoke anyway. "With no emphatic gesture, and no rising intonation in his voice,"[4] he revealed his futile negotiations with the Progressive National Committee and with Nicholas Murray Butler. His overstated Butler's reaction to the Lodge suggestion. He left it "to the [Progressive] party to decide" on whether he might still run.

"Then your decision is not final yet?"

"No, my decision is not final yet," he answered, though, as the *Sun* observed, it was "in a hopeless sort of way, as if he were repeating something somebody else had said rather than a sentiment of his own. Then, straightening up a little, he said with a show of vigor: 'I am not going to yield pay gravel.'"[5]

He dodged a question regarding Hughes's recent statement of acceptance before concluding, "And now, gentleman, I'll say good-by. There's no use of your coming up here again or staying in town. I'll have nothing to say at all."

He advanced forward, shaking hands as if taking his leave forever.

"But you'll say something when the Progressive committee reports to you."

"Maybe, but that news will come from them. Good-by. I hate to see you go, for you add to the scenic features of Oyster Bay."[6]

He ushered them outside to the veranda. Anxious photographers awaited him.

"No, no; no pictures," he regretfully responded. "I am out of politics."[7]

The press went one way, he another, walking slowly and alone into the big house on the hill.

No one dared guess what sort of Roosevelt might emerge again.

Theodore Roosevelt possessed a great many skills—perhaps too wide an array for measure. His political skills wafted him ever skyward through the years, but it cannot be said that his rise was without its missteps: his affidavit of Washington residency, his hurried barring of a 1908 candidacy, his tossing away of the black vote at Brownsville and at the first Bull Moose convention, his endorsement of William Howard Taft, and, perhaps most injurious of all, his failed 1912 candidacies.

The sinking Progressive ship: an unhappy TR meets with 1914 Ohio Bull Moose candidates, his former interior secretary James Rudolph Garfield (for governor) and industrialist Arthur L. Garford (for U.S. Senate) (courtesy of the Library of Congress).

WELL, "HE KEPT *US* OUT OF WAR."

A September 1917 cartoon in the *New York Sun* noting "He kept us out of war" contained a particularly rueful twist for both TR and Leonard Wood (collection of the author).

Edith Roosevelt Derby in her nurse's uniform. She served alongside her surgeon husband, Dr. Richard Derby, in France (collection of the author).

Immediately following TR's death, the noted sculptor James Earle Fraser rushed to Sagamore Hill to slather the deceased's head in grease before carefully applying plaster-soaked bandages to craft this death mask (collection of the author).

Archibald Roosevelt (left) suffered grievous wounds in France and was billeted stateside before the Armistice. "An absolutely selfless gladiator," marveled a comrade, "who insisted on being the first to smell the enemy's bad breath" (courtesy of the Harvard Library).

Woodrow Wilson marches in Washington's June 14, 1916, Preparedness Day Parade. A month earlier, 125,683 Preparedness advocates had streamed for a full twelve hours down New York's Fifth Avenue. "The significance of 160,000 men [*sic*] marching to-day," said TR, "means that the nation is waking to understand that a weakling never earns anything but contempt" (courtesy of the Library of Congress).

TR despised both the politics and the personality of Wilson's first secretary of state, William Jennings Bryan, "The Great Commoner." TR dismissed Bryan as "a professional yodeler, a human trombone" (courtesy of the Library of Congress).

Albany's Republican boss William F. Barnes Jr. sued TR for libel in 1915—and soon regretted it. "In its political sense," said Barnes, "progress means nothing good" (courtesy of the Library of Congress).

William Allen White was the nationally renowned editor of the *Emporia (Kansas) Gazette*. "I put his heel on my neck," he said of his loyalty to TR, "and I became his man. . . . [H]e became my lifetime liege and I became his yeoman in his service" (courtesy of the Library of Congress).

German-American poet George Sylvester Viereck first supported TR but later broke with him over the war. "I hated him and I loved him," wrote Viereck of TR. "If I attacked him bitterly, the arrow intended for him entered my own heart" (courtesy of the Library of Congress).

In March 1917, TR and noted marine scientist and hunter Russell J. Coles harpooned devilfish off the Florida coast. Roosevelt, Coles recalled, "made a perfect cast, and for twenty-six minutes he had truly a great fight. The boat was towed two miles, and looking back I could see a broad band of blood more than fifty feet wide" (courtesy of the Library of Congress).

Inauguration Day, 1909: TR and William Howard Taft's friendship would soon begin to fray. "The truth is," Taft would conclude, "he believes in war and wishes to be a Napoleon and to die on the battlefield. He has the spirit of the old berserkers" (courtesy of the Library of Congress).

Still toying with the idea of another presidential run, TR addresses his followers at Sagamore Hill, May 1916 (courtesy of the Library of Congress).

TR at his Sagamore Hill library in 1912—not yet permanently weakened from the effects of his near-fatal Brazilian expedition. "I wonder," he would say to Edith on the very eve of his death, "if you will ever know how I love Sagamore Hill" (courtesy of the Library of Congress).

A gaunt TR returns from his disastrous 1913–1914 "River of Doubt" expedition. "You can get out," he at one point informed Kermit. "I will stop here" (courtesy of the Library of Congress).

Brothers Theodore Roosevelt Jr. and Kermit Roosevelt. They learned of their father's death while serving in occupied Germany. "It is foolish to think of oneself," Kermit wrote his mother shortly afterward, "but you will know how the bottom has dropped out from me" (courtesy of the Library of Congress).

TR's funeral at Christ Church, Oyster Bay, January 1919. "Theodore," the church's rector, Dr. George E. Talmadge, prayed as he ended the service, "the Lord bless thee, and keep thee. The Lord make his face to shine upon thee, and be gracious unto thee. The Lord lift up his countenance upon thee, and give thee peace, both now and evermore. Amen" (courtesy of the Library of Congress).

TR at his desk in New York. "I hope to continue earning a good salary until all of you come home," he wrote Quentin in September 1917, "so that I can start Archie and you all right. Then I intend to retire" (courtesy of the Library of Congress).

The paths of glory lead but to the grave. The grave of Quentin Roosevelt, shot down over enemy territory on July 14, 1918. "It is rather awful to know," wrote TR, "that he paid with his life, and that my other sons may pay with their lives, to try to put in practice what I preached. Of course I would not have it otherwise" (courtesy of the Library of Congress).

George Walbridge Perkins, Wall Street powerhouse and financial angel for TR's renegade Bull Moose Party. "Mr. Perkins," Progressive journalist William Allen White declared, "had paid his good money for the [Progressive] party, and in him rested the title of the party" (courtesy of the Library of Congress).

Pennsylvania GOP senator Boies Penrose was the very epitome of standpat GOP leaders despised by TR and his fellow Progressives. "I don't like him," Penrose confessed in 1918. "I once despised him. But that doesn't alter the fact that Theodore Roosevelt is now the one and only possible Republican candidate in 1920" (courtesy of the Library of Congress).

Newton D. Baker, Wilson's second secretary of war, rejected Roosevelt's request to command a combat regiment in France. The avowed pacifist Baker, TR concluded, was merely the sort of gentleman who was "charming at ladies' pink tea" (courtesy of the Library of Congress).

TR unsuccessfully supported pro-Preparedness John Purroy "The Boy Mayor" Mitchel for reelection as New York City's chief executive in 1917. "Mitchel," TR concluded, "has given us the best municipal administration we have had for fifty years. He was not popular" (courtesy of the Library of Congress).

Germany's May 1915 sinking of the RMS *Lusitania* cost 1,198 lives and enraged Theodore Roosevelt. Germany's policy of unrestricted submarine warfare, TR averred, "can be justified only by a plea which would likewise justify the wholesale poisoning of wells in the path of a hostile army, or the shipping of infected rags into the cities of a hostile country: a plea which would justify the torture of prisoners and the reduction of captured women to the slavery of concubinage" (courtesy of the Library of Congress).

TR's old Spanish-American War comrade and his greatest ally in the fight for Preparedness, General Leonard Wood. In December 1914, Wood warned, "A government is the murderer of its people which sends them to the field uninformed and untaught" (courtesy of the Library of Congress).

Wisconsin senator "Fighting Bob" La Follette—a progressive, but no friend of TR—with American Federation of Labor president Samuel Gompers. In 1917, TR flayed La Follette as "the worst enemy that democracy has now alive" (courtesy of the Library of Congress).

The four Roosevelt siblings who served overseas: Kermit, the badly wounded Archie, Ethel, and Ted Jr. (courtesy of the Library of Congress).

A trio of Progressive era powerhouses: California's governor and senator Hiram Johnson, Idaho's William E. Borah, and Illinois's J. Medill McCormick. "Keep Hiram Johnson in touch with me," TR requested of George Perkins in June 1916, "so he won't fly off the handle and think I am neglecting him." Charles Evans Hughes would soon discover how dangerous it was to neglect Hiram Johnson (courtesy of the Library of Congress).

Vitagraph Studio's J. Stuart Blackton, producer of the TR-endorsed Preparedness epic *The Battle Cry of Peace*. "I wish I had it in my power," TR told the press, "to make a law compelling every man, woman and child in the United States to see 'The Battle Cry of Peace,' particularly the young pacifists. . . . It is the most educational drama I have ever witnessed. I did not think that motion pictures were so capable of impressing the human mind" (courtesy of the Library of Congress).

Charles Evans Hughes served as governor of New York, associate justice of the U.S. Supreme Court, and the GOP's reluctant 1916 presidential candidate. "When you see me in my coffin," Hughes warned his wife regarding his White House run, "remember I did not want to take this burden on myself" (courtesy of the Library of Congress).

Smokeless gunpowder inventor Hudson Maxim's 1916 book *Defenseless America* inspired J. Stuart Blackton's blockbuster film *The Battle Cry of Peace*. "Mr. Maxim," the pacifist Henry Ford alleged in a barrage of paid newspaper advertisements, "was merely advertising his wares and playing on your fears to make a market for his goods. Mr. Maxim has something to sell—war munitions" (courtesy of the Library of Congress).

Massachusetts's U.S. senator Henry Cabot Lodge, one of TR's longest-standing friends, shared TR's pro-Preparedness enthusiasms and anti-Wilson animus. "Lord, I am feeling warlike with this Administration!" TR wrote to Lodge in February 1915 (courtesy of the Library of Congress).

Ohio senator Warren Gamaliel Harding, chair of the 1916 GOP convention, vigorously opposed TR in 1912 before later reconciling with him. "There had been talk of . . . Harding setting [1916's] convention aflame with his oratory," wrote the *New York Times*, "so that the lightning would strike . . . to name a dark horse. But . . . Harding could not stampede any convention" (courtesy of the Library of Congress).

Future Mount Rushmore sculptor Gutzon Borglum was a long-time TR acolyte—but TR's machinations at the 1916 GOP and Bill Moose conventions taxed his loyalty. "I would not enlist under Roosevelt to charge a strawberry patch, or anything else," he fumed. "I have lost every bit of confidence I ever had in the man, and I say that with genuine regret" (courtesy of the Library of Congress).

Assistant Secretary of the Navy Franklin D. Roosevelt (TR's "fifth cousin by blood and nephew by law!") and his boss Navy Secretary Josephus Daniels. "My cousin's death," FDR wrote Daniels in January 1919, "was in every way a great shock[,] for we heard just before leaving that he was better—and he was after all not old. But I cannot help think that he himself would have had it this way and that he has been spared a lingering illness of perhaps years" (courtesy of the Library of Congress).

In 1912, Elihu Root, TR's former secretary of state, supported William Howard Taft, leading to a long-standing feud. Root, TR had expounded in 1910, "is as sane and cool-headed as he is high-minded . . . the wisest and safest of advisers" (courtesy of the Library of Congress).

Edith Kermit Carow Roosevelt, TR's childhood sweetheart and level-headed second wife. "I am glad you did not speak of Quentin," Roosevelt advised the visiting Will Hays in July 1918. "Edith could not have stood it. I don't think I could have stood it myself" (courtesy of the Library of Congress).

Sawdust-circuit evangelist Billy Sunday. "The plain people are with you to a man," he informed TR in 1916, "and if you run this fall, they are going to give you the biggest majority ever piled up by an American candidate" (courtesy of the Library of Congress).

TR's obstreperous oldest daughter, Alice, was also the wife of Ohio congressman (and future House Speaker) Nicholas Longworth. "All our lives before and after," she mourned, "have just been bookends for the heroic, tragic volume of the Great War" (courtesy of the Library of Congress).

The stateside-bound Theodore Roosevelt with his family in August 1918. From left to right: Archie Roosevelt's infant son Archibald Jr., TR, Mrs. Archibald Bulloch Roosevelt, Richard Derby Jr., Edith Roosevelt, baby Edith Derby, Ethel Roosevelt Derby.

The proud grandfather: Theodore Roosevelt with granddaughter Edith Roosevelt Derby. At Christmas 1918, TR wrote to his older sister, Anna "Bye" Roosevelt Cowles, regarding his daughter Ethel's children: "Richard and little Edie are the darlingest small souls you have ever known. Little Edie is the busiest person imaginable, and runs around exactly as if she was a small mechanical toy" (courtesy of the Harvard Library).

The Roosevelt boys at the front (clockwise): Archie, Kermit, Ted, and Quentin. All eventually served in France, through Kermit initially served with distinction with British forces in Mesopotamia. "There is much more of me in the war, now," TR unburdened himself to his friend, Ferdinand Cowle Iglehart, "than though I were there myself, for these boys are my heart of hearts, they are the life of my life" (courtesy of the Harvard Library).

Quentin Roosevelt as a recruit in 1917. "We run with the torches until we fall," TR wrote after Quentin's death, "content if we can then pass them to the hands of other runners. The torches whose flame is brightest are borne by the gallant men at the front, and by the gallant women whose husbands and lovers, whose sons and brothers, are at the front. . . . These are the torch-bearers; these are they who have dared the Great Adventure" (courtesy of the Harvard Library).

And what of his recent decisions? How sound had they proved? He commenced the year with the Bull Moose nod in his pocket—and tossed it away. Hemming and hawing and blustering toward a GOP anointing, at day's end he was lucky to have accumulated a pitiful eighty-five convention votes, even fewer than those tendered to such historical footnotes as a Weeks or a Fairbanks.

For TR to have fared better (let alone triumphed) at the Coliseum, he would have needed to place a loaded gun to the GOP's head: Nominate me, or I run third party. I run third party, and you lose. By 1916, TR wielded a thoroughly tarnished and quite unloaded political firearm—and, according to Progressive Party secretary O. K. Davis, the GOP knew it. They didn't even have to guess.

"The Republicans had information, on which they knew they could rely," Davis later revealed, "that Colonel Roosevelt would not under any circumstances head another third ticket. That was all they needed to defeat him in their own convention. The Republican leaders had that information from sources so close to Colonel Roosevelt himself that it could not be denied. That was a situation which the progressives could not meet. No bluff would work against such an inside revelation of the facts."[8]

Were these mysterious "sources" men like Henry Cabot Lodge, Gussie Gardner, or perhaps Theodore's own son-in-law, Representative Nicholas Longworth?

Or an even higher source?

Politicians then spoke with startling frequency to reporters—but were almost never quoted directly, their sentiments being invariably described as emanating from those particularly "close" (wink, wink) to said official. Thus reports emanating from sources so close to Colonel Roosevelt himself that they could not be denied meant they originated, in one way or another, from none other than TR himself.

If his initial gambits on 1916's chessboard were profoundly misplayed, his latter moves proved hardly better, the most embarrassing being, of course, the ludicrous and insulting Lodge stratagem. Taft privately characterized it as a reflection of his "desperate condition of mind . . . he was groggy," adding, for good measure, "He is not a good loser. He is a squealer, with all his boasted sportsmanship."[9]

Taft chortled. Leonard Wood confessed to feeling "very much disgusted."[10] In Chicago, Progressives shouted, "We've been delivered. We've been thrown down." And as party brass mulled their infinitesimal options, female Progressives stormed their party's executive committee session. "We are going to be delivered like a lot of pigs," one screamed. "Let's demand another party."[11]

"It was nearly midnight," recalled William Allen White, "when I . . . called [my wife] Sallie on the phone in Emporia, and spent nine dollars and eighty-five cents bawling like a calf into the receiver. At least I had release and relief. She cut me off when she thought I had spent enough money, and I went to bed at peace, and slept. It was the end of a great adventure, politically and emotionally probably the greatest adventure of my life."[12]

As *The Nation* observed, not without some satisfaction, "The seeds of [the party's] death were planted from the first, because it began as a personal party, pure and simple. It was made the appanage of an attractive and versatile politician, who was certain to seek to use it as a means to glut his revenge and an instrument of his ambition. And when it broke in his hands, as it did last week, there was never any doubt that he would drop it in disgust."[13]

TR did drop it in disgust, dispatching the following self-satisfied, self-unaware nonsense to his sister "Bye": "Well, the country was'n't [*sic*] in heroic mood! We are passing through a thick streak of yellow in our national life. This has been a perfectly easy campaign for me, and it has'n't [*sic*] left me with even the smallest feeling of personal chagrin. I shall of course support Hughes; with how much heartiness, his own attitude must decide."[14]

⌒

The music ended; the dance continued.

Telegrams swamped Oyster Bay. So did visitors, Raymond Robins, Harold Ickes, and Hiram Johnson among them.[15] But all was not well, and neither was TR. As he hurried to Manhattan's Pier No. 9 to greet the arrival of his son Kermit and daughter-in-law Belle (just recovering from typhoid) from Panama, the Colonel found himself engulfed in coughing. Chest pains—and fear of a heart attack—followed. "He paced nervously about," noted the *Brooklyn Eagle*, "and looked like a very ill man, his face changing from gray to carmine."[16] Physicians traced the matter to his embarrassing May 1915 riding mishap.[17]

William Allen White wrote to Theodore, ostensibly to commiserate about TR's health but more likely regarding Hughes: "The personal differences between Hughes and Wilson are on the whole too unimportant to warrant much excitement. . . . Don't get in a place where you will be held responsible for Hughes as you were . . . for Taft. There is too much judicial mind . . . to warrant you fretting your spirit or mortifying your flesh over it."[18]

TR brushed aside such sentiments. Soon he met with—and endorsed—Hughes, suddenly touting "The Bearded Iceberg" as quite the decent chap after all. "Hughes is an able, up-right man whose instincts are right," TR assured his English friend James Bryce, "and I believe in international matters he will learn with comparative quickness, especially as I hope he will put Root into office as Secretary of State. Under these circumstances there is in my mind no alternative but to support him. At his worst he will be better than Wilson, and there is always the chance that he will do very well indeed."[19]

By June 26, the Progressive National Committee reconvened in Chicago to rubber-stamp the Hughes-Fairbanks ticket. Bitter-enders, led by Captain John M. Parker, Bainbridge Colby, and Boston's Matt Hale, proposed Victor Murdock as TR's replacement but lost a proxy-fueled 32–6 vote to forces led by Perkins, Robins, Mac McGrath, and James R. Garfield. Nine members abstained. Three didn't even bother showing up. In an off-key coda to his doomed party's forlorn requiem, Parker remained its vice presidential pick.[20] Eventually, he—alongside Murdock, Colby, Hale, Amos Pinchot, Walter Lippmann, Felix Frankfurter, California's Francis Heney, Missouri's Judge Albert Nortoni, former party treasurer J. A. H. Hopkins, and former congressmen William Kent and Ole Hanson—endorsed Woodrow Wilson. So did James Garfield's eighty-four-year-old mother, former First Lady Lucretia Garfield, and eleven of the nineteen drafters of the 1912 Bull Moose platform.[21]

TR's willingness to campaign for Hughes alienated his radical flank but reaped regular Republican admiration. Warren Harding in particular commended TR's "unselfishness . . . [and] desire to serve our common country. It will re-enlist the devotion of thousands of republicans who have never been lacking in their personal esteem, but were arrayed against you . . . because of party differences. I believe you will have a high reward in the high esteem of your fellow countrym[e]n."[22]

Woodrow Wilson effortlessly secured his own renomination, his campaign fueled by former New York governor Martin Glynn's suspiciously past-tense nominating-address mantra: "He kept us out of war."

Buttressing his point, Glynn imparted what the *New York Tribune's* Heywood Broun described as an "inspiring tale of Americans killed and captured in piping times of peace, of ships molested and sunk and the various far-flung outrages."[23]

Broun was only half kidding. Democrats *were* inspired. The *New York Times* noted,

Men jumped up in their seats and danced about the aisles and waved American flags, shouting like school boys and screaming like steam-sirens. . . .

What was going on in their minds was as easily read as if it had been printed. When Glynn first began to deal with the historic instances there was an expression of dawning bewilderment, which was changed to half-incredulous joy and then to rapture. It was plain to see that they had been supplied with a reason for their faith. Pacifism had been jeered at and made to seem in opposition to Americanism, until they had come to feel almost apologetic about it. Now they were told that they had been right all the time, that one could be patriotic and pacifistic, that it was the historic American policy to submit to great provocation and historically un–American to go to war over it; and they could not contain themselves.[24]

William Jennings Bryan wept with pride.[25] TR would have vomited.

Until 1932, candidates eschewed official campaigning until receiving formal notification of their selection: in Wilson's case, until Saturday afternoon, September 2, before a twenty-five-thousand-person crowd outside his rented New Jersey summer White House, Shadow Lawn.

Hughes received his notification before a Carnegie Hall audience of three thousand on the sweltering Monday evening of July 31. Overshadowing Hughes was TR, gracing his first GOP gathering since 1912's great schism—and prefiguring a campaign-long eclipse of the phlegmatic Hughes.

His shaky June vow of silence long lay in the garbage heap. At Oyster Bay's Independence Day festivities, he followed up his standard pro-Preparedness utterances with a vow to personally raise a regiment should full-blown war erupt with Mexico.

"If there is war I shall go," he thundered to ten thousand listeners. "You have known me for a great many years. I have never said anything in my life that I did not try to make good, and if we have any trouble ... I should give the young men of Oyster Bay ... a chance to make good, and I won't ask them to do anything that I and my sons won't do."[26]

No, he wouldn't. As early as 1886, he had "offered to raise some companies of rifle horsemen . . . in the event of trouble with Mexico."[27] He essentially repeated that offer to Taft in March 1911.[28]

"The bald fact," observed Progressive era historian George E. Mowry, "was that Roosevelt liked war—its noise, its smoke, its action were a part of his soul. War made heroes, and Roosevelt had to be a hero. Had he been a nobody in a country village he would certainly have been a member of the volunteer fire department."[29]

On July 6, 1916, he wrote to Secretary of War Baker requesting his commission in "event of a war with Mexico and volunteers being called."[30] Three days later, he produced a blueprint of his officer corps (Parker, Ted, Archie, Dick Derby, and Henry Stimson among them) and every detail of its structure from its cavalry and artillery, machine guns and ambulances, to plans for retrieving "some of our American aviators back from France for our aerosquadron."[31]

War did not come, and Roosevelt did not go—except once more to the campaign trail.

Republicans faced huge problems. Wilson *had* kept America out of war—or at least not blundered into it. Thanks to its neutrality, the nation enjoyed unprecedented prosperity. In 1916, a third of all U.S. millionaires had reached that status in just the past year. U.S. Steel's profits bounded from $76 million in 1915 to $272 million a year later. Armour & Company's meatpacking profits tripled. Wheat prices doubled.[32] Unemployment tumbled from 14.3 percent in 1915 to 7.1 percent in 1916.[33]

Beyond that, TR may have manipulated his faltering party into oblivion, but he had hardly convinced its former members of either the charms of the GOP in general or those of Charles Evans Hughes specifically. Despising Woodrow Wilson might prove sufficient reason for TR to cast a Hughes-Fairbanks ballot, but few Americans, let alone Progressives, hated Wilson as much as he.

Hughes, previously a formidable statewide candidate, quickly emerged as an uninspiring, if not dismal, national standard-bearer. "Six years on the bench . . . had deanimated, dehydrated, and almost dehumanised him," observed O. K. Davis. "He had become an automatic, dry-as-dust law machine . . . practically worthless as a leader in a great political campaign."[34]

But in inheriting such a fractured party, even the most skillful of politicians might have fumbled. "All the colors," concluded Walter Lippmann, "are represented in the Hughes following. Mr. Hughes trying to be very efficient as a candidate . . . has mixed the violent contrasts, and the result of course is a dull gray."[35]

Hughes scored a quick point by going beyond the GOP platform (and Wilson) to advocate a constitutional amendment granting women the vote,[36] but somehow gold always turned to sawdust in his hands. As early as August, Wilson explained to Bernard Baruch why he was not attacking his opponent: "I am inclined to follow . . . the rule to never murder a man who is committing suicide, and clearly this misdirected gentleman is committing suicide slowly but surely."[37]

In September, a trainload of prominent female Hughes supporters (the "Hughesettes"), including novelists Mary Roberts Rinehart, Edna Ferber, Zona Gale, and Elizabeth (Mrs. Raymond) Robins, *New York Evening Mail* syndicated columnist Rheta Childe Dorr (a former Socialist), and pioneering New York social workers Belle Moskowitz, Katherine Bement Davis, and Mary Dreier (Elizabeth Robins's sister-in-law), embarked upon a groundbreaking, cross-country Women's Campaign Special. A prospective coup turned into a liability as Democrats and newspapers (particularly the *New York Times*) pilloried their expedition as the jaunt (the "Golden Special") of well-to-do East Coast matrons out of touch with the rest of the nation.[38]

Hughes prattled on about issues few now cared about, about Democratic federal patronage[39]and about the tariff.[40] When the National Association for the Advancement of Colored People solicited his views on race and lynching, he ignored the query.[41] "I can think of several reasons why I might vote against Wilson," puzzled one independent, "but I can't think of one why I should vote for Hughes."[42] By November, *The Nation*, initially pro-Hughes, confessed finding itself "WITHOUT ALTERNATIVES."[43]

Hughes's mid-August swing through California emerged as a textbook fiasco. He never should have visited the state. At the very least, he might have waited until its bitter GOP primary concluded. In San Francisco, he alienated labor by lunching at a private club staffed by strikebreakers. At Long Beach's opulent Hotel Virginia, he inadvertently neglected to meet with Hiram Johnson, who by coincidence and unbeknownst to him was also at the establishment. The ever-prickly Johnson (never a Hughes admirer) trumpeted the incident as an unforgivable slight.[44]

A nervous Republican hierarchy begged TR to "perform a personal rescue act."[45] Audiences cheered his words. Huge crowds greeted him lustily. But large crowds gawking to see a larger-than-life celebrity could not obscure a very unpleasant fact: 1916's political horserace was galloping at a far faster pace than TR's political instincts could carry him.

The Mexican miasma had quickly lifted. Neither Wilson nor Venustiano Carranza had any great reason to prolong matters, and peace delegates soon convened at New London, Connecticut.[46] Though German sabotage continued afoot (most spectacularly in July 1916's Black Tom munitions explosion), Berlin's May 1916 *Sussex* Pledge traveled a great distance in allaying war jitters.

Yet pro-Preparedness forces pushed on. In New York, TR's old ally, Robert Bacon ("I am an avowed unneutral"[47]), launched a last-minute challenge to heavily favored Brooklyn congressman William M. Calder for the state's open U.S. Senate seat. Bacon, who, as the *Times* noted, "fairly shrieked his sympathy for the Allies,"[48] enjoyed not only TR's support but also Elihu Root's, Joe Choate's—and, even more remarkably, Billy Barnes's.[49] Bacon fell just short in September's primary. That he got any traction at all amazed observers and encouraged Preparedness advocates—TR included—that their issue remained a winning one.

⌒

Charles Whitman also ran in 1916.

Few people liked him. TR certainly didn't.

The Colonel did admire the patrician reformer Samuel Seabury. In 1913, Seabury, an anti-Tammany Democrat, ran on the otherwise doomed Progressive line for a seat on the New York Court of Appeals, the state's highest court. Finishing third, he polled a respectable 193,798 votes, and TR continued to encourage his ambitions. They dined at Sagamore Hill in July 1914, and Roosevelt gushingly wrote him, "I want you on the Court of Appeals, or a Senator, or as Governor!"[50] So encouraged, Seabury again competed for a court of appeals seat, securing both Democratic and Bull Moose endorsements. Bucking a Republican tide that elected Barnes's candidates, Whitman and James W. Wadsworth Jr., and decimated Progressives in the state legislature, he won by 56,054 votes.

Two years later, Roosevelt pledged his vigorous support should Seabury challenge incumbent governor Whitman, whom TR ("The truth is not in Whitman"[51]) vowed never to support. Seabury proved skeptical. Would the Colonel really boost Seabury while Seabury backed Wilson? "I will support [Hughes]," said TR, "but that will in no way interfere with my giving you my support for the governorship. I have considered the whole problem from every angle. . . . If you secure the Democratic nomination, my support will insure your election."[52]

In August, Seabury resigned from his fourteen-year Court of Appeals term to seek the Democratic and Progressive nominations for governor. Barely a fortnight later, a bombshell landed. TR's reenlistment in Republican ranks, it seemed, required not merely deserting surviving Progressive forces but also bayonetting their wounded.

Samuel Seabury was not merely expendable; he was doomed.

Still, TR proved skittish about stabbing him in the back and entrusted the task to George Perkins and Mac McGrath, the latter just removed from TR's payroll.[53] McGrath's announcement that TR now backed Whitman over Seabury dumbfounded Seabury's supporters. The New York State Assembly's sole surviving Progressive, Hamilton Fish (Ted Jr.'s classmate at Harvard), incredulously rejected the news as "preposterous and unworthy of credence."[54]

But it was true. And soon TR publicly confirmed it.[55]

Irate, Seabury rushed to Oyster Bay, confronted Roosevelt, and reminded him of his now broken promises. He waved his "I want you on the Court of Appeals, or a Senator, or as Governor!" letter in his face. TR wouldn't budge. "Mr. President," Seabury exploded, "you are a blatherskite!"[56]

Seabury complained to friends, "The truth is not in Roosevelt."[57] Some already suspected as much. Amos Pinchot fired off a fifteen-hundred-word missive not so much to console Seabury as to publicly lacerate Roosevelt:

> *The Colonel is merely running true to recent form. You stand squarely for the things the Progressive party has stood for in the past; about as squarely as Whitman stands against them. I do not think that anybody would question this, not even the Colonel. But, for quite a good while, it has been fairly clear to the majority of us that Roosevelt, Perkins and the steel trust, the Old Guard group around them, have not been interested in the things which the Progressive party stood for.[58]*
>
> *... For them there was no escape from the Progressive party, with its tiresome principles and undistinguished personnel, unless a paramount issue could be discovered [by] which the progressivism of 1912, social justice, democracy and all that sort of politically useless rot could be gracefully abandoned.*
>
> *So if some ... of us feel that a good deal of this so-called "Americanism" is in reality not so much a paramount issue as a paramount gangplank, to get back, without loss of face, into old guard Republicanism, it is our misfortune.[59]*

Charles Whitman swamped Samuel Seabury in September's Progressive primary.

And again that November.

In October 1917, the precious few remaining Progressives convened in Chicago, struggling to merge with a ragbag coalition of Prohibitionists, "Single Taxers," and pro-war "Social Democrats."[60]

They could not even decide on a name for their new party.

And nobody seemed to notice . . . or care.

The nation's agenda was quickly shifting back toward domestic matters. The year 1916 witnessed a spectacular renewal of progressive legislation: the Federal Farm Loan Act, the Owens-Keating Child Labor Act, the Kern-McGillicuddy Workmen's Compensation Act protecting five hundred thousand federal employees, inheritance and excess-profit taxes, and, though one might today surmise it to have been Teddy Roosevelt's handiwork, even creation of the National Park Service.[61]

But overshadowing all this was the threat of a nationwide rail strike. Virtually all the nation's commerce and passenger travel depended upon train traffic, and a nationwide walkout would bring the economy—and Wilson's reelection hopes—to a painful halt. It would also obstruct war materiel shipments to the beleaguered Allies. "The Allies are fighting our battle," Wilson warned labor and management, "the battle of civilization, across the way. They cannot 'carry on' without supplies and means of sustenance which the railroads of America bring to them."[62]

Accordingly, Wilson dispatched legislation (the Adamson Act) to Congress mandating an eight-hour workday (ten was standard) for railway employees. Hughes damned Wilson's action as egregiously contravening the principle of arbitration. His vigorous excoriation of the bill cost him labor votes he could ill afford to spare.

TR also orated about such issues, but perhaps even less fervently than the "iceberg" Hughes. To Lodge, in 1894, he had confessed to "a tinge of economic agnosticism";[63] he admitted much the same thing to *McClure's* Ray Stannard Baker in 1906.[64]

Neither laborers nor, for that matter, farmers had ever done much to swell Bull Moose ranks. By 1915, at the latest, TR's economic radicalism, while hardly extinct, was conspicuously overshadowed by his fixations on Preparedness and hyphenated-Americans.

Such drumbeating was not without effect. Wilson uttered louder pro-Preparedness noises. He marched at massive Preparedness and Flag Day parades. He echoed Rooseveltian warnings of a hyphenated menace. When, in August, the pro-German Irish-American activist Jeremiah A. O'Leary sharply rebuked his policies, the president tartly responded, "Your telegram received. I would feel deeply mortified to have you or anybody like you vote for me. Since you have access to many disloyal Americans and I have not, I will ask you to convey this message to them."[65]

Woodrow Wilson's words hardly stilled TR's passions. The Colonel demanded deeds not diplomatic notes, consistency not "weasel words." At Battle Creek, on September 30, thirty thousand greeted his arrival, and thirty thousand more lined his route.[66] For "fourteen months," Roosevelt charged,

President Wilson took forty-one different positions about prepared-ness and the measures necessary to secure it; and each of these forty-one positions contradicted from one to six of the others. In many of his speeches the weasel words of one portion of the speech took all the meaning out of the words used in another portion of that speech; and these latter words themselves had a weasel significance as regards yet other words. He argued for preparedness, and against preparedness. He stated that our army was ample; and that we did not have enough troops to patrol the Mexican border in time of peace. He said the world was on fire, and that sparks were liable to drop anywhere and cause us to burst into flame; and he also said that there was no sudden crisis; and then again that he did not know what a single day would bring forth. He said that we were on the verge of a maelstrom; and then that there was no special or critical situation. He said the danger was constant and immediate; and also that we were not threatened from any quarter. He said that there was no fear among us; and also that we were in daily danger of seeing the vital interest and honor of the country menaced and the flag of the United States stained with impunity. He said that we were in very critical danger of being involved in the great European struggle; and also that there was no need to discuss the question of defense, or to get nervous or excited about it.[67]

On Tuesday evening, October 3, TR addressed a massive Union League Club unity dinner held on behalf of Hughes. The Old Guard was, of course, there, such men as Root and Butler, W. Murray Crane and Boies Penrose, even old Chauncey Depew. But so was Roosevelt's crowd: Perkins, Bacon, George von L. Meyer, Albert B. Fall, and even the multiply erstwhile Albert Beveridge. And so was William Howard Taft.

Some predicted a TR-Taft rapprochement. Less Pollyannaish types scoffed at the idea. Some anticipated (or desired) a barely controlled brawl. A "very considerable part of the low-minded press," Taft wrote to his younger brother Horace, "[has] given the impression that if Roosevelt and I met, he would curse me and I would curse him, and each would kick the other in the stomach."[68]

But if the dinner was a peace conference, it featured little conferencing. "The inventor of morality [TR]," jeered the *Times*, "laughed and jested with Mr. Penrose, but for Taft [he had] only the briefest, formal greeting. Was it worthwhile for the Republican managers to stage this 'reunited' party scene, which did but exhibit the leaders of the two factions as irreconcilable enemies?"[69]

Taft dutifully sat through Roosevelt's dinner comments. "He talked well and ill," he wrote his wife, Nellie (who still thoroughly detested Roosevelt). "But he talked long. He spoke six minutes longer than Hughes."[70]

In mid-October, Theodore commenced a twelve-day, sixty-three-hundred-mile cross-country tour. Taft sniped to Horace, "Roosevelt is going clear out to Arizona . . . and I am glad of it. The further he goes away the better."[71]

At coal-mining Wilkes-Barre, TR addressed workers "as one union man to other union men."[72] He spoke during drenching rain at Louisville, visited Emporia at William Allen White's pleading, and paused in one-hundred-degree, sweat-soaked Phoenix. From Albuquerque, it was on to Las Vegas (population eight hundred) and then to Denver, where "Wilson hecklers stirred [him] to a terrible rage and he called them several kinds of scoundrels in his own, patented smashing style."[73] In Chicago, he teamed up with the Hughesettes' campaign train. At Elkhart, Indiana, spying a babe in its mother's arms, he recalled the infants lost on the *Lusitania*: "The blood of those babies is on the lintels of the White House. Why is it not atoned for?"[74] Back in Brooklyn, curious, but not necessarily sympathetic, Mexican members of the Mexican-U.S. arbitration conference absorbed his orations from nearby box seats.[75]

Not all Republicans desired his presence. GOP leaders canceled scheduled appearances in heavily Germanic St. Louis and Cincinnati. Dovish California Progressives wanted no part of his warlike ways and ordered him kept beyond Golden State borders.[76]

In Washington, DC, German ambassador Johann Heinrich von Bernstorff cabled Berlin, "Four months ago a Republican victory seemed certain, to-day Wilson's success is very possible. [But since then] Mr. Hughes has made, no permanent impression as a speaker, whereas Roosevelt blew the war trumpet in his usual bombastic fashion. If Hughes should be defeated he can thank Roosevelt. The average American is, and remains, a pacifist."[77]

The campaign turned uglier by the day—from all angles. Whispers swirled of alleged Wilson infidelities during his first marriage with a certain Mrs. Mary Allen Peck, who supposedly blackmailed him ("Peck's Bad Boy") to the tune of $75,000 in hush money paid through Samuel Untermyer. In return—so the rumors said—Wilson appointed Untermyer's coreligionist Louis Brandeis to the Supreme Court.[78]

Democrats assaulted Hughes as either a TR puppet bent on plunging the nation into war with Berlin or a cringing ally of powerful German- and Irish-American voting blocs—pointing specifically to a meeting of Hughes with Jeremiah O'Leary's German-financed American Independence Conference.[79]

In Massachusetts, Cabot Lodge faced a strong challenge from Boston mayor John "Honey Fitz" Fitzgerald (John F. Kennedy's grandfather).

How Lodge might fare in a statewide popular election was anybody's guess, as he had previously relied on mere legislative action. Facing similar circumstances, Elihu Root retired. But Lodge fought on, and some observers (Henry Stoddard included[80]) theorized that TR delivered his absurd Lodge-for-president suggestion largely to boost his embattled friend's reelection.

In late October, Lodge alleged that during May 1915's *Lusitania* crisis, Wilson had pondered secretly advising Berlin against taking his official note seriously and that certain cabinet members threatened resignation if he did. Lodge had it only partially right: Wilson's "hint" would not go directly to Berlin; it would be planted in a friendly newspaper. No cabinet members directly warned Wilson; instead, Secretary of War Garrison and future secretary of state Lansing employed Wilson's secretary, Joe Tumulty, to carry that message to him.

Taking advantage of Lodge's imperfect grasp of events, Wilson carefully crafted a largely misleading public statement (meant to be wired to obscure Democratic operative A. Jonas Lippmann but in a mix-up dispatched to Walter Lippmann[81]) excoriating Lodge's "untrue" statement. Lodge backed down, though he suspected that he might be more correct than Wilson suggested.[82] Democratic newspapers mocked Lodge. The *Times* pilloried his "puerile partisan falsehood."[83]

The imbroglio could not have pleased TR. It certainly severed the already frayed Wilson-Lodge relationship.

Nor was TR's mood improved by Amos Pinchot's constant sniping. To Pinchot, the Colonel had degenerated into "the bell hop of Wall Street," "Colonel Sit-by-the-Fire," and (sarcastically) "The Only Patriotic American." Exasperated, TR rejoined, "When I spoke of the Progressive Party as having a lunatic fringe, I specifically had you in mind. On the supposition that you are of entire sound mind, I should be obliged to say that you are absolutely dishonorable and untruthful. I prefer to accept the alternative."[84]

No, TR was thus not amused on the night of Friday, November 3, when he addressed a packed GOP rally of twenty-five hundred at Yiddish actor Boris Thomashefsky's National Theatre. Ten thousand people jammed Lower East Side streets to catch a glimpse of him. Fifty police patrolled the area, as Democrats, Socialists, and former Progressives protested. Inside, Republicans presented a tableau of remarkable diversity. The German-born Jew Oscar S. Straus oversaw proceedings. Former collector of internal revenue for New York's Second District, Charles W. Anderson (the first black man to hold that position), sat alongside TR. Recently returned from their oft-maligned national tour sat Katherine Bement Davis, the lesbian Mary Dreier, and their band of Hughesettes.

Earlier that evening, a ten-minute ovation greeted TR as daughters Alice and Ethel escorted him to Cooper Union's historic stage. The upper-class audience "yelled and cheered and whistled and stamped its feet in the effort to show him he was with friends," noted the *Times*. "Everybody yelled, 'Teddy!' but not a single person even whispered the name of Mr. Hughes. It was a 'Teddy' crowd, and, everybody, even the Colonel, knew it."[85]

Seventy-eight-year-old department store magnate John Wanamaker chaired the Cooper Union session. Wanamaker and Roosevelt had been at odds since Benjamin Harrison's administration, when they tussled over patronage issues. In 1912, Wanamaker seconded Taft's renomination.[86] Four years later, he served as a member of Pennsylvania's Penrose-led delegate slate.[87] But tonight he sat at the very desk and chair used by Lincoln in February 1860 and provided TR's introduction. Yes, TR was back in the GOP.

The Colonel's thirty-five-hundred-word address (brief by his standards) deployed verbal missiles that no ex-president had ever dared launch against a successor. It climaxed with

Mr. Wilson now dwells at Shadow Lawn. There should be shadows enough at Shadow Lawn: the shadows of men, women, and children who have risen from the ooze of the ocean bottom and from graves in foreign lands; the shadows of the helpless who Mr. Wilson did not dare protect lest he might have to face danger; the shadows of babies gasping pitifully as they sank under the waves; the shadows of women outraged and slain by bandits; the shadows of troopers who lay in the Mexican desert, the black blood crusted round their mouths, and their dim eyes looking upward, because President Wilson had sent them to do a task, and then shamefully abandoned them to the mercy of foes who knew no mercy.

Those are the shadows proper for Shadow Lawn: the shadows of deeds that were never done; the shadows of lofty words that were followed by no action; the shadows of the tortured dead.[88]

TR's words thrilled those whom they thrilled but only terrified those who feared far more American dead under a Roosevelt-influenced Hughes administration than might perish with a thousand *Lusitanias* sent to ocean bottom. In late October Hearst's *New York American* editorialized,

If the Republican Party wants to win this election, it should repudiate Roosevelt and his outbursts of rage and spite.

If Mr. Hughes wants to be elected, he should plainly state that he does not approve of Colonel Roosevelt's utterances. If the Republican candidate permits the country to believe that he approves of Colonel Roosevelt's violent and unreasonable outbursts of hate and rage—a thousand times more unbecoming and indecent since Mr. Roosevelt was once President—then we suspect that the next President will not be the Republican candidate.

Thousands of American citizens who have been a good deal ashamed of Mr. Wilson's foreign policies are apt to decide that they would rather endure four years more of futility than to risk four years of an administration that might follow the advice of Colonel Roosevelt.[89]

The pro-Wilson *New York World* could not be bothered to print a syllable of TR's Cooper Union address. It did join in publishing this powerful Wilson campaign ad:

You Are Working;
—Not Fighting!
Alive and Happy;
—Not Cannon Fodder!

Wilson and Peace with Honor?
or
Hughes with Roosevelt and War?

Roosevelt says we should hang our heads in shame because we are not at war with Germany in behalf of Belgium!

Roosevelt says that following the sinking of the Lusitania he would have foregone diplomacy and seized every ship in our ports flying the German flag. That would have meant war! . . .

Hughes Says
He and Roosevelt Are
in Complete Accord!
. . .

The Lesson is Plain:
If You Want WAR, Vote for—HUGHES!

If You Want Peace With Honor
VOTE FOR WILSON!
and Continued Prosperity[90]

Peace and Prosperity is a tough ticket to beat; yet the warlike Roosevelt and the bore-like Hughes tag team might yet triumph. Election Day betting odds deemed Hughes a 10–6 favorite.[91] A *Literary Digest* straw poll showed Hughes carrying five key battleground states: New York, New Jersey, Indiana, Illinois, and Ohio.[92]

Two days prior to the voting, Wilson, fearing the worst, concocted a scheme to radically shorten the November 1916 to March 1917 election-to-inauguration interregnum. He would force Vice President Thomas R. Marshall to resign, appoint Hughes to replace Robert Lansing as secretary of state, and then resign himself, leaving Hughes as president. It was either nobility or sour grapes—a verdict for the reader to decide.[93]

An ill omen greeted the Colonel on Election Day, as his chauffeur backed his vehicle into the polling place. "For goodness sake don't knock the polling place over," TR shouted, "or I'll be arrested before I vote."[94]

Perhaps still wrestling with his conscience, he required five minutes to mark his ballot.

When the polls closed, Hughes shot to a solid lead in the Northeast, even carrying Wilson's home state, New Jersey. He won a majority of the vote in the nation's ten largest cities.[95] Atop Times Square's Astor Hotel, searchlights blazed. Red lights flickered. A huge electric sign flashed "HUGHES" to signify his victory.[96] The *Times* and then the *World* forlornly conceded his triumph.[97] At New York's Biltmore Hotel, Franklin Roosevelt (facing unemployment) put his best face on matters, joking that he might open his own law practice or even don a military uniform.[98]

At 9:30 p.m., Wilson phoned Tumulty, mournfully confiding, "it looks as if we were licked. But I have no regrets. We have tried to do our duty."[99] A thousand jubilant Republicans trooped to Hughes's Astor Hotel lodgings, expecting a victory statement. Cautious as ever, he kept silent.[100] At Oyster Bay, TR didn't. "In view of the latest returns I have received," he informed reporters, "it appears that Mr. Hughes is elected. I wish to express my profound gratitude, as an American of his country, that the American people have repudiated the man who coined the phrase about this country, that is, 'Too proud to fight,' and whose Administration has done so much to relax the fibre of the American conscience and to dull the sense of honorable obligations in the American people. We are all of us sincerely to be congratulated on the victory of Mr. Hughes."

Sincerely or not, he noted, "Let me add, in view of certain letters and telegrams which have already begun to come in to me, that I will not make any recommendations to Mr. Hughes for appointments, nor any requests about legislation."[101]

In Washington, Nick Longworth installed a wire in his office to receive returns. Someone thanked heaven that the party had nominated Hughes—TR could never have pulled off a victory. The comment absolutely infuriated Alice Roosevelt Longworth, who, barely containing herself, advised against such enthusiasm.[102]

But as the night dragged on, Wilson swept more than the South and most of the Far West. Assisted by the Adamson eight-hour law, he captured normally Republican Ohio. By midnight, he had inched into a precarious 251–247 lead, with California's thirteen electoral votes still in play. The next day, Franklin Roosevelt wrote to wife Eleanor ("Dear Babs") that this was "the most extraordinary day of my life. After last night, Wilson may be elected after all. It looks hopeful at noon."[103] Hopeful indeed—but still incredibly dicey.

In California, Hiram Johnson walloped George S. Patton Sr. for the state's open Senate seat by 296,815 votes. Hughes lost the state by 3,422 votes. Nationwide, an estimated 20 percent of TR's 1912 vote defected to Wilson.[104] Socialists also defected. In 1912, their candidate, Eugene V. Debs, had drawn 901,551 votes, or 6 percent of the total. Four years later the party's vote total plunged to just 590,524, or 3.19 percent. Most defected to Wilson, including an estimated thirty thousand Californians.

Mothers had indeed not raised their boys to be soldiers. Women voted in twelve states, including California. Wilson carried ten of those twelve.[105]

It was damn close. A flip of only 87,760 votes in thirteen key states would have generated a 342–189 electoral college landslide victory for Hughes,[106] but that was not to be. Woodrow Wilson remained president.

In Washington, Princess Alice savored "the malicious pleasure of announcing to Nick and my mother-in-law . . . that Wilson was with us for another four years."[107]

Late one night, as TR's 1916 campaign tour concluded, he confided to George Perkins and Henry Stoddard, "Old trumps, let me tell you something. . . . I'm finishing . . . my last Presidential campaign. I've done my 'bit' for Hughes; I am not going to tour for any future Presidential candidate . . . I've done my full share of it; I am now entitled to go on the exempt list. I am positively through campaigning forever."[108]

"I shall be out of it," he reiterated to the *New York Tribune*'s Jack Leary at Oyster Bay on Election Eve, when Leary inquired of his post-Hughes victory plans. "I shall ask for nothing from him and will recommend nobody. He will not ask my advice. So I will just be an elderly literary gentleman of quiet tastes and an interesting group of grandchildren."[109]

He spoke similarly to other newsmen—but with a crucial caveat: "Gentlemen, remember this, if Mr. Hughes is elected Nov. 7, I shall never be seen in politics again, I'm through."[110]

But Hughes was not elected.

And Roosevelt was not finished either.

"I'm only asking to be allowed to die"

TR HAD MORE TO CONVEY TO JACK LEARY THAN YET ANOTHER FAITH-less vow to exit politics.

For Leary had also prodded him to forecast Woodrow Wilson's course of action should he somehow overcome Charles Evans Hughes. TR responded,

> *He will muddle along just as he has been, writing notes that are brave, but doing nothing to back them up until Germany decides it wants us in this war and kicks us into it. Against that contingency he will do nothing and war will find us as unprepared as we were two years ago. . . .*
>
> *He will . . . be in a position to do big things. But he won't do them. He'll simply write notes until something so audacious is done that he will wake up to the fact that Germany has been making war upon us while he has been writing.*[1]

For once, the Colonel and the Professor shared proximate views. "I can't keep this country out of war," Wilson had confessed to Josephus Daniels. "They talk of me as though I were a god. Any little German lieutenant can put us into war at any time by some calculated outrage."[2]

From May 1916, when Germany grudgingly extended its *Sussex* Pledge, American neutrality seemed, if not ensured, at least immensely strengthened. But 1916 was a horrible year, even by Great War standards, with February's German Verdun offensive designed to "bleed France white," then May's Battle of Jutland, June's death at sea of British war minister Lord Kitchener, and July's massive British advance along the Somme.

And that was just on the western front.

Italians and Austrians battled in the Alps; British Empire forces invaded Mesopotamia. April witnessed Dublin's bloody Easter Rebellion; Romania joined the Allied cause in August—and Bucharest fell to the Central Powers that December. A June Russian offensive captured 350,000 Austro-Hungarian prisoners but endured a million losses before falling back. That same month, Arabs revolted against Ottoman rule.

So when a pacifist delegation visited the White House that May, Woodrow Wilson, with more than ample reason, declared 1916 "a year of madness."[3]

Berlin still enjoyed its successes. But they came at great cost. All the while, Britain's blockade slowly strangled Germany's economy, starving women and children. Germans railed against what they regarded as American indifference to British (but not German) violation of the freedom of the seas. "The hate of Americans grows daily," America's ambassador to Berlin, James W. Gerard, recorded in his diary in September 1916, "if indeed it is possible to be greater."[4]

Flushed with electoral triumph, Wilson pondered mediating an accord between the two warring camps and grandly proposed a "peace without victory" (a phrase that infuriated TR). Berlin had other ideas. Desperate for victory before both its economy and its entire regime collapsed, it opted in January 1917 to resume unrestricted submarine warfare. Wilson quickly (or finally, depending upon one's viewpoint) severed diplomatic relations. Shortly thereafter, British intelligence revealed Germany's ill-considered Zimmermann Telegram, proposing a military alliance and promising Mexico a generous slice of U.S. territory if America joined the Allies.

Suddenly, TR again marched alongside—if not led—public opinion. From Oyster Bay on February 3, he informed reporters, "Of course I shall in every way support the President in all that he does to uphold the honor of the United States and to safeguard the lives of American citizens." His magnanimity possessed its motives; his next sentence read, "Yesterday I wrote to the War Department asking permission to raise a division if war is declared and there is a call for volunteers. In such event I and my four sons will go."[5]

War—a very personal war—obsessed him. In 1916, he requested of New York's Police Department that "in the event of war" they supply him with two "horses with good manners who will stand fire and the like without making a fuss," diffidently adding that an "elderly Major General who had been President of the United States and who had broken all kinds of bones, needs a hardy and well-bitted horse."[6]

Provided with good-mannered equines or not (and, after all, cavalry charges were distinctly passé on the western front by 1916), TR stood ready to fight in France—but not at Madison Square Garden. In late February 1917, the New York branch of the left-wing Congress of Forums invited TR and William Jennings Bryan to debate "the issue of national preparedness." Bryan readily acceded, envisioning a traveling roadshow involving not merely New York but also Washington, St. Louis, Chicago, and San Francisco—just for starters. "I regard it as a waste of time to debate non-debatable subjects," the Colonel said angrily, ducking the challenge on February 28—the very day the Zimmermann Telegram was revealed. "To debate with Mr. Bryan his views against national preparedness would, in my judgment, be precisely on a par with debating the undesirability of monogamous marriages, or the morality of abolishing patriotism, or the advantage of the reintroduction of slavery, or the right of judges to accept bribes from suiters, or the duty of submission to the divine right of kings, or the propriety of action such as that of Benedict Arnold. . . . [I]t is only the more backward among elderly Chinese reactionaries who would treat Mr. Bryan's thesis as debatable."[7]

Yes, TR wanted in on the game—and, in at least one small way, Woodrow Wilson responded, approving a commission for a major of infantry in the Officers' Reserve Corps—for Ted Jr.[8] TR and Edith quickly canceled a trip to Jamaica and the West Indies[9] as TR also planned for a war not yet declared. Instead, the Roosevelts embarked upon an island trip of a different sort—via tugboat to Governor's Island in New York Harbor—where alongside Leonard Wood, they would watch fresh recruits train. "I have . . . seen the airplanes," TR told reporters afterward. "I also saw the 'rookies' drill with broomsticks. I admired their wonderful patriotism, but was filled with wonder and shame that a great people like ours should be in such a state of unpreparedness."[10]

On Monday, March 5, Chief Justice Edward Douglass White swore Wilson in for his second term. That evening, TR dispatched a brief message to an angry pro-Preparedness mass meeting at Carnegie Hall,[11] where well-heeled audience members (many in formal attire) howled "Traitor!" and "Hang Them!" regarding the "little group of willful men" (including Robert La Follette and Albert B. Cummins) who had recently blocked Wilson's plan to arm merchant ships. Mistaking one speaker's remarks as pro-German, they shouted, "Shut up!" and "Throw him out!"[12]

The country didn't march to war. It galloped.

Two days later, TR, Hughes, and Elihu Root spoke at the Union League Club's grill room. TR ("let us show that Americans are willing to pay with their bodies for their souls' desire"[13]) for once held his thunder against Wilson, but only barely and with much calculation, still hoping to personally fight—and die—in France. "Do you really mean that?" an astonished Root asked of his near-suicidal desire. TR answered yes. "Theodore," Root retorted, "if you can convince Wilson of that I am sure he will give you a commission."[14]

His ambition to fight—and die—was hardly new. During his 1912 campaign, former San Juan Hill Rough Rider (and Yale football and baseball star) John C. "Jack" Greenway shyly inquired, "Colonel, I've long wanted to ask you something."

"Go right ahead," answered TR, "what is it?"

"Well, Colonel, I've always believed that it was your ambition to die on the field of battle."

CRASH!

Roosevelt slammed his fist upon a nearby table.

"By Jove, how did you know that?"

"Well, Colonel," Greenway continued, "do you remember that day in Cuba, when you and I were going along a trail and came upon [a member of the regiment] propped against a tree, shot through the abdomen? It was evident that he was done for. But instead of commiserating him, you grabbed his hand and said something like this, 'Well, old man, isn't this splendid!' Ever since then I've been sure you would be glad to die in battle yourself."

TR grew solemn.

"You're right, Jack," he answered. "I would."[15]

In 1917, TR's anger festered. To Henry Cabot Lodge, he grumbled, "I am so utterly sick of the gush about 'supporting the President.'... Taft, Hughes and even Root take part in the general idiot cry which aligns us behind the President, right or wrong—and he is 99 per cent wrong."[16]

He soon cut loose, though recognizing that his words jeopardized his chances of any military commission. Within a single forty-eight-hour period, U-boats torpedoed three American merchant steamships, the *City of Memphis*, the *Vigilancia*, and the *Illinois*. All flew the American flag conspicuously. Fifteen seamen (including five Americans) perished when the *Vigilancia's* lifeboat swamped. Enraged, Roosevelt lambasted the administration:

Words are wasted on Germany. What we need is effective and thorough-going action.

Seven weeks have passed since Germany renewed ... submarine war against neutrals and noncombatants ... itself a declaration of war and should have been treated as such.... [S]he has steadily waged war upon us ...; she has killed American women and children as well as American men upon the high seas. She has sunk our ships, our ports have been put under blockade. She has asked Mexico and Japan to join her in dismembering this country. If these are not overt acts of war, then Lexington and Bunker Hill were not overt acts of war.

Seven weeks ago we broke relations with Germany. This was eminently proper. But it amounted to nothing, it was an empty gesture, unless it was followed by vigorous and efficient action....

[A]rmed neutrality is only another name for timid war; and Germany despises timidity as she despises all other forms of feebleness. She does not wage timid war herself, and she neither respects nor understands it in others.

Seemingly her submarine warfare has failed.... We are profiting and shall profit by this failure. But we have done nothing to bring it

about. It has been due solely to the efficiency of the British Navy. . . .
We have been content to shelter ourselves behind the fleet of a foreign
power.

Such a position is intolerable to all self-respecting Americans. . . .
Let us dare to use our own strength in our own defense and strike
hard.[17]

In early February 1917, TR commenced badgering Secretary of War
Baker to allow him "to raise a Division of Infantry, with a divisional brigade of cavalry in the event of war."[18] Baker averred that no such action
could be undertaken "without the express sanction of Congress,"[19] but
such arguments failed to impress the man who "took the Canal Zone and
let Congress debate." TR reiterated his nineteenth-century qualifications
to lead men half his age into twentieth-century combat:

I wish respectfully to point out that I am a retired Commander in
Chief of the United States Army, and eligible to any position of
command over American troops to which I may be appointed. As for
my fitness for command of troops, I respectfully refer you to my three
immediate superiors in the field. . . . In the Santiago Campaign I
served in the first fight as commander first of the right wing and
then of the left wing of the regiment; in the next, the big fight, as
Colonel of the Regiment; and I ended the campaign in command of
the brigade.

The regiment, 1st United States Volunteer Cavalry, in which I
first served as Lieutenant Colonel, and which I then commanded as
Colonel, was raised, armed, equipped, drilled, mounted, dismounted,
kept for two weeks on a transport, and then put through two victori-
ous aggressive fights, in which we lost a third of the officers, and a fifth
of the enlisted men, all within little over fifty days.[20]

Baker—whose own alcoholic younger brother, Julian, now volunteered to serve under TR[21]—for some reason was not at all intrigued by
any strategy, however heroic, that involved losing "a third of the officers,
and a fifth of the enlisted men, all within little over fifty days."

Baker closed one door. Roosevelt pounded upon another, entreating Britain's Cecil Spring-Rice and France's ambassador Jean Jules Jusserand for permission to raise an American volunteer regiment on Canadian soil. "Of course," he reassured Jusserand, "I would not attempt to raise it *so far as I can now see*, unless this country went to war, because I gravely doubt the propriety of an ex-President of the United States attempting to go to war unless his country was at war" (emphasis added).[22]

Wilson scheduled a special session of Congress for April 2. Wise observers expected war. Stymied by Baker, TR scheduled a monthlong combination devilfish (i.e., giant manta ray) and shark hunt in Florida. His expedition turned out to be surprisingly productive. Practice makes perfect. And Roosevelt had practiced his harpooning techniques on Long Island Sound as well as alongside his host, Virginia tobacco planter and noted amateur marine hunter and naturalist Russell J. Coles, prior to their arrival in Florida. Coles (an uncanny William Howard Taft look-alike) detailed their first day's action to the *New York Sun*:

We had not been out on the water of the Gulf more than thirty minutes before we ran into a school of eight or ten of these strange monsters. Although Col. Roosevelt had never stood before in the bowels of a small launch in a choppy sea, or had never hurled a heavy harpoon at a living creature, he promptly stepped out with me, and I had the boat run squarely upon a large devilfish.

At the word from me the Colonel hurled his harpoon two feet and four inches through the tough hide, bone and sinew of the fish. We were instantly deluged with water by the stricken creature and the fight was on. Col. Roosevelt was absolutely cool headed throughout and he did every word I said. He recognized the fact that I knew my work. Finally when I had the boat placed just right I told him to strike and instantly he sent the great spade lance crashing through its vitals and the fight was over.

Just eleven minutes after he first struck it with a harpoon we towed the fish three-quarters of a mile to shore. The fish was a magnificent adult male specimen, measuring thirteen feet, two inches across its back. . . .

We then ran the boat back into the school of devilfish, and in cruising around among them I selected the largest. Running the launch up on it, I again told the Colonel to strike. In almost the same spot where he struck the first, which was through its heart, he again made a perfect cast, and for twenty-six minutes he had truly a great fight. The boat was towed two miles, and looking back I could see a broad band of blood more than fifty feet wide.

At last the fish turned and rushed the boat, not giving a good chance for a blow. I instructed the Colonel to hold until I gave the word. The fish lifted the boat well out of the sea and covered all with blood and water, but in coming from under the boat it gave the chance that I was looking for. I exclaimed "Now!" and again the heavy spade lance was driven into the creature.

On towing this fish to the beach we found it to be a grand female specimen measuring sixteen feet in width and being the next to the largest ever officially recorded.[23]

TR harpooned. War-weary Russia toppled its ancient tsarist regime. And fifteen hundred persons packed 34th Street's Manhattan Opera House to salute the false dawn of Russian freedom. In a gathering chock-ablock with TR's old adversaries—Republicans Root, Nicholas Murray Butler, and the aged (and soon dead) Joe Choate and Democrats Alton B. Parker and William McCombs (Wilson's 1912 campaign manager)—each mention of him generated huzzahs. Choate advanced the regret that TR "has gone . . . to harpoon devilfish . . . I wish he had stayed here, for there are plenty of devilfish for him to harpoon in New York City in German spies, Austrian plotters, and mad pacifists without number."[24]

On Monday evening, April 2, 1917, Wilson ("The world must be made safe for democracy") addressed Congress to demand war. Pacifists prowled congressional hallways to protest, including a delegation from Boston's Emergency Peace Federation (its ranks embracing two young Socialists, Stuart Chase and the Reverend A. J. Muste[25]). "National degeneracy and cowardice are worse than war," Cabot Lodge told them. "I must do my duty as I see it."[26]

That offended one of the group's leaders—a Swiss-born 1906 Princeton graduate and former minor-league infielder named Alexander W. Bannwart.[27] "Anyone who wants to go to war is a coward," he thundered.[28] "You're a damned coward!"[29]

"You're a damned liar!"[30] exclaimed the diminutive sixty-seven-year-old Lodge as he punched the thirty-six-year-old Bannwart in the jaw. Avowed pacifist Bannwart counterpunched Lodge, and a general melee ensued until a pint-sized twenty-year-old Western Union telegraph messenger, David B. Herman, happened by and wisely chose to throw himself upon Bannwart rather than Lodge. Police hauled Bannwart—along with a Cambridge suffragette, Mrs. Anna May Peabody ("She is a divorced woman"[31])—off to a nearby precinct house.

That was Monday.

Tuesday saw TR and Coles, their devilfish hunt complete, speeding northward by rail. En route, TR received word that the War Department had exacted its price for Leonard Wood's long-standing impudence, bypassing him for command of the army's key Eastern Department, thus essentially blackballing him from leadership of any European expeditionary force.[32]

In mid-afternoon, TR detrained at Washington's Union Station. He rushed to the White House for an impromptu confrontation with Woodrow Wilson.

Ten minutes earlier, Wilson had departed for a cabinet meeting at the nearby Executive Office Building. TR meekly deposited his calling card with White House chief usher Irwin "Ike" Hoover[33] and sped off to Cabot Lodge's Massachusetts Avenue home. Lodge ("the man who put the fist in pacifist"[34]) wasn't home either.[35]

Before departing for New York, TR extended some rare praise for Wilson, advising reporters,

The President's message is a great state paper which will rank in history with the great state papers of which Americans in future years will be proud. It now rests with the people of the country to see that we put in practice the policy that the President has outlined and that

we strike as hard, as soon, and as efficiently as possible in aggressive war against the Government of Germany.

We must send troops to the firing line as rapidly as possible. Defensive war is hopeless. We must by vigorous offensive warfare win the right to have our voice count for civilization and justice when the time for peace comes.

Then came his real message: "I, of course, very earnestly hope that I may be allowed to raise a division for immediate service at the front."[36]

Conciliation abounded. The following afternoon, Alexander Bannwart contritely pledged to local authorities that he would mend his ways. Simultaneously, Lodge dropped charges against the man he had struck first. That evening, Bannwart stunned his Emergency Peace Federation comrades first by declining to sign their no-enlistment pledge and then by urging support for Wilson ("It is a joyous privilege to take part in such a war"[37]). Shouting him down, they chased him from the premises. Bannwart scurried to the White House to provide his personal encouragement to Wilson. Wilson didn't see him either.[38]

Bannwart might abandon hope of a presidential interview after a single failed attempt. TR would not.

Days passed. TR heard nothing regarding his precious commission. Congress declared war on Good Friday, April 6. Six senators voted no—Robert La Follette and George W. Norris among them. Cabot Lodge, of course, voted yes. So did William E. Borah, who later regretted it,[39] and Warren Harding, his decision infuriating his vociferously pro-German paramour, Mrs. Carrie Phillips.[40]

That same Good Friday, TR wrote Lodge regarding the latter's recent adventure: "If you had knocked down that pacifist last May my message to the Republican Convention would have borne fruit in your nomination! I think you are at present the most popular man in the United States, which is growing relieved to find that it isn't quite as anaemic as it feared that it was."[41]

On Easter Monday, April 9, TR and Leonard Wood visited John D. Rockefeller Jr.'s eight-story 10 West 54th Street mansion for a private luncheon honoring Billy Sunday, about to commence a ten-week

Manhattan crusade. At West 168th Street and Broadway, organizers constructed a temporary sixteen-thousand-seat tabernacle for Sunday's use.[42] Two thousand voices comprised his choir that night. Every seat was taken. Four to five thousand persons stood for the entire program. A half dozen army recruiting stations ringed the building. From open automobiles, women harangued passersby to enlist.

Sunday's literal flag-waving sermon ("God's Grenadiers") featured more patriotism than piety. "The soldier who breaks every regulation," he orated, "yet is found on the firing line in the hour of battle, is better than the God-forsaken mutt who won't enlist, and does all he can to keep others from enlisting. In these days all are patriots or traitors, to your country and the cause of Jesus Christ."[43]

Behind Sunday sat Rockefeller Jr.—but not TR. At 11:00 that evening he arrived unannounced at Washington's Union Station. Nick and Alice Longworth conveyed him to their M Street home,[44] where Cabot Lodge awaited him.[45] TR's agenda: another attempt to personally entreat Wilson. "I'll take my chances on his trying to snub me," TR seethed. "He can't do it! I'd like to see him try."[46]

At 11:00 the next morning, TR and Alice (she considered Wilson a "slimy hypocrite"[47]) motored past a small gaggle of banner-wielding suffragettes to arrive at the White House's front door.[48]

Again, TR had not called ahead. But word of his visit had leaked out, and Joe Tumulty stood ready to escort him into the Red Room, where an edgy Wilson awaited him. The president, however, soon "'thawed out' and was soon laughing and 'talking back.'"[49]

"Nothing could have been pleasanter or more agreeable than this meeting," Tumulty recalled. "They met . . . in the most friendly fashion, told each other anecdotes, and seemed to enjoy together what the Colonel was accustomed to call a 'bully time.' The object of the Colonel's call was discussed without heat or bitterness."[50]

"I put before the President my proposals," TR wrote to his friend Cal O'Laughlin, "and the reasons therefor, substantially as I have put them in public. He evidently felt pleased that I was going to support his [conscription] bill. . . . He suddenly entered into a defense of his past conduct, saying that he had for a long time felt what he now said in his speech to Congress, but that the American people were not awake to the need, and that he had to bide his time; and he added that many people had misunderstood him (hastily interpolating, with obvious insincerity, that he did not mean me)."[51]

And so, TR answered (perhaps with similar insincerity), "Mr. President, what I have said and thought, and what others have said and thought, is all dust in a windy street, if now we can make your message good. Of course, it amounts to nothing, if we cannot make it good. But, if we can translate it into fact, then it will rank as a great state paper, with the great state papers of Washington and Lincoln. Now, all that I ask is that I be allowed to do all that in me is to help make good this speech of yours—to help get the nation to act, so as to justify and live up to the speech, and the declaration of war that followed."[52]

To O'Laughlin, Roosevelt revealed, "I added that I felt that the situation was as if Jefferson, after the *Leopard* attacked *Chesapeake*, had gone to war with Great Britain, in which case it would have been Light-Horse Harry Lee's duty instantly to support to the best of his power and ability such action; and that I wished to act [thusly] toward him."[53]

Yet the Colonel could not abandon his long-standing condescension to—and suspicion of—his frustratingly invincible foe:

I found that, though I had written plainly enough, there was confusion in [Wilson's] mind as to what I wanted to do. I explained everything to him. He seemed to take it well, but—remember I was talking to Mr. Wilson. . . .

He has promised me nothing definitely, but as I have said, if any other man than he talked to me as he did I would feel assured. If I talked to another man as he talked to me it would mean that that man was going to get permission to fight.

But I was talking to Mr. Wilson. His words may mean much; they may mean little. He has, however, left the door open.[54]

The session lasted somewhere between thirty and sixty minutes. Tumulty escorted TR out to meet with an excited gaggle of reporters. TR revealed to the *New York Tribune*'s Jack Leary that as Tumulty ushered him out, "by way of a half joke, [he] said he might go to France with me."[55]

"By Jove, Tumulty," TR boomed, slapping him on the back, "you are a man after my own heart! Six children, eh? Well now, you get me across and I will put you on my staff, and you may tell Mrs. Tumulty that I will not allow them to place you at any point of danger."[56]

His bonhomie coated a huge dollop of cynicism. "I would [have sent Tumulty], too," he would recollect to Leary, "but it would n't [*sic*] be the place [Tumulty] thinks. It is possible he might be sent along as sort of a watchdog to keep Wilson informed as to what was being done. He would n't [*sic*] be, though. He'd keep his distance from headquarters except when he was sent for."[57]

By now, a crowd of three hundred onlookers clustered at the White House gate.[58] On the Executive Mansion's steps, TR dodged reporters' questions[59] but issued a prepared statement: "I am heart and soul for the proposal of the Administration for universal obligatory military training and service. I would favor it for 3,000,000 men. You can call it conscription if you wish, and I would say yes. The division that I ask permission to raise would be raised exclusively among men who would not be taken under the conscription system. They would either be over 25 or of the exempted class, and they would eagerly enlist to go to the front."[60]

Either deluded that Wilson had granted his wish or merely hoping to box the administration into so doing, he meekly turned to Tumulty and, fairly kowtowing, said, "If I say anything I shouldn't, be sure to censor it. I'm already under orders."[61]

Not quite—not at all—though his meeting went far better than anyone might have predicted. "Well, and how did the Colonel impress you?" Wilson asked Tumulty, who indicated that he was impressed by their uninvited visitor's "buoyancy, charm of manner, and his great good nature."

"Yes, he is a great big boy," Wilson agreed. "I was, as formerly, charmed by his personality. There is a sweetness about him that is very compelling. You can't resist the man. I can easily understand why his followers are so fond of him."[62]

But Woodrow Wilson, master of weasel words, had not said that *he* was fond of Roosevelt.

TR returned to the Longworths. Recently, he had comported himself as if commanding a government in exile. His exile now seemed over. He received not only such Republican and Progressive friends and acolytes as Lodge, Hiram Johnson, and Medill McCormick but also Republican standpatters like "Uncle Joe" Cannon, John W. Weeks, and James Wadsworth Jr. Ambassadors Cecil Spring-Rice, Jean Jules Jusserand, and Japan's Aimaro Satō came to call, as did numerous active-duty military officers. By day's end, Franklin Roosevelt and even Secretary Baker had paid homage.[63] TR took Baker by the arm to an upstairs bedroom for a private—and inconclusive—chat, confessing that he "had not enough experience to lead a division myself. But I have selected the most experienced officers from the regular army for my staff."[64]

All in all, he retained little more genuine respect for Baker than he did for Wilson or Tumulty:

> *I had a good talk with Baker—I could twist him about my finger could I have him about for a while. But he does not realize what he is trying to do.*
>
> *He is exactly the type of man Mr. Wilson wants about him. He will do exactly what Mr. Wilson tells him to do, he will think exactly as Mr. Wilson wants him to think, and when Mr. Wilson changes his mind, he will change with him. If Mr. Wilson should agree with me to-morrow, Mr. Baker would be perfectly sure he always agreed with me. He's a pleasant enough type socially, but impossible in his present place because he is inefficient and is unable to grasp the fact that he is inefficient.*
>
> *He has the blindest faith in the General Staff and the graduates of West Point. He does not realize that a muttonhead, after an education at West Point or Harvard, is a muttonhead still.*[65]

Acting Army Chief of Staff Tasker Bliss had supplied Wilson with an eight-page memorandum, detailing reasons aplenty why a TR-led division was a bad idea.[66] Joseph Leiter, president of the Army League, also opposed it. TR angrily resigned as the league's honorary vice president. "I thought at first that your intentions were inspired by patriotism," Leiter retorted. "I am now constrained to believe that your own schemes of political and personal aggrandizement lie at the bottom of the agitation."[67] Missouri Democratic senator William J. "Gumshoe Bill" Stone blasted the Colonel as "unfit to command even a regiment" and possessing "no respect for authority, constitutional or otherwise."[68] John J. Pershing's memoirs betray a singular lack of eagerness for the idea.[69]

No word came approving TR's fading dream.

Everyone else now headed for the service. In Boston, on May 7, even ex-pacifist Alexander Bannwart was allowed into the reserves.[70] A week later, a new avenue opened up for Roosevelt to serve. Charles Whitman, perhaps grateful for TR's 1916 sandbagging of Samuel Seabury, offered the Colonel a generalship in the New York National Guard—a plan designed to provide TR with a regular army commission when Washington federalized the state militias. TR—still wary of Whitman—said no.[71]

John M. Parker endorsed Woodrow Wilson in 1916 but soon emerged as a key backer of the Colonel's military plans. He trekked to the White House to argue Roosevelt's cause.

The meeting went long—but not well. Scheduled for ten minutes, it stretched to more than thirty-five, as Parker bluntly accused Wilson of acting as "a czar and a dictator."[72] "In all the civilized world," he asserted, "there is no greater autocrat or more arbitrary ruler than Woodrow Wilson, President of the United States."[73]

Not even TR dared defy Wilson so boldly. "He was not only irritated at the frankness with which I spoke," Parker detailed, "but the color in his cheeks and the glint in his eye satisfied me that he was thoroughly angered when he made his response."[74]

"Sir, I am not playing politics," Wilson snapped. "Nothing could be more advantageous than to follow the course you suggest. . . . Colonel Roosevelt is a splendid man and a patriotic citizen, as you say, but he is not a military leader. His experience in military life has been extremely short. He and many of the men with him are too old to render efficient service, and in addition to that fact he as well as others have shown intolerance for discipline."[75]

Woodrow Wilson stood fast. Signing the Selective Service Act on May 18, he formally quashed TR's entreaty.

It would be very agreeable to me to pay Mr. Roosevelt this compliment and the Allies the compliment of sending to their aid one of our most distinguished public men, an ex-President who has rendered many conspicuous public services, and proved his gallantry in many striking ways. Politically, too, it would no doubt have a very fine effect and make a profound impression. But this is not the time or the occasion for compliment or for any action not calculated to contribute to the immediate success of the war. The business now in hand is undramatic, practical, and of scientific definiteness and precision.[76]

Wilson spoke.

Roosevelt did not hear.

He quickly telegraphed Wilson requesting permission to immediately raise two regiments, plus two more if necessary (one being "a negro regiment"[77]). His officer corps would be heavy on old Rough Riders and political allies like Parker, McCormick, Borah, James R. Garfield, Robert Bacon, Henry Stimson, Gussie Gardner, and Jack Greenway.[78] Wilson responded the following day with an even firmer no[79]—one even TR might comprehend. Shattered, the Colonel plunged into a truly "black mood," as his valet James Amos recalled, "a state of great depression such as I seldom saw him in. However, he quickly recovered himself and said: 'Well, I must be a good soldier and do what I am told—just carry on here the best way I can.'"[80]

At his private Fifth Avenue recruiting office, TR gathered the subordinate officers—Parker, Garfield, and Dick Derby among them—about him.[81] "Never, except in a house of death," observed Jack Leary, "have I noticed a greater air of depression. All except the Colonel showed it plainly. He, it was apparent to those who knew him best, felt worse than any other."[82] A day or two later, O. K. Davis saw him at the Harvard Club. The Colonel's mood had improved not a bit. Like James Amos, Davis "never saw [TR] in a blacker mood. . . . He was angered to the core."[83]

"Wilson," TR sputtered privately, "that skunk in the White House!"[84]

In politics yesterday's skunk may be tomorrow's rose.

And so it was with Warren Harding.

As war became a reality, no stranger alliance evolved than that of the unrepentant Progressive ex-president and the unapologetic future standpatter chief executive. Upon this unlikely bridge, TR, rejected now in two disastrous elections, might coexist with his more conservative fellow party leaders.

TR not only returned to the Republican reservation but also resolved to reclaim his forfeited title of chief—if not *the* chief, then at least *a* chief. A big chief. In January 1917, he summoned a conference of GOP leading lights (Harding included) to discuss the future of their dispirited party.[85]

"We did not dwell on the differences of 1912," Harding told a close friend, "for that was an old story. He thought his course was justified and we jointly deplored the results. But he did insist we must all get together and save the country to a Republican restoration; that the Republican party was the one agency to give the highest service to our country, and the compact of council and co-operation was made then and there."[86]

Political parties may rest upon such platitudes. More so, they are built on personal rapport. The Harding-Roosevelt relationship was only just beginning.

"My interview . . . was not of significant importance," Harding revealed to his friend Ed Scobey.

I went over at his request and was very glad to have the meeting, and found it a very satisfactory one. He made a rather more favorable impression on me than I have ever had heretofore, but I cannot say as to what impression I left with him. My best guess is that the Colonel is looking forward to a candidacy in 1920, and felt that it might not be unwise to be on friendly terms with me. Later developments have tended to confirm this impression. The most enjoyable part of the interview was the revelation of his thorough understanding of the Republican members of the Senate. He had the Progressives down to

an ant's heel, called one of them an S.O.B. and suggested that another
was impossible.[87]

The two men now corresponded regularly. Harding took up the cudgels to authorize TR's volunteer legions, not only proposing such legislation but also shepherding it through the Senate with what Cabot Lodge informed TR was "great skill and tact."[88]

"I deeply appreciate your patriotic work,"[89] TR complimented Harding on April 17, conflating his own fortunes with the national good.

In early May, Ed Scobey joked to Harding, "Mrs. S. says she is like you, she wants T.R. to go to the front; the farther in front the better."[90]

Unamused, Harding responded, "You can say all you please about [Roosevelt], he has a personality which cannot be put aside and he has the qualities of Americanism, which have largely restored him in the affections of the people. He and I are getting to be quite Buddy, but I do not think you need to have any apprehension of seduction. I mean to maintain my virtue at all hazards."[91]

Warren Harding did not always guard his virtue with such determination.

The House of Representatives included Harding's volunteer regiment amendment in its final version of the Selective Service Act. Merely permitting volunteer divisions, it left their ultimate disposition to presidential discretion. Wilson, possessing no inclination ever to implement them, gladly signed the measure.[92]

Conceding defeat, Harding proclaimed the issue "settled."[93] Others retained hope. Former New York City Republican congressman William S. Bennet speculated, "If no other way can be found for Colonel Roosevelt to go, then I expect him to get an individual passport and go to France as a private soldier. I am not afraid to bet he will do something like that."[94]

From Paris, Georges Clemenceau (not yet again prime minister) publicly begged Wilson to send the Colonel to the Allies' aid. TR's name, gushed "The Tiger of France," was "one . . . which sums up the beauty of American intervention. . . . He is an idealist, imbued with simple, vital idealism. . . . You are too much of a philosopher to ignore that the influence on the people of great leaders of men often exceeds their personal merits, thanks to the legendary halo surrounding them. The name of Roosevelt has this legendary force in our country. . . . [Y]ou must know, Mr. President, more than one of our *poilus* asked his comrade: 'But where is Roosevelt?'"[95]

The answer remained Oyster Bay.

The jig was up. TR disbanded his two hundred thousand volunteers,[96] issuing a fifteen-hundred-word statement, which, while commencing with unusual sanguine magnanimity, steadily evolved into a familiar anti-Wilson apologia, from sullen depression into clenched-teeth enmity.[97]

In mid-May, command of the newborn American Expeditionary Force fell to "Black Jack" Pershing rather than Leonard Wood. Wood barely escaped being shipped to Hawaii or Manila.[98] Gutzon Borglum also sought service unsuccessfully.[99] Billy Sunday hankered to see France. Wilson hankered to say no.[100]

As TR complained to William Allen White, the "Washington people would rather make this a paper war, if possible; but if not that they want to make it a Democratic war."[101]

Worst of all, TR now feared that his four sons would also be refused the chance to serve. "His bitterness," recalled O. K. Davis, "was inexpressible."[102]

His grief would be more so.

"I wish I could get my hands on him!"

ARCHIE ROOSEVELT'S APRIL 14, 1917, WEDDING TO BACK BAY'S GRACE Stackpole Lockwood was hastily rescheduled owing to an emergency.

The couple had announced their engagement only eight days previously,[1] but impending war rather than impending maternity governed events. Twenty-three-year-old army reservist Archie, anticipating being called up, desired to be a married man when he was. His slim, dark-haired bride wore white satin. His corpulent father still dreamed of wearing khaki and reminisced to reporters about his old commanding officer in Cuba.[2]

TR remained stateside. The great majority of Roosevelts marched off to battle. Volunteering was more than patriotic; it was fashionable. At Harvard, beyond being the first to join the reserves, Archie helped recruit a thousand more warriors.[3] Grace graduated from the Navy League's Chevy Chase, Maryland Women's Preparedness Camp[4]—"A Woman's Plattsburgh."[5] Ted and Kermit held Officers Training Camp commissions.[6] Rumors circulated of Archie's best man, Quentin (still a Harvard sophomore), traveling to Canada for aerial combat training.[7]

"The war party," Amos Pinchot observed the previous September, "is also essentially a moneyed, or leisure-class party."[8] In 1917–1918, it fairly jumped at the chance to fight. Henry Cabot Lodge's son-in-law, the fifty-one-year-old Gussie Gardner, resigned his House seat to enlist. Newly defeated New York City mayor John Purroy Mitchel, his police commissioner Arthur Woods, and newly elected East Harlem congressman Fiorello La Guardia joined the Army Air Corps. Henry Stimson and Frank Knox served with the artillery. The *Chicago Tribune*'s Cal O'Laughlin served as a major with the Quartermaster Corps.

Harold Ickes, fortyish and bespectacled, volunteered with a YMCA unit supporting the 35th Infantry Division to ultimately serve on the Meuse-Argonne. Robert Bacon performed with the American Field Service Corps in France and later with Pershing's staff (though Pershing soon dispensed of his services). Jack Greenway won the Croix de Guerre, the Legion of Honor, and the Distinguished Service Cross, serving with the 101st Infantry. Assemblyman Ham Fish served as a captain with the African-American "Harlem Hellfighters" infantry regiment. Episcopal bishop of Rhode Island James DeWolf Perry commanded all Red Cross chaplains in France.

They served. TR did not.

⸝⸏

He was nothing if not resilient. The day following the dirgeful disbanding of his prospective volunteer officer corps, he welcomed to Sagamore Hill his daughter Ethel; her husband, Dr. Richard Derby; and their three-year-old son, Dick, TR's first grandchild. "Late that afternoon," TR would write to Kermit's wife, Belle Willard Roosevelt, "I found them in the North Room; the Victrola was playing 'Garry Owen,' while Ethel, Richard and Dick, hand in hand, executed a dance-step march to the tune, whereupon I joined in and executed pigeon-wings in time, opposite them, while the enthralled Richard gazed at my feet."[9]

Even warriors take time to be grandparents.

He kept plugging to give his boys the chance to do their bit—and sooner, very much sooner, than later. On May 20, he entreated "Black Jack" Pershing to allow Ted and Archie "to enlist as privates under you, to go over with the first troops. . . . [T]hey are keenly desirous to see service; and if they serve under you at the front, and are not killed, they will be far better able to instruct the draft army next fall."[10]

But before he lay his pen aside, his thoughts turned—as always—to his own increasingly humble ambitions: "P.S. If I were physically fit, instead of old and heavy and stiff, I should myself ask to go under you in any capacity down to and including a sergeant; but at my age, and condition, I suppose that I could not do work you would consider worth while in the fighting line (my only line) in a lower grade than brigade commander."[11]

Ted Jr. and Archie embarked for France, Ted as a major and Archie as a second lieutenant. Ted's elevated rank triggered rumors of favoritism and gibes that "there ought to be a rule that no reserve officer shall be appointed to command a battalion without the consent of his parents or guardian."[12]

When American doughboys paraded down Parisian boulevards on July 4, 1917, Ted and Archie marched with them—and heard French crowds shout, "Teddy! Teddy! Long Live the Teddies!" (as the French dubbed the long-awaited doughboys).[13] Among the enthusiastic throngs was TR's friend (and Edith's distant cousin), the expatriate American novelist Edith Wharton. She thought the arriving Americans were a "really splendid" sight and invited the two Roosevelts to enjoy her hospitality.[14] Soon Ted and Archie would lead the first American raid on a German position.[15]

Kermit, meanwhile, enlisted as an honorary captain in the British army, contracted malaria while passing through Italy,[16] and faced the Ottoman Turks in Mesopotamia, initially with the machine-gun corps and later with army transport.

Quentin departed not to Canada for aerial training but to nearby Mineola,[17] unleashing practice "bombs" of flowers and paper upon his parental lawn. Dick Derby received a major's commission in the Medical Officers Reserve Corps.[18] Edith Roosevelt's younger sister, fifty-two-year-old Miss Emily Tyler Carow, a longtime expatriate, volunteered as a Red Cross nurse on the Italian front.[19] TR's sister Corinne's sons, Theodore and Monroe Robinson, served with the artillery and the infantry, respectively.

And TR did not.

Before America fought Germany, it fought itself. On July 2, 1917, rioting rocked East St. Louis, Illinois, where white union members (and just plain racists), incensed by the recent influx of blacks from Mississippi and East

Tennessee—and fearful of their impact on local labor conditions—invaded black neighborhoods. Officially eight whites and thirty-nine blacks died. Unofficial estimates of African-American fatalities varied from one hundred to even double that. Six thousand blacks were left homeless.

Roosevelt's record on racial issues was confusingly mixed. An enthusiastic admirer of Abraham Lincoln, he proudly characterized his Georgia-born mother as "entirely 'unreconstructed' to the day of her death."[20]

True, he had invited Booker T. Washington to the White House in October 1901 and provided James Weldon Johnson, author of "Lift Every Voice and Sing" (as well as the less well-recalled "You're All Right, Teddy"), with a pair of consular appointments.[21] But he had outraged blacks with his handling of August 1906's Brownsville Incident.

At a 1905 New York Lincoln Day dinner speech titled "The Negro Problem," while declaring that "all men should stand on an equal footing as regards civil privileges," he declaimed against any "social intermingling of the races; a question which must, of course, be left to the people of each community to settle for themselves," averring that "race purity must be maintained."[22]

He blew hot—and then decidedly frigid—regarding black appointments in the South. And while in April 1906 he assured author Owen Wister that he did not "know a white man of the South who is as good a man as Booker Washington,"[23] he agreed with him that "as a race and a mass [Negros] are altogether inferior to whites." In 1910, following Jack Johnson's victory over James J. "The Great White Hope" Jeffries, he joined in the racially charged fight to outlaw not only the interstate transport of prizefight films but also all professional boxing.[24] Outraged by William Howard Taft's control of southern black delegates at 1912's GOP convention, he banned them from his resultant Progressive gathering.[25]

Yet it must also be admitted that TR never begrudged a black person of talent and determination advancement in any profession. In his "Negro Problem" address, he approvingly quoted North Carolina Episcopal bishop Robert Strange, who answered the question of "What should the white men of the South do for the negro?" thusly:

*They must give him a free hand, a fair field, and a cordial godspeed,
the two races working together for their mutual benefit and for the
development of our common country. He must have liberty, equal
opportunity to make his living, to earn his bread, to build his home.
He must have justice, equal rights, and protection before the law.*

*He must have the same political privileges; the suffrage should be
based on character and intelligence for white and black alike. He must
have the same public advantages of education; the public schools are
for all the people, whatever their color or condition. The white men of
the South should give hearty and respectful consideration to the exceptional men of the negro race, to those who have the character, the ability and the desire to be lawyers, physicians, teachers, preachers, leaders
of thought and conduct among their own men and women. We should
give them cheer and opportunity to gratify every laudable ambition,
and to seek every innocent satisfaction among their own people.[26]*

Or, as he wrote Lyman Abbott the previous July, "I would not be
willing to die for what I regard as the untrue abstract statement that all
men are in all respects equal, and are all alike entitled to the same power;
but I would be quite willing to die . . . for the proposition that each man
has certain rights which no other man should be allowed to take away
from him."[27]

"Ugh!" he wrote Columbia University's Brander Matthews in 1913.
"There is no more puzzling problem in this country than the problem of
color. It is not as urgent, or as menacing, as other problems but it seems
more utterly insoluble. The trouble is that the conflict in many of its
phases is not between right and wrong, but between two rights."[28]

In February 1916, when Theodore and Edith sailed for the Caribbean, Edith devoured a 1912 study of American race relations, *Le Negro
aux États-Unis* (*The Negro in the United States*), penned by a Roosevelt
family friend, the South Carolina–born but now Paris-based journalist
Warrington Dawson, and presenting the usual southern case for Recon-
struction, the first Ku Klux Klan, and racial segregation. To Dawson she

soon wrote, "Alas, we can't send every negro in the U.S. to Africa & I suppose could we do so we would still have some moral responsibility towards them. I have stopped at nine of the West India islands and cannot feel that their method is any better than ours. I can't begin to write all I have seen and heard but am still firmly convinced that any mixture of races is an unmitigated evil."[29]

That having been said, while Edith or Theodore may or may not have condoned race "mixture," neither could stomach lynching or rioting—and East St. Louis's violence soon triggered a volcanic TR reaction. On Friday evening, July 6, 1917, the Friends of the New Russia hosted a massive rally in honor of Russia's nascent revolutionary, pre-Bolshevik government, featuring Roosevelt, American Federation of Labor president Samuel Gompers, various Russian dignitaries, the Russian Symphony Orchestra, and actual film of the recent revolution. All aimed to bolster democracy in Russia—and, more important, to keep that beleaguered nation in the Allied camp.

That was the idea.

Another idea haunted TR.

Two mornings previously, he had addressed a Fourth of July celebration in Queens and interjected a stinging denunciation of the violence in East St. Louis. A concern for justice may have inspired him—so might mere politics. East St. Louis was represented by Republican congressman William Rodenberg. During 1916's elections, Democrats accused Rodenberg of encouraging a "colonization scheme"[30] of first his district and then all Illinois through massive organized voter fraud (Illinois required a one-year residency to vote). In early November 1916, Attorney General Thomas W. Gregory warned of the recent influx of sixty thousand blacks northward in just three months, "a number of [whom] have registered in violation of [the law] and have expressed the intention of voting in these states."[31] Assistant Attorney General Frank C. Dailey warned of a "gigantic vote fraud conspiracy,"[32] alleging, "More than 300,000 Negroes of votable ages have been brought from the south and colonized in Illinois, Indiana, and Ohio. This colonization has been going on for eighteen months."[33]

Two days later, Woodrow Wilson, using language suspiciously close to Dailey's allegations of "conspiracies to intimidate employes [*sic*],"[34] warned of "industrial coercion"[35] and of the work of "conscienceless agents of the sinister forces"[36] to steal the election. The *Chicago Herald* warned, "60,000 Bogus Votes for Hughes; Plot to Steal Doubtful States."[37]

Republicans saw it differently. Republican National Committee Chairman William Willcox angrily denounced the administration's charges as "a bold attempt to disenfranchise negro voters by the Democrats who have long been expert in the disenfranchisement of negroes in the South."[38]

Having so sown, Democrats possessed little inclination to reflect upon the deadly crop others now reaped. And Woodrow Wilson maintained an awkward silence on the incident despite numerous appeals from the press and the black community.[39]

At Carnegie Hall, an uproarious crowd greeted Roosevelt, ostensibly there to welcome Russia's new ambassador, Boris Bakhmeteff. Instead, as the *New York Tribune* recorded, TR "shouted in his most piercing voice,"[40]

> *Before we do justice to others, it behooves us to do justice within our borders, I refer to . . . a race riot for which, so far as I can see, there was no provocation.*
>
> *It behooves us to express our condemnation of acts that give the lie to our laws, and to say that it is impossible that there should be justification for mob violence. It is our duty to demand that the governmental authorities shall use with ruthless severity every power at their command to punish those guilty of murder, whether committed by whites against blacks or by blacks against whites.*[41]

Gompers followed TR but, before commending the new Russia, felt compelled to answer TR's comments—since East St. Louis's racial acrimony was tied not only to partisan politics but also to issues of unionism and the hiring of cheap black labor to replace whites.

"I join with you," said Gompers, "and with him," here turning to TR, "in expressing my detestation of the brutalities committed in the East St.

Louis race riots. However, I wish that I had with me a telegram received only last night from Victor Olander, secretary of the Illinois Federation of Labor, which explains the real cause of the trouble."

To Gompers, the blame ultimately lay with local management, "who were bringing the colored men from the South . . . to undermine the white workers. . . . [T]housands were brought in and had not a place where to lay their heads. The whole thing was an exercise of tyrannical power like that which existed in old Russia."[42]

"At first," reported the *Brooklyn Eagle*, "the Colonel seemed to regard the words of Mr. Gompers as innocuous enough, but as [he] proceeded with his 'explanation' the Colonel became more and more wrought up and, leaping to his feet, asked permission to say one word more. His words issued from him like molten lava from a volcano."[43]

Mayor John Purroy Mitchel struggled to introduce Ambassador Bakhmeteff, but TR waved "a programme in his right hand and obviously boiling with suppressed feeling . . . [bit] off each word as if it were a soft nosed bullet."[44]

"May I say another word?" he sharply demanded. "I am not willing that a meeting called to commemorate the birth of a democracy in Russia shall even seem to have given any approval or accepted any apology for the brutal infamy imposed on negroes, on colored men."

Audience members sprang from their seats. The *New York Sun* thought they yelled and screamed in TR's favor. The *Tribune* disagreed: "A shout went up, but its tone was different from the applause which had greeted the other addresses. It was high and angry [with] audible 'Boos.'"[45]

"Justice," TR plowed onward, "is not merely words. It is to be translated into living acts, and how can we praise the people of Russia if we by explanation, silence or evasion apologise for murdering the helpless." Here there were cheers. "In the past I have listened to the same form of excuse from the Russian autocracy for the pogroms inflicted on the Jews. Shall we by silence acquiesce in this amazing apology for the murder of men, women and children in our own country?"[46]

The *Sun* noted,

There was noise all over the hall, but it was all in the Colonel's favor. Hitting the speaker's table with his fist after every word, he said: "I'll do everything for the laboring man except that which is wrong, and that I will not do for any man or cause."

"I care not a snap of my finger"—here the Colonel walked over to Mr. Gompers and shook his fist within a foot of the Gompers nose— "for a telegram from the head of the strongest labor union in Illinois. This thing took place in a Northern State, where the whites outnumber the negroes twenty to one, and if in that city white men cannot protect their rights by their votes against an insignificant minority and have to murder women and children, then the state that sent Abraham Lincoln to the Presidency must bow its head in shame."[47]

TR stood barely five feet, eight inches. The roly-poly sixty-seven-year-old Gompers measured just five-foot-four.[48] He bounded from his chair brandishing his own fist at the former president. A battle royal loomed, threatening to engulf not merely Gompers and Roosevelt but also the rally's five thousand attendees.

"Why don't you accuse after the investigation?" Gompers demanded, retaking his seat.

TR ("burning red and waving his arms up and down"[49]) advanced toward him: "Mr. Gompers, why don't I accuse afterward? I'll answer now, when murder is to be answered!"[50]

Pandemonium erupted. Finally TR continued, "I will go to any extreme to bring justice to the laboring man, but when there is murder I will put him down."[51]

Gompers attempted to rise, but others pushed him back down.[52] And "with that," noted the *Chicago Tribune*, "the Colonel brought down on Mr. Gompers' shoulder his open left hand which he had raised above his head. At this juncture many of the men on the platform leaped to their feet and there was a storm of hisses, cheers, and 'boos' from all parts of the house."[53]

Added the obviously amazed *New York Times*, "And then [TR] took his seat, while the crowd raged at him or at Mr. Gompers, with groups downstairs howling at groups upstairs, women shrieking and waving their arms, sailors shouting at men in boxes opposite or in the dress circle above. . . . All over the house people were standing up, yelling outbursts which were indistinguishable in the general din, but as Mayor Mitchel tried to quiet them the volume of sound rolled higher."[54]

A "babel of indistinguishable sounds" enveloped the hall, mourned the *Sun*. "Whether most of the shrieks of disapproval were directed at Col. Roosevelt or the labor leader was impossible to tell. Apparently some of the hullabaloo was meant for both. Through it all, however, ran a strong current of handclapping and cheering for the Colonel, to whom men yelled as if they thought they were watching a prize fight."[55] The event concluded, two city police inspectors escorted TR to his car. Amazed reporters demanded a statement.

"I meant everything I said," snapped the Colonel. "I stand by it."

"How about the slap on Mr. Gompers' shoulder?"

"That wasn't a hard blow," TR contended. "It was only a gentle touch. I did that to emphasize my point. I have no personal grievance against Mr. Gompers."[56]

"For a moment," noted the *Sun*, "it seemed he would go back to look for Mr. Gompers, but [Mayor Mitchel's secretary] Theodore Rousseau and other friends prevailed upon him to drive away."[57]

"I wish I could get my hands on him!" TR smoldered before motoring off. "I can scarcely keep my hands off him."[58]

Yes, something strange was happening—and not merely at Carnegie Hall.

The Colonel drew ever closer to his party's Old Guard; yet his domestic policies—overshadowed though they might be by the war— still inched steadily leftward. To daughter Ethel one evening he confided his thoughts on social issues. She shared them with her husband: "After declaring that all men are equal we cannot expect that permanently the 3% will own the property & have the power: the 97% will become restless, are restless. And perhaps the best way to meet it is that the 3%

recognize the claim of all the others—& give them sickness insurance & old age pensions & a share in the stock & profits etc."[59]

Yet he was no Socialist. He hated Socialists.

Power, not policies, divided his camp from theirs. Beyond that, they were not of his sort. TR shared little power with even his fellow aristocrats. He would not share any with mere Socialists.

No, not at all—and, unquestionably, not with a war on. In 1914, European Socialists largely deserted pacifist internationalism for militant nationalism. American Socialists held firm, blasting America's war as one fought between "predatory capitalists." In June 1917, federal authorities arrested former Socialist presidential candidate Eugene V. Debs on ten counts of sedition—for opposing wartime conscription. In New York, Lower East Side Socialist leader Morris Hillquit boasted that he wanted no part of purchasing Liberty Bonds to finance a capitalist war.[60] Authorities indicted Milwaukee Socialist congressman Victor Berger for Espionage Act violations.

John Purroy Mitchel reluctantly sought reelection in 1917. Four years earlier, TR had entreated Mitchel, hitherto the Democrat president of the board of aldermen, to run for mayor as a "fusion" candidate. He triumphed over Charles Whitman (then district attorney and, of course, an actual Republican) to secure the GOP endorsement.[61] With Progressive Party support (though no formal endorsement), Mitchel won November's general election by the largest popular margin in the history of consolidated New York.

Mitchel offered the police commissionership to George Perkins. Perkins declined it but later accepted the chairmanship of a blue-ribbon committee investigating high wartime food prices.[62] TR, in turn, praised Mitchel for providing voters with "the best administration the city has ever had."[63] But efficiency only goes so far in overcoming monumental political ineptness. TR privately condemned Mitchel's "arrogance . . . his being out of touch with the man in the street."[64] A modern historian assessed him as "a one-of-a-kind amalgam of urban visionary and priggish dolt."[65]

In 1913, William Randolph Hearst had ardently supported Mitchel. By 1917, he merely derided him and seemed on the verge of running himself. But powerful elements within Tammany Hall—Al Smith included—

not only opposed Hearst but also hated him.[66] Eventually, Tammany and Hearst united behind a challenger, a remarkably unimpressive Kings County judge named John Francis "Red Mike" Hylan (so dubbed for his hair, not his politics). Morris Hillquit ran on the Socialist ticket.

Against such competition, TR gladly stuck with "The Boy Mayor" Mitchel, an early graduate of the Plattsburgh camp (Archie Roosevelt had escorted him to the train station where he received his pup tent[67]) and a foursquare advocate for Preparedness.

"A Vote for Mayor Mitchel is a Vote for the U.S.A.,"[68] declared a Mitchel campaign pamphlet.

At the Brooklyn Academy of Music, Rabbi Stephen Wise, no longer so pacifist as in 1916, warned a three-thousand-person audience that in order to keep the city from becoming "the American suburb of Berlin, you have got to vote for Mitchel."[69]

Yet John Purroy Mitchel was too foursquare for Preparedness in a city still featuring large amounts of German, Irish, and Jewish antiwar sentiment. As Hearst's *New York American* gibed, "What impression does Mr. Mitchel bring to your minds when he puts himself up on the billboards dressed in [Plattsburgh camp] khaki? What would you think of yourself if you had your picture posted everywhere in a khaki uniform trying to get votes posing as a hero? He wraps puttees around his thin legs, buttons on his person a khaki suit that looks like cotton goods wrapped around a piece of kindling wood, tops off the magnificent war-like picture with a slouch hat, and . . . says, 'Vote for me, I'm a hero. Don't you see my picture in khaki on the billboards?'"[70]

On Monday, October 29, TR addressed three three-thousand-person crowds for Mitchel, speaking twice in Harlem and then moving on to Park Slope's Prospect Hall to address Brooklyn Scandinavians. At East 126th Street's Harlem River Casino, a Socialist heckler awaited his arrival. TR, reported the *Herald*, "walked over toward him, shaking his finger and prepared to take care of him."[71] Two men rushed to eject the troublemaker. TR shooed them away—he wanted his antagonist to hear him excoriate Hillquit as "the Hun inside our gates."[72]

More Socialists ambushed the Colonel (and Mitchel—and Harlem's Abyssinian Baptist Church pastor, Adam Clayton Powell Sr.) at their next stop, before "3,000 cheering negroes"[73] at West 135th Street's Palace Casino. Harlem's pioneering African-American weekly newspaper, the *New York Age*, reported,

These rowdies, who espouse the cause of the Socialist candidate, made themselves obnoxious by hissing and frequently interrupting the speakers, and had not three-fourths of the audience been decidedly friendly to . . . [f]usion the disturbance makers would have broken up the meeting, which they seem bent on doing.

Even Theodore Roosevelt, . . . the most fearless champion in America in demanding that the Negro be given a square deal, was insulted by these ruffians, [following] a programme . . . arranged some hours before. They insulted everybody, even the prominent colored ministers who spoke.

This element was made up of negroes who are seeking to secure a real democracy in this country by advocating violence and who are opposed to the right of free speech and their anarchistic tendencies were fully emphasized during the evening, making a powerful impression on the minds of those who believe in law and order.[74]

One man's free speech is another man's sedition.

A sizable segment of the population now considered the Colonel's anti-Wilson drumbeat unpatriotic and seditious. Missouri senator "Gumshoe Bill" Stone denounced TR as "the most seditious man of consequence in the country . . . whether willingly or out of sheer madness the most potent agent the Kaiser has in America."[75]

If TR could be accused of sedition, who might not? The very night before TR invaded Harlem, antiwar Cincinnati minister Herbert S. Bigelow, a Socialist, was kidnapped, beaten, and literally horsewhipped in nearby Newport, Kentucky.[76] On Election Eve, Monday, November 1, 1917, in presumably more sophisticated Manhattan, the Metropolitan Opera not only banned stage productions in German but also dismissed two performers bearing an "avowedly pro-German attitude."[77] Meanwhile, the Boston Symphony Orchestra's renowned German-born conductor, Dr. Karl Muck, faced withering criticism ("a creature of Germany and a dangerous enemy alien"[78]) for ignoring a request to include "The

Star-Spangled Banner." Said TR, "I think that if he will not play 'The Star-Spangled Banner,' he ought to be interned."[79] In March 1918, Muck (actually a Swiss national) indeed was.[80]

That Election Eve, fifty thousand John Purroy Mitchel partisans processed in five separate torchlight parades, featuring "the blare of a hundred or more brass bands,"[81] all heading toward Madison Square Garden for one great, last-minute gesture. TR (a late arrival, having just also spoken in Astoria, Queens) personally commanded the contingent advancing down Second Avenue.

He who would command a division on the western front barely made it through Midtown East. "The marchers became excited," noted the *Herald*, "and the organizations, moving in opposite directions, became entangled in a mass that held up traffic for more than fifteen minutes and almost exhausted their leaders before the jam was straightened out and the procession, in single colums [*sic*], began again its march behind Mr. Roosevelt's automobile toward the Garden."[82]

There, TR addressed matters military not municipal, of patriotism not potholes. "The American pacifist," he thundered, "has been the great ally of the German militarists. If we don't fight the war through to a successful conclusion, if we let it be a draw . . . your children and my children will have to fight here beside their ruined hearthstones in the end to defend themselves."[83]

Respectful silence enveloped the hall, followed by a ripple of applause. Suddenly "a piping, rasping voice"[84] in the second gallery interrupted: "Why don't you go over, then, and fight? You go ahead over."[85]

"Instantly, the great building was in an uproar," reported the *Herald*.

Flushed with anger, his jaws snapping and his eyes flashing the acceptance of the challenge which his voice could not carry over the din raised by the audience, Mr. Roosevelt pleaded for quiet.

Mr. Roosevelt's arms were outstretched as he futilely implored the crowd to let him answer. Charles E. Hughes, who presided at the meeting, was pounding his gavel for quiet which did not come. Thousands in the audience stood on their chairs and waved flags, one of which had been given to every one who entered the hall.[86]

"He [Roosevelt] wants to go over there!" a woman shouted.

"Just wait a minute," bellowed TR. "I didn't catch the question. You asked why I didn't go over there? Wait."

The crowd, the *Herald* reported, thundered "its applause in a manner that again brought virtually every person in the building to his feet shouting. Confusion was everywhere."

"They wouldn't let you go over," a man yelled. TR grinned broadly.

"Wait a minute, friend," the Colonel begged his audience, "wait a minute. Let me answer. Don't put him out. Let me answer him. Now, wait a minute please! I understand the gentleman to ask why I don't go over there; you have got to ask somebody else that question."

Twelve thousand voices drowned him out.

"I did my level best."

Again came a deafening roar.

"I asked not only to go over, but I came with a hundred thousand men in my hands to help."

"Here's one of them, Teddy," a doughboy in the audience shouted, literally waving the Stars and Stripes above his head. Another ovation roared through the Garden.

"Wait a minute," TR pled. "I found that as I was concerned, this was a very exclusive war. And I was blackballed by the Committee on Admissions. But I will tell you, you man over there [here he pointed an accusing finger at the heckling Socialist], I have sent over my four sons!"

That blew the roof off Madison Square Garden. "Shouts to have the socialist put out of the place," noted the *Herald*, "became so multiplied that a squad of policemen and detectives hurried up to the gallery where the offender sat."

"I have sent over—" Roosevelt continued, barely heard above the tumult.

"Let that man stay here and listen," TR insisted. "I have sent over four boys, and each of whose life I care a thousand times more than I care for my own if you can understand that, you man over there!"[87]

Yes, Colonel Roosevelt indeed cared for them.

And would soon have reason to fear for them even more.

"Everybody works, but father"

THEODORE ROOSEVELT, CHARLES EVANS HUGHES, AND EVEN TR'S 1904 opponent, Alton B. Parker[1]—so many of the best people—supported Mayor John Purroy Mitchel on that Monday evening of November 1, 1917. So did William Howard Taft, Elihu Root,[2] and 1916 gubernatorial rivals Charles Whitman[3] and Samuel Seabury.[4] After all, who else stood between city hall and "Hearst, Hylan, the Hollenzollerns, and the Hapsburgs"?[5]

"Red Mike" Hylan maintained a maddening silence during the campaign. Morris Hillquit turned his guns on TR, whom he termed "the most serious menace to American Democracy."

"It is not socialism," he charged, "but Rooseveltism that is the true enemy within the gates."[6]

On Election Day, November 2, Tammany's Hylan crushed Mitchel by a two-to-one margin. "The Boy Mayor" barely garnered ten thousand votes more than Hillquit. He finished third in the Bronx and barely ahead of Hillquit in Brooklyn and Queens.[7]

And spent a million dollars doing so—a phenomenal $8.60 per vote.[8]

Which was horrible enough. But antiwar Socialists reelected antiwar Lower East Side congressman Meyer London and sent eleven party members to the New York State Assembly and seven more to the city council.[9] Worse, Mitchel faltered in that September's Republican primary, narrowly beaten by an obscure former Manhattan state senator. A week later, TR (who had predicted that Mitchel would not even have a primary[10]) confided to O. K. Davis, "The direct primary . . . initiative, referendum, and recall . . . should all be exceptional remedies. It should be possible to invoke them in exceptional cases to control the boss and the machines; but they simply do damage if habitually invoked."[11]

Or when they failed to support his own favored candidates.

The world was moving very fast now. The day following Mitchel's inglorious November rout, American doughboys in France finally saw combat.

Ted Jr. and Archie reached France that June, as did Ted's twenty-eight-year-old wife, Eleanor, who volunteered with the YMCA. TR opposed any female Roosevelts serving in France. He strongly resisted Eleanor's going, as she was the mother of a five-year-old girl and two boys, a three-year-old and a one-and-a-half-year-old. She went anyway.[12]

Princess Alice participated in the war effort—though in her own distinctive style. Remaining in Washington, she dabbled in wartime volunteer work ("I dished out ice cream to soldiers coming through and things like that, but nothing very serious"[13]) but soon wearied of it.

In summer 1917, she enthusiastically joined in some high-profile counterespionage—or, as she gleefully put it, the chance "to look over transoms and peep through keyholes."[14] Forty-seven-year-old War Industries Board chairman Bernard Baruch's latest extramarital fling involved glamorous twenty-one-year-old New York banking heiress Eugenie Mary "May" Ladenburg. Intelligence officers suspected her (without much good reason) of relaying Baruch's pillow talk to agents of the Central Powers. They recruited Alice not only to recommend the best locations within Ladenburg's M Street home for primitive bugging devices but also to accompany "three or four absolutely charming"[15] agents in surreptitiously planting them. Cousin Franklin Roosevelt had prepared false naval intelligence documents for Baruch to pass on to Miss Ladenburg and now joined Alice in eavesdropping on the unsuspecting lovers from the vantage point of a nearby stable. Little came of the episode, though the gossip-loving Alice later pronounced her "most disgraceful" adventure to be "sheer rapture."[16]

Kermit, his father's companion in Africa and the Amazon, was always a bit of a morose odd duck—not to mention an alcoholic. Edith once described him—her blondest offspring—as "the one with the white head and the black heart."[17]

Far less eager for combat than either Ted or Archie, Kermit nonetheless received an "honorary" captaincy in the British army ("Wouldn't it be wonderful to be at the fall of Constantinople?"[18]) and headed for action in Turkish Mesopotamia. By spring 1918, he had transferred to an American Expeditionary Force artillery unit. The previous November, Dick Derby had sailed for France to serve with the American Medical Corps.[19]

"There is much more of me in the war, now," TR unburdened himself to his friend, Ferdinand Cowle Iglehart, "than though I were there myself, for these boys are my heart of hearts, they are the life of my life."[20]

The septuagenarian Iglehart had never seen Roosevelt "so serious and it was the first time he ever looked to me as though he wanted to cry; his words were spoken with such deep emotion."[21]

"Colonel," Iglehart tried reassuring him, "we know that the boys will do brave fighting and we will hope and pray that God will send them back to you."

"It is my constant prayer to God," TR responded, "that, in His mercy, He will spare them, use them in the battle and then let them come home to us again." He paused before continuing, "It is not likely that all will come back from such a deadly war, but we will have to leave them in the hands of a good God, Who doeth all things well."[22]

The popular novelist and short story writer Mary Roberts Rinehart witnessed similar anguish. She and TR both kept quarters at Manhattan's Hotel Langdon, and he would periodically visit for company. She had interviewed him during 1916's convention season but now found

little left of the boyishness which had [then] characterized him. . . . We did not agree on many things, and he worked himself into a very real rage at those times. But in the main we talked of the war. One day he had a letter from young Ted, in France; it was a fine letter, full of fighting spirit, but his men needed shoes. I gathered that they also needed many other things, but shoes seem to remain in my memory. And I think I am correct when I say that the Colonel had sent a check to buy shoes for those men.

But much deeper things were troubling him. He knew, and I knew, that his boys would try to live up to his own fighting reputa-

tion, and that this endeavor might kill them. That must have been a bitter thought. . . .

Sometimes, however, he was very cheerful. One morning before I was dressed he rapped at my sitting room door, and brought in his sister [presumably Corinne] to see me. . . . Always I had admired him, but now I began to feel a great affection for him. He was solid and fine and substantial.[23]

TR worried most of all for Quentin, his youngest—young enough so that on his last night at Sagamore Hill before shipping off for Europe, his mother literally tucked her baby in for the night.[24]

Alice traveled from Washington to see him off. She saw how hard his leaving was on both their mother and their father. "The old Lion perisheth for lack of prey," she recollected from the Book of Job, "and the stout lion's whelps are scattered abroad."[25]

"It was hard when Quentin went," Edith conceded. "But you can't bring up boys to be eagles, and expect them to turn out sparrows."[26]

In most public moments, TR now played the part less of the loving father than of the stern household god of war. When *The Outlook*'s Lawrence F. Abbott protested to the Roosevelts that perchance Quentin might have better remained among his classmates, the Colonel coldly retorted, "I would not have stopped him if I could, and I could not have stopped him if I would. The more American boys from nineteen to twenty-one join the army the better it is for the country. To take them out of our civil life entails the smallest economic loss upon the nation, and because of their elasticity and powers of recuperation they are its greatest military asset."[27]

Quentin was indeed a mere Harvard sophomore—and a rather undistinguished one at that. His older brothers were already men of business—of sorts. Ted surprised just about everyone by taking a menial $6-per-week wool-sorting position in a small-town Connecticut carpet mill. Later, he peddled bonds in New York, learning the hard way that his father's "malefactors of great wealth" rhetoric earned his sons few friends—or clients—on Wall Street.[28] Archie survived expulsion from Groton to graduate from Harvard but followed Ted's rather halting footsteps into the carpet industry. Kermit was a banker in Buenos Aires.

But beyond such matters was Quentin's questionable physical fitness. He longed to be an aviator—a dashing, devil-may-care knight of the air. However, he suffered from poor eyesight—and a bad back incurred in July 1913, when a pack horse rolled over him during a Grand Canyon rock slide.[29] Memorizing the eye chart advanced him past the former barrier.[30] But not the latter.

Quentin's older brothers had already wed: Archie in his hurried April 1917 ceremony; Ted, in June 1910, to New York socialite Eleanor Butler Alexander (the church filled with an ample quotient of uniformed ex–Rough Riders[31]); and Kermit, in June 1914, to Belle Wyatt Willard, daughter of the American ambassador to Madrid. Quentin left behind not a wife but rather a fiancée—the barely twenty-year-old Flora Payne "Foufie" Whitney.

Roosevelt-Whitney family relations needed work. Quentin's father famously excoriated the "malefactors of great wealth"; Flora's father, Harry Payne Whitney, was richer than Croesus—or at least wealthier than all the many Roosevelts put together. Her mother, Gertrude Vanderbilt Whitney, was the great-granddaughter of Commodore Cornelius Vanderbilt. Her great uncle, Oliver Hazard Payne, had helped found both Standard Oil and United States Steel. Worse, Flora's family were Democrats. Her aunt Dorothy Payne Whitney's husband, Willard Straight, bankrolled the pro-Wilson, now anti-TR *New Republic*. Flora's great-grandfather Henry Payne had served as Democratic U.S. senator from Ohio, her paternal grandfather, William C. Whitney, as Grover Cleveland's secretary of the navy, sharing his conservative "Bourbon" Democrat politics. Most pointedly, had death not claimed William Whitney in February 1904, he most certainly would have sought to personally oust Theodore Roosevelt from the White House. It could not have improved either TR's or Edith's mood that Flora's mother, an accomplished sculptor, had in 1916 famously allowed herself to be painted wearing—gasp!—pants.

Yet, though TR eyed the Whitneys with more than a little suspicion (and vice versa), since 1914 he possessed no great compunction about accepting a $25,000-per-year salary from *Metropolitan Magazine*—owned by none other than Harry Payne Whitney.[32] In any case, love finds its own way, and when Quentin proposed in May 1917,[33] Flora quickly accepted—but did take more time to inform her family.[34] TR soon resolved his own uncertainties ("After some hesitation and misgiving, Mother and I have become much pleased"[35]) and found Flora to be "a dear."[36]

By now, TR was returning to normal, jokingly mourning his noncombatant status ("Everybody works, but father"[37]) and protesting for the umpteenth instance that his useful public life was *finie*. In September 1917, he wrote Quentin,

> *I hope to continue earning a good salary until all of you come home, so that I can start Archie and you all right. Then I intend to retire. An elderly male Cassandra has-been can do a little, a very little, towards waking the people now and then; but undue persistency in issuing Jeremiads does no real good and makes the Jeremiah an awful nuisance. . . .*
>
> *I make a few speeches; I loathe making them; among other reasons because I always fear to back up the Administration too strongly lest it turn another somersault.[38]*

That same month he returned to Kansas City. He did not back up the administration. With Leonard Wood in tow, he roused a boisterous throng of twenty-five thousand at an amusement park amphitheater—plus another twenty thousand just beyond. They cheered for twenty-five minutes before the mayor could introduce him. Fireworks blazed his image in the sky. He attacked Robert La Follette ("the worst enemy that democracy has now alive"[39]). He reiterated warnings of German—or even Japanese—invasion:

> *If at this moment, while we are still helpless, France and England were defeated, the German fleet would be at our doors in a fortnight and an army of conquest would have landed here within a month. . . . [I]f Germany could land a single small army of 60,000 men in this country we would be wholly unable to match it for we have neither artillery nor airplanes that could be put against them. If at this*

moment our allies suddenly made peace, we would be a helpless prey to
Germany or any other first-class European or Asiatic military power.[40]

Enemies foreign.

Enemies domestic.

The San Francisco that Charles Evans Hughes blundered into in mid-August 1916 was a seething cauldron of labor unrest. Barely a month previously, 51,319 persons, 52 bands, and 2,134 organizations had marched in the city's Preparedness Day Parade—an event as much about supporting the local antiunion "Open Shop" movement as sustaining Preparedness. Local unions boycotted it. Unionists and radicals threatened it. "If I were in a heroic mood like Roosevelt," a prominent Socialist warned at a massive rally, "I might advise somebody to shoot in the back of the neck, or some other spot in the back, every representative of a corrupt munition maker or corporation in the parade."[41]

Barely a half hour after the parade kicked off, a suitcase filled with explosives and shrapnel detonated along its route. Ten died. Sixty more suffered injuries.

District Attorney Charles M. "Legs" Fickert obtained convictions for two union-organizer Socialists, Tom Mooney and Warren Billings (both previously arrested for dynamite possession), but soon faced charges of manufacturing evidence and suppressing testimony—as well as a December 1917 recall election. Leading the charge against him were *San Francisco Bulletin* editor Fremont Older and San Francisco sugar magnate Rudolph Spreckels, who in 1906 had convinced TR to lend federal prosecutor Francis J. Heney to the city to cleanse its rampant corruption. "You are in a fight for plain decency, for the plain democracy of the plain people, who believe in honesty and in fair dealing as between man and man," Roosevelt wired Spreckels in 1908. "Do not become disheartened. Keep up the fight."[42]

In 1909, Fickert defeated Heney for the district attorneyship and settled into protecting San Francisco's grafters and vice lords. Nonetheless, in September 1917, *Pittsburgh Leader* publisher Alexander Moore, a prominent 1912 Progressive, secured TR's intervention on Fickert's behalf. Roosevelt telegrammed Fickert,

The issue between you and your opponents is that between patriotism and anarchy. . . . [A]ll who directly or indirectly assail you for any such reason should be promptly deprived of citizenship.

Anarchist bomb throwers are murderers, worse than ordinary murderers, and all men who sympathize with them or give them aid and support are enemies of the country and should at least be disenfranchised and furthermore punished to any extent possible.[43]

The Colonel's endorsement stunned many of his longtime California allies. Initially, they imagined it to be a hoax. It wasn't. Older, Spreckels, and former Northern California congressman William Kent (by now a Wilson appointee to the Tariff Commission) telegrammed him in protest, arguing that none of the accused were anarchists and that two other suspects indicted by Fickert were quickly found not guilty.

TR remained unmoved. "I am sorry to say," he answered Older, "that all the information I have is to the effect that the excellent gentlemen connected with your league are being used simply as a shield behind which the enemies of Americanism, the friends of Germany, and the advocates of anarchy and disaster, can punish Mr. Fickert, because he had had the courage to attack the assassins who committed wholesale murder of innocent people with dynamite."[44]

Privately, he thought even less of Older, Kent, and Spreckels, confiding to another veteran Progressive, *Fresno Morning Republican* editor Chester H. Rowell,

It is quite impossible that any substantial injustice was done Mooney and Billings. . . . As for Fremont Older, Rudolph Spreckels and Willie Kent, not only do I regard their judgment as hopelessly unsound but I feel they have gradually grown to be downright sympathizers with anarchy and murder, and this to the extent in the case of Older at least of becoming an accessory to the gravest wrongdoing. . . . I feel that it is perfectly clear that Billings and Mooney were among those responsible for the bomb outrages. I am inclined to think that the verdicts are absolutely just, and I am certain that the evidence is such that would warrant and require the execution of both men under the procedure of martial law; and martial law is the proper way for dealing with outrages of this character when it proves impossible to get at the criminals under the ordinary process of civil law. . . .

If Billings and Mooney were not anarchists, were not bomb-throwers, were not murderers and were really entirely innocent, well-behaved, law-abiding men, then the Bolsheviki people at home and abroad would be utterly indifferent to their fate.[45]

Publicly, he doubled down, telegraphing that "all the opponents of law and order, all the pro-Germans and all the men against straight United States sentiment will be exultant if Mr. Fickert is recalled."[46]

Fickert coasted to victory. He wired TR, "Patriotism has triumphed over anarchy."[47]

Which did not end matters.

A former top assistant to Henry Stimson, Felix Frankfurter (enthusiastically for TR in 1912—"I was devoted to him"[48]), had by now moved on to serving as secretary and counsel of the President's Mediation Committee, probing wartime labor issues. At Wilson's personal behest, he investigated the Mooney case, which Wilson explained was "greatly disturbing to our allies, Russia [the new Kerensky government] and Italy."[49] Alarmed by TR's public endorsement of Fickert, Frankfurter—in conjunction with Chester Rowell[50]—wired his friend Emory Buckner (another Stimson protégé and Mayor Mitchel's 1917 campaign manager) to intercede with the Colonel:

VERY URGENT . . . EVIDENTLY SOMEONE HAS BEEN DRAWING ON TR'S GOOD NATURE AND PATRIOTISM TO GET HIM LINED UP IN THIS LOCAL FIGHT FOR HIS OWN SAKE HE OUGHT NOT TO MIX IN AT LONG RANGE BECAUSE IT MUDDIES THE WATER CONSIDERABLY FROM THE POINT OF VIEW OF CREATING THE RIGHT KIND OF WAR SPIRIT ON THE COAST PLEASE SEE THE COLONEL AND TELL HIM THAT I AM HERE INVESTIGATING THE SITUATION AND GOING TO THE BOTTOM OF THE THING THAT HE

*OUGHT NOT TO ALLOW HIMSELF TO BE MADE USE
OF AND THAT THE ISSUE IS NOT WHAT HE HAS BEEN
TOLD IT IS TO MAKE HIM REALIZE THAT I AM WRIT-
ING THIS SOLELY FROM THE POINT OF VIEW OF
THE MOST EFFECTIVE PROSECUTION OF THE AIMS
WHICH HE HAS MOSTLY IN MIND.*[51]

TR was not to be mollified.

Not improving his mood were anti-Preparedness sentiments exhibited by many of District Attorney Fickert's severest critics. Fremont Older,
for example, had declaimed, "Most men can remember when they thought
exactly as Colonel Roosevelt does about war. All boys who are worth their
salt want to be Indians, pirates, bandits, and soldiers. All boys who are
boys play at fighting. Most boys like to punch each other's faces. Sometimes the liking lasts over in mature life, but generally, with many other
traits of varying ethical value, it is lost. The trouble with Colonel Roosevelt
is that he never did lose his boyish pugnacity. He wouldn't grow up."[52]

Nor would he have been pleased by the fact that Frankfurter's sole
fellow staff member was attorney George Stanleigh Arnold, son-in-law
of William Kent.[53]

Immediately following Fickert's recall triumph, TR exploded at
Frankfurter, "You have taken, and are taking, on behalf of the Administration an attitude which seems to me to be fundamentally that of
Trotsky and the other Bolsheviki leaders in Russia: an attitude fraught
with mischief to this country."[54]

In addition, he charged,

*Fremont Older and the [Industrial Workers of the World (IWW)]
and the "direct action" anarchists and apologists for anarchy are never
concerned with justice. They are concerned solely in seeing one kind
of criminal escape justice, precisely as certain big business men and
certain corporation lawyers have in the past been concerned in seeing
another kind of criminal escape justice. . . .*

*It is the Hearsts and La Follettes, and [Victor] Bergers, and
Hillquits, the Fremont Olders and Amos Pinchots and Rudolph*

Spreckels who are the really grave danger. These are the Bolsheviki of America, and the Bolsheviki are just as bad as the Romanoffs, and are, at the moment, a greater menace to orderly freedom.[55]

Further enraging Roosevelt were Frankfurter's findings[56] regarding a fractious July 1917 IWW copper strike in Bisbee, Arizona, where armed vigilantes corralled 1,286 strikers, packed them into twenty-seven manure-caked cattle cars, and dumped them in the New Mexican desert. Prominent among the round-up's leaders was that "old friend" of the Colonel, Jack Greenway—a former Rough Rider and 1912 Progressive and most recently among the officer corps of Roosevelt's stillborn volunteer regiments. For good measure, his wife, Isabella, was a bridesmaid at Franklin and Eleanor's wedding.

"No human being," Roosevelt lectured Frankfurter, as he noted Greenway's role in the controversy, "in his senses doubts that the men deported from Bisbee were bent on destruction and murder."[57]

"I submit," Frankfurter countered, "it is not fair to your own standards of impartial justice, to your characteristic of being open-minded to facts, for you, some 3,000 miles away from the scene of action, away from an intimate study of the facts—the circumstances, the personnel, the industrial conflict. . . . I say it is not fair for you to pass judgment upon the deportations just on Jack Greenway's say-so, to brush aside the conclusions of a trained and impartial investigator whose desire and ability to obtain the truth, you have heretofore had many occasions never to find wanting."[58]

Fremont Older first assumed the bomber "must be Mooney."[59] He soon shifted to Mooney's spirited, though not always ethical, defense—for as one admirer pointed out, Older would "bribe or do anything for justice."[60] In November 1918, outraged by Older's methods (or merely his audacity), the two-decades younger, former Stanford football star Fickert accosted Older in the Palace Hotel lobby, cursed him, punched him in the face, knocked him to the floor, and proceeded to kick him as he lay helpless on the ground. Rumors—false—spread of Older's death.[61]

In the summer of 1918, *Bulletin* ownership, weary of Older's Tom Mooney crusade, stood ready to fire him after a quarter century of service. TR might have danced with joy—but for what followed.

William Randolph Hearst hired him to run his *San Francisco Call and Post*.[62]

⸺

TR turned on Felix Frankfurter.

But not on Madison Grant.

They were very old friends. When TR returned from the Badlands, the patrician conservationist Grant was among the handful of intimate friends invited to dine with him. In October 1916, Grant published his masterwork, *The Passing of the Great Race: Or, The Racial Basis of European History*, a purportedly "purely scientific"[63] examination of the dangers facing the Nordic race. To his theories of "race suicide" and the superiority of blond, blue-eyed Nordics over relatively deficient "Mediterraneans" and "Alpines" (Slavs), Grant inserted a generous eugenic component:

> *A rigid system of selection through the elimination of those who are weak or unfit—in other words social failures—would solve the whole question in one hundred years, as well as enable us to get rid of the undesirables who crowd our jails, hospitals, and insane asylums. The individual himself can be nourished, educated and protected by the community during his lifetime, but the state through sterilization must see to it that his line stops with him, or else future generations will be cursed with an ever increasing load of misguided sentimentalism. This is a practical, merciful, and inevitable solution of the whole problem, and can be applied to an ever widening circle of social discards, beginning always with the criminal, the diseased, and the insane, and extending gradually to types which may be called weaklings rather than defectives, and perhaps ultimately to worthless race types.*[64]

Provided a copy of *The Passing of the Great Race* by Grant, TR vowed "not just to read but to study it."[65]

Study it he did, writing Grant, "This book is a capital book; in purpose, in vision, in grasp of the facts our people most need to realize. It shows a habit of singularly serious thought on the subjects of most commanding importance. It shows a fine fearlessness in assailing the popular and mischievous sentimentalities and attractive and corroding falsehoods which few men dare assail. It is the work of an American scholar and gentleman; and all Americans should be sincerely grateful to you for writing it."[66]

Well, perhaps not all Americans.

"I would not have it otherwise"

THE BILL FOR NATIONAL GLORY QUICKLY CAME DUE. IN MID-AUGUST, Gussie Gardner—having resigned from Congress to take a colonelship with the 121st Infantry Regiment—died of pneumonia while training at Macon, Georgia's Camp Wheeler.

In late January 1918, Leonard Wood, hitherto exiled to commanding the 89th Infantry Division at Kansas's Camp Funston, toured Europe, indiscreetly bad-mouthing everyone from Wilson ("that rabbit"[1]) and Pershing on down. At Fère-en-Tardenois, near Soissons, he inspected a French field mortar. It exploded, propelling shrapnel into his arm. Wood recalled, "The explosion was so violent that it stunned us all for a time. My right sleeve was torn by the piece which killed the man on my right. One was disemboweled and another had an ugly wound from which he later died. I found the front of my coat covered with the brains of the man on my left."[2]

Wood insisted that the more seriously wounded be cared for first. Rather than take their place on any ambulance, he walked a mile to the nearest hospital. As Wood spent three weeks recuperating in Paris, Pershing simmered to Newton Baker, "[Wood] is very hostile to the administration and has criticized the War Department very freely. . . . His attitude is really one of disloyalty, in fact he is simply a political general and insubordination is a pronounced trait in his character. He is not in any sense true, and seemingly cannot control his overwhelming ambition for notoriety. . . . It would settle his pernicious activities if he could be retired and then recalled for some unimportant duty."[3]

Pershing invited Wood to his headquarters at Chaumont. Wood's tactless comments continued, and Pershing sent him packing stateside.[4]

In Washington, Wood only further infuriated the administration (if that were possible) with three and a half hours of negative testimony before the Senate Military Affairs Committee.

Wood had long endured bad health, having suffered a severe concussion while military governor of Santiago de Cuba. By 1910, he suffered a heavy limp, tremors, seizures, and a partly immobile left arm. That February, he underwent pioneering brain surgery. The seizures and tremors stopped. He regained full use of his arm. His limp improved, though it never left him, and he would always wear a steel plate inside his cap to shield his damaged skull.[5] After touring Plattsburgh, Newton Baker recalled Wood as having "panted and labored so obviously that I [concluded] that his health was bad, and when I later [chose] between Pershing and Wood that recollection influenced the choice."[6]

Pershing now ordered Wood to undergo a physical, hoping to cashier him. Wood passed easily. "How in the hell any board could . . . believe that General Wood is fit for active service is more than I can understand," Pershing raged. "He is a cripple and that is all there is to it, and there is no use in sending cripples over here to do men's work."[7]

Wood aimed to confront Wilson with his grievances. Wilson wouldn't see him. Nonetheless, Wood anticipated resuming command of the 89th Infantry, soon to deploy for France. Pershing stripped him of his command. Shocked and humiliated, Wood personally entreated Baker, who informed him that if he were in command in France, he wouldn't want him there either. Wood desperately stooped to repeating decade-old (and officially disproved) rumors of Pershing's fathering several illegitimate Filipino children while in Manila. Baker dismissed his accusation as "irrelevant and unworthy of consideration."[8]

Wood again demanded to see Wilson—and Wilson relented. Wood tried flattery. It failed. He resorted to the same bastard-siring smear that had failed with Baker. It worked no better with Wilson.

Wood departed, remaining livid with Pershing, spreading the same allegations, and inventing new ones. "No one ever hated anyone as much as Wood hated Pershing," Alice Longworth recalled. "How he talked! There was nothing he didn't say about him!"[9]

By now, Wood had fully reconciled with TR. In summer 1918, they were perhaps closer than ever.[10] That July, Wood entreated Theodore, "Imagine yourself in my position. The majority of Pershing's commanders are older than I. . . . Not one of them has ever had any important command experience. They are men who served under me as majors and captains in various parts of the world."[11]

Roosevelt urged restraint: "My dear Leonard, do let me beg you not to yield to your most natural and most bitter resentment at the infamous way in which you have been treated and say anything which your enemies can get hold of. Remember it isn't Pershing and it isn't Baker that is to blame; it is President Wilson and nobody but President Wilson."[12]

Wood responded, "I shall not permit myself to be baited into a position such as I know the people you refer to would like to put me."[13]

After all, 1920 was coming faster than the Democrats might ever desire.

On March 11, 1918—six weeks after Wood's field mortar mishap—red-hot German shrapnel shredded Archie's left arm and leg, severing a nerve above his elbow and mangling his knee. Amputation of that leg seemed likely, but the crisis soon passed. The threat of lifetime infirmity remained.

Two mornings later, a United Press reporter appeared at Oyster Bay. He bore news of Archie being awarded France's Croix de Guerre—and being wounded, though not too seriously. Theodore informed Edith. At lunch, the normally staid Roosevelt grande dame not only toasted Archie's heroics with a glass of rare Madeira but also shocked everyone (most likely including herself) by triumphantly smashing her empty glass on the floor. Only later did Ted Jr. (blown skyward by the same blast that injured Archie[14]) cable home to reveal the horrid severity of his brother's condition.[15]

In Mesopotamia, Kermit faced German aerial bombardment, taught himself Arabic (he was a skilled linguist), and won the British Military Cross. At Tikrit, armed only with a swagger stick, he bluffed a sizable number of Turks into surrendering. Soon he would be off to France to serve as an American captain of artillery.[16] In transit, he stopped off in Egypt to meet T. E. Lawrence.[17]

Ted Jr. had already been appointed commander of the 26th Infantry, 1st Battalion, of the American Expeditionary Force's (AEF) 1st Division.[18] In January 1918, Brigadier General George B. Duncan praised him as "an officer of unusual ability. He is most conscientious in the performance of every duty, never falters, has been an excellent commander of men, and is today probably the best battalion commander in the 1st Division—I know he is superior to any [other]."[19] In late May, as the Germans stormed the Aisne, he was gassed. "I have never seen anyone look so ghastly," recalled his wife, Eleanor. "His face was scorched and inflamed, and the whites of his eyes an angry red. He was thickly covered with dust and shaken by a racking cough."[20]

He was, without exaggeration, a better soldier than his fabled father. Colonel George C. Marshall, then a staff officer at Pershing's headquarters, later wrote him,

> *With no idea of flattery and with absolute honesty I will tell you that [I] consider your record one of the most remarkable in the entire A.E.F. . . . I consider your conduct as a battalion commander . . . among the finest examples of leadership, courage and fortitude that came to my attention during the war.*
>
> *I do not believe I have ever before indulged myself in such frank comments of a pleasant nature to another man, but I derived so much personal satisfaction as an American from witnessing the manner in which you measured up to the example of your father.*[21]

Quentin, also now in France, was not nearly ready for combat. He was still, as his second cousin Nicholas Roosevelt assessed him, "the gayest and most whimsical and most promising"[22] of the Sagamore Hill brood. In France, he was well liked and even admired by his colleagues. He was "gay, hearty and absolutely square in everything he said or did," remembered the famed American ace Captain Eddie Rickenbacker. "We loved him purely for his own natural self."[23]

One incident in particular endeared him to his comrades. They stood guard in freezing mud and rain. They contracted pneumonia and influenza. But their red-tape-bound quartermaster, a captain, refused to issue them rubber boots. Quentin protested—but to no avail. He demanded an explanation. However, captains do not gracefully provide explanations on demand to mere lieutenants. He ordered Quentin out of his office. Quentin wouldn't budge.

"Who do you think you are?" the captain demanded. "What is your name?"

Quentin was not the type to seek favors based on his surname. "I'll tell you my name," he shot back, "after you have honored this requisition, but not before."

This response enraged his superior even more. Quentin challenged, "If you'll take off your Sam Browne belt and insignia of rank I'll take off mine, and we'll see if you can put me out of the office. I'm going to have those boots for my men if I have to be court-martialed for a breach of military discipline."

Two officers pulled them apart. Quentin headed for the battalion's commander, a major. He convinced him of his cause and departed. Soon after, his adversary stormed in, demanding his court-martial. "Who is the lieutenant?" the major asked

"I don't know who he is," came the answer, "but I can find out."

"I know who he is," the major answered. "His name is Quentin Roosevelt, and there is no finer gentleman nor more efficient officer in this camp, and from what I know, if anyone deserves a court-martial you are the man. From now on you issue rubber boots to every cadet who applies for them, army regulations be damned."[24]

Yet Quentin shared with his father not only a taste for heroic glory and the military life but also a nearly suicidal obsession with death. Beyond that lay a far stranger side. "At one time," noted Kermit, "he was greatly interested in demonology and witchcraft, and combed the second-hand bookstores for grimy tomes on this subject."[25] Roosevelt family historian Edward J. Renehan noted how Quentin "tended to churn out macabre tales of madness, desperation and suicide that he did not dare to show his parents. . . . Every hero was a tragic, thoughtful, existential intellectual: brave but doomed."[26]

In France, he penned a morose short story about a conscience-stricken U-boat commander's suicide that commenced and concluded with the thought "The service pistol is a merciful thing."[27] A poem of his climaxed, "Yes. Ah, yes! Death, death and oblivion are God's greatest gifts."[28]

In early December 1917, ill with pneumonia,[29] he did not write home at all. On Christmas Eve, TR, ignorant of his son's plight, chided,

> *Dearest Quentin,*
>
> *Mother, the adamantine, has stopped writing to you because you have not written to her—or to any of us—for a long time. That will make no permanent difference to you; but I write about something that may make a permanent difference. Flora spoke to Ethel yesterday of the fact that you only wrote rarely to her. She made no complaint whatever. But she knows that some of her friends receive three or four letters a week from their lovers or husbands (Archie writes Gracie rather more often than this—exceedingly interesting letters).*
>
> *Now of course you may not keep Flora anyhow. But if you wish to lose her, continue to be an infrequent correspondent. If however you wish to keep her write her letters—interesting letters, and love letters—at least three times a week. Write no matter how tired you are, no matter how inconvenient it is; write if you're smashed up in a hospital; write when you are doing your most dangerous stunts; write when your work is most irksome and disheartening; write all the time! Write enough letters to allow for half being lost.*
>
> *Affectionately*
> *A hardened and wary old father*[30]

Quentin took that hint—and another one: that he bring Flora to France for matrimony: "As for your getting killed, or ordinarily crippled, afterwards, why she would rather have married you than not married you under those conditions; and as for extraordinary kinds of crippling, they are rare, and anyway we have to take certain chances in life."[31] But Flora did not go; the War Department would not allow it.[32]

Quentin fitfully continued learning how to fly—a harder process than one might think. His father was unfortunately right about Preparedness. American industry seemed incapable of turning out the aircraft the new American Air Service needed. Two thousand American pilots shuffled around their French training base, grounded not by enemy air superiority but by a simple lack of planes. "They are not going to send any more pilots over here from the states for the present," Quentin wrote home in April 1918, "which is about the first sensible decision that they have made as regards the Air Service. As it is they must have two thousand pilots over here, and Heaven knows it will be ages before we have enough machines for even half that number."[33]

In late March 1918, while still in training, Quentin cracked up his plane. "I smashed [it] up beautifully," he wrote back home. "It was really a very neat job, for I landed with a drift, touched one wing, and then, as there was a high wind, did three complete summersaults (spelling?) ending up on my back. I crawled out . . . with nothing more than a couple of scratches."[34]

He attracted some antiaircraft fire in late June ("I had a hole through my wing"[35]) but didn't see actual aerial combat until July 11, 1918, when, after cavalierly veering off from his fifteen-plane squadron and "returning" to its rear, he discovered he was accidentally trailing three enemy aircraft.

"Quentin," reminisced Eddie Rickenbacker, "fired one long burst. . . . The aeroplane immediately preceding him dropped at once and within a second or two burst into flames. Quentin put down his nose and streaked it for home before the astonished Huns had time to notice what had happened. He was not even pursued!"[36] Elated, Quentin set off to Paris, celebrating at the swank Ciro's with Ted's wife.[37] Just about then, Archie faced additional surgery on his nerve-damaged left arm. "The severed nerve was so shrunken," recalled Eleanor, "that there was a gap of some inches between ends."[38] Months passed before his recovery was ensured.

As Quentin was preparing for his first kill, John Purroy Mitchel, now an overaged army major flight cadet, trained at Lake Charles, Louisiana's Gerstner Field. His plane lurched into a tailspin. Mitchel, more reckless even than Quentin, had neglected to fasten his seatbelt and plunged five hundred feet to his death.[39] Five days later—as Quentin notched that first kill—the City of New York turned out for "The Boy Mayor's" funeral as it had not for his reelection. A million souls lined city streets, from city hall to St. Patrick's Cathedral, silently witnessing the horse-drawn gun caisson that bore Mitchel's flag-draped casket. Their numbers—larger than those mourning either Ulysses S. Grant or William Tecumseh Sherman—stunned observers. Elihu Root, Nicholas Murray Butler, Colonel Edward Mandell House, George W. Perkins, George von L. Meyer, and, yes, Theodore Roosevelt served among Mitchel's honorary pallbearers.[40]

The world moved very fast now. The dance of death whirled wildly, particularly for pilots. Eighty percent died in combat.[41] Once aloft in their "flaming coffins,"[42] they had a combat life expectancy of a mere eleven days.[43] Such unpleasant facts counted for little with Quentin Roosevelt. "He was [so] reckless," reminisced Rickenbacker, "that his commanding officers had to caution him repeatedly about the senselessness of his lack of caution. His bravery was so notorious that we all knew that he would either achieve some great, spectacular success or be killed in the attempt. Even the pilots in his own flight would beg him to conserve himself and wait for a fair opportunity for a victory. But Quentin would merely laugh away all serious advice."[44]

Sunday, July 14, was Bastille Day, and French airmen serving alongside Quentin's unit hoped to celebrate their national holiday with some authentic American entertainment. Quentin helped by rounding up what talent he could, even participating in his troupe's rehearsal on the evening of July 13. He was, a superior remembered, "the life of the party, inspiring everybody with his enthusiasm."[45]

At 8:20 the following morning, Quentin's squadron headed toward Château-Thierry. At forty-three hundred meters, seven Fokker triplanes appeared. Quentin pursued one of them, but it was a trap. Three other higher-flying German pilots descended upon him. Two machine-gun bullets ripped through his skull, killing him instantly. Spiraling downward, he crashed in enemy territory near the village of Chamery, ten kilometers north of the Marne.[46]

The next day, a group of American prisoners trudged past the twisted wreckage of his wrecked biplane. The 110th Infantry's Captain James E. McGee later wrote Ted,

In a hollow square about the open grave were assembled approximately one thousand German soldiers, standing stiffly in regular lines. They were dressed in field gray uniforms, wore steel helmets, and carried rifles. Officers stood at attention before the ranks. Near the grave was the smashed plane, and beside it was a small group of officers, one of whom was speaking to the men.

I did not pass close enough to hear what he was saying. . . . At the time I did not know who was being buried, but the guards informed me later. The funeral certainly was elaborate. . . . [T]hey paid Lieut. Roosevelt such honor not only because he was a gallant aviator, who died fighting bravely against odds, but because he was the son of Colonel Roosevelt, whom they esteemed as one of the greatest Americans.[47]

Quentin's German adversaries buried him with full military honors—but also photographed his remains lying alongside his wrecked craft. In Germany, the photo was issued as a postcard. It sold like hotcakes.

At Oyster Bay, the afternoon following Quentin's crash, TR was dictating to his secretary, the forty-year-old Miss Josephine M. Stricker, when Associated Press correspondent Philip Thompson rapped upon his door conveying puzzling news: the *New York Sun* had received a cable from France reading, "WATCH SAGAMORE HILL FOR—" with the remainder of the message censored. TR feared trouble. Some family member was wounded—or, worse, slain. "It can not be Ted and it can not be Archie," he speculated, "for both are recovering from wounds. It is not Kermit, for he is not in the danger zone at just this moment. So it must be Quentin. However, we must say nothing of this to his mother to-night."[48]

At 7:30 the following morning, Thompson interrupted the Colonel's breakfast with word that Quentin had been shot down over enemy lines. But was he wounded? Dead? Alive? He had survived one accident. His Nieuport had, after all, once crashed without catching fire. Might he walk away from another?

TR knew enough of war not to deceive himself. And he knew Edith could not be deceived either.

For the longest time, he said nothing. Finally, he exclaimed, "But—Mrs. Roosevelt! How am I going to break it to her?"[49]

He trudged upstairs. A few hours later he returned, accompanied by Edith. Thompson recalled, "[Her] eyes [were] bright and voice steady." Yet it was plain she had been told. As the Colonel walked away, Mrs. Roosevelt confided that she and the others in the house would do everything to help him. The burden must not be on his shoulders, she thought, and it was her duty to help him.

Her voice choked. They were just an American father and mother, who had been called overnight to the supreme sacrifice for their flag and who were trying, each without seeking aid from the other, to shield the other, to soften the great blow, to help and inspire.[50]

Just after 1:00 p.m., TR issued a manly, stiff-upper-lip statement ("Quentin's mother and I are very glad that he got to the front and had the chance to render some service to his country and to show the stuff that was in him before his fate befell him"[51]). Later, he walked alone to Sagamore Hill's stables. There, wrote the *Sun*, he "stopped before the stall of a fat, old and rheumatic Shetland pony, 'Algonquin,' which 'was breathing laboriously under the strain of his twenty years.'"[52] Years before, this tiny old Shetland had been Archie and Quentin's pony. It was Algonquin that five-year-old Quentin had so famously transported up the White House elevator back in 1903 to cheer the ailing eight-year-old Archie.[53]

"In the seclusion of the stable," the *Sun* continued, "the iron of a Spartan father's soul gave way . . . and with tears in his eyes he threw his arms around the old pony's neck."[54]

Reports filtered in, providing false hope of Quentin's survival. Quentin's best friend and fellow aviator, Lieutenant Hamilton Coolidge, reassured Edith, "The fact that his plane was neither spinning nor in flames as it came down makes me believe that [Quentin] landed safely."[55] Eleanor wired home, "The chance exists that he is a prisoner."[56] Dick Derby did much the same ("Companion aviator confident Quentin landed unhurt"[57]).

It was not until Saturday, July 20, that German pilots dropped a note confirming his death—and his identification bracelet—behind American lines.[58] Two days later, German authorities at Geneva notified their American Red Cross counterparts.[59] Eventually, Quentin's last letters home ("We lost another fellow from our squadron three days ago.

However, you get lots of excitement to make up for it"[60]) reached Oyster Bay.[61] And thus, day after day, a son died again and again in a mother and father's broken hearts.

On July 17, TR informed Edith of the terrible news about Quentin. He phoned Flora. *And he kept on working.* Choking back tears, he continued, as if all were normal, with his dictation. His only concession to tragedy was to cancel an afternoon business appointment in Manhattan.

On the following afternoon, he was to address the Republican State Convention at Saratoga Springs. No one would dare reprove him for his absence.

Corinne telephoned with condolences. She knew the grief he felt. She, too, had lost her youngest child. In February 1909, nineteen-year-old Stewart Douglas Robinson had committed suicide by plunging to his death at Harvard.

That year—1918—Corinne's other son, State Senator Theodore Douglas Robinson, had boomed TR for the governorship of New York. Billy Barnes ("Every man should be able to put aside subjects that are closed"[62]) even circulated a petition for him to run. Elihu Root and Nicholas Murray Butler, both New York U.S. senators, and William Howard Taft's younger brother Henry all signed.[63]

But Quentin was dead.

And so, Corinne advised her brother that he need not travel to Saratoga.

She recalled his answer as being "almost harsh in its rapidity: '. . . I will meet you in Saratoga as arranged. It is more than ever my duty to be there. . . .' The very tone of his voice made me realize the agony in his heart, but duty was paramount."[64]

That evening, Edith accompanied Theodore to Manhattan's Hotel Langdon. She and Ethel (hurriedly back from a Maine vacation[65]) would await his return the following night—there rather than at a home now haunted by too many memories.

Two thousand delegates and alternates—six thousand Republicans in all—greeted TR at Saratoga's Convention Hall. Warming up the crowd, former congressman J. Stoat Fassett spoke of sending his three sons to war, triggering massive weeping throughout the hall. Fassett, reported the *Sun*, was so "overcome with emotion . . . at one time he could hardly go on."[66]

Republicans wept. Nearby, a fatigued[67] TR rested at the United States Hotel, consoled only by Corinne; her husband, Douglas Robinson; their son, Theodore Douglas Robinson; and his wife, Helen (daughter of FDR's half brother James "Rosie" Roosevelt).[68]

Theodore Robinson escorted his uncle ("His face . . . set and grave"[69]) into the hall. "The crowd [rose] as one man and the cheers were deafening," the local paper noted. "To many it seemed the greatest ovation [he] ever received."[70]

The cheers were loud but not long—three minutes in all. Halfway through them, TR, weary in body as well as spirit, sat down to rest. When he spoke, no trace of a smile graced his lips; initially, reported the *Sun*, he had "a more subdued manner than is his custom and at first he used few gestures, but as he warmed up to his subject the old fire and vigor came out."

His subject was war.

Speaking from a manuscript, almost on autopilot, he gushed the old patriotic bromides: "The Hun within our gates," he proclaimed, is "the worst traitor to this republic, and we must treat agitation for a premature or inconclusive peace as treason. . . . The German spy, the alien enemy here at home, and the even fouler and more despicable native American who serves the alien should be interned at hard labor or . . . buried. The surest way to stop . . . spies and plotters is to shoot every one of them who is caught in a flagrant offence."[71]

Only in the most oblique manner did he discuss Quentin. Now speaking extemporaneously, he "bit off his words here in the old Roosevelt fashion."[72]

"That is the only kind of peace," he vowed, "that will atone to us for the blood that has been shed to win it."[73]

His audience, observed the *Sun*, "thought of Quentin and their heart went out to the speaker."[74]

There would be no nomination for governor.

"I motored him back to Albany and took the train with him for New York," recalled Corinne.

His attitude was one of ineffable gentleness. Never was he more lov-
ing in his interest about me and mine; never was he less thoughtful
of self. I realized that he needed quiet, and when I found that my
seat was in a different car from his, although several people offered
to change their seats with me, I felt that after our drive together, it
would do him more good to be alone and read than to try to talk to
me. I told him I would order our dinner and would come back for
him when it was time for the meal, and I left him with his usual
book in his hand. When I came back, however, I stood behind him for
a moment or two before making myself known to him again, and I
could see that he was not reading, that his sombre eyes were fixed on
the swiftly passing woodlands and the river, and that the book had
not the power of distracting him from the all-embracing grief which
enveloped him. When I spoke, however, he turned with a responsive
smile, and during our whole meal gave me, as ever, the benefit of his
delightful knowledge of all the affairs of the world.[75]

They returned that night to Edith at the Langdon. The next morning, reporters badgered him for his plans. "There is only one thought in my heart and you know what that is,"[76] he responded. The *New York World* thought he laid "his hand over his heart for an instant."[77]

On Saturday, July 20, newly installed Republican National Committee chairman Will Hays lunched at Sagamore Hill. "I am glad you did not speak of Quentin," Roosevelt advised him as they walked toward the library. "Edith could not have stood it." His voice broke, before he added, "I don't think I could have stood it myself."[78] That afternoon, official word arrived from President Wilson: Quentin was dead.[79]

Twenty minutes later, TR addressed a delegation from the Japanese Red Cross ("Any man who works at this time against the interests of Japan is a traitor to civilization and humanity"[80]). Trubee Davison, himself a badly injured army pilot, considered TR's behavior that day the "most magnificent exhibition of self-control and courage"[81] he ever saw.

The Japanese departed. Again, word arrived from France.

Ted was wounded.

Helmetless, at Ploisy near Soissons the previous morning, he had led a charge against a German machine-gun nest.[82] A bullet ripped through his left leg just above and behind the knee. Unable to find an ambulance, he headed for Paris. That evening, he arrived at his wife Eleanor's Avenue de Boies du Boulogne home. A tag affixed to his shirt read, "GUNSHOT WOUND SEVERE."[83] With perfect sangfroid, he called for a hot meal and champagne. Eleanor demanded that Dick Derby treat her husband's wound. He arrived to find his brother-in-law gushing blood, his wound dangerously filled with dirt and uniform cloth. "It's in a bad place," Derby informed Ted. "If it's not opened and thoroughly cleaned out right away it will get infected and you may lose the leg."[84] An operation saved the leg but not the feeling in Ted's left heel.

"No cause for anxiety,"[85] Eleanor calmly wired her in-laws.

"There is no use pretending that we do not bitterly mourn," TR wrote to Ted and Eleanor, "but [Quentin] had his crowded hour, of a life that was not only glorious but very happy; he had got his man; he had rendered service; he had a fortnight or three weeks when he stood on a crest of life which cannot even be seen by sordid and torpid souls who know neither strife in our honor and our love, and who live forever in a gray fog at the lowest level."[86]

Wars do not pause for a parent's heartbreak. The following month, Theodore Douglas Robinson enlisted as a lieutenant of U.S. Army artillery.[87] In September, Franklin Roosevelt traveled to France. At Mareuil, near the Meuse, he fired a 155-mm howitzer at Germans: "I shall never know how many, if any, Huns I killed."[88] Returning home, he took grievously ill—enabling Eleanor to discover her former social secretary's love letters to her husband. Thus, among war's very real casualties was a Roosevelt marriage. A month afterward—on TR's sixtieth birthday—Quentin's best friend, twenty-three-year-old Hamilton Coolidge, died from antiaircraft fire over the Argonne.[89]

In late 1918, when cousin Nicholas Roosevelt was about to pack off for France, he visited Sagamore Hill. It nearly proved too much for the stoic Edith. "When she saw me in uniform her eyes filled with tears and she turned away," Nicholas recalled. "Then she put her hand on my right arm and said, 'I'm all right, Nick; I'm all right.'"[90]

"It is rather awful to know," TR would write in late July to an acquaintance of Quentin's, a Miss Mary L. Brown, who wrote Theodore and Edith with information about him, "that he paid with his life, and that my other sons may pay with their lives, to try to put in practice what I preached. Of course I would not have it otherwise."[91]

Three weeks afterward, he confided to Edith Wharton, "There is no use of my writing about Quentin; for I should break down if I tried. His death is heart breaking, but it would have been far worse if he had lived at the cost of the slightest failure to perform his duty."[92]

Barely five weeks later, Wharton herself lost her cousin, twenty-three-year-old Lieutenant Philip Newbold Rhinelander—shot down on his first mission over German lines.[93]

Yet even then, TR *had* committed to writing about Quentin—or at least about death and dying and sacrifice, and everyone knew of what and whom he actually wrote. In the October 1918 *Metropolitan Magazine*, he gritted his teeth and spat in death's eye:

Only those are fit to live who do not fear to die; and none are fit to die who have shrunk from the joy of life and the duty of life. Both life and death are parts of the same Great Adventure. Never yet was worthy adventure worthily carried through by the man who put his personal safety first. Never yet was a country worth living in unless its sons and daughters were of that stern stuff which bade them die for it at need; and never yet was a country worth dying for unless its sons and daughters thought of life, not as something concerned only with the selfish evanescence of the individual, but as a link in the great chain of creation and causation, so that each person is seen in his true relations as an essential part of the whole, whose life must be made to serve the larger and continuing life of the whole. Therefore it is, that the man who is not willing to die, and the woman who is not willing to send her man to die, in a war for a great cause, are not worthy to live. . . .

Woe to those who invite a sterile death; a death not for them only, but for the race; the death which is ensured by a life of sterile selfishness.

But honor, highest honor, to those who fearlessly face death for a good cause; no life is so honorable or so fruitful as such a death. Unless men are willing to fight and die for great ideals, including love of country, ideals will vanish, and the world will become one huge sty of materialism. And unless the women of ideals bring forth the men who are ready thus to live and die, the world of the future will be filled by the spawn of the unfit. Alone of human beings the good and wise mother stands on a plane of equal honor with the bravest soldier; for she has gladly gone down to the brink of the chasm of darkness to bring back the children in whose hands rests the future of the years. But the mother and, far more, the father, who flinch from the vital task earn the scorn visited on the soldier who flinches in battle. . . .

In America to-day all our people are summoned to service and sacrifice. Pride is the portion only of those who know bitter sorrow or the foreboding of bitter sorrow. But all of us who give service, and stand ready for sacrifice, are the torch-bearers. We run with the torches until we fall, content if we can then pass them to the hands of other runners. The torches whose flame is brightest are borne by the gallant men at the front, and by the gallant women whose husbands and lovers, whose sons and brothers, are at the front. . . .

These are the torch-bearers; these are they who have dared the Great Adventure.[94]

Only Quentin's Great Adventure had concluded.

His father stood upon the brink of one last Great Adventure: the reconquest of the White House in 1920.

"I have kept my promise"[1]

As Theodore and Corinne traveled from Saratoga Springs to Manhattan that mournful late afternoon of July 18, 1918, they reviewed only briefly the question that so agitated Republican convention-goers: Would he seek the governorship?

"He used an expression," Corinne remembered, "which gave me at once a sense of almost physical apprehension. Looking at me gravely, he said: 'Corinne, I have only one fight left in me, and I think I should reserve my strength in case I am needed in 1920.' The contraction of my heart was swift and painful, and I said: 'Theodore, you don't feel really ill, do you?' 'No,' he said; 'but I am not what I was and there is only one fight left in me.'"[2]

His party indeed stood ready to welcome him back, not merely as a foot soldier but as its commander. All was somehow magically forgiven. "The growing murmur," observed Corinne, "rose louder and louder that [he] was the only candidate to be nominated. . . . The men who had parted from him in 1912, the men who had not rallied around him in 1916, were all eagerly ranging themselves on [his] side."[3] At Columbus, Ohio, in September 1918, he dined with Warren Harding's major political factotum, Harry M. Daugherty, and with Daugherty's even shadier crony, Jess W. Smith. To some, like Henry Allen, in February 1918, TR remained coy ("All that is near to me in the male line, is in France. If they do not come back what is the Presidency to me?"[4]), but to Daugherty that night he confided that 1920 indeed lay in his plans—even dangling a Roosevelt-Harding ticket as bait for Daugherty's support.[5]

Gossip of the Colonel's anticipated 1920 effort circulated even before Hughes's 1916 defeat. TR had promised to be "positively through campaigning forever,"[6] but even the least experienced observers knew better. "The American people, however, will [n]ever permit him to retire," the *New York Tribune*'s Edwin N. Lewis, just barely out of Columbia, wrote home from 1916's campaign trail. "Just as sure as Wilson is re-elected, there will be a demand for Theodore Roosevelt in 1920. He knows it and he is trying to start the talk now through us to show that it is the last thing on earth he cares to do."[7]

Rapprochement bloomed everywhere. TR's prodigal acolyte Gutzon Borglum now fancifully entreated him to run for the House—"the most wonderful campaign since 1860"[8]—as a stepping stone to House Speaker. If such as Borglum, Barnes, and Root might forgive and forget, might even "Big Bill" Taft?

In late May 1918, TR, en route to a Des Moines speaking engagement, stopped at Chicago's Blackstone Hotel. Taft, returning from business in St. Louis, coincidentally also lodged there. Heading to his room, he learned that TR was dining downstairs. Ordering his elevator back down, he clumsily rushed toward the blissfully oblivious Roosevelt. TR recalled looking up "just as Taft reached the table with his hand stuck out. There was so much noise being made by the people in the room[,] I am not quite sure what he said. I think it was 'Theodore, I am glad to see you.' I grabbed his hand and told him how glad I was to see him. By Godfrey, I never was so surprised in my life. . . . But, wasn't it a gracious thing for him to do? . . . I never felt happier over anything in my life. . . . It was splendid of Taft. . . . I've seen old Taft and we're in perfect harmony on everything."[9]

Soon TR courted Taft (as he had done with Root) by forwarding him speeches for review.[10] But "perfect" harmony hardly existed between them. Taft's wife, Nellie, still roundly detested Theodore. TR and Taft would soon diverge regarding Wilson's proposed League of Nations—Taft strongly for it, TR predictably opposed to whatever Wilson advocated.[11]

"I want to get along with those fellows and especially with Will Taft in the matter of the League of Nations," TR said privately later that year, "but I will follow them just so far and no farther. . . . If the League of Nations means that we will have to go to war every time a Jugo-Slav wishes to slap a Czecho-Slav in the face, then I won't follow them. For

I don't believe our people will do it, and we don't want any more scraps of paper."[12]

As far as other issues were concerned, he had, of course, long since enlisted in the pro–woman suffrage ranks and, by 1918, had endorsed a federal Prohibition amendment.[13] But above all he remained very much a man of the Left.

"I wish to do everything in my power," he vowed to William Allen White in April 1918, "to make the Republican Party the party of sane, constructive radicalism, just as it was under Lincoln. If it is not that, then, of course, I have no place in it."[14]

A month earlier, he had lectured the Maine Republican Convention, "We cannot afford any longer to continue our present industrial and social system. Or rather no-system of every-man-for-himself and devil-take-the-hindmost."[15]

Love is blind. Blinder still is a political party thirsting for electoral victory. Otherwise orthodox Republicans, lusting for power, patronage, and revenge against Woodrow Wilson, now firmly shut their eyes to their savior's radicalism.

Yes, the long-stalled TR train was finally leaving the station. Delegates to that Maine Republican convention proclaimed TR "the next President of the United States."[16] The *New York Herald* categorically designated him as "the Republican candidate for President in 1920."[17]

By now, Progressives were a spent—though still highly acrimonious—force. A dead party walking. Harold Ickes, Medill McCormick, Raymond Robins, Gifford Pinchot, Chester Rowell, and William Allen White had renewed their pleas for George Perkins's exile from Progressive councils.[18] In January 1917, Perkins counterattacked, skewering Gifford Pinchot in a letter to TR: "I doubt if I know any more contemptible character than this fellow Pinchot, unless it is his brother Amos. I think him thoroughly insincere, selfish, and never stood for anything that he thought did not further his own interest."[19]

The following month, White tendered a blistering missive to Perkins:

You didn't appreciate the tremendous sincerity and deep democratic feeling of that big [1916] Bull Moose Convention. . . . You were not frank with it. . . . You man-handled it and in man-handling it you crucified Colonel Roosevelt. . . . The whole tactics . . . put him in the attitude of intriguing on the long-distance telephone with a lot of high-binders with whom he could have no honest relations. . . . That convention had an everlasting right to nominate Colonel Roosevelt Thursday and it had a right to demand that he should come down to the convention Friday—put all the cards before the convention himself . . . and then ask that convention as his good friends . . . to join him in an attempt to save the country from Wilson. But to make that convention think it was going to nominate Roosevelt without the knowledge that you had and that I had . . . that he did not want the nomination and would not take it as a third party nominee against Hughes—was dishonest and wicked. . . . The people of the Middle West and far West were shocked and insulted and they rebelled.[20]

In February 1918, Republicans convened to select a new national chairman. TR, though hardly uninterested, remained uncharacteristically restrained, while Perkins labored noisily for Indiana GOP chair Will Hays, to whom TR had offered a campaign position in 1912.

Hays's uphill victory against incumbent party vice chairman John T. Adams stemmed more from wartime GOP jingoism than from any Republican desire to suddenly turn more Progressive, as Perkins's allies tied the "taint of pro-Germanism"[21] to Adams ("Having failed in every other effort to dictate the organization of the Republican Party, George W. Perkins has undertaken to cast doubt upon my patriotism"[22]). It also stemmed from Boies Penrose's last-minute support—and, certainly not inconsequentially, from a package deal involving the outright bouncing of Perkins from any official connection to GOP leadership, a move Ickes gleefully pronounced "entirely satisfactory."[23]

The outcome, nonetheless, inflamed Perkins's ego. Following a visit to an ailing TR in New York, he boasted to reporters of a newfound (in truth, largely fanciful) Progressive influence on the GOP. "Already the Progressives, headed by . . . Perkins," noted the *New York Times*, "are laying their plans to draft the Colonel for the big national contest."[24]

Since 1916, Perkins's influence over TR had been in free fall. This was the last straw. From his hospital bed, the Colonel dispatched an almost fourteen-hundred-word missive excoriating his longtime patron, first for daring to reveal their visit and, further, for his "inevitably creat[ing] the impression that you were speaking as my representative." For good measure, TR lacerated Perkins's attitude toward Josephine Stricker ("You seem to feel a resentment that Miss Stricker was not on telephone [with you]"[25]).

"Much of your letter, it does not seem to me, worth while to discuss," Roosevelt blustered on. "If any advice I gave could be heeded I should give with all possible emphasis to everyone, the following advice: To quit talking in the papers."[26]

Most fatal to Perkins was this line: "I am exceedingly sorry that you feel as you do about [Connecticut Republican National committeeman John T.] King. As you know I do not share your views any more than I share the views of the men who come to me to attack you."

Touché.

Perkins had angrily demanded that TR sever relations with the Old Guard–leaning King,[27] a successful but not always reputable politician who essentially operated as Connecticut's version of Billy Barnes, having converted the Democrat stronghold of Bridgeport into his own patronage-rich Republican fiefdom. At least as early as June 1916, Roosevelt and the anti-Hughes King had conferred on political strategy. It was King, together with Cabot Lodge, who devised TR's ultimately disastrous tactic of delaying his Progressive nomination. It was King—not Perkins—whom the press described as TR's "personal representative"[28] at the recent Republican National Committee session. Some even said that it was King—not Hays—who was Roosevelt's choice for chair.[29] That was not true, though it was not that far off, as evidenced by TR's February 6 dispatch informing Hays that "John King is very close to me. He will present you this letter. He will do everything he can for you, or if you and the others deem it impossible to elect you and possible to elect somebody else, he will work with you to elect that other person. Will you treat him as my particular and confidential friend, and consult and advise with him?"[30] Moreover, the *Chicago Tribune* had reported that King was "clothed with authority from Mr. Roosevelt to give the colonel's approval, not only to the elevation of Hays, but to the erasure of Perkins."[31]

King, conferring with Hays and Penrose in Indianapolis, had said pretty much the same thing as had Perkins—he, too, sought TR's nomination in 1920.[32] TR didn't mind *that*—because he didn't mind *King*. Almost immediately, news reports floated of King's replacing Perkins as TR's chief political adviser.[33]

Roosevelt's alliance with King outraged old-line Progressives. "You are [now] surrounded by . . . leaders . . . of political criminality," Gutzon Borglum angrily warned Roosevelt.[34] But TR had his own priorities. "John supplies the efficiency," TR cynically quipped, "and I supply the morals."[35]

At King's request, in autumn 1918 TR invited Boies Penrose and his fellow standpatter, Indiana's freshman senator James "Sunny Jim" Watson, to a Hotel Langdon peace conference. Beforehand, Penrose advised his senatorial allies, "There is but one candidate for president. He is the only candidate. I mean Theodore Roosevelt. . . . I don't like him. I once despised him. But that doesn't alter the fact that Theodore Roosevelt is now the one and only possible Republican candidate in 1920. He will surely receive the nomination."[36]

Penrose and Watson arrived in New York. TR "bounded" up from a couch to greet them, chatting of the Amazonian fever that still periodically sidelined him but soon declaiming on the party's future. Screwing up his face "with one of those peculiar twists . . . that nobody has ever been able to describe," he even backpedaled on the recall of federal judges—a stance particularly terrifying to conservatives. Watson considered him full of "buoyancy and . . . vitality." Penrose kept his silence, reduced to "monosyllables" when he did speak.

Penrose and Watson motored off. Finally, Penrose spoke.

"Jim, the Colonel won't be with us very long."

"What do you mean by that?" the startled Watson asked.

"Why," Penrose replied, "didn't you see that he is a marked man?"

"I certainly did not," Watson responded. "He seemed to me just as vigorous and as explosive and as full of life as ever, and I don't know what you discovered to lead you to believe that he is anywhere near dissolution."

"My father," Penrose now explained, "was as great a doctor as ever lived in Pennsylvania, my brother is a natural diagnostician of great ability, and I have a sort of intuition or instinct in sizing up a man physically. I tell you now that Colonel Roosevelt will not be alive in three months and that your promise to support him will prove of no avail."[37]

Penrose was no progressive and no great fan of TR but also no fool. To many (particularly his adulatory admirers), the Colonel was indestructible. Laid terribly low in 1913 by jungle fever, he bounced back, as he had from being hit by a runaway streetcar in Pittsfield or a .38-caliber slug in Milwaukee. It required more than a bacillus or a bullet to stop a Bull Moose.

Yet, if not stopped, he had been slowed down—and with increasing frequency and severity. As mentioned, he suffered two broken ribs falling off a horse in May 1915. In March 1916, an unusual incident occurred as he returned from his Caribbean "Heroic Mood" trip. As the *Sun* reported, "About 2 o'clock one morning huge waves ... flooded the Colonel's cabin. Nothing could stop him from jumping out of his berth in his pajamas and bailing out his state room with a bucket. The labor occupied him for a full hour, and when he landed here he described it as 'a bully good time.' But the soaking he received proved too much, and ... his physicians at Oyster Bay prescribed a complete rest for several days."[38]

That June, when "a strained ligament on a rib" triggered "a severe attack of pleurisy," physicians advised that he "give up violent exercise."[39] "Well," the Colonel grimly explained to reporters, "one doesn't care, you know, to exercise very hard when one has pleurisy."[40]

By October 1917, Edith had resolved to do something regarding his "too substantial form"[41] (Edmund Morris estimates he had ballooned to 250 pounds[42]) and bludgeoned him into enrolling in former prizefighter Jack Cooper's Stamford, Connecticut, Health Farm. To Cooper, the Colonel confessed that he was "slipping a bit both mentally and physically."[43] Cooper feared that his new client (his *only* client, a circumstance designed to preserve the old Rough Rider's privacy) teetered "on the verge of collapse."[44] TR reluctantly dieted, jogged, and exercised on Cooper's excruciating "Reducycle." The regimen "bored [him] to extinction,"[45] but he (temporarily) lost nearly four inches of waistline. Still, Edith confided to her diary, "Cooper's not a success,"[46] most likely referring to her husband's mental state. "At times the horrid futility of beating the air comes upon him in a great wave,"[47] as she confessed to Corinne before packing him off to Cooper's.

Rumors—quite true—now circulated of arteriosclerosis. "I have had arterio-sclerosis for a long time," he divulged to Jack Leary. "Ever since I was about forty, I have had to cut out violent exercises one after the other until now there is nothing left except what a grandfather might expect."[48] Concurrently, the public finally learned of TR's loss of his left eye while boxing in the White House.[49]

In January 1918, he invaded Washington, addressing the National Press Club, making the rounds ("TR came to town to set up a rump gov. but failed,"[50] thought Josephus Daniels), socializing with Cabot Lodge and Billy Sunday,[51] and triggering a rush of reporters to his quarters at the Longworths' (by actual count Alice numbered thirty-three in her foyer[52]). Again, ill health struck, this time in the form of acute indigestion so severe that Alice summoned a doctor, who ordered him to bed.[53]

Far worse was soon to come.

On Monday, February 4, 1918, St. Luke's Hospital's Dr. Walton Martin operated on him for a rectal abscess—not in New York or in any hospital but at Sagamore Hill—employing only a local anesthetic. The following day, Theodore and Edith motored to Manhattan for a whirlwind day of meetings, jumping from his *Metropolitan Magazine* offices to the Harvard Club to his Hotel Langdon quarters.

He conferred with standpatters and progressives alike. With John T. King, he plotted installing Will Hays as national chairman.[54] Later, he spoke with the *Wichita Beacon's* Henry J. Allen ("Take good care of yourself, Colonel; you are the only bet for 1920"[55]). He reconnoitered with Princess Alice, in town by sheer coincidence. Still tormented from the previous day's operation, he hoped to see Dr. Martin.

That night he was to return to the Harvard Club to address a farewell dinner for John Purroy Mitchel, thrown by the Vigilantes, a group of more than four hundred "patriotic" writers and artists. On the morrow, he would entrain for Boston and a talk to the American Red Cross.

He reached neither Boston nor the Harvard Club. Dictating correspondence at the Langdon to Josephine Stricker, he looked gray and exhausted. His eyes closed from weariness. She suggested that their work might wait till the morrow. "Miss Stricker," he snapped, "when I was President I instituted a rule to clear my desk each day of the day's work, and I shall stick to it."[56]

Wracked by pain, he slugged down a rare "stiff hooker of whiskey."[57] Weaker still, he lay down ("What a jack I am!"[58])—and bled. A minute later, he passed out (some said he also fainted during lunch[59]), tumbling off his now blood-red divan and onto the floor.

Dr. Martin arrived. The Colonel refused his help in walking into the next room, but Martin summoned nurses and ordered TR to cancel the remainder of his schedule. Late the next morning, TR departed for Roosevelt Hospital. He insisted on doing so via his own private automobile and largely under his own power.[60] By now, Ethel (residing at Oyster Bay since Dick Derby had entered the service), Corinne, and Corinne's thirty-year-old son Monroe had arrived. Also present was TR's cousin W. Emlen Roosevelt, his close friend, personal financial adviser, and summertime next-door neighbor. Most important (on this day), he was also president of Roosevelt Hospital.[61]

Just before 4:00 p.m., Theodore—fully anesthetized—underwent two hours under the knife. At his request, his three surgeons also examined his ears. A large abscess had developed in the left; a smaller, embryo abscess, in his right. Everything seemed to go well ("The operation proved successful. No unpleasant results. Resting comfortably. Respiration normal"[62]). The condition of his ears seemed so minor, it was not even mentioned.

Infection soon raged through his left ear. Fever engulfed him. His life hung in the balance, his condition so "hopeless"[63] that his surgeons feared to operate again. They stationed three nurses to attend to him and, absent any real option, waited things out. Edith took a room adjacent to Theodore's second-floor bedside. Emlen occupied quarters elsewhere in the hospital. It was now a "death watch," and rumors flashed of TR's demise, first down to Wall Street and, within hours, to far-off Oklahoma and Michigan.[64] The *New York Tribune's* editorial page pled, "*Theodore Roosevelt—Listen! You must be up and well again; we cannot have it otherwise; we could not run this world without you.*"[65]

Corinne waited patiently outside her brother's room. Finally allowed in, she feared this might be her last visit. Doctors advised her to draw very close to Theodore to avoid causing him to stir, as even the slightest movement might kill him. When he spoke, it was ever so haltingly. "I am so glad that it is not one of my boys who is dying here," he rasped, "for they can die for their country."[66]

Woodrow Wilson wired Edith his "warmest sympathy,"[67] and TR—perhaps just to spite Wilson—pulled through. With more bluster than truth, he wrote to Kermit describing his ordeal as "entirely trivial."[68] It wasn't. Edith retained her hospital quarters for another fortnight. Departing on March 4, TR headed not for Sagamore Hill but back to the Langdon, obviously hedging his bets against any setback. Worse, the operation on his pus-filled left ear had destroyed its canal, leaving that ear permanently deaf[69] and making "his gait unsteady." As he phrased it, he was "compelled . . . to learn to walk again."[70]

"It will be some months," his doctors explained, "before he will recover complete . . . equilibrium, or before he will cease to find himself dizzy at quick or unexpected motion. . . . [D]uring these months he must be cautious about—his activities."[71]

Doctors proposed. TR disposed. Soon he was off to the hustings, rousing patriotic fervor, encouraging enlistments, and selling Liberty Bonds by the millions. His "was the voice of emotion," noted his biographer Henry F. Pringle, "but it did untold service. . . . Roosevelt at home, unhappy and vengeful, was far more useful than he could have been in France."[72]

Physical adversity dogged him. In Boston, on May 1, 1918, ptomaine poisoning laid him low.[73] On an early June midwestern speaking tour, he refused hospitalization despite contracting erysipelas, a painful skin infection, in his left foot and suffering from renewed fever.[74] "In spite of intense suffering," the *Times* later noted, "he made speeches at Omaha, Indianapolis, and St. Louis. Taking his physician with him he made a 120-mile automobile trip to keep speaking engagements and returned to Indianapolis leaving his physician a 'wreck,' while he was fresh and vigorous physically though in a good deal of pain. He came home by train and spent a part of his first day chopping wood."[75]

In Philadelphia, TR lunched with Raymond Robins and Owen Wister before motoring off to nearby Chester. "We were talking about matters wholly interesting to Roosevelt," Wister would recall. "As the conversation went on, we noticed his head bent forward, and his eyes closed. He was asleep." Wister, accustomed to TR's inexhaustible vigor, found the episode "ominous."[76]

The intense pain of a son's loss never departed. "He kept his peace," recollected his valet and bodyguard James Amos, "but it was eating his heart out."[77] His associate, Harvard professor Hermann Hagedorn, concluded, "The boy in him had died."[78]

"Quentin's death shook him greatly," Edith wrote Kermit in late October. "I can see how constantly he thinks of him and not the happy silly recollections which I have but sad thoughts of what Quentin could have counted on in the future."[79]

He could not escape reminders of the boy. In late October, a well-meaning YMCA worker announced plans to gift TR with the seat ("not charred or burned in any way"[80]) from Quentin's aeroplane. Almost simultaneously, the Colonel learned that, following victory, all servicemen interred abroad—Quentin included—would be brought stateside for reburial. Horrified, TR wrote to Pershing's chief of staff, General Peyton C. March, begging for that not to happen:

> *The inclosed [sic] clipping states that all the American dead will be taken home after the war, according to orders received by the army chaplains. I do not know whom to write to in the matter, so I merely ask that you turn this over to whomever has charge of it.*
>
> *Mrs. Roosevelt and I wish to enter a most respectful but most emphatic protest against the proposed course so far as our son Quentin is concerned. We have always believed that*
>
> *Where the tree falls,*
> *There let it lie.*
>
> *We know that many good persons feel entirely different, but to us it is painful and harrowing long after death to move the poor body*

from which the soul has fled. We greatly prefer that Quentin shall continue to lie on the spot where he fell in battle and where the foemen buried him.

After the war is over Mrs. Roosevelt and I intend to visit the grave and then to have a small stone put up saying it is put up by us, but not disturbing what has already been erected to his memory by his friends and American comrades in arms.

With apologies for troubling you.[81]

As TR mournfully confessed to a friend, "I feel as though I were a hundred years old and had *never* been young."[82]

He nonetheless counted himself as more than fit to combat Woodrow Wilson, his vitriol only increasing as the war progressed without him. In early October 1917, Abilene, Texas, mayor E. N. Kirby blasted TR in a letter to the *Fort Worth Star-Telegram*: "The Roosevelt article appearing in your paper of this date is nothing short of the expression of the thoughts of a seditious conspirator who should be shot dead, and the Editor-in-Chief of your paper should be tarred and feathered for publishing it, and your paper should be excluded from the mails.... You may publish this if you wish, and stop my paper."[83]

Two days later, Secretary of the Navy Josephus Daniels recorded in his diary, "T. R. at large, writing and speaking in disparagement of America's preparation for war, is helping Germany more than the little fellows who are being arrested for giving aid and comfort to the enemy. Can [the] *Kansas City Star*, containing his allusions to soldiers training with broom-sticks, be excluded from the mails along with other papers spreading what is construed as seditious? B—— [probably Postmaster General Albert Burleson] said he was having paper read carefully and would not hesitate to act."[84]

In January 1918, the American Labor Council denounced his remarks as seditious.[85] That November, *The Nation* asked, "Why Is Roosevelt Unjailed?"[86]

Wilson retained his usual sangfroid. "The best way to treat Mr. Roosevelt is to take no notice of him," he remarked to Joe Tumulty in December 1917. "That breaks his heart and is the best punishment that can be administered. After all, while what he says is outrageous in every particular, he does, I am afraid, keep within the limits of the law, for he is as careful as he is unscrupulous."[87]

Or, as the journalist Mark Sullivan observed, "Wilson knew not only how to be subtle with words but subtle with silence."[88]

Still, TR maintained a machine-gun-like fire on his usual targets—the hyphenated-Americans, the pacifists, and those who neglected to prepare for war. In April 1918, he wrote,

And we deserve to be brayed in a mortar if we are ever again guilty of . . . our foolish failure to prepare our strength in efficient fashion during the last three and a half years. The women of this country who love their husbands and sons should realize now that only by thorough prepared-ness in advance can war be avoided, if possible, or successfully waged if it has to come. Recently men in high position whose own bodies are safe have stated that they are glad that we were not prepared in advance to do our duty when this war came. These men have purchased their own safety and advantage by the blood of our sons at the front.[89]

In May 1918, he locked horns with Postmaster General Albert Burleson regarding the administration's handling of the Hearst press (which, TR said, "opposed the war or attacked our Allies or directly or indirectly aided Germany"[90]) versus such outlets as *Metropolitan Magazine, Collier's Weekly,* and the *New York Tribune* ("which have consistently upheld the war, but which told the small portion of the truth about the Administration's failure to conduct the war efficiently"[91]). When Burleson retorted that he had received more complaints from the public against TR than against the Hearst newspapers, Roosevelt snarled, "In view of Mr. Burleson's record and actions there is small cause for wonder in this. Every German and anti-American, every believer in a feeble American war and a triumphant German peace, every man who follows Mr. Hearst would naturally appeal for sympathy to Mr. Burleson in denunciation of what I have done."[92]

Occasionally, he added new targets, such as birth control ("It is not well for a nation to import its art and its literature; but it is fatal for a nation to import its babies"[93]) and the Bolsheviks ("crack-brained fanatics and foolish, simple people"[94]). To Kermit, in March 1918, he worried, "The Bolshevists seem to have absolutely ruined Russia. Apparently the Russians for the time being lost all national spirit. For centuries they have cruelly persecuted the Jews, and now the Jew leadership in Russia has been a real nemesis for the Russians."[95]

"Theodore is the same old darling," TR's old friend Major Winthrop Astor "Winty" Chanler observed to Cecil Spring-Rice.

> *He too is older. His egotism has grown on him, but so has his fat. These are trifles, the warty growths on a magnificent oak tree.*
>
> *A man cannot be at the top—the real top—for six or seven years the leader of the world and not show the effects. And no man who went through such a phase in the world's history, perhaps, has come out of it so little harmed and changed. That he will ever be President or even candidate again is open to every doubt, political turn or popular fancy. Look at his victory, and look at his defeat. He remains through it all the man we know and have known.*[96]

Other observers proved less amenable. *The Nation* looked into the future (or maybe just the present) to pen this satire:

> *OYSTER BAY, L. I., July 4, 1921—Ex-President Theodore Roosevelt to-day dedicated an heroic monument to himself as a Rough Rider, which is his final gift to the town. The pedestal is conspicuous because of a lion couchant and a wild hyena rampant, in memory of his African explorations. His four-hour oration was a well-emphasized and earnestly-gesticulated review of his career in the light of history. Any historian who might differ from him he consigned in advance to the Ananias club. The oration will be published (at Mr. Roosevelt's usual rates) in six numbers of Scribner's Magazine.*[97]

TR was not America's only egoist. In May 1918, Wilson stood before Congress ungrammatically vowing that "Politics are adjourned"[98] for the war's duration. Yet he had already dispatched Vice President Thomas

Marshall to campaign in a special Wisconsin Senate election. Marshall accused Republicans of banking on the "sewage vote . . . of the German sympathizer, . . . the traitor, . . . the seditionist, . . . the pacifist."[99]

Marshall's overheated rhetoric backfired. But Wilson learned nothing from the experience. In late October, he appealed to voters to elect a Democratic Congress, claiming that a GOP victory would be "interpreted on the other side of the water [i.e., primarily in Berlin] as a repudiation of my leadership."[100]

TR was ailing. Ghastly arthritic pain in his right arm and leg sidelined him for a full ten days in late October,[101] but Wilson's remarks reenergized him. "He is a partisan leader first and president of all the people second,"[102] TR thundered that very evening, as he prepared for another round of speeches against his foe. Telegramming Cabot Lodge, Hiram Johnson, and Washington State's Miles Poindexter, he blasted the idea of any peace based on Wilson's Fourteen Points (a "thoroughly mischievous" foundation). "Let us dictate peace by the hammering guns," he snarled, "and not chat about peace to the accompaniment of the clicking of typewriters."[103]

He called for reelecting such Republicans as Charles Whitman,[104] Albert B. Fall,[105] ("you embody the best American spirit"[106]), and John W. Weeks[107]—though he felt that Weeks, while "an honorable man" and "a genuine patriot," was "a reactionary by conviction" who lacked "foresight."[108] He endorsed Senate hopefuls Medill McCormick, Truman Newberry (running against Henry Ford[109]), and former Idaho governor Frank Gooding. William E. Borah, running to retain the state's other Senate seat, rejected his endorsement.[110]

During 1916's chaotic Republican National Convention, Boston department store owner Frank W. Stearns had suggested newly elected Massachusetts lieutenant governor Calvin Coolidge as a compromise presidential candidate. The Massachusetts delegation burst out laughing. When the news was conveyed to Lodge, he exclaimed, "Calvin Coolidge! My God," and the laughing resumed. But in 1918, Lodge, hungry to elect GOP candidates, dutifully suggested to TR that he endorse Coolidge ("a very able, sagacious man of pure New England type"[111]) for promotion to the governorship.

TR, perhaps assuming that Coolidge (a Murray Crane protégé) was a bit more progressive than he actually was, meekly complied: "Mr. Coolidge is a high-minded public servant of the type which Massachusetts has always been honorably anxious to see at the head of the state government; a man who has the forward look and who is anxious to secure genuine social and industrial justice in the only way it can effectively be secured, that is, by basing a jealous insistence upon the rights of all, on the foundation of legislation that will guarantee the welfare of all."[112]

The Colonel addressed a packed Carnegie Hall rally on Monday evening, October 29—"attired in full dress . . . his famous smile beaming left and right . . . teeth click[ing] audibly."[113] His twenty-thousand-word speech lasted for more than two hours, flaying all things Wilsonian, most pointedly "his famous Fourteen Points" and the Princetonian's "naked eagerness for partisan success."[114] That TR had issued similar partisan electoral pleas in both 1906 and 1908 escaped his renowned memory—though not Democrats'.[115]

The following Friday, November 2, he and Taft joined in calling for electing a "better qualified" GOP Congress.[116]

Archie, still convalescing, had arrived stateside.[117] "Of our four hawks one has come home," TR informed Kermit, "broken-winged, but his soul as high as ever. Never did four falcons fly with such daring speed at such formidable quarry."[118] TR lied. Archie's soul did not soar as high as ever. Depression dogged him. He concocted unfounded conspiracies regarding alleged high-command plots aimed at denying his brother Ted a well-deserved promotion. Not even the sight of his infant son cheered him.[119]

That Friday evening, Archie ("tall and slim, his injured arm still encased in leather, his face just recovering its color"[120]) accompanied his father to the Metropolitan Opera House. Alongside John D. Rockefeller Jr., they appeared before a cheering, whistling five-thousand-person audience supporting the Boys' Victory Mobilization.

The following evening, the Colonel addressed a Carnegie Hall benefit for the Circle for Negro War Relief. The National Association for the Advancement of Colored People's W. E. B. Du Bois presided, and near bedlam greeted TR's impromptu 11:00 p.m. entrance. As the black *New*

York Age reported, "Everybody acted uproariously and none too dignified."[121] In 1899, TR had damned black troopers as "peculiarly depen-
dent on their white officers," adding that "under the strain the colored
infantryman begins to get a little uneasy and to drift to the rear."[122] Now,
he saluted "the gallantry and efficiency [of] the colored men . . . at the
front." His extemporaneous remarks included warnings against both the
Russian Bolsheviki and the scourge of Negro crime. "The worst offender
against the colored race is the colored criminal," TR warned. "He is the
man who does more to keep the Negro down than any white man can
possibly do. And I ask you colored men to of all things hunt down, hunt
out, the colored criminal of every type."[123]

TR returned to Oyster Bay limping. Edith remembered him as being
in "great pain."[124] His foot was so swollen that he could not put a shoe
upon it.[125] On November 5, still feeling "wretchedly"[126] and ignoring
his physician's orders,[127] he had his cousin Nicholas (already returned
from France) drive him to his polling station at Oyster Bay's blacksmith
shop.[128] The evening's results exhilarated him. The nation had reproached
Wilson. Both houses of Congress went Republican. For TR, the results
were a mixed bag. Fall, McCormick, Newberry, and Coolidge all triumphed. Whitman, "poor gallant"[129] Weeks, and Idaho's Gooding all
met narrow defeat, while Borah, running sans TR's endorsement (but
with Wilson's), romped to victory. Nonetheless, he eagerly gloated at the
overall outcome. "Mr. Wilson," he pronounced, "has no authority whatever to speak for the American people at this time. His leadership has
been emphatically repudiated . . . and all his utterances every which way
have ceased to have any shadow of right to be accepted as expressive of
the will of the American people."[130]

Yet 1918's Republican victory had less to do with the human cost of
war than with the price of wheat. Twenty-one of the GOP's twenty-five
new congressmen hailed from the agricultural Midwest, an area irate over
Wilson's veto of a wartime wheat price while allowing southern-pro-
duced cotton prices to soar.[131] And while wheat farmers seethed, eastern
financial interests damned alleged Southern Democrat congressional
moves to "pay for the war out of taxes raised north of the Mason and
Dixon line."[132] GOP candidates in both regions (skillfully managed by

Will Hays) charged that "the South [was] in the saddle."[133] Their accusation worked.

Revenge is sweet. But it cannot heal an aching body. TR remained housebound. He who had orated with an assassin's bullet lodged near his heart and traveled to Saratoga Springs with his heart broken forever now canceled a speaking engagement at Pittsburgh. On Monday afternoon, November 11, mere hours after the armistice, he returned to Roosevelt Hospital, suffering from what doctors officially termed "an attack of lumbago."[134]

Whatever it was, it hurt like hell and laid him low for weeks. Throughout November and December 1918, his English-born general practitioner, the thirty-nine-year-old Dr. John H. Richards, supplied the public with shifting versions of TR's ailments. The diagnosis ranged from lumbago[135] to sciatica to rheumatism.[136] With good reason, TR had long feared rheumatism ("I have a tendency to rheumatism, or gout or something of the kind, which makes me very stiff"[137]), which had largely crippled his sister "Bye."[138]

"Doctor, you have deceived me," he jocularly accused Richards, "and I think purposely, withheld from me the facts. At one time you said I had acute arthritis, and at another time [Dr.] Josh Hartwell told me that I had a low-grade infection, and, oh, how I hate anything low-grade! This morning, innocently enough, my daughter Ethel, who is married to a doctor and for that reason knows a great deal of medicine, told me the truth. She told me that I had inflammatory rheumatism, and that is a disease that I know all about."[139]

Perhaps Richards did not know himself what ailed TR. But he knew this: TR's pain was so excruciating that it required morphine.[140] Beyond that, the Colonel had entered the hospital with a 102-degree fever.[141] It peaked at 104.[142] These facts Richards withheld from public view. Nor did he report a bout of near pneumonia,[143] a "curious trouble with [TR's] chest,"[144] and even far worse news. In mid-December, TR suffered a near-fatal pulmonary embolism. His doctors feared a second.[145] Too sick to return home, he reluctantly delegated to Archie his annual performance as Santa (he had arrived in a sleigh the previous year bearing not presents but yet another lecture on Preparedness[146]) at Oyster Bay's Cove School.

He managed to maintain his usual flow of personal correspondence. He continued writing articles and columns. He received far too many visitors. Corinne visited daily, coming and going as she pleased.[147] Former commerce secretary Oscar Straus came often.[148]

Another old friend, the agrarian novelist Hamlin Garland, visited on November 21. They chatted of old acquaintances, mutual Western experiences, and even of Dickens. Garland offered to help fund a memorial at the site of Quentin's grave, and TR's eyes "misted" up. TR had greeted his visitor with all the bonhomie he might muster, but Garland wasn't fooled. "I found him in bed propped up against a mound of pillows," Garland worried to his diary. "He looked heavier than was natural to him and his mustache was almost white. There was something ominous in the immobility of his body. That he is a very sick man is evident to me."[149]

They spoke of politics but once. "I wanted to see this war put through," said the Colonel, "and I wanted to beat Wilson. Wilson is beaten and the war is ended. I can now say *Nunc dimittis*, without regret."[150]

Garland returned four days later. In the interim, TR had two teeth extracted. He "appeared stronger," noted Garland.

He had gained in vitality[, but was] both old and sad, and in his voice (when speaking of his sons) I heard something indicative of decay. That he was in worse condition than the bulletins stated was obvious to me. He lay like a man who could not move. His feet were covered thickly with blankets and when he reached his right hand to me he did so without moving his shoulders, a motion which alarmed me. It suggested immobility. For a moment I could not control my voice, but he spoke of his condition as though it was only a temporary disability. . . .

Never were we closer than at that moment. But when I took his hand at parting, I had a clear premonition that I would not see him again.[151]

Elihu Root and the veteran diplomat Henry White visited on November 26 to discuss postwar conditions but found him too weak to talk. White, soon to accompany Wilson to Versailles, departed feeling that TR supported Wilson's proposed League of Nations.[152] If TR somehow did, he would have envisioned more an anti-German alliance than anything resembling Wilson's idealistic dream. At TR's request, Cabot Lodge spent two full mornings discussing the League.[153] Corinne Robinson had helped arrange their meeting (Lodge even stayed with her) and sat in on their first session. Lodge's later reservations about the League, she recalled, "were tentatively formulated at the bedside of the Colonel. . . . [O]n the fundamental issues of 'America First' . . . they stood invariably as one man."[154]

In mid-December, *Le Matin* editor in chief Stéphane Lauzanne, ready to return to Paris, visited, inquiring of what sentiments he might convey to the French people. "I have no message to send to France," TR responded. "I have given her the best I had. If over there you speak of me, tell them simply that I have but one regret, that I was not able to give myself."[155]

William Allen White, heading for Paris to cover the peace conference for the *Red Cross Magazine*, stopped in. He found the old Rough Rider "propped up in a bed, sweet as a cherub"[156] but "going very fast."[157] White conveyed rumors of a prospective Leonard Wood White House bid. "Well," TR responded, "probably I shall get in this thing in June [1919],"[158] and he revealed news of his own: the support of both Penrose and Barnes.

Yet TR continued to deny any further presidential ambitions. "Let 1920 take care of itself when it comes," he declared to Henry Stoddard, "but I shall not be the candidate."[159] To the British adventure novelist H. Rider Haggard, he went even further: "I doubt if I will ever again go back into public life. I have had to go into too much bitter truth telling. Like you I am not certain about the future, I hope Germany will suffer a change of heart but I am anything but certain. I don't put much faith in the League of Nations, or any corresponding cure-all."[160]

Nonetheless, should the trumpet sound once more, he would enlist. "But if the leaders of the party come to me," he explained to his close friend Joseph Bucklin Bishop, "and say that they are convinced that I am the man the people want and the only man who can be elected, and that they are all for me, I don't see how I could refuse to run."[161]

To others he was far less circumspect, as when he advised the vociferously anti-German Wall Street attorney James M. Beck, "I don't want you to run for Governor because in all probability I will be the next President. If I am I want you to be Secretary of State."[162]

"It was clear," recalled his valet James Amos, "that he would have to be the Republican candidate in 1920. And I think he contemplated the outlook with a little horror."[163]

As always, the rumor mill ran wild, whether regarding his intentions—or his health. Accurate accounts of his condition would have been shocking enough, but the *American Magazine*[164] alleged that a tick bite to his cheek, inflicted in the Amazon jungle, had produced "the complete degeneration of his mental organs."

"I suppose I have cause for a libel suit," TR pondered to Dr. Richards.

I will send this to my lawyer, but if he does advise a libel suit I do not think that I will undertake it, for I have been pretty successful in my libel suits and one can easily get the habit. I think a better way to answer that will be to go to Florida harpooning devilfish in March. I expect to take that trip with Archie then, providing we are both well enough. A picture harpooning devilfish in a description of the performance will answer this better, I think, than a libel suit would. The public have always exaggerated such reports. I do not know what they think I will do. Some people will think that I take the harpoon in between my teeth, swim out to where the devilfish is, drive the harpoon into the devilfish and, with the rope over my shoulder, swim to the shore with a devilfish in tow.[165]

Just before Christmas, Corinne came once more to comfort her bathrobe-clad[166] brother, though she, too, required comforting. Three months earlier, a sudden heart attack had claimed her sixty-four-year-old husband, Douglas Robinson, and she remained in black mourning garb.[167]

On this day, thought Corrine, her brother "seemed particularly bright and on the road to recovery. His left arm was still in bandages, but with his strong right hand he gesticulated as of old, and sitting in his armchair, his eyes clear and shining, his face ruddy and animated, he seemed to me to have lost nothing of the vigorous and inspiring personality of earlier days."[168]

They chatted of family, of course, with TR repeating his earlier strong desire (*all* his desires, after all, were *strong* desires) for four of Corinne's grandchildren to visit Oyster Bay during the upcoming holidays, with particular emphasis on having thirteen-year-old Douglas (the only boy among those four[169]) view TR's impressive trophy room. As Theodore once admitted, "I'm not a good shot, but I shoot often."[170]

Indeed, he did.

At Roosevelt Hospital, he paused to muse upon his recent birthday—his sixtieth—on Sunday, October 27, 1918. On that date, the already ailing TR had written, more truthfully than jocularly, to Kermit, "I am glad to be sixty, for it somehow gives me the right to be titularly as old as I feel."[171]

To Corinne, Theodore now continued, "Well, anyway, no matter what comes I have kept the promise that I made to myself when I was twenty-one."

"What promise, Theodore?" Corinne asked in her normally high-pitched voice, one akin to their niece Eleanor's.[172] "You made many promises to yourself, and I am sure have kept them all."

"I promised myself," TR responded, slamming his fist upon his chair, "that I would work up to the hilt until I was sixty, and I have done it. I have kept my promise, and now, even if I should be an invalid—I should not wish to be an invalid—but even if I should be an invalid, or if I should die"—and here he suddenly and sharply snapped his fingers—"what difference would it make?"

To TR, death—like life itself—must always be heroic, for himself and for the entire Roosevelt tribe. And so Corinne pressed, "Theodore, do you remember what you said to me nearly a year ago when you thought you were dying in this same hospital? You said that you were glad it was not one of your boys that was dying at that time in this place, for they could die for their country. Do you feel the same way now?"

When TR instantly responded, "Yes, just the same way. I wish that I might, like Quentin, have died for my country," she answered,

I know you wish it, but I want to tell you something. Every one of us—even those not as courageous, not as patriotic, as you are—would, I feel sure, if our country were in peril, be willing to bare

our breasts to any bullet, could we, by so doing, protect and save our country; but the trouble is that the very people who, in peril, will give themselves, with absolute disregard of the consequences, to their country's service, fail, utterly, in times of peace, to sacrifice anything whatsoever for their country's good. The difference, Theodore, between you and the majority of us is that you not only are willing and anxious to die for your country, but that you live for your country every day of your life.[173]

Each day, he focused on Quentin. Dr. Richards recalled that on Monday morning, November 18, "a joint that had cleared up had once again become inflamed and the prospects of an early recovery appeared even more remote than usual." TR remarked to him, "I have always wanted to live until the last of my children should be twenty-one. Tomorrow will be Quentin's birthday, and I suppose I might as well go. Doctor, I have had an abundant life. I have done everything from shooting lizards to being President, and on the whole I have been happy."[174]

Happy but now in tormenting pain. Still, as ever, he somehow grinned and blustered his way through it. When Richards rigidly prescribed a new diet, he responded—perhaps tongue in cheek, perhaps not—"Do what you consider best. I want you to know that I have no habits that I cannot correct and no ideas I cannot control."[175]

Following TR's departure, the hospital's superintendent, Dr. Charles B. Grimshaw, recalled of his most famous patient:

During all the time he was here he was absolutely his old self. The pain that he suffered intermittently could not subdue his vital spirit. He was cheerful even in his suffering, which he jested about.

He spoke in his usual emphatic manner choosing his words carefully, usually avoiding political discussions, although he did talk with some of his many callers about the European trip of President Wilson. His main topic was the war and the problems growing out of it.

Dr. Richards had put the Colonel on a diet, and this was the occasion of many lively debates in which the Colonel described many dishes that he said he wanted but which he knew he could not have.

*He was an excellent patient, however. He joked with his attendants,
but he obeyed. . . .*

*Every hour or so he suffered severe pain, in which he seemed to
take an almost impersonal interest, making it a game to guess how
long the pain would last. When the first twinge came he would look
at the clock and say:*

*"This pain will last two minutes." Or "three minutes," or "four,"
and he would congratulate himself as a good guesser when he hit it
about right, which he frequently did.*

*He joked, too, about the way the pain shifted from place to place,
now in the left knee, now in the right great toe. Always he was
cheerful.*[176]

A surgeon was less impressed: "The folks here do not give him orders.
They think they do. He . . . captivated everybody in the place, and comes
pretty near to running things. It's what I suspect he does everywhere.
Personally I'll be glad when he gets out. Why? Because the nurses and
some of the fool doctors here can then think of something beside[s]
Colonel Roosevelt."[177]

TR departed shortly thereafter—demanded to leave, actually. Dr.
Grimshaw recounted,

*A week before Christmas, he announced that he had decided to spend
the holidays at home at Oyster Bay. He was advised to stay two weeks
longer, but his condition was not dangerous in any way at that time
and the point was not insisted upon.*

*On Christmas Day, true to the programme he had made for him-
self, he arose and dressed. Instead of calling a taxi he walked out of the
hospital, went to the subway, took a train to the Pennsylvania Station
and then a train to Oyster Bay.*[178]

In the hospital elevator, vertigo kicked in, and as TR faltered, Dr.
Richards reached out to catch him. "Don't do that, Doctor," TR objected.
"I am not sick and it will give the wrong impression."[179] Downstairs, he
allowed only Edith to stand with him.[180]

More than mere stumbling should have given cause for alarm. Dr. Richards's public statement upon his patient's release was guarded at best and disconcerting at worse: his patient was "sufficiently recovered to return home on Christmas"—not *fully* recovered—and would not be "able to take up his usual duties [for] six weeks or two months."[181] At one point, doctors warned TR that he might be permanently confined to a wheelchair ("tied to a chair"). "All right!" he blustered. "I can work and live that way too."[182]

It was a Christmas Day of "three generations,"[183] as he described it to still far-off Ted—Theodore and Edith; Archie and Gracie; Alice and Ethel; and Ethel's two children, the sickly four-year-old Richard (TR's first grandson) and eighteen-month-old Edith. "Come, grandpa," Richard yelled from Sagamore Hill's lawn as his grandfather approached, "we must go in and see what Santy has brought for Christmas."[184] However, there was to be no freshly slaughtered young pig as per family custom. The uncertainty of TR's release hamstrung (so to speak) its demise and necessitated substituting turkey.[185]

"Richard and little Edie," TR wrote "Bye," "are the darlingest small souls you have ever known. Little Edie is the busiest person imaginable, and runs around exactly as if she was a small mechanical toy."[186]

"I'm feeling Bully," TR proclaimed to the scrum of neighbors and reporters who greeted him upon his veranda, "and I was treated well at the hospital. The sciatica got the best of me for a time, but I'm alright."[187] He wasn't. Merely watching Edie at play tired him, and he spent the remainder of the afternoon at rest.[188] Ethel worried that he looked "very white."[189]

He continued with his correspondence and columns—and with loathing Wilson. While still at the hospital, he burbled to Dr. Richards, "If this left wrist were a little better I would like to be left alone in this room with our great and good President for about fifteen minutes, and then I would be cheerfully hung."[190]

On December 30, he wrote his friend, the renowned eugenicist Madison Grant, to lecture him on the value of "men of foreign parentage" as U.S. soldiers.[191] On New Year's Day, he dictated letters to Russell J. Coles, accepting a March invitation for him and Ted to come to Florida to devilfish,[192] and to *New York Tribune* editor Ogden Mills Reid, admonishing,

"For Heaven's sake never allude to Wilson as an idealist or militaire or altruist. He is doctrinaire . . . always utterly and coldly selfish."[193] On Thursday, January 2, he dictated a fresh column for the *Kansas City Star*, lambasting Wilson's League of Nations ("we do not intend to take a position of an international meddlesome Matty"[194]).

The following day, writing to a midwestern banker friend, he conceded that while he "frequently erred in judgement," he had "unlike Mr. Wilson . . . never erred in intellectual honesty and moral straightforwardness."[195]

That same day, John T. King visited, departing not only confident of TR's health but also certain of his eventual 1920 triumph.[196] TR also busied himself dictating to Josephine Stricker some brief comments for Archie to deliver in his stead when the American Defense Society gathered that Sunday evening at Sixth Avenue's cavernous Hippodrome Theatre:[197]

I cannot be with you and so all I can do is to wish you Godspeed. There may be no sagging back in the fight for Americanism merely because the war is over.

There are plenty of persons who have already made the assertion that they believe the American people have a short memory and that they intend to revive all the foreign associations which more directly interfere with the complete Americanization of our people. Our principle in this matter should be absolutely simple.

In the first place we should insist that if the immigrant who comes here does in good faith become an American and assimilates himself to us, he shall be treated on an exact equality with everyone else, for it is an outrage to discriminate against any such man because of creed or birthplace or origin. But this is predicated upon the man's becoming in very fact an American and nothing but an American.

If he tries to keep segregated with men of his own origin and separated from the rest of America, then he isn't doing his part as an American.

We have room for but one flag, the American flag, and this excludes the red flag which symbolizes all wars against liberty and

*civilization just as much as it excludes any foreign flag of a nation
to which we are hostile. We have room for but one language here and
that is the English language, for we intend to see that the crucible
turns our people out as Americans, and American nationality, and not
as dwellers in a polyglot boarding house; and we have room for but
one soul loyalty, and that is loyalty to the American people.*[198]

At some point (we know not exactly when), TR jotted a note regarding Will Hays and how best to avoid new Republican fissures now that old ones had healed:

Hays
    *see him; he must go to Washington for 10 days; see Senate &
House; prevent split on domestic policies*[199]

On Christmas Day, another sorrow burdened the Colonel. His beloved terrier, "Shady," his constant companion on walks about Sagamore Hill, had been stolen. Each day he would inquire of his longtime black chauffeur, Charles H. Lee, whether there was any news. Each day, there was none.[200]

Sagamore Hill was not the best place to winter. Jutting into Long Island Sound and poorly insulated, its two furnaces and numerous grate fireplaces fought a losing battle with the cold.[201] As Edith dryly observed to "Bye" that February, "Sagamore is just as warm as it ever was in cold weather. We have plenty of coal but a bird cage is hard to heat."[202]

On December 28, writing to Leonard Wood, TR claimed to be "on the high road to recovery,"[203] and on December 29 and 30, Edith accompanied him on hourlong drives to the village.[204] On New Year's Eve, his fever blazed red hot yet again—reaching 103 degrees. Particularly excruciating pain plagued one finger.[205]

On New Year's Day, rheumatism engulfed his swollen right hand, leaving him largely confined to his room.[206] Doctors visited on a regular basis: Oyster Bay's Dr. George W. Faller (a fellow member of the village's Mattinecock Masonic Lodge #806) came twice daily, and Dr. Richards from the city and two other doctors from Brooklyn traveled up on occasion. Richards advised Edith to secure a live-in nurse, and she engaged a local resident, the twenty-nine-year-old Miss Alice F. Thom, a 1905 nursing school graduate of Brooklyn's Cumberland Street Hospital.[207] Dr. John A. "Josh" Hartwell, a prominent New York City surgeon, longtime friend, and Edith's distant in-law,[208] now warned that Theodore's recovery might prove even longer than Dr. Richards's original guarded estimate.[209] Edith confided to Ethel that Theodore was "suffering day and night. . . . [I]n this last attack he has felt as miserable as at any time in the hospital, except the time he had that curious trouble in his chest."[210]

The big house emptied out. Alice returned to Washington. On Friday, January 3, Ethel and her brood headed south to winter at Major Thomas Hitchcock's three-thousand-acre Aiken, South Carolina, estate.[211] Archie received disturbing news from Back Bay Boston that his father-in-law, Thomas S. Lockwood, was dying. Jettisoning plans to substitute for his father at the Hippodrome, he accompanied Gracie northward.[212] Corinne planned to visit that Friday. TR felt so poorly that he advised her to wait until Monday.[213] "Father was so melancholy,"[214] Edith wrote Ethel.

Theodore did receive Ted's wife, Eleanor, recently returned home from France. "You know, Father," she dared to comment, "Ted has always worried for fear he would not be worthy of you."

"Worthy of me? Darling, I'm so very proud of him. He has won high honor not only for his children but, like the Chinese, he has ennobled his ancestors. I walk with my head higher because of him. . . . [M]y war was a bow-and-arrow affair compared to Ted's, and no one knows it better than I do."[215]

With fewer persons to turn to (Eleanor remained with her family at Port Chester), on Saturday morning, January 4, Edith phoned James Amos, importuning him to pack a valise, take a leave from his regular position at the William J. Burns Detective Agency, and remain at Saga-more Hill to assist with the Colonel's care.[216]

Josephine Stricker arrived to take dictation but, finding her once indefatigable boss asleep, departed without accomplishing a thing.[217]

James Amos arrived that evening, disturbed by his former boss's appearance:

His face bore a tired expression. There was a look of weariness in his eyes. It was perfectly plain that he had suffered deeply. And it made me sick at heart to see him so.

It seemed unnatural for Theodore Roosevelt, whom I had seen always so full of vigor and life, to be thus brought down. He asked me to give him a bath and change his pajamas. This I did. He was in great pain and I had to be exceedingly careful. When I was through he said: 'By George, you never hurt me a little bit.' My heart swelled with happiness to know I had been able to do this. Then he got me to turn his chair so he could look out toward [Long Island Sound's] Centre Island. He had played there as a boy. And he sat looking out of the window into the darkness very quietly for a little while. Later he asked me to put him to bed. This I did and watched with him through the night.[218]

On Sunday, January 5, Edith responded in his stead to an invitation from the Independent Citizens Committee on Welcoming Returning Soldiers, which had recently named him its honorary chairman. "Rheumatism," she wrote, "has invaded Mr. Roosevelt's right hand and he wants me to write that he has telegraphed his acceptance. This is to assure you that he will be at your call by springtime."[219] She hardly exaggerated his infirmity. Having dictated Friday's epistle to Ogden Reid, he could not even sign it, leaving the task to Miss Stricker.[220]

Rheumatism or not, he remained the avid naturalist, and in a letter written that same day to the famed ornithologist William Beebe regarding Beebe's four-volume *A Monograph of the Pheasants*, he displayed his own remarkable knowledge of his abiding first great love—birding:

Dear Beebe:

I have read through your really wonderful volume. . . . I cannot speak too highly of the work. Now, a question: on Page xxiii, final paragraph, there is an obviously incorrect sentence about which I formerly spoke to you. Ought you not call attention to it and correct it in the second volume? In it you say by inference that the grouse of the Old World and the grouse of the New World are in separate families, although

I believe that three of the genera and one of the species are identical. Moreover, you say that the family of pheasants includes not only the pheasants but the partridges and quail of the Old and the grouse of the New World, and furthermore red-legged partridges and francolins, which of course you have already included in the term of partridges and quail of the Old World. Obviously someone has made a mistake, and I cannot even form a guess of what was originally intended. Do you mind telling me, and I can say in my [forthcoming] review that this slip of the printer will be corrected in some subsequent edition?

Faithfully yours, T.[221]

TR had remained attached to Quentin's fiancée, Flora Payne Whitney ("Remember, Flora, that as long as I live I shall love you as if you were my own daughter"[222]). She visited that Sunday,[223] and after TR dictated a letter to Kermit,[224] she appended a postscript that Theodore was "having a horrid painful time."[225]

Almost on a lark, the British poet Alfred Noyes motored over to Sagamore Hill, hoping to drop in. In 1914, TR had written Noyes, complimenting him on his poetry and, not surprisingly, excoriating "the ultra-pacifist type. . . . They hold little futile peace parades, and send round peace postage-stamps with a dove on them, and get up petitions for peace in the public schools; but they do not venture for one moment to condemn any man who has done wrong."[226]

TR remained too sick to welcome Noyes but retained enough strength to yell downstairs to Edith (and loudly enough for Noyes to hear), "Tell him I'm a pacifist, but I do believe in common sense."[227]

Cousin Emlen visited, as he had each day. Finding TR asleep, he departed without seeing him.[228]

Sixty-three-year-old Dr. George Faller called each morning and also each evening at eight. On January 5, he arrived at two in the afternoon,[229] just before TR received his Italian-born Oyster Bay barber, Giovanni Michael Gerardi. The stocky forty-year-old Gerardi recalled,

The Colonel rose to greet me and then said "Hello, John," and to the physician, "Here's my Feast of St. Rocco friend." You know St. Rocco is

an Italian patron saint whose day the Italians of Oyster Bay celebrate each year.

Then he said to me, "The doctor here can tell you more about St. Rocco than you know," adding, "John, you do not have to write to me for a subscription for your fund. All you have to do is come here and get it."

The physician was about to depart then, and after telling the Colonel what he could have to eat departed.

The Colonel was always particular how he was shaved. He would rub his hand over his face, and if there was a tiny rough spot he would call my attention to it.

Sunday he rubbed his palm over his face and said pointing to his chin, "John, you have left some hair there." I went over the spot lightly and then he rubbed his palm over his face and said, "John, that is good."

He looked well and he was just as cheerful as ever when I departed. I had no worry about my good friend when I left the house.[230]

TR remained upon the sofa in his library for the day, reading and chatting with Edith. It was, despite everything, "a happy and wonderful day,"[231] thought Edith.

Still, there was pain. Edith would soon write Ted,

The last attack of rheumatism was a little better. Everything had been adjusted. . . . He had a happy day. People came in and I went down to see them.

Father was in your old nursery and loved the view, of which he spoke, and as it got dusk he watched the dancing flames and spoke of the happiness of being home, and made little plans for me. I think he had made up his mind that he would have to suffer for some time to come & with his high courage had adjusted himself to bear it. He was very sweet all day. Since Quentin was killed he has been sad, only Ethel's little girl had the power to make him merry.[232]

She played solitaire as he read. At one point, he peered up and said, "I wonder if you will ever know how I love Sagamore Hill."[233]

"When I called on him [the previous] night at 8 o'clock," Dr. Faller recalled, "I wanted to know his condition, but I could not get him to tell me anything about his case. He talked about almost everything except himself and his condition of health. His months of illness had not made much change in his appearance. He was ruddy, and, to outward appearances, nearly as sturdy as ever. I left him . . . apparently improving rapidly and feeling first-rate."[234]

Dr. Richards was scheduled to visit that evening. Delayed in the city, he phoned to explain he could not come. Edith advised him not to worry. All was fine.[235]

That would soon change. To Edith, TR complained that he felt he was no longer breathing. "I am perfectly all right but I have a curious feeling. I know it is not going to happen, but it is such a strange feeling."[236]

Edith gave her husband some smelling salts.[237] Nurse Thom phoned Dr. Faller, and he raced back by auto.[238] "I felt as if my heart was going to stop beating," TR informed him. "I couldn't seem to get a long breath."[239]

No one seemed too concerned. "I found Colonel Roosevelt looking about the same," Faller recalled. "He was interested in his condition, but not worried. He had no idea that he was in danger. After I had been with him for some time he said that he felt better."[240]

Yet his pain remained. Edith recalled how their Boston friend, Dr. Thomas Sturgis Bigelow, had suggested morphine when ptomaine struck TR the previous May. She begged Faller to inject her husband with the drug to ease his sleep. She had taken it in June 1912 for facial erysipelas.[241]

At Roosevelt Hospital TR had received opiates for his sleeplessness. Two days previously, Dr. Faller, for reasons lost to history, had injected two hypodermics of arsenic into him.[242] He agreed to the morphine, and Nurse Thom injected the hypodermic.[243] Twenty minutes after arriving, Faller departed.[244]

It was late for even the healthiest of patients on a wintry January night, and around midnight TR turned to James Amos for assistance. "I could see plainly enough the look of great weariness in his face," Amos would write.

He did not talk much and a little later said: "James, don't you think I might go to bed now?"

That was his way of asking for a thing, so I removed his robe and had to almost lift him into bed. Mrs. Roosevelt was in and out of the room and . . . kissed him good-night and retired. The nurse had gone to bed. . . . Just after Mrs. Roosevelt left the room; Mr. Roosevelt said: "James, will you please put out the light?"²⁴⁵

The house was lit entirely in those days by old-fashioned lamps. There was a very small one on the dresser which lit the large room with a dim yellow light. I put it out and sat in a chair where I could see the bed. It was a winter's night and there was nothing stirring outside. The large house was very still. Soon my eyes became accustomed to the dark and I could see him lying there on the bed very still and I could tell by his breathing that he was asleep. I was alone with Theodore Roosevelt as he slept in a sound and peaceful slumber. . . . About four o'clock in the morning I was startled by his irregular breathing. Very quickly it became so uncertain that I got up and went to his side.²⁴⁶

To a *New York World* reporter, Amos would soon explain, "He had stopped snoring or breathing hard, and there was something queer about the way his breath came. I could hear a breath, then I could count one-two-three-four-five, then there would be another breath, kind of quiet, like a sigh. I put my hand on his forehead, but there didn't seem to be a sweat or anything. Still, I thought something was wrong. So I called the nurse."²⁴⁷

"When she came," he wrote, "I asked her to call Mrs. Roosevelt. It was about 4:15. In a few moments Mrs. Roosevelt came in. She was calm and went to her husband's side. She leaned over him and called—'Theodore darling!' But there was no answer."²⁴⁸

Edith directed Amos to summon the Roosevelts' black family chauffeur, Charles Lee.²⁴⁹ Dr. Faller returned once more to find TR, as the *Sun* noted, "on his left side with his arms folded in an attitude of natural sleep. His expression was serenity itself."²⁵⁰

At six, Edith phoned Corinne.[251] Cousin Emlen arrived just before seven and learned of Theodore's death.[252] Edith phoned Miss Stricker in Manhattan, instructing her to dispatch word to the world beyond the immediate family.[253]

"In the morning, after the undertaker had left, Mrs. Roosevelt told Lee . . . and myself to come with her," recalled Amos. "We went to the quiet bedroom where our dear friend lay in his last sleep. Mrs. Roosevelt, Lee, and I knelt beside the bed and recited the Lord's Prayer. Her voice was steadiest and bravest of the three."[254]

Months before, Norwegian-born sculptor Sigurd Neandross had entreated TR for permission to create yet another bust of the great Rough Rider. Roosevelt agreed only following additional lobbying from Anthony Fiala, one of his companions in exploring the Amazon. TR sat for Neandross at his magazine offices and at the American Museum of Natural History but entered Roosevelt Hospital before Neandross could complete his work.[255]

If TR could not be sculpted alive, he would be sculpted dead. On the morning of his death, James Earle Fraser arrived at Sagamore Hill. Years before, Fraser had created TR's bust for the U.S. Senate's Vice Presidents Gallery and designed the Indian Head nickel. Today, he slathered the deceased's head and right hand in grease before carefully applying plaster-soaked bandages. His mission: to create a death mask preserving his subject's features for posterity, as had been done with George Washington, Abraham Lincoln, and William McKinley. TR's hand cast bore no hint of the rheumatism that inflicted such agony. His face, heavier than history remembers it—his nose larger, his moustache bushier, his hair closer cropped from his barber's recent work—seemed at great peace.[256]

The news reached Archie and Gracie as they sped toward Boston. Archie detrained, leaving Gracie to proceed alone to mourn her now deceased father, as he returned to Oyster Bay to mourn his. Arriving only past nightfall,[257] he cabled Ted and Kermit, both now stationed in occupied Germany: "The old lion is dead."[258]

That Sunday, Robert Bacon visited Ted and Kermit before returning to his quarters for the night. Kermit dined at Coblenz. Ted was the first to hear the news. He found his brother, returned from town and sipping wine at his tent. They spent the night, sleepless in sorrowful conversation. Not until 2:00 a.m. did Bacon learn of his friend's death. He roused Dick Derby from his sleep. Together, they joined the Roosevelt brothers. They decided it should be Derby to return stateside. At 6:00 the next evening, Derby, with Bacon escorting him as far as Trier, headed home.[259]

"It is foolish to think of oneself," Kermit soon wrote his mother, "but you will know how the bottom has dropped out from me."[260]

At Camp Funston, *Kansas City Star* managing editor Ralph Stout interrupted Leonard Wood's breakfast to convey the information. "Sad, sad business," Wood wrote in his diary. "I have lost my best friend."[261]

William Howard Taft was on the road. From Harrisburg, he cabled Edith Roosevelt his sympathies, referring not only to his "great sorrow" and "personal loss" but also to her husband's now dashed personal ambitions ("The country can ill afford . . . to lose one who . . . could in the next decade have done so much for it and humanity"[262]). He solicited an invitation to the funeral and, returning to New York, slogged through snow-covered streets to purchase a proper silk top hat before embarking on a specially chartered train car to Oyster Bay.[263]

Woodrow Wilson also traveled by train en route from Turin to Paris. At Modane, on the Italian-French border, a French messenger boarded his car with a telegram. Suspecting nothing unusual, reporters milled about outside his window, occasionally staring inside. In 1968, the *Louisville Courier-Journal*'s Arthur Krock would describe Wilson's first reaction as "a kind of spontaneous relaxation," then a "distinctly a sad one."[264] Decades earlier, Krock and another member of the traveling press, author Bellamy Partridge, had told a startlingly different tale to author Henry F. Pringle. Pringle reported that Krock and Partridge first witnessed an expression of "surprise" flash across Wilson's face. "Then," said Pringle, "came pity. Then a look of transcendent triumph."[265]

Wilson's staff prepared a telegram of condolence to Edith. As he struggled to edit it, his own wife Edith knitted, and the words "another White House widow"[266] blazed through her mind. Her husband shortened "deeply grieved" to "grieved"[267] before settling on merely "shocked." He shunned any reference to his predecessor's vexatious crusade for Preparedness, instead lauding his alerting of the nation "to the dangers of private control which lurked in our financial and industrial systems."[268]

Later, in Paris, David Lloyd George offered his sympathy and stood "aghast at the outburst of acrid detestation that flowed from Wilson's lips."[269]

Other Americans in Paris did mourn. William Allen White breakfasted at the Hôtel Vouillemont and saw the headlines in Frank Munsey's *Paris Herald*. "Not since my father's death has death stabbed me so poignantly," he recalled.[270]

"Again and again," he added, "I looked at the headlines to be sure that I was reading them correctly."[271]

As he did, Wilson's press secretary, his friend Ray Stannard Baker, arrived, and White cried out, "Ray, Ray, the Colonel is dead—Roosevelt!"[272] Baker, already aware, moved to comfort him.

"All day," White wrote his wife, Sallie, back in Kansas, "I have been on the verge of tears."[273]

"He and death did not rhyme," mourned Hamlin Garland. "His going leaves a vacant place in my horizon, something like the sudden sinking of a mountain peak."[274]

Within days, Edith Wharton composed a poem, narrating how the dead themselves, great multitudes of them upon Long Island Sound, welcomed their newest comrade:

> Softly they came, and beached the boat, and gathered
> In the still cove under the icy stars,
> Your last-born, and the dear loves of your heart,
> And all men that have loved right more than ease,
> And honor above honors; all who gave
> Free-handed of their best for other men,
> And thought their giving taking: they who knew
> Man's natural state is effort, up and up—
> All these were there.[275]

From Washington, Cabot Lodge wired Edith Roosevelt, "Words fail me. I am overwhelmed."[276] A month later, before a joint session of

Congress, he would eulogize his departed friend for a full hour and fifty minutes. As he ended, noted the *New York Times*, his "voice broke, and he had to steady himself as he sank into his chair. A deep hush fell over the throng."[277]

Franklin and Eleanor Roosevelt heard the news in the mid-Atlantic. "My cousin's death was in every way a great shock[,] for we heard just before leaving that he was better—and he was after all not old," Franklin wrote to Josephus Daniels. "But I cannot help think that he himself would have had it this way and that he has been spared a lingering illness of perhaps years."[278]

After all, how might anyone ever run for the White House confined to a wheelchair?

Back home, everyone from Bryan and Hughes, Seabury and Root, Barnes and Penrose, Alton B. Parker and Joe Tumulty, to even his attempted assassin, John Schrank ("a great, good man and honest . . . I never hated him"[279]), expressed regret. Gutzon Borglum proposed—what else?—an immense equestrian monument blasted into the cliffs of the Hudson River Palisades.[280]

In Worcester, fifty-eight-year-old Charles E. Burnham, the 1904 Prohibition Party candidate for Massachusetts state auditor and a 1912 Bull Mooser, obsessed over press accounts of his hero's life and death. Grief stricken, he ingested cyanide. His wife found his body the next morning.[281]

Corinne and her son Douglas had hastened to Oyster Bay. Late that afternoon, she and Edith strolled forlornly through Sagamore Hill's woods and along its Long Island Sound shore. As winter's darkness fell, they heard the buzz of aeroplanes. "They must be planes from the camp where Quentin trained," said Edith, choking with emotion. "They have been sent as a guard of honor for his father."[282]

A delegation from Mattinecock Lodge paid respects, offering Masonic ceremonies for their brother lodge member.[283] Episcopal bishop David Greer of New York offered the Cathedral of St. John the Divine.[284] Edith respectfully declined both, vetoing any large ceremony, any repeat of John Purroy Mitchel's monster observance. On the morning of Theodore's funeral, she hosted a private family gathering at Sagamore Hill beforehand, but neither she nor Corinne attended the church service or the burial.[285]

The most modest of rituals greeted mourners at Oyster Bay's green wood-framed, red-gabled Christ Church.[286] The coffin was of oak. A silver plate upon it read:

Theodore Roosevelt
Born October 27, 1858. Died January 6, 1919.[287]

There was no eulogy. No flowers. No honorary pallbearers. Not even any music, though Christ Church's gaunt rector, Dr. George E. Talmadge, recited the words of the Colonel's favorite hymn, No. 636 in the Episcopal hymnal, "How Firm a Foundation, Ye Saints of the Lord."[288] Its last stanza read,

The soul that on Jesus hath leaned for repose,
I will not, I will not desert to its foes;
that soul, though all hell shall endeavor to shake,
I'll never, no, never, no, never forsake.

"Theodore," Dr. Talmadge prayed at the end of the service, "the Lord bless thee, and keep thee. The Lord make his face to shine upon thee, and be gracious unto thee. The Lord lift up his countenance upon thee, and give thee peace, both now and evermore. Amen."[289]

Admission was by ticket only. Outside, the Colonel's grief-stricken neighbors crowded snow-covered Main Street. Archie, Ethel, Alice, and Nick Longworth attended, as did Ted's wife, Eleanor. "Bye," crippled by her own rheumatism, proved too sick for travel from her Farmington, Connecticut, home. George Perkins was also absent, in Europe on business. Mac McGrath—still with Perkins—did attend.[290] So did Lodge and Root, Warren Harding and Hiram Johnson, Leonard Wood and General Peyton Marsh,[291] Gifford Pinchot and Oscar Straus, Henry Stoddard and John T. King, Rough Riders and Boy Scouts and twenty-five New York City police, Charles Evans Hughes and William Howard Taft, James Amos, chauffeur Charles Lee, Madison Grant, and TR's devilfish-hunting companion Russell J. Coles.

Outside Christ Church, Taft pondered that his erstwhile friend "would never have been happy to live the life of an invalid."[292] Usher William Loeb, TR's old White House secretary, bade him inside to sit alongside the family servants. Archie bade the former president to come forward, installing him in the pew ahead of Cabot Lodge. "You're a dear personal friend," Archie consoled Taft, "and you must come up farther."[293] Taft did, and when all progressed to TR's snow-covered hillside grave, no one, it is said, wept more deeply than William Howard Taft.

The nation honored him. "Businesses, schools, and social affairs," noted a press report, "will be suspended in nearly every city and town of the Central and Western States. . . . Arrangements have been made in many places to stop street cars and at various forts salutes will be fired."[294] At Roosevelt, New Jersey (so named for TR), employees at its various fertilizer factories halted work.[295] The Boy Scouts of America pledged to plant a minimum of sixteen-thousand trees in his honor.[296]

At noon in the city, schools dismissed eight hundred thousand students. Wall Street closed a half hour later, and the entire city observed a minute of silence. The *New York Times* noted,

Patrolmen on traffic duty or elsewhere on their posts bared their heads for a minute, and great throngs in all parts of the town followed their example.

Power on the traction lines was shut off for a minute and many thousands of citizens halted at the ticket gates. Lights in the trains were lowered and the passengers took off their hats in tribute.[297]

Woodrow Wilson, of course, remained in Europe, about to fashion the League of Nations that TR had proved too wary of. It fell to his vice president, Thomas R. Marshall, to represent the administration at Christ Church.

"Death," Marshall observed, "had to take him sleeping, for if Roosevelt had been awake, there would have been a fight."[298]

And not even Marshall dared predict the winner.

Epilogue
"Death was the only relief"

WHAT IF DEATH HAD NOT TAKEN THEODORE ROOSEVELT?
What if he had taken death?

The idea struck slowly—before striking hard.

It commenced simply enough. A brief endnote marked the incidence of suicide among TR's followers. Senator Medill McCormick overdosed on barbiturates in his Washington, DC, hotel room in 1925.[1] Chicago furniture magnate Alexander H. Revell jumped from a ninth-floor window in 1931. Studebaker's Albert R. Erskine shot himself through the heart two years later. Amos Pinchot unsuccessfully slashed the veins of his upper arm in August 1942.[2] Kermit Roosevelt—long haunted by moodiness, alcoholism, and depression—put a Browning Colt .45 to his head while on duty in the Aleutians in June 1943.[3]

But other family suicides accompanied Kermit's. TR's immensely troubled younger brother Elliott died of a seizure in August 1894 after flinging himself out the window of his mistress's West 102nd Street home. He had allegedly attempted suicide three times previously.[4]

Corinne's nineteen-year-old son Stewart Douglas Robinson either fell or jumped to his death from a Harvard dormitory widow in February 1909. "Detectives here," noted a press report, "who have investigated the case are skeptical in regard to the theory that young Robinson's death was accidental. They cannot understand how he could have fallen from the window of his brother [Monroe]'s room on the sixth floor of the Hampton Hall dormitory, as the sill of the window is five and a half feet from the floor."[5]

In April 1938, Kermit's troubled thirteen-year-old son Dirck went missing from Groton, leaving a note reading, "If a man feels it necessary to take his own life, should he be condemned?"[6] In January 1953, he committed suicide at his mother's Sutton Place townhouse.[7] His family claimed a heart attack felled him, a rather unconvincing explanation for the death of a twenty-eight-year-old.[8]

TR's granddaughter, Paulina Longworth Sturm (Alice's daughter sired illegitimately by William E. Borah), ended her own life in January 1957. Like Kermit, Archie, and Elliott, she suffered from depression. Like Medill McCormick, she overdosed—in her case, washing down twelve barbiturates and forty-eight sleeping pills with hard liquor. She very likely first attempted suicide before departing Vassar; she certainly attempted it again in New York in May 1952.[9] Her suicide—like Dirck's, Kermit's, Robinson's and McCormick's—was covered up.

Paulina's cousin Judith, Ethel's daughter, sick with cancer and wracked by her own alcoholism and depression, never took her own life but talked "incessantly of suicide, its different aspects . . . and would wake from sleep crying" before her own September 1973 death.[10]

Quentin, of course, died in aerial combat. But while in France, awaiting his chance to fly, he penned a short story about a U-boat captain's suicide containing this passage: "Suddenly there was the roar of a Shot. . . . He lay bent over his desk, the pistol still clutched in his hands. . . . Perhaps he was right, after all. The service pistol is a merciful thing."[11]

I finally recalled that TR himself had very earnestly deliberated suicide during his disastrous 1913–1914 "River of Doubt" expedition. "You can get out," he informed Kermit. "I will stop here."[12] But Kermit would not let him, admonishing his father that he was going back to civilization—one way or another—and it would be easier for all concerned if his carcass were as ambulatory as possible.

That incident highlights TR's significant suicidal streak. "I've always made it a practice on such trips to take a bottle of morphine with me," he informed Oscar King Davis, "because one never knows what is going to happen. I always meant that, if at any time it became inevitable, I would have it over with at once, without going through a long-drawn out agony from which death was the only relief."[13]

How persistent was that urge? Too persistent. His friends and family feared his suicide not only as he fought back against the agony of his wife's and mother's deaths in February 1884[14] but even before that, as he courted Alice Lee and remained uncertain of his success. "He was once found wandering in the woods at night," records Sylvia Jukes Morris, "too restless to sleep, and apparently suicidal."[15]

His 1917 request to fight in France was, after all, "only asking to be allowed to die."[16]

His attitude hardly escaped notice. In September 1911, William Howard Taft observed to Philander Knox, "The truth is he believes in war and wishes to be a Napoleon and to die on the battlefield. He has the spirit of the old berserkers."[17]

In September 1914, Owen Wister dared broach the issue of TR's supposed death wish to Edith. She thought the idea rubbish but conceded that the new world war might be good for him, a distraction from his recent political failures.[18] By January 1919, that distraction was over.

Many, perhaps most, recoil from suicide for fear of divine retribution. TR may not have been among them. He was churchgoing. He was religious. But his belief in any sort of afterlife was slim at best. Invariably, he spoke of death as only a "blackness" or "darkness."[19] He exhibited little faith in any Christian-style afterlife.

His faith was in himself—but not always. He was a warrior but not always a happy warrior.[20]

Depression dogged him, particularly in early 1916 ("the blackest period of [TR's] life. He felt . . . all his efforts had been well-nigh useless"[21]), when Harold Ickes found him "deep down into the doldrums."[22] James Amos described his "great depression"[23] on being denied the opportunity for active duty. "There is not one among us in whom a devil does not dwell," Roosevelt wrote that March. "At some time, on some point, that devil masters each of us."[24]

Devils haunted the upper middle class. Greater—or at least more gilded—demons tormented what passed for an American aristocracy. Questions chased them as to what they might achieve and should achieve, questions that fortune and breeding could not mask but only inflame.

The man to whom Theodore Roosevelt wrote of devils knew his own. He was a poet decidedly down on his luck, a threadbare, alcoholic young man, when in January 1904 Kermit, then at Groton, introduced his work to his father. President Roosevelt publicly gushed over his literary output in *The Outlook*,[25] pulled publishing strings for him, and even provided him with a handsome sinecure at the New York Customs Office—perhaps the only such patronage appointment the civil service–minded TR ever stooped to.[26] His name was Edwin Arlington Robinson, and among the poems TR so admired was this:

> Whenever Richard Cory went down town,
> The people on the pavement looked at him:
> He was a gentleman from sole to crown,
> Clean favored, and imperially slim.
>
> And he was always quietly arrayed,
> And he was always human when he talked;
> But still he fluttered pulses when he said,
> "Good-morning," and he glittered when he walked.
>
> And he was rich—yes, richer than a king—
> And admirably schooled in every grace.
> In fine, we thought that he was everything
> To make us wish that we were in his place.
>
> So on we worked, and waited for the light,
> And went without the meat, and cursed the bread;
> And Richard Cory, one calm summer night,
> Went home and put a bullet through his head.[27]

Yes, there was something in the air back then, something tragic and romantic—and deadly.

And Theodore Roosevelt was not immune.

"There was a melancholy side to T.R.'s soul," reflected historian Edward Wagenknecht, "and it reveals itself even in what seem superficially to be expressions of the opposite character. It shows in his furious energy, his determination to cram his days more full than they can hold, as if life would otherwise be intolerable."[28] TR hinted at such a motivation when he himself observed, "Black care rarely sits behind a rider whose pace is fast enough."[29]

Wagenknecht buttressed his case by citing three of Roosevelt's associates: Henry Cabot Lodge, Owen Wister, and his key foreign policy adviser, the diplomat Lewis Einstein. Their observations bear repeating at somewhat greater length.

"You are always so buoyant and fearless that everybody thinks that you are one of the most sanguine of men," Cabot Lodge wrote to him in September 1903. "I am one of the two or three people in the world who know better," Lodge continued. "I know you are, and always have been, a pessimist in regard to yourself and your prospects, and . . . it does make you see things sometimes too darkly."[30]

"Time and again in his career [the] fear of failure in public life preyed on his mind," Einstein concluded in *Roosevelt: His Mind in Action*. "Roosevelt's buoyant exuberance and the confidence which impressed people were only veils hiding the doubt, the depression often gnawing his soul, the secret of which he unbared only to his intimates. . . . His mercurial temperament swayed between elation and moods of utmost depression."[31]

Wister described "the wistfulness [which] blurred his eyes—the misty perplexity and pain, which [the portraitist John Singer] Sargent has caught so well. This look was the sign of . . . his determination to grasp his optimism tight, lest it escape him in the many darknesses that rose around him along his way."[32]

Or recall Lawrence F. Abbott's words: "No man that I have known liked personal approval more than Roosevelt. . . . [H]e was really hurt when those to whom he was attached were displeased with him. There are people who thought he was thick-skinned. On the contrary, he was highly sensitive."[33]

"I cannot remember to have seen a man so cast down by political defeat,"[34] an associate recalled following his 1886 mayoral debacle. Confronted in September 1898 by the good-government Independents he had betrayed in securing the GOP gubernatorial nomination, he "cried like a baby. . . . [H]e could hardly walk when he left. . . . The poor fellow is broken up."[35] To Lodge, he confessed that he "hardly had been able to eat or sleep."[36]

Yet he always bounced back. But what if, in January 1919, the pain, the darkness, the depression that his immense, toothy grin veiled so well finally grew so intense as to momentarily shatter his iron will? What if the realization hit him that he existed only at the horrid beginning of an ever-worsening physical spiral? He was half deaf, half blind, wheelchair bound, his arm in a sling, tormented by massive pain. Unable to sleep or even sign his name, he was too ill to even receive Josephine Stricker or Emlen Roosevelt, Alfred Noyes or his sister Corinne.

And, as always, there was Quentin.

"It is rather awful," he had confessed, "to know that he paid with his life, and that my other sons may pay with their lives, to try to put in practice what I preached."[37]

"I can now say *Nunc dimittis*,"[38] he informed Hamlin Garland at Roosevelt Hospital. *Nunc dimittis*—the beginning of the prayer of the aged Simeon in the Gospel of Luke: "Nunc dimittis servum tuum, Domine, secundum verbum tuum, in pace."

"Now, Master," Simeon had entreated the Lord his God, "you can let your servant go in peace, just as you promised."

The servant was ready to go.

Circumstances resembling TR's involve former New York governor Martin H. ("He kept us out of war") Glynn. Returning from a Boston hospital in December 1924 and suffering intense back and arthritic pain, he shot himself. The suicide was covered up. Psychologist Dr. James Rossè noted that Glynn exhibited

classic symptoms of hopelessness, helplessness and hurting. He was in pain for about 38 years of his 53. The last two being the most intense. Pain of such severity and length wears one down. He had reached the stage of becoming an invalid. . . . He became inactive. He reached out continuously to God for relief and it did not seem to come. . . . The ending of the hope and relief he received in Boston was too much. Pain is irrational, it reduces sleep, eliminates pleasure and causes deep depres-

sion. It focuses on the hopelessness of the human being's life. Demons attack in the night when one cannot sleep. Reason and the ability to reason end. That last night must have been terrible. He . . . had lost a child. . . . Also the Christmas season has often triggered suicides.[39]

Morphine.

It was Oscar King Davis's mention of morphine that caught my eye. For I instantly recalled another mention of that drug nestled within my narrative.

Dr. George W. Faller visited Sagamore Hill at 8:00 p.m. on that Sunday, January 5, 1919. Edith begged him to administer the opiate to her suffering husband. Certainly, her husband needed something to ease his pain and sleeplessness. But that injection might ultimately also serve a darker purpose: to provide a reason for the drug to be discovered in any autopsy.

"About four o'clock in the morning I was startled by his irregular breathing,"[40] his valet James Amos recalled. "He had stopped snoring or breathing hard, and there was something queer about the way his breath came. I could hear a breath, then I could count one-two-three-four-five, then there would be another breath, kind of quiet, like a sigh."[41]

Amos's description of Roosevelt's last moments is consistent with "the most life-threatening morphine overdose symptom"—that is, a "decreased respiratory rate of less than 12 breaths per minute."[42]

The official cause of death, however, was a pulmonary embolism— again, a side effect of a morphine overdose.

TR had suffered such an embolism at Roosevelt Hospital the previous December. That Sunday evening, his breathing was odd ("I felt as if my heart was going to stop beating. I couldn't seem to get a long breath"). Thus, the diagnosis was not at all suspicious—in 1919, anyway.

In 2010, however, Dr. Paul Marks, president emeritus of Memorial Sloan-Kettering Cancer Center, and Dr. Andrew R. Marks, cardiologist and professor at Columbia University College of Physicians and Surgeons, concluded that "embolism is unlikely since Faller recorded [just six hours before Roosevelt's death] 'normal heart and pulse'—and this is very unlikely associated with a pulmonary embolus."[43] While concluding that a "myocardial infarction" (i.e., a heart attack) ultimately felled Roosevelt, they nonetheless allow (in author Edmund Morris's words) "that the undisclosed amount of morphine administered to the patient four hours before his death may have caused the respiratory depression noticed by James Amos."[44]

Theodore Roosevelt worked up to the very end. But had his ominous heartbeat and breathing shouted to him what he wanted never to hear? A message he could no longer avoid. He was a sick man, growing weaker, not stronger. There would be no more tours. No more speeches. No third term. And barely much of himself.

The game was up.

"I would have it over with at once, without going through a long-drawn out agony from which death was the only relief."

His death mask reveals a countenance peaceful, at rest, as if fallen eternally asleep from just the right (or rather wrong) amount of morphine.

His funeral was oddly muted—not held at the Capitol or the massive Cathedral of St. John the Divine. No spouse or sister attended. No music accompanied it. It was as if there was something to be ashamed of or nervous about.

What if Edith found an empty vial and knew enough of her husband to grasp its significance?

In any case, there was no autopsy.

It is impossible to know what happened.

We surmise what we can. We dissect what evidence exists of our subject's final actions and the hints—no, not defining proof but certainly ample hints—of means, motive, and opportunity. We dare not present a final answer. But we do respectfully present these facts.

"What I have found remarkable is that infirm people want to hold onto life," a friend has commented to me. "It's the young Gods who destroy themselves. I think [Roosevelt] would have considered it a coward's way out." Many readers, perhaps most, may agree with that assessment; others may disagree. We respect either conclusion—or those reaching no conclusion at all.

If, however, in those last moments, Theodore Roosevelt gave in to despair, let our knowledge—or even our mere suspicion—of that enable us to better appreciate the price of his glory.

But what if he *had* withstood grief, pain, and even heredity to firmly fight unto death?

Such a last ounce of courage—that last war—would indeed be Theodore Roosevelt's grandest triumph.

ACKNOWLEDGMENTS

WRITING ABOUT THEODORE ROOSEVELT IS LIKE SCALING A MOUNTAIN that doubles in elevation every forty-eight hours. Suffice it to say, there is a lot of mountain out there, and, as always, I extend sincere thanks to the many wonderful institutions that have in some sense or another assisted in the compilation of my work, in this case, the Schaffer Library of Union College, Schenectady, New York; the University Library at the University at Albany, Albany, New York; the Begley Library at Schenectady County Community College, Schenectady, New York; the New York Public Library; the New York Public Library for the Performing Arts; the Schenectady County Public Library, Schenectady, New York; the Lucy Scribner Library, Skidmore College, Saratoga Springs, New York; the Franklin D. Roosevelt Presidential Library and Museum, Hyde Park, New York; the District of Columbia Public Library, Washington, DC; the William K. Sanford Town Library, Colonie, New York; the Sage Libraries, Russell Sage College, Troy, New York; the Richard G. Folsom Library of Rensselaer Polytechnic Institute, Troy, New York; the Townsend Memorial Library of the University of Mary Hardin-Baylor, Belton, Texas; the Mountain Top Library, Tannersville, New York; the National Museum of the U.S. Air Force; the Chicago Public Library; the National Archives; and the Library of Congress.

Sincere thanks are also extended to Michael Jones; Kevin Fitzpatrick; John Thorn; Robert N. Going; Mindy January Ronson; Matt K. Lewis; Whit Stillman; George H. Nash; Paul M. Audino; Cathy Cardillo; Sue Sarna, curator of the Sagamore Hill National Historic Site; Elizabeth DeMaria, museum technician of the Sagamore Hill National Historic Site; Heather Cole, curator of the Theodore Roosevelt Collection of Harvard University's Houghton Library; Aaron M. O'Donovan, local history librarian at the Columbus (Ohio) Metropolitan Library; Helen Ferrell and Gerri Reaves of the Southwest Florida Historical Society; Karen Kasper of the Ishpeming Area Historical Society; and Ann Schroeder, administrator of the United States Ski & Snowboard Hall of Fame, for their assistance in completing *TR's Last War*. Thanks also go out to my editors at Lyons Press—Eugene Brissie, Keith Wallman, Patricia Stevenson, Jen Kelland, and Emily Eastridge—and to Lyons publicists John Priest and Jessica Kastner—and, particularly, to my agent and friend, Robert Wilson, at Wilson Media.

And, of course, to my beloved wife, Patty.

NOTES

"WE MUST NOT WEEP"

1. *New York Times*, July 18, 1918, p. 1; *New York Times*, October 4, 1918, p. 15; K. Roosevelt (*Quentin*), pp. 169–71.

2. *Literary Digest*, April 13, 1918, p. 94; Brands (*Letters*), p. 635; Jeffers, pp. 98, 108.

3. *New York Times*, July 21, 1918, p. 1; *New York Times*, July 24, 1918, p. 6; Jeffers, pp. 103, 108.

4. *New York Times*, July 11, 1917, p. 2; *New York Times*, July 22, 1918, p. 1.

5. E. Morris (*Colonel*), p. 346.

6. TR put his money where his heart was, personally subscribing to $73,000 in Liberty Bonds (*Trusts & Estates*, October 1919, p. 344). Thanks, however, to his cousin FDR essentially outlawing gold in 1933 and 1934, his estate lost 41 percent of the bonds' gold-based value. Casting the deciding Supreme Court vote to uphold FDR's policy was Charles Evans Hughes.

7. *Spokane Spokesman-Review*, September 29, 1918, p. 6.

8. J. B. Bishop, p. 390.

9. Amos, front matter. Most likely his last.

10. *Columbus Dispatch*, September 30, 1918, p. 1; *Cincinnati Enquirer*, October 1, 1918, p. 1.

11. Renehan, p. 213.

12. *Columbus Dispatch*, September 30, 1918, p. 1; *Cincinnati Enquirer*, October 1, 1918, p. 1.

13. *Columbus Dispatch*, September 30, 1918, p. 1; *Marion (OH) Star*, October 1, 1918, p. 7.

14. *Columbus Dispatch*, September 30, 1918, p. 1.

15. *Columbus Dispatch*, September 30, 1918, p. 17.

16. Amos, pp. 160–61.

17. *Columbus Dispatch*, October 1, 1918, p. 2.

18. *New York Times*, October 1, 1918, p. 8.

19. *Norwalk (OH) Reflector-Herald*, October 1, 1918, p. 4.

20. *Norwalk (OH) Reflector-Herald*, October 1, 1918, p. 4.

21. *Norwalk (OH) Reflector-Herald*, October 1, 1918, p. 4.

"Murder on the High Seas"

1. Van Winkle, pp. 130–35; Pringle (*Roosevelt*), pp. 234–38. Also indicted was the *Indianapolis News*.
2. F. Russell (*President Makers*), p. 85.
3. *Outlook*, September 12, 1903, p. 140.
4. Dalton, pp. 331–32.
5. Manners, p. 229.
6. *New York Times*, May 12, 1912, p. SM2.
7. *New York Times*, May 12, 1912, p. SM2.
8. *Logansport (IN) Journal-Tribune*, June 1, 1913, p. 1; W. E. Roosevelt, pp. 12, 435.
9. *Saturday Evening Post*, December 9, 1922, p. 42. At this very same time, Ted's heavy drinking caused his mother great discomfort (S. J. Morris [*Edith*], pp. 393–94).
10. T. H. Watkins, pp. 126–27.
11. Wagenknecht, p. 106. The same cannot be said for his family. His father-in-law, Charles Carow, brother Elliott, son Kermit, nephews G. Hall Roosevelt (Elliott's son) and Stewart and Monroe Robinson (Corinne's boys), son-in-law Nicholas Longworth, granddaughter Pauline Longworth Sturm, and her husband Alexander Sturm were all alcoholics. Ted Jr. and Theodore Douglas Robinson were also heavy drinkers (Felsenthal, p. 152; Caroli, pp. 187, 281–84; Donn, p. 155).
12. E. Morris (*Colonel*), p. 183.
13. W. E. Roosevelt, *passim*.
14. Dalton, p. 423.
15. *New York Times*, January 5, 1908, p. 2; *New York Times*, May 28, 1913, p. 2.
16. Abbott, pp. 281–85; Dalton, pp. 423–24.
17. The author deals with Whitman's district attorneyship at length in his *Rothstein: The Life, Times, and Murder of the Criminal Genius Who Fixed the 1919 World Series*. See pp. 66–91.
18. *New York Times*, June 23, 1914, p. 1; Van Winkle, p. 4; Drinker and Mowbray, p. 436.
19. *New York Times*, April 18, 1915, p. 1; *Syracuse Journal*, April 20, 1915, p. 3.
20. *Presidential Studies Quarterly* 19, no. 1, p. 96.
21. Stimson and Bundy, p. 68.
22. *Record of the Constitutional Convention of the State of New York 1915*, pp. 1804–5; Stimson and Bundy, pp. 68–69.
23. *New York Times*, June 29, 1930, p. 29.
24. *Chicago Examiner*, June 18, 1912, p. 1; *New York History* 60, no. 2 (April 1979), p. 197; Pringle (*Roosevelt*), p. 403; Gardner, p. 329; Eaton, pp. 212–13; Martin, pp. 96–97.
25. J. B. Bishop, p. 366; Gilman, p. 351; Pringle (*Roosevelt*), p. 576; Busch, pp. 302–3.
26. *Current Literature*, March 1911, p. 268.
27. *Presidential Studies Quarterly* 19, no. 1, p. 100.
28. *New York Times*, May 3, 1915, p. 1; Wickware (*1915*), p. 797; Van Winkle, p. 15.
29. Burns, p. 56.
30. *New York Press*, May 5, 1915, p. 8; Van Winkle, p. 86.

31. *New York History* 60, no. 2 (April 1979), pp. 211–12.
32. *New York Evening Post*, September 22, 1914, p. 1.
33. *New York Times*, April 12, 1915, p. 4.
34. *Brooklyn Daily Eagle*, May 2, 1915, p. 7; Wickware (*1915*), pp. 797–98.
35. Thompson, p. 66.
36. Morison, pp. 921–22; E. Morris (*Colonel*), pp. 416–17.
37. *New York Sun*, May 1, 1915, p. 1; *Brooklyn Daily Eagle*, May 1, 1915, p. 22.
38. *Freeman*, December 8, 1920, p. 306; Viereck (*Hate*), p. 66. In 2008, despite the effects of decades of ocean water, divers located four million rounds of ammunition adjacent to the ship's wreckage (E. Morris [*Colonel*], p. 695; Pines, p. 58).
39. *Christian Advocate*, May 20, 1915, p. 675.
40. Sullivan (Vol. 5), p. 115.
41. TR to Kermit and Belle Roosevelt, May 27, 1915, http://www.theodoreroosevelt center.org/Blog/Item/A%20Trial%20in%20Syracuse.
42. J. B. Bishop, p. 377; Busch, p. 303.
43. J. B. Bishop, p. 376; Busch, p. 303.
44. *Christian Science Monitor*, May 10, 1915, p. 9.
45. J. B. Bishop, pp. 376–77. Seven Republicans sat on the jury (*New York Times*, May 22, 1915, p. 1).
46. N. Miller (*Life*), p. 546fn.
47. N. Miller (*Life*), p. 546.
48. O'Toole, pp. 276, 446.
49. *New York Times*, May 12, 1915, p. 3.
50. *Chicago Tribune*, May 10, 1916, p. 1.
51. *Syracuse Journal*, May 10, 1915, p. 6.
52. *New York Tribune*, May 8, 1915, p. 8.
53. *New York Sun*, May 8, 1915, p. 6; *New York Times*, May 8, 1915, p. 10.
54. *Syracuse Journal*, May 10, 1915, p. 6.
55. E. Morris (*Colonel*), p. 420.
56. *New York Times*, May 11, 1915, p. 1.
57. *New York Times*, May 12, 1915, p. 3.

"A NOISE LIKE 10,000 BABIES"

1. *Los Angeles Herald*, May 22, 1915, p. 1; T. H. Russell, p. 252.
2. *New York Times*, May 22, 1915, p. 1.
3. *Los Angeles Herald*, May 22, 1915, p. 1; Van Winkle, p. 117–21; Wickware (*1915*), pp. 75, 798.
4. S. J. Morris (*Edith*), p. 406; E. Morris (*Colonel*), p. 696.
5. Thayer, p. 400; E. Morris (*Colonel*), p. 696.
6. E. Morris (*Colonel*), p. 696.
7. *New York Times*, March 25, 1911, p. 10.
8. Villard, p. 151.
9. Villard, p. 151.

10. Villard, p. 151.
11. *Chicago Tribune*, October 28, 1934, p. 2.
12. C. R. Robinson (*Poems*), pp. 24–25.
13. Brands (*T.R.*), p. 289. In 1895.
14. Martin, p. 77.
15. Chace, p. 17.
16. Sullivan (Vol. 4), pp. 331–32.
17. N. Miller (*Chronicles*), p. 276.
18. Eaton, p. 209; Martin, pp. 83–84.
19. Gunther, pp. 171, 714.
20. Eaton, p. 209.
21. *Christian Science Monitor*, September 1, 1910, p. 6.
22. Chamberlain, p. 236.
23. Eaton, p. 211.
24. *New York Times*, February 27, 1912, p. 1.
25. *New York Times*, February 28, 1912, p. 10.
26. *New York Times*, February 27, 1912, p. 1.
27. *Duluth (MN) Herald*, February 23, 1912, p. 12.
28. *Chicago Tribune*, February 22, 1912, p. 1.
29. Wolraich, pp. 210–11. Historians nearly always inaccurately conflate these two statements into a single quote.
30. *Independent*, May 2, 1912, p. 964.
31. Goodwin (*Pulpit*), p. 696; N. Miller (*Chronicles*), p. 277.
32. *New York Times*, May 16, 1912, p. 1; Mowry, pp. 234–35.
33. Eaton, p. 213.
34. *New York Evening Telegram*, May 4, 1912, p. 2.
35. McKenna, p. 123.
36. Chace, p. 118.
37. Manners, pp. 253–54; Martin, pp. 146–49; Dalton, pp. 390–91; Eaton, pp. 222–23.
38. *Chicago Tribune*, June 23, 1912, p. 1.
39. *New York Times*, August 6, 1912, pp. 1–2.
40. Dalton, p. 407.
41. *New York Sun*, May 29, 1912, p. 2.
42. *The Public*, August 16, 1912, p. 772.
43. *Wadesboro (NC) Messenger and Intelligencer*, August 22, 1912, p. 1.
44. *Christian Science Monitor*, October 15, 1912, p. 7.
45. *Los Angeles Times*, October 15, 1912, p. 12; *Washington Post*, October 15, 1912, pp. 1–2; *Chicago Tribune*, October 15, 1912, p. 1.
46. *New York Times*, May 29, 1952, p. 26.
47. E. Morris (*Rise*), p. 574. TR may have known what he was doing. Choate lost in the legislature 142–7.
48. *New York Times*, September 25, 1898, p. 1; Villard, pp. 146–48; Cohen, pp. 76–90; Brown, pp. 50–51; Chessman, pp. 42–44; N. Miller (*Life*), pp. 310, 14–16; E. Morris (*Rise*), pp. 700–701, 709–11.

49. Villard, p. 147.

50. *Literary Digest*, October 8, 1898, p. 425; Pringle (*Roosevelt*), p. 204; Jessup, p. 198. A similar affidavit endeavored to free him from taxes in Oyster Bay. TR later remitted to the state the $995.28 he had hoped to save.

51. Chessman, p. 47.

52. *New York History*, January 1953, p. 60; Chessman, p. 48.

53. Hart and Ferleger, p. 542.

54. *Boston Globe*, January 1, 1911, p. 47; *Trenton Evening Times*, June 4, 1911, p. 9; *Chicago Tribune*, August 11, 1911, p. 5.

55. Hodgson, p. 6; Dos Passos, p. 95.

56. George and George, p. 163.

57. E. Morris (*Rex*), p. 578.

58. *Baltimore Sun*, March 4, 1896, p. 8.

59. Pringle (*Roosevelt*), p. 545. The opinion of the *Baltimore News*.

60. *Baltimore Sun*, March 4, 1896, p. 8.

61. Cooper (*Warrior*), p. 60.

62. Pringle (*Roosevelt*), pp. 545–46.

63. Pringle (*Roosevelt*), p. 546.

64. Chace, pp. 65–66; Cooper (*Warrior*), p. 60.

65. Cooper (*Warrior*), p. 60.

66. Link (*Papers*, Vol. 11), p. 515.

67. Kohlsaat, pp. 96–97; E. Morris (*Rex*), pp. 18, 577.

68. Cooper (*Warrior*), p. 60; E. Morris (*Rex*), p. 578.

69. Walworth, p. 141.

70. *New York Times*, October 24, 1901, pp. 1–2.

71. Link (*Papers*, Vol. 12), p. 262.

72. E. Morris (*Rex*), p. 578.

73. Link (*Papers*, Vol. 12), p. 454.

74. Cooper (*Warrior*), p. 60.

75. Wagenknecht, p. 159.

76. *New York Times*, September 4, 1902, pp. 1–2.

77. *New York Times*, October 19, 1902, p. 1; N. Miller (*Life*), p. 372; Baker (*Princeton*), p. 140; Chace, pp. 65–66.

78. Cooper (*Warrior*), pp. 130, 382; Startt, p. 24.

79. Walworth, p. 141.

80. Walworth, p. 141.

81. Walworth, p. 141. This odd incident absolutely incensed Pulitzer Prize–winning Wilson biographer Arthur Walworth, who characterized TR's "manners" as being "of the jungle." Almost all other biographers have averted their eyes.

"A TRUE LOGOTHETE, A REAL SOPHIST"

1. Cooper (*Warrior*), p. 131.

2. *New York Times*, November 24, 1907, p. SM1; Pringle (*Roosevelt*), p. 546.

3. Cooper (*Priest*), p. 131.

4. Abbott, p. 285.
5. Baker (*Governor*), p. 316. Wilson to Edith Gittings Reid, May 8, 1912.
6. Tilchin and Neu, p. 77.
7. McAdoo, p. 337.
8. Shachtman, p. 95.
9. Wickware (*1915*), p. 75.
10. Morison, p. 790.
11. Miller (*Life*), p. 542; Dalton, p. 443.
12. Kazin (*Bryan*), p. 221.
13. Loizillon, pp. 115–16.
14. O'Toole, p. 264.
15. Thompson, p. 28.
16. *New York Times*, February 7, 1914, p. 1; *The (New London, CT) Day*, March 18, 1914, p. 1. Wilson's actions resulted as much from a desire to obtain Britain's opposition to Huerta's regime as from any desire to satisfy previous treaty legalities (Dos Passos, pp. 78, 84).
17. Thompson, p. 22.
18. C. Seymour, p. 118; Ellis, p. 153.
19. K. S. Davis, p. 382.
20. *Christian Science Monitor*, August 28, 1914, p. 5.
21. Dos Passos, pp. 17–18, 85.
22. Brands (*T.R.*), p. 749.
23. E. B. Roosevelt (*Yesterday*), pp. 67–68.
24. Hagedorn (*Bugle*), p. 8.
25. Bishop (*Roosevelt*), p. 258; Hart and Ferleger, p. 651.
26. Viereck (*Roosevelt*), p. 100.
27. *Outlook*, October 23, 1914, p. 1011.
28. *Outlook*, August 22, 1914, p. 1012.
29. *Outlook*, September 23, 1914, p. 169.
30. *Outlook*, September 23, 1914, p. 170.
31. *Outlook*, September 23, 1914, p. 169.
32. *New York Times*, October 4, 1914, p. 33.
33. *Outlook*, September 23, 1914, p. 173.
34. *New York Times*, October 11, 1914, p. SM2; T. Roosevelt (*America*), p. 65; Hart and Ferleger, p. 651.
35. Hoover, p. 202.
36. Brands (*Letters*), p. 575.
37. Brands (*Letters*), p. 581.
38. Page, p. 315.
39. Berg, p. 362.
40. *Chicago Tribune*, May 10, 1915, p. 1.
41. Traxel, p. 170.
42. Patton (*Pattons*), p. 160.
43. *Philadelphia Record*, May 9, 1915, p. 6; Nasaw, p. 244.

44. Link (*Papers*, Vol. 50), p. 724.
45. E. B. G. Wilson (*Memoir*), pp. 60–61.
46. Tribble, p. 9.
47. Link (*Papers*, Vol. 33), p. 112; Tribble, p. 12.
48. Link (*Papers*, Vol. 50), p. 161; Tribble, p. 22; Traxel, p. 170.
49. C. Seymour (Vol. 1), p. 434.
50. Page, p. 2.
51. Ellis, p. 204.
52. Page, p. 6.
53. Kazin (*Bryan*), p. 236.
54. *New York Press*, May 14, 1915, pp. 1–2.
55. Millis, p. 186.
56. Cherny, p. 149.
57. Dos Passos, p. 128.
58. Millis, p. 190; Kazin (*Bryan*), p. 240.
59. *Syracuse Herald*, June 12, 1915, p. 8.
60. *New York Times Current History*, July 1915, p. 642.
61. Levin, p. 86.
62. Wister, p. 344.
63. Richardson, p. 8066.
64. Wister, p. 344.
65. Brands (*Letters*), p. 575. In August 1914.
66. Hagedorn (*Bugle*), pp. 64–65.
67. Largey, p. 39.
68. B. Alexander, p. 73.
69. *Harper's Weekly*, December 12, 1914, pp. 556–59.
70. Doenecke, p. 105.
71. *North American Review*, August 1915, p. 181.
72. *New York Times*, December 9, 1915, p. 5.
73. Doenecke, p. 106.
74. *Congressional Record* 56, pt. 12, p. 440.
75. *The Fatherland*, October 27, 1915, p. 205.
76. Garraty (*Lodge*), p. 95; Bell, p. 162.
77. Sullivan (Vol. 5), p. 203.
78. *Harper's Weekly*, July 3, 1915, pp. 9–10.
79. Daniels (*Era*, Vol. 1), p. 579.
80. Morison, p. 922; Brands (*Letters*), pp. 592–93.
81. Cobelle, p. 18.
82. *New York Times*, November 3, 1928, p. 14; Kolko, pp. 194–95; Eaton, p. 210.
83. Hoover, p. 120.
84. Chace, p. 205.
85. Taliaferro, p. 141.
86. *Munsey's Magazine*, February 1913, pp. 729–33; Cobelle, pp. 92–94.
87. McGeary, p. 253.

88. *New York Times*, November 5, 1914, p. 5.

89. Richberg (*Hero*), p. 65. Donald R. Richberg's assessment. McCormick was an alcoholic and highly unstable, treated, in fact, by Zurich's Dr. Carl Jung in early 1909. He committed suicide in 1925 (A. Smith [*Titan*], pp. 174–76).

90. Ickes, pp. 166–67.

91. White (*Autobiography*), p. 517.

92. Thompson, pp. 21, 42, 303.

93. Pinchot, p. 212; J. B. Bishop, pp. 356–58.

94. Mayer, p. 339.

95. Mayer, p. 339.

96. Karsten, pp. 545–46.

97. Hollander, p. 215.

98. *New York Times*, July 20, 1915, p. 20.

99. *Friends' Intelligenser*, September 4, 1915, p. 562.

100. J. B. Bishop, pp. 381–83.

101. Morison, p. 940.

"PRETTY BOYS WHO KNOW ALL OF THE LATEST TANGO STEPS"

1. Thompson, p. 74.

2. *New York Times*, May 28, 1915, p. 1. This was not his first equine accident. In October 1904, his horse somersaulted ("I landed on my head"), and he badly skinned his forehead.

3. Brands (*Letters*), p. 599.

4. Pringle (*Roosevelt*), p. 5.

5. Ellis, p. 147.

6. Palmer, pp. 40–41.

7. Palmer, p. 57.

8. Thompson, p. 48.

9. T. Roosevelt (*America*), p. 273.

10. T. Roosevelt (*America*), p. 273.

11. Stimson and Bundy, p. 86. TR, however, bore some responsibility for events. By 1906, he had slashed the army by 25 percent (Wagenknecht, p. 254).

12. N. Roosevelt, p. 177.

13. Doenecke, p. 145.

14. Doenecke, p. 145.

15. Cook (Vol. 1), p. 531; Burns, p. 60.

16. Cook (Vol. 1), p. 531.

17. Morgan, pp. 155–56.

18. Lash (*Eleanor*), p. 103.

19. K. S. Davis, pp. 390–91.

20. K. S. Davis, p. 391.

21. *Boston Evening Post*, December 8, 1915, p. 8. In July 1943, FDR confessed to Belle Willard Roosevelt that in reading his own pre-1917 letters, he was shocked by the "bit-

ter criticism and intolerance of Wilson in them" and by his own "lack of understanding." "In view of my own [later] experience," he continued, "I realize he could not have made the American people declare war then" (Lelyveld, pp. 60, 349).

22. Brands (*Traitor*), pp. 96, 833.
23. Brands (*Traitor*), pp. 96, 833.
24. Brands (*Traitor*), pp. 96, 833.
25. *New York Times*, November 22, 1914, p. SM2; K. S. Davis, pp. 163–64.
26. Link (*Papers*, Vol. 31), p. 32.
27. S. J. Morris (*Edith*), p. 408.
28. Pearlman, p. 68; Collier and Horowitz, p. 125; Jeffers, p. 62.
29. Wagenknecht, p. 202.
30. Leary, pp. 234–35.
31. *American Legion Monthly*, July 1934, p. 43.
32. *New York Times*, March 1, 1915, p. 1; Richard Bleiler, "A History of Adventure Magazine," Galactic Central, http://www.philsp.com/articles/magazines/adventure.html. This is not the American Legion Ted Jr. founded in February 1919. This earlier version disbanded in April 1917.
33. Brands (*Letters*), p. 222.
34. Brands (*T.R.*), p. 289.
35. Wagenknecht, p. 283; Brands (*T.R.*), p. 289.
36. E. Morris (*Rise*), p. 594.
37. *The Cosmopolitan*, December 1892, p. 232; Wagenknecht, p. 285.
38. *American Monthly Review of Reviews*, August 1900, p. 186; Roosevelt (*Autobiography*), p. 8. Yes, *The Cosmopolitan* is now *Cosmopolitan*.
39. McCullough, pp. 56–58; Brady, pp. 22, 70–71.
40. J. C. Lane (*Wood*), p. 26. To Lodge in 1897.
41. Villard, pp. 157–58.
42. Villard, p. 158.
43. J. C. Lane, pp. 191, 298.
44. McCallum, p. 262.
45. J. C. Lane, p. 188.
46. Finnegan, p. 59.
47. Villard, p. 158.
48. Finnegan, p. 58.
49. *New Outlook*, August 30, 1916, unnumbered page; *Saturday Evening Post*, May 6, 1916, p. 44.
50. Finnegan, p. 68.
51. *New York Times*, June 30, 1915, p. 6; E. B. Roosevelt (*Day*), pp. 70–71; J. B. Bishop, p. 397; Hart and Ferleger, p. 656; Clifford, pp. 72–73.
52. Pearlman, pp. 58–59; Clifford, p. 182.
53. Finnegan, p. 72; Clifford, pp. 182–85.
54. O'Toole, p. 286.
55. *New York Times*, August 26, 1915, pp. 1, 4; *Independent*, September 6, 1915, p. 319.
56. Doenecke, p. 112.

57. *New York Times*, August 26, 1915, pp. 1, 4; *New York Times Current History*, October 1915, p. 18; Drinker and Mowbray, p. 431; Holme, p. 190.

58. Holme, p. 191; Howland, p. 264.

59. *New York Times*, July 30, 1911, p. SM5. In 1911, Straight did marry Dorothy Payne Whitney, aunt of Quentin Roosevelt's future fiancée Flora Payne Whitney.

60. Clifford, p. 87fn.

61. *Literary Digest*, September 11, 1915, pp. 514–15.

62. *New York Herald*, August 28, 1915, p. 1.

63. *New York Times*, August 29, 1915, p. 2.

64. Howland, p. 264.

65. *Washington Post*, August 28, 1915, p. 1.

66. *Washington Post*, August 28, 1915, p. 1.

67. *Life*, September 9, 1915, p. 469.

68. Roosevelt and Lodge, p. 458.

69. Daniels (*Life*), p. 176.

70. Daniels (*Life*), pp. 177–78.

71. Daniels (*Life*), p. 178. Forty thousand Americans resided in Mexico in 1910 (*Pan-American Magazine*, August 1915, p. 226).

72. Berg, p. 288.

73. T. Roosevelt (*Americanism*), p. 18. Some precedent existed for Wilson's policy of nonrecognition. Neither Abraham Lincoln nor Andrew Johnson ever recognized Emperor Maximilian I's Mexican government. Further, TR evinced no problem with Wilson's subsequent nonrecognition of Lenin's Soviet regime.

74. Dos Passos, p. 90.

75. *New York Times*, April 21, 1914, p. 1; *New York Times*, April 22, 1914, p. 1.

76. Kazin (*Bryan*), p. 231.

77. *The Forum*, September 1916, p. 271.

78. *New York Times*, December 6, 1914, p. SM1.

79. *New York Times*, December 6, 1914, p. SM1.

80. *New York Times*, February 24, 1915, p. 8.

81. *Atlanta Constitution*, February 23, 1915, p. 2.

82. Kazin (*Bryan*), p. 231.

83. Katz, p. 499.

84. Katz, p. 499.

85. *Oswego Palladium-Times*, February 2, 1917, p. 2; Nasaw, p. 248; Swanberg, p. 297; Hurst, p. 7; Procter, pp. 49–50; Katz, p. 500.

86. Morison, p. 1249.

"THE MOST EDUCATIONAL DRAMA I HAVE EVER WITNESSED"

1. *Fort Wayne (IN) Daily News*, February 19, 1917, p. 10.

2. *Uniontown (PA) Morning Herald*, April 3, 1917, p. 8.

3. *Motion Picture News*, April 22, 1916, pp. 2446–47.

4. *Motion Picture News*, May 27, 1916, pp. 3198–99.

5. *Motion Picture News*, June 10, 1916, p. 3526.

6. *Motion Picture News*, June 10, 1916, p. 3526.
7. *Motion Picture News*, June 10, 1916, p. 3526.
8. *Moving Picture World*, March 1916, p. 1644.
9. *Variety*, September 15, 1916, p. 23; *Motion Picture World*, September 16, 1916, p. 1822.
10. *Motion Picture News*, August 19, 1916, p. 1084.
11. Ellis, p. 246.
12. Pizzitola, pp. 66–68; Dewey, pp. 56–59.
13. Blackton, p. 9.
14. *Variety*, September 17, 1915, p. 23.
15. *New York Sun*, October 24, 1915, p. 5.
16. *New York Dramatic Mirror*, August 1915, exact date and page unknown.
17. Dewey, p. 162.
18. Ramsaye, p. 727; Soister and Nicolella, p. 27.
19. *The Fatherland*, March 29, 1916, p. 121; *Motion Picture News*, April 15, 1916, p. 2145.
20. Soister and Nicolella, p. 27.
21. *New York Clipper*, August 14, 1915, p. 19. Only a few nitrate-stock scraps of it still exist.
22. *New York Times*, August 7, 1915, p. 8.
23. TR's remarkable chronicler Edward Wagenknecht observes, "Literally the only dramatic film I find any record of his having seen is *The Battle Cry of Peace*" (Wagenknecht, p. 78). Wagenknecht chose his words carefully: a private screening of the documentary *The American Ambulance Boys at the Front* was arranged for TR in 1916 (Isenberg, p. 70).
24. *New York Times*, October 27, 1915, p. 11; *Boston Post*, October 28, 1915, p. 10.
25. *Boston Globe*, November 2, 1915, p. 3.
26. Morison, pp. 989–91.
27. *New York Times*, August 7, 1915, p. 8; Soister and Nicolella, p. 26.
28. Trimble, p. 75; Soister and Nicolella, p. 26.
29. *Washington Post*, April 9, 1916, p. 5; *New York Times*, April 23, 1916, p. 6; Soister and Nicolella, p. 26.
30. Ramsaye, p. 727; Trimble, p. 78; Isenberg, p. 102.
31. Trimble, pp. 78–79.

"GO HOME TO GERMANY"

1. *Review of Reviews*, August 1895, p. 169.
2. *The Forum*, April 1894, p. 202.
3. *New York Dramatic Mirror*, August 1915, exact date and page unknown; Trimble, p. 68; Dewey, p. 177.
4. Viereck (*Roosevelt*), p. 68; Viereck (*Hate*), p. 232; N. M. Johnson, p. 11.
5. Viereck (*Hate*), p. 232.
6. *The Dial*, August 16, 1912, p. 104.
7. Viereck (*Roosevelt*), p. 81; Viereck (*Hate*), p. 232; N. M. Johnson, p. 14.
8. Gable, pp. 121–22; Chace, pp. 205–6.

9. Viereck (*Armageddon*), p. 21.
10. Gertz, p. 109; N. M. Johnson, p. 16.
11. *New York Tribune*, August 17, 1912, p. 4. A bull moose later replaced the hollow square.
12. Gertz, p. 101.
13. *New York Sun*, February 2, 1913, p. 6.
14. Viereck (*Hate*), p. 75; Gertz, p. 139; N. M. Johnson, p. 23.
15. H. Blum (*Invasion*), p. 340.
16. Viereck (*Hate*), p. 51; Gertz, pp. 139–40; N. M. Johnson, p. 25.
17. *The International*, January 1916, pp. 24–25.
18. Viereck (*Roosevelt*), p. 113.
19. Viereck (*Roosevelt*), p. 114.
20. Viereck (*Roosevelt*), pp. 117–18.
21. Viereck (*Roosevelt*), p. 118.
22. Viereck (*Roosevelt*), p. 119.
23. Viereck (*Roosevelt*), p. 125; Hart and Ferleger, pp. 201–2.
24. Viereck (*Hate*), pp. 255–56; Viereck (*House*), pp. 161–62. Viereck's account is verified by none other than TR himself, who, in Kansas City in September 1917, declared, "Some years ago I saw openly published in Germany a pamphlet written by a member of the German general staff containing a well worked out plan for the conquest of the United States which the German staff regarded as easy" (*Topeka [KS] State Journal*, September 25, 1917, p. 7).
25. *New York World*, August 15, 1915, p. 1; *New York Herald*, August 15, 1915, p. 10; *Chicago Tribune*, August 15, 1915, pp. 1, 4; Viereck (*Hate*), pp. 68–74; H. Blum (*Invasion*), pp. 340–44; Peterson, pp. 154–55; Dos Passos, pp. 137–39; Gertz, pp. 137–40; Millman, pp. 31–32. Despite such pro-Allied activity on McAdoo's part, British ambassador Sir Cecil Spring-Rice once quipped, "Wilson is the little shepherd of his people, and McAdoo is his crook."

"The Country Is Not in a Heroic Mood"

1. Schickel, p. 269.
2. Ramsaye, pp. 641–44; Schickel, p. 270; Brownlow and Kobal, pp. 40–44, 62–67.
3. Slide, p. 91.
4. *New York Times*, February 11, 1916, p. 1; *Outlook*, February 23, 1916, pp. 401–2.
5. Morgan, p. 169.
6. Craig, p. 141.
7. Wickware (*1915*), p. 802.
8. *Outlook*, May 10, 1916, p. 194.
9. Wickware (*1916*), p. 801; Whalen, p. 61.
10. *New York Times*, February 18, 1916, p. 1.
11. Whalen, pp. 61–62.
12. Whalen, p. 62.
13. Whalen, p. 62.
14. Wickware (*1916*), p. 803.

15. Butler, p. 251.
16. Wickware (*1916*), p. 26.
17. *New York Times*, February 16, 1916, p. 1.
18. *New York Times*, February 16, 1916, p. 4.
19. *New York Times*, February 16, 1916, pp. 1–4.
20. *New York Times*, April 8, 1916, p. 1; *North American Review*, March 1916, p. 643; *Literary Digest*, April 22, 1916, p. 1193; Wickware (*1916*), p. 26.
21. Sullivan (Vol. 3), p. 279.
22. Link (*Confusions*), pp. 98fn–99fn.
23. *Pittsburgh Post-Gazette*, November 20, 1991, p. 8.
24. Pines, p. 91.
25. Dos Passos, p. 156.
26. C. Seymour (Vol. 1), p. 361.
27. Pines, p. 63.
28. *Independent*, September 13, 1915, p. 351.
29. Knock, pp. 60–61; Carlisle and Kirchberger, pp. 171–72; Hull, pp. 262–63.
30. Millis, pp. 287–93, 297–300; Carlisle and Kirchberger, pp. 172–73; Knock, pp. 73–75.
31. T. Roosevelt (*Fear God*), p. 124.
32. Pines, p. 96.
33. S. J. Morris (*Edith*), p. 408; Dalton, p. 463.
34. *New York Times*, May 13, 1916, p. 1; *New York Herald*, May 14, 1916, p. 12.
35. Lurie, p. 182.
36. Braeman, pp. 240–43; Lovell, p. 12.
37. Lovell, p. 12.
38. *Saturday Review*, April 21, 1951, p. 14.
39. Thompson, pp. 62–63, 307.
40. White (*Autobiography*), p. 531.
41. Dalton, p. 459.
42. Dalton, p. 459.
43. *New Republic*, December 12, 1914, p. 5; Steel, p. 76.
44. A. Johnson, p. 233. *New Republic* editor Alvin Johnson's autobiography is the source for TR's denigration of *New Republic* staff but does not directly quote him.
45. Steel, p. 4.
46. Steel, p. 76.
47. Steel, pp. 97–98.
48. Steel, p. 98.
49. *New York Times*, July 20, 1915, p. 20.
50. *New York Times*, July 20, 1915, p. 20; *New York Times*, July 21, 1915, p. 20; *Trenton Evening Times*, July 21, 1915, p. 11; *York (PA) Daily*, July 21, 1915, p. 3.
51. *Boston Post*, July 22, 1915, p. 1.
52. *Boston Post*, July 22, 1915, p. 6.
53. Todd, p. 95.
54. *Philadelphia Inquirer*, July 6, 1913, p. 4.

55. *New York Times*, October 21, 1916, p. 22.

56. *Oakland Tribune*, July 24, 1915, p. 5; *Woodland (CA) Daily Democrat*, August 7, 1915, p. 2.

57. Drinker and Mowbray, pp. 431, 454.

58. Morison, p. 993. To the painter and naval expert Henry Reuterdahl.

59. Drinker and Mowbray, p. 432.

60. *New York Times*, December 19, 1915, p. 7.

61. Cobelle, p. 94. Perkins also raised at least $200,000 for TR in 1904; Edmund Morris places the figure at $450,000.

62. Cobelle, pp. 72–75.

63. Kolko, p. 199.

64. Kolko, p. 200.

65. Mowry, pp. 297–98.

66. Pinchot, p. 189.

67. Pinchot, p. 57.

68. Pinchot, p. 217.

69. Garraty (*Perkins*), pp. 332–33.

70. Pinchot, p. 217.

71. *Harper's Weekly*, July 3, 1915, p. 10.

72. *Literary Digest*, December 18, 1915, p. 1404; Jessup, p. 335.

73. *New York Times*, April 8, 1916, p. 1; *North American Review*, March 1916, p. 643; *Literary Digest*, April 22, 1916, p. 1193.

74. Jessup, p. 333.

75. E. Morris (*Colonel*), p. 205.

76. Jessup, pp. 333–34.

77. Hughes, p. 148.

78. Wesser, pp. 209–25; Pusey, pp. 233–39, 300–301.

79. Perkins, p. 51; Pusey, p. 301.

80. Lurie, p. 182.

81. *Literary Digest*, December 18, 1915, pp. 1404–5.

82. *Scribner's*, May 1921, p. 557; Scott, p. 28.

83. Pearlman, p. 72.

84. Pearlman, p. 75.

85. Pearlman, p. 72.

86. Finnegan, p. 70; Pearlman, p. 75.

87. Pearlman, p. 75.

88. *New York Times*, April 1, 1916, pp. 1, 4; Baker (*Facing War*), p. 233.

89. Gardner, p. 345; J. C. Lane, p. 206. Bacon had already facilitated a rapprochement between TR and Henry Stimson, at Oyster Bay, in late 1915 (Stimson and Bundy, p. 91).

90. *New York Times*, April 1, 1916, p. 1; *New York Sun*, April 1, 1916, p. 4; *Boston Post*, April 1, 1916, p. 7.

91. *New York Times*, April 1, 1916, p. 1; *Boston Post*, April 1, 1916, p. 7.

92. Mowry, p. 342.

93. J. C. Lane, p. 206.
94. *New York Times*, April 1, 1916, p. 1.
95. *New York Herald*, April 1, 1916, p. 1.
96. Harbaugh, p. 211; Pearlman, p. 147.
97. *New York Herald*, April 1, 1916, p. 1.
98. J. B. Bishop, pp. 396–97; Hart and Ferleger, p. 656.
99. Doenecke, p. 165.
100. Doenecke, p. 192.
101. Morison, p. 1012. TR to Lodge.
102. J. B. Bishop, p. 401.
103. Gardner, p. 341; Thompson, p. 114. To her he wrote, "The country is not in a heroic mood."
104. *New York Times*, January 11, 1916, p. 1.
105. Brands (*Letters*), p. 599.
106. Thompson, p. 64.
107. Brands (*Letters*), p. 599.
108. S. J. Morris (*Edith*), pp. 408, 553.
109. *New York Times*, March 8, 1916, p. 5.
110. *New York Sun*, March 4, 1916, p. 4.
111. *New York Press*, March 12, 1916, p. 3.
112. *New York Evening Telegram*, February 25, 1916, p. 12; *New York Times*, March 8, 1916, p. 5; *New York Press*, March 12, 1916, p. 3; E. Morris (*Colonel*), pp. 446–49.
113. *New York Evening Mail*, pp. 596–97; *New York Times*, March 8, 1916, p. 5.
114. Stoddard (*Knew*), 429.
115. Stoddard (*Roosevelt*), p. 22.
116. Stoddard (*Knew*), p. 311. John J. Leary and the *New York Times*'s Charles Willis Thompson—and TR himself—all confirm Stoddard's appraisal of TR's decision-making process (N. Roosevelt, pp. 64–65; Davis [*Publication*], p. 133).
117. Stoddard (*Knew*), p. 430.
118. *New York Times*, March 10, 1910, p. 20; *Independent*, March 27, 1916, p. 450; *Current Opinion*, April 1916, p. 233; Executive Committee of the Progressive National Committee, p. 11; *New York Evening Mail*, pp. 596–97; Baker (*Facing War*), p. 233; J. B. Bishop, pp. 404–5.
119. *Brooklyn Daily Eagle*, March 9, 1916, p. 1.
120. *Review of Reviews*, May 1916, p. 552.

"RULES IS RULES HERE"

1. "Teddy Roosevelt Tours Breton Island Louisiana," video posted to YouTube by US Fish and Wildlife Service, May 20, 2010, https://www.youtube.com/watch?v=JbRp2DqkiXM.
2. E. Morris (*Colonel*), p. 428.
3. *New York Herald*, March 29, 1916, p. 1.
4. *New York Sun*, March 29, 1916, p. 1.
5. *Barnes v. Roosevelt*, 87 Misc. 55 (N.Y. Misc. 1914), p. 184.

6. O. K. Davis, pp. 377, 381.

7. *New York Times,* July 12, 1914, p. 5.

8. *New York Sun,* March 29, 1916, p. 1.

9. *Buffalo Express,* March 29, 1916, p. 3.

10. *New York Herald,* March 29, 1916, p. 1.

11. *New York Herald,* March 29, 1916, p. 1.

12. *New York Herald,* March 29, 1916, p. 1.

13. *New York Sun,* March 29, 1916, p. 1.

14. *Brooklyn Daily Eagle,* October 22, 1915, p. 2; *Brooklyn Standard Union,* March 29, 1916, p. 1.

15. *Rochester Democrat & Chronicle,* January 15, 1904, p. 1.

16. *New York Times,* August 7, 1915, p. 8; *Philadelphia Inquirer,* August 7, 1915, p. 1.

17. *Brooklyn Daily Eagle,* October 22, 1915, p. 2; *Brooklyn Standard Union,* March 29, 1916, p. 1.

18. *Buffalo News,* March 30, 1916, p. 20.

19. *New York Herald,* March 30, 1916, p. 1.

20. *New York Times,* October 21, 1916, p. 8.

"When a weasel sucks eggs"

1. Ickes, p. 176.

2. O. K. Davis, p. 447.

3. *New York Times,* January 9, 1919, p. 5.

4. *New York Times,* January 14, 1919, p. 4.

5. Lovell, p. 16.

6. *North American Review,* March 1916, p. 332.

7. *North American Review,* March 1916, p. 332; Colby, p. 484.

8. *North American Review,* March 1916, p. 332; Colby, p. 722.

9. Colby, p. 722.

10. *New York Times,* April 5, 1916, p. 24; *Literary Digest,* April 22, 1916, p. 1193; Colby, p. 722.

11. *New York Times,* April 20, 1916, p. 7.

12. *New York Times,* April 20, 1916, p. 7.

13. *New York Sun,* April 25, 1916, p. 4; Colby, p. 722.

14. *The Fatherland,* January 26, 1916, p. 431.

15. Colby, p. 722.

16. *New York Times,* April 17, 1916, p. 20.

17. Butler, p. 251.

18. *St. Johnsbury (VT) Caledonian,* May 17, 1916, p. 1; "Vermont Presidential Primaries," Vermont Secretary of State, https://www.sec.state.vt.us/media/62790/Vermont-PresidentialPrimary.pdf; Colby, pp. 722, 767.

19. J. B. Bishop, p. 407.

20. Lovell, p. 19.

21. Thompson, p. 116.

22. *New York Tribune,* April 6, 1916, p. 1; *Independent,* April 17, 1916, p. 98.

23. Roosevelt and Lodge, p. 475.
24. *New York Herald*, April 9, 1916, p. 4.
25. *New York Press*, April 9, 1916, page unknown.
26. *New York Tribune*, April 13, 1916, p. 8; *New York Press*, April 13, 1916, p. 4.
27. Beers, p. 48.
28. Butler, p. 249; Eaton, p. 250; Lovell, p. 191.
29. *American Heritage*, December 1957, p. 100.
30. *American Heritage*, December 1957, p. 100; Garraty (*Perkins*), p. 336; Robertson, p. 19.
31. *Saturday Evening Post*, May 13, 1916, pp. 67–70; *Fourth Estate*, May 13, 1916, p. 6; *Printer's Ink*, May 25, 1916, p. 1916.
32. Lovell, p. 19.
33. *New York Press*, April 10, 1916, p. 3.
34. *New York Times*, April 25, 1916, p. 1; *New York Sun*, April 25, 1916, p. 4.
35. *New York Times*, May 13, 1916, p. 1; *New York Tribune*, May 12, 1916, p. 3.
36. *New York Times*, May 13, 1916, p. 1; *New York Tribune*, May 12, 1916, p. 3.
37. *New York Press*, May 16, 1916, page unknown; *Syracuse Journal*, May 22, 1916, p. 14; *New York Times*, May 26, 1916, p. 3.
38. *New York Press*, May 16, 1916, page unknown; Dalton, p. 399; Mowry, p. 343.
39. Mowry, p. 343.
40. *New York Sun*, May 23, 1916, p. 4.
41. J. B. Bishop, pp. 399–400.
42. Hart and Ferleger, p. 451.
43. Thompson, p. 125.
44. Thompson, p. 125.
45. *Everybody's*, Vol. 52 (1925), p. 184.
46. *Women's Home Companion*, October 1919, pp. 7–8; *Literary Digest*, October 18, 1919, p. 48.
47. Mowry, p. 344.
48. *Washington Times*, May 31, 1916, p. 1.
49. *Washington Herald*, May 31, 1916, p. 1; *Washington Times*, May 31, 1916, p. 1; *Wilmington (DE) News Journal*, May 31, 1916, p. 6; Mowry, p. 344.
50. *Wilmington (DE) News Journal*, May 31, 1916, p. 6; Frankenberg, p. 202.
51. Hart and Ferleger, p. 451; Executive Committee of the Progressive National Committee, p. 55.
52. *New York Times*, June 1, 1916, p. 4.
53. *New York Times*, June 1, 1916, p. 1.
54. *New York World*, May 31, 1916, p. 1; J. B. Bishop, pp. 410–11.
55. Morison, p. 1026.
56. Morison, p. 1078.
57. *Current Literature*, October 1905, pp. 377–81; Garraty (*Perkins*), pp. 182–83; Pusey, p. 156; O'Toole, p. 293.
58. Hughes, p. 126; Garraty (*Perkins*), p. 182.
59. Pusey, pp. 177–78.

60. Pusey, p. 178.
61. Brown, pp. 141–42; Sullivan (Vol. 3), pp. 281–87; Wesser, pp. 163–66; Fausold (*Wadsworth*), pp. 61–65.
62. Stoddard (*Knew*), pp. 440–41.
63. *New York Times*, February 1, 1908, pp. 1–2; O. K. Davis, pp. 69–72; Pusey, pp. 236–38; Wesser, pp. 218–20.
64. Sullivan (Vol. 4), p. 304fn; Pusey, p. 238; Wesser, p. 220.
65. O'Toole, pp. 293, 448; Thompson, pp. 65, 308.
66. O'Toole, p. 293.
67. Stoddard (*Costs*), p. 114.
68. *New York Evening Telegram*, April 14, 1916, p. 3; Pusey, p. 320.
69. *North American Review*, May 1916, p. 649; Pusey, p. 320.
70. Pusey, p. 320.
71. *Brooklyn Daily Eagle*, April 9, 1916, p. 4.
72. Pusey, p. 234; Eaton, p. 248.
73. Stoddard (*Knew*), p. 432.
74. Stoddard (*Knew*), p. 451.
75. *New York Times*, June 1, 1916, p. 4; *New York Press*, June 1, 1916, page unknown.

"One colossal figure of American manhood"

1. Mayer, p. 341.
2. Executive Committee of the Progressive National Committee, p. 9.
3. Richberg (*Tents*), p. 72.
4. *Topeka (KS) State Journal*, June 1, 1916, p. 1; *Philadelphia Evening Public Ledger*, June 2, 1916, p. 1.
5. *Philadelphia Evening Public Ledger*, June 2, 1916, p. 1.
6. *New York Evening Telegram*, June 3, 1916, page unknown.
7. *Topeka (KS) State Journal*, June 1, 1916, p. 1.
8. *New York Times*, January 11, 1916, pp. 1, 6.
9. Fausold (*Pinchot*), p. 220.
10. *New Republic*, June 17, 1916, p. 164; Editors of the *New Republic* and Straight, p. 154.
11. G. L. Hart, pp. 92–93.
12. *New York Times*, June 9, 1916, p. 1.
13. Cobelle, pp. 80–81.
14. Morison, pp. 1051–52. TR's sister "Bye" remained firmly antisuffrage (Caroli, pp. 122–23).
15. *Chicago Examiner*, June 8, 1916, p. 2.
16. *New York Tribune*, June 8, 1916, pp. 1, 4; *Chicago Examiner*, June 8, 1916, p. 2; *Washington Times*, June 10, 1916, p. 2; Downes, pp. 250–52.
17. *New York Press*, June 7, 1916, p. 4.
18. *New York Tribune*, June 8, 1916, p. 4; Downes, p. 252.
19. *New York Times*, June 8, 1916, p. 12.
20. *New York Times*, June 8, 1916, p. 1.
21. Downes, p. 175; Sinclair, p. 50.

22. *New York Times*, February 29, 1920, p. 7.
23. *Marion (OH) Star*, September 21, 1912, p. 6.
24. *Helena (MT) Independent*, June 27, 1920, p. 8.
25. *Ardmore (OK) Daily Ardmorite*, October 12, 1920, p. 4.
26. Downes, p. 189.
27. White (*Autobiography*), p. 522.
28. Robenalt, pp. 171–75.
29. *New York Times*, June 10, 1916, p. 4; Lovell, p. 44.
30. Lovell, p. 44.
31. Mowry, p. 346.
32. von Weigand, p. 213.
33. Glad, p. 78; Kazin (*War*), p. 138.
34. Brown, p. 271.
35. *New York Sun*, June 11, 1916, p. 2; Brown, p. 283.
36. Butler, p. 254.
37. *Brooklyn Daily Eagle*, June 9, 1916, p. 2.
38. *Washington Herald*, June 10, 1910, p. 2.
39. *Topeka (KS) State Journal*, June 9, 1916, p. 2.
40. *Topeka (KS) State Journal*, June 9, 1916, p. 2. She claimed to be "Mrs. Thomas Root," Elihu's daughter-in-law. She might well have been, save that no Root offspring bore the name Thomas (*Keokuk [IA] Gate City*, June 9, 1916, p. 1).
41. Hart (*Proceedings*), p. 148; *Chicago Tribune*, June 10, 1916, p. 3.
42. Hart (*Proceedings*), p. 149; *New York Times*, June 10, 1916, p. 4; Eaton, p. 254.
43. Hart (*Proceedings*), p. 149.
44. *Chicago Tribune*, June 10, 1916, p. 3.
45. Thompson, p. 131.
46. *Chicago Tribune*, June 10, 1916, p. 10.
47. *New York Tribune*, June 8, 1916, pp. 1, 4; *Washington Herald*, June 8, 1916, p. 1.
48. *New York Tribune*, June 9, 1916, p. 3.
49. *Washington Herald*, June 8, 1916, p. 2.
50. Pinchot, p. 57.
51. White (*Autobiography*), pp. 521–22.
52. McKenna, p. 138.
53. McKenna, p. 138.
54. *New York Evening Telegram*, June 3, 1916, page unknown.
55. Hart (*Proceedings*), p. 186.
56. *Chicago Tribune*, June 9, 1916, p. 4.
57. *New York Tribune*, June 8, 1916, p. 1.
58. *Decatur (IL) Daily Review*, May 31, 1916, p. 1. TR's long-distance convention conversations were transcribed by Perkins's trusted longtime secretary, Miss Mary Kihm, to whom he left $50,000 in his will, plus $6,000 annually for life ("The provisions for said Mary Kihm are to be deemed absolute") (*New York Times*, June 23, 1920, p. 1).
59. *New York Tribune*, June 9, 1916, p. 1.
60. *New York Tribune*, June 9, 1916, p. 1.

61. *New York Tribune*, June 9, 1916, p. 1.
62. *New York Times*, May 29, 1916, p. 1.
63. *New York Times*, May 30, 1916, p. 1; C. T. Thomas, p. 122.
64. *New York Times*, May 29, 1916, p. 1.
65. C. T. Thomas, p. 121.
66. *New York Times*, May 31, 1916, p. 1; *Fourth Estate*, June 3, 1916, p. 30; C. T. Thomas, p. 123.
67. *New York Tribune*, June 9, 1916, p. 1.
68. *New York Tribune*, June 8, 1916, p. 1.
69. *Chicago Tribune*, April 3, 1916, p. 11.
70. N. Roosevelt, p. 108; Hagedorn (*Wood*), p. 187.
71. Hagedorn (*Wood*), pp. 187–88.
72. Hagedorn (*Wood*), p. 188.
73. Hagedorn (*Wood*), p. 188; McCallum, p. 266.
74. Hagedorn (*Wood*), p. 188.
75. *New York Times*, June 6, 1916, p. 3; *Los Angeles Times*, June 6, 1916, p. 5; *Washington Times*, June 6, 1916, p. 2.
76. Morison, pp. 1051–52.
77. Lovell, pp. 20, 191.
78. Lovell, pp. 194–95.
79. *Chicago Examiner*, June 9, 1916, p. 2.
80. *Washington Herald*, June 7, 1916, p. 1.
81. Morison, p. 1039.
82. Garraty (*Lodge*), p. 323.
83. *Washington Times*, June 8, 1916, p. 2.
84. White (*Autobiography*), p. 523.
85. *New Republic*, June 17, 1916, p. 165.
86. Butler, p. 259.
87. Garraty (*Perkins*), p. 339.
88. *Chicago Tribune*, June 10, 1916, p. 2; Hart (*Proceedings*), pp. 176–82.
89. *Chicago Tribune*, June 10, 1916, p. 2; Hart (*Proceedings*), pp. 182–86.
90. Hart (*Proceedings*), p. 192.
91. Hart (*Proceedings*), p. 192.

"THE COWARDLY STAB"

1. *American Heritage*, December 1957, p. 103; Garraty (*Perkins*), p. 341.
2. *American Heritage*, December 1957, p. 104; Garraty (*Perkins*), p. 343.
3. *American Heritage*, December 1957, p. 104; Garraty (*Perkins*), p. 344.
4. Garraty (*Perkins*), p. 344.
5. *Washington Star*, June 1, 1916, p. 1.
6. *American Heritage*, December 1957, p. 104; Garraty (*Perkins*), p. 344.
7. Rosenthal, pp. 187–91.
8. Morison, p. 1128.
9. *American Heritage*, December 1957, p. 105; Garraty (*Perkins*), p. 345.

10. Mowry, p. 341.
11. N. Roosevelt, p. 40.
12. Felsenthal, pp. 147–49; Cordery (*Alice*), pp. 303–4, 525; Hernon, p. 141.
13. Garraty (*Perkins*), pp. 345–47.
14. *American Heritage*, December 1957, p. 107; Garraty (*Perkins*), pp. 348–49.
15. Hart (*Proceedings*), pp. 193–95; Roosevelt and Lodge, pp. 486–89.
16. Morison, p. 1062fn.
17. Garraty (*Perkins*), pp. 359–60.
18. *St. Louis Post-Dispatch*, June 11, 1916, p. 32. Clark McAdams was Clark Clifford's uncle.
19. *St. Louis Post-Dispatch*, June 11, 1916, p. 32.
20. Lovell, p. 49.
21. *American Heritage*, December 1957, p. 101; Garraty (*Perkins*), p. 338.
22. Hart (*Proceedings*), pp. 195–97.
23. *St. Louis Post-Dispatch*, June 11, 1916, p. 33.
24. Hart (*Proceedings*), pp. 197–98.
25. *New York Sun*, June 11, 1916, p. 4; *Los Angeles Herald*, June 11, 1916, p. 1.
26. *New York Times*, June 11, 1916, p. 3.
27. *New York Times*, June 11, 1916, p. 3.
28. *New York Sun*, June 11, 1916, p. 4.
29. *New York Herald*, June 11, 1916, p. 5.
30. Pinchot, p. 221.
31. *New York Sun*, June 11, 1916, p. 4.
32. *North American Review*, May 1891, p. 602.
33. *New York Sun*, June 11, 1916, p. 4.
34. *New York Sun*, June 11, 1916, p. 4.
35. Pinchot, p. 221.
36. *New York Times*, June 11, 1916, p. 2.
37. *New York Sun*, June 11, 1916, p. 4.
38. *New York Sun*, June 11, 1916, p. 4.
39. *New York Herald*, June 11, 1916, p. 5.
40. *Chicago Examiner*, June 11, 1916, p. 4.
41. *Chicago Examiner*, June 11, 1916, p. 4.
42. *Philadelphia Inquirer*, June 11, 1916, p. 14.
43. *Xenia (OH) Gazette*, June 9, 1916, p. 4.
44. *Portsmouth (OH) Daily Times*, June 6, 1916, p. 3.
45. *Chicago Examiner*, June 11, 1916, p. 4.
46. *New York Times*, June 11, 1916, p. 3.
47. *Chicago Examiner*, June 11, 1916, p. 4.
48. *New York Times*, June 11, 1916, p. 10.
49. *Chicago Examiner*, June 11, 1916, p. 4.
50. Pinchot, p. 221.
51. *Chicago Tribune*, June 11, 1916, p. 10.
52. Garraty (*Perkins*), p. 351.

53. Hart (*Proceedings*), pp. 207–12; *Boston Post*, June 10, 1916, p. 8; *New York Sun*, June 11, 1916, p. 2.

54. *American Heritage*, December 1957, p. 108; Garraty (*Perkins*), pp. 351–52.

55. *American Heritage*, December 1957, p. 108; Garraty (*Perkins*), p. 352.

56. *New York Tribune*, June 11, 1916, p. 1.

57. *Chicago Examiner*, June 11, 1916, p. 4.

58. White (*Autobiography*), p. 527.

59. Pinchot, p. 7.

60. Pinchot, p. 8.

61. Goodwin (*Pulpit*), p. 539.

62. *St. Louis Post-Dispatch*, June 11, 1916, p. 33; Wickware (*1916*), p. 30.

63. White (*Autobiography*), p. 527.

64. *Washington Herald*, June 11, 1916, p. 4.

65. *Duluth (MN) Herald*, June 12, 1916, p. 11.

66. *New York Times*, June 11, 1916, p. 1.

"BLACK BLOOD CRUSTED ROUND THEIR MOUTHS"

1. Garraty (*Perkins*), p. 351.

2. *New York Times*, June 11, 1916, p. 1.

3. *New York Sun*, June 11, 1916, p. 1.

4. *New York Sun*, June 11, 1916, p. 1.

5. *New York Sun*, June 11, 1916, p. 1.

6. *Chicago Tribune*, June 11, 1916, p. 11.

7. *New York Sun*, June 11, 1916, p. 1.

8. O. K. Davis, p. 449. "I made an unannounced visit to Oyster Bay about two weeks before the Republican convention," revealed Chicago city treasurer Charles H. Sergel. "From my conferences with Colonel Roosevelt, I feel positive that he not only will withdraw unconditionally, but will campaign actively for the Republican nominee" (*New York Times*, June 12, 1916, p. 1).

9. Pringle (*Taft*), p. 893.

10. J. C. Lane, p. 207.

11. *New York Sun*, June 11, 1916, p. 2.

12. White (*Autobiography*), p. 527.

13. *The Nation*, June 15, 1916, pp. 636–67.

14. Morison, p. 1063. Written on June 16, 1916. Wagenknecht notes that beneath the surface of TR's superhuman memory lurked a substandard speller (Wagenknecht, p. 74).

15. *New York Times*, June 15, 1916, p. 1; *New York Herald*, June 15, 1916, p. 1; *New York Tribune*, June 15, 1916, p. 1; *Brooklyn Daily Eagle*, June 15, 1916, p. 1.

16. *Brooklyn Daily Eagle*, June 15, 1916, p. 1.

17. *New York Times*, June 15, 1916, p. 1; *Brooklyn Daily Eagle*, June 15, 1916, p. 1; *New York Herald*, June 15, 1916, p. 1; *New York Tribune*, June 15, 1916, p. 1; Dalton, pp. 466, 636.

18. W. Johnson, pp. 168–69.

19. J. B. Bishop, p. 412.

20. *Chicago Tribune*, June 27, 1916, p. 1; *New York Times*, June 27, 1916, p. 5; Eaton, p. 257.

21. *New York Times*, November 1, 1916, p. 5; Link (*Papers*, Vol. 5), p. 125; Lovell, p. 106. Press reports indicated that William Allen White also endorsed Wilson; they appear to be incorrect (W. Johnson, p. 171).

22. Downes, p. 247.

23. *New York Tribune*, June 15, 1916, p. 3.

24. *New York Times*, June 15, 1916, p. 2.

25. *New York Times*, June 15, 1916, p. 1; Kazin (*War*), p. 113.

26. *New York Tribune*, July 5, 1916, p. 5.

27. Stoddard (*Knew*), p. 317; Pringle (*Roosevelt*), p. 589.

28. J. B. Bishop, pp. 311–12; Pringle (*Roosevelt*), pp. 589–90.

29. Mowry, p. 313.

30. Morison, pp. 1087–88.

31. Brands (*Letters*), p. 609.

32. *Garment Worker*, December 14, 1917, p. 2; Thelen, p. 129.

33. "Annual Estimates of Unemployment in the United States, 1900–1954," National Bureau of Economic Research, http://www.nber.org/chapters/c2644.pdf (retrieved May 15, 2017).

34. O. K. Davis, p. 450.

35. *New Republic*, September 30, 1916, p. 210.

36. Wickware (*1916*), p. 806.

37. Baker (*Facing War*), pp. 50–51.

38. *New York Sun*, September 6, 1916, p. 4; *New York Times*, October 9, 1916, p. 11; *New York Times*, October 15, 1916, p. 6. A good many, including Robins, Dreier, and Davis, had been for TR.

39. Wickware (*1916*), p. 806.

40. *New York Times*, August 17, 1916, p. 7.

41. Sherman, p. 122.

42. *The Nation*, November 2, 1916, p. 411.

43. Villard, pp. 317–18.

44. *New Outlook*, November 22, 1916, pp. 644–45; Pusey, pp. 340–49.

45. Dalton, pp. 467, 636.

46. Wickware (*1916*), p. 807.

47. *New York Times*, September 21, 1916, p. 10; Scott, p. 270; Brown, p. 284. In March 1918, Bacon wrote his wife, "Between you and me . . . not to be repeated to my friend T. R., who thinks me already an Anglophile, I am proud to be of Anglo-Saxon breeding and race" (Scott, p. 357).

48. *New York Times*, September 21, 1916, p. 10.

49. Scott, pp. 461–62.

50. Mitgang, p. 112.

51. Mitgang, pp. 113, 118.

52. Mitgang, p. 113.

53. *New York Evening Telegram*, September 17, 1916, p. 4.

54. *New York Evening Post*, September 16, 1916, p. 4.
55. *New York Sun*, September 17, 1917, p. 6.
56. Mitgang, p. 118.
57. Mitgang, p. 118.
58. *Indianapolis News*, September 28, 1916, p. 9.
59. *Indianapolis News*, September 28, 1916, p. 9.
60. *Chicago Tribune*, October 3, 1917, p. 17; *Ardmore (OK) Daily Ardmorite*, October 3, 1917, p. 1; *Chicago Tribune*, October 4, 1917, p. 17. They eventually settled on the name "The National Party." It quickly fell apart.
61. Wickware *(1916)*, p. 807; Berg, p. 399.
62. Tumulty, p. 201.
63. Morison, p. 408.
64. Cooper *(Warrior)*, p. 80.
65. O'Leary, p. 46.
66. *Oshkosh Northwestern*, September 30, 1916, p. 1.
67. T. Roosevelt *(Americanism)*, p. 44.
68. Manners, p. 298.
69. *New York Times*, October 5, 1916, p. 10; Manners, p. 299.
70. Manners, p. 299.
71. Manners, p. 299. Horace also detested TR. The scathing analysis of Roosevelt found in his memoirs makes for bracing reading (Taft, pp. 127–38).
72. *New York Times*, October 11, 1916, p. 13.
73. Dalton, p. 471. The observation of *New York Tribune* reporter Ned Lewis.
74. *New York Sun*, October 28, 1916, p. 4.
75. *New York Times*, October 29, 1916, p. 1.
76. *New York Sun*, October 18, 1916, p. 4; *New York Sun*, October 28, 1916, p. 4; Dalton, pp. 470–72.
77. Bernstorff, pp. 296–97.
78. Dall, pp. 140–41; Devlin, p. 530.
79. Link *(Progressive)*, p. 245.
80. Stoddard *(Knew)*, p. 436.
81. Schriftgiesser, p. 284fn.
82. Garraty *(Lodge)*, pp. 329–32.
83. *New York Times*, October 30, 1916, p. 8.
84. Tobin, p. 36.
85. *New York Times*, November 4, 1916, p. 4.
86. *Detroit Free Press*, June 4, 1916, p. 4.
87. *Philadelphia Inquirer*, May 14, 1916, p. 6.
88. *New York Times*, November 4, 1916, p. 4.
89. *The Fatherland*, November 1, 1916, p. 203.
90. *New York World*, November 4, 1916, p. 9.
91. N. Miller *(F.D.R.)*, p. 229.
92. *Literary Digest*, November 4, 1916, pp. 1155–56; Weed, pp. 34–35.
93. Cooper *(Wilson)*, pp. 356–57.

94. *Chicago Examiner*, November 8, 1916, p. 6.
95. Weed, p. 33.
96. *New York Times*, November 8, 1916, p. 2; Baker (*Facing War*), p. 295.
97. Villard, p. 318; Devlin, p. 531.
98. N. Miller (*F.D.R.*), p. 229; Morgan, p. 174.
99. Palmer, p. 73.
100. *New York Times*, November 8, 1916, p. 2; Devlin, p. 531.
101. *New York Times*, November 8, 1916, p. 1.
102. Longworth, pp. 241–42.
103. Morgan, p. 174.
104. Devlin, p. 529.
105. Kazin (*War*), p. 134.
106. G. S. Thomas, pp. 166–67.
107. Longworth, p. 242.
108. Stoddard (*Knew*), p. 321.
109. Leary, p. 76.
110. Dalton, pp. 472, 638.

"I'M ONLY ASKING TO BE ALLOWED TO DIE"

1. Leary, pp. 76–77.
2. Cooper (*Wilson*), p. 352.
3. *Chicago Tribune*, May 9, 1916, p. 2.
4. Gerard, p. 120.
5. *New York Times*, February 4, 1917, p. 1.
6. Cramer, p. 110.
7. *New York Times*, March 5, 1917, p. 10.
8. *New York Times*, February 6, 1917, p. 6.
9. *New York Times*, February 5, 1917, p. 6.
10. *New York Times*, February 18, 1917, p. 15.
11. *Arizona Republic*, March 6, 1917, p. 1.
12. *New York Times*, March 6, 1917, p. 1.
13. *Utica (NY) Herald-Dispatch*, March 21, 1917, p. 10.
14. Manners, p. 299. A very similar bon mot is often ascribed to Colonel House (TR: "After all, I'm only asking to be allowed to die"; House: "Oh? Did you make that point quite clear to the President?"), supposedly uttered immediately following April 10, 1917's TR-Wilson session. That version's original source is Belle Willard Roosevelt's March 5, 1940, diary entry indicating that she had heard the tale from Winston Churchill, who heard it from House himself (Renehan, p. 129; Collier and Horowitz, pp. 194, 498; Auchincloss, p. 132; Brady, pp. 73–74). However, House's own diary places him in Manhattan on that April 10, conferring with Democratic operative Robert Wooley (actor Monty Wooley's father) and later dining at Delmonico's with Mr. and Mrs. Ignaz Jan Paderewski (MS 466, Edward Mandell House Papers, Series II, Diaries, Vol. 5, p. 104, Yale University Library Digital Collections, http://digital.library.yale.edu/cdm/compoundobject/collection/1004_6/id/4658/rec/1).

15. Howland, pp. 270–71.
16. Brands (*Letters*), p. 622.
17. J. B. Bishop, pp. 419–20.
18. Roosevelt and Lodge, p. 509.
19. Roosevelt and Lodge, p. 510.
20. Brands (*Letters*), pp. 623–24.
21. Cramer, p. 110; Craig, p. 303.
22. Morison, p. 1152; Brands (*T.R.*), p. 778.
23. *New York Sun*, April 4, 1917, p. 8.
24. *New York Times*, March 26, 1917, p. 4.
25. *Boston Post*, April 3, 1917, p. 2.
26. Garraty (*Lodge*), p. 334.
27. *Washington Star*, April 3, 1917, p. 1; Garraty (*Lodge*), pp. 333–34; Wiggins, p. 228; "Senator Attacks Constituent," United States Senate, http://www.senate.gov/artand history/history/minute/Senator_Attacks_Constituent.htm.
28. *Washington Star*, April 3, 1917, p. 1; Garraty (*Lodge*), pp. 333–34; Wiggins, p. 228.
29. Garraty (*Lodge*), p. 334.
30. Garraty (*Lodge*), p. 334.
31. *Boston Post*, April 3, 1917, p. 2.
32. Dos Passos, p. 211.
33. *Washington Herald*, April 4, 1917, p. 4.
34. *New York Times*, April 4, 1917, p. 10.
35. *New York Sun*, April 4, 1917, p. 1.
36. *New York Times*, April 4, 1917, p. 4.
37. *New York Times*, April 5, 1917, p. 4.
38. *New York Times*, April 4, 1917, p. 10.
39. McKenna, p. 143.
40. Robenalt, pp. 243–44.
41. Roosevelt and Lodge, p. 507.
42. *New York Times*, April 12, 1917, p. 22.
43. *New York Times*, April 9, 1917, p. 1.
44. *New York Times*, April 10, 1917, p. 3.
45. *Washington Star*, April 10, 1917, p. 2.
46. Leary, p. 93; E. Morris (*Colonel*), p. 486.
47. Cordery (*Alice*), p. 258.
48. *New York Times*, April 11, 1917, p. 2.
49. Link (*Papers*, Vol. 42), p. 31.
50. Tumulty, p. 285.
51. Brands (*Letters*), pp. 624–25.
52. Brands (*Letters*), p. 625.
53. Brands (*Letters*), p. 625.
54. Leary, pp. 95–96; Tumulty, p. 288.
55. Leary, p. 96.
56. Tumulty, p. 286; Daniels (*1917–1923*), p. 286.

57. Leary, p. 96; Tumulty, p. 288.
58. *New York Times*, April 11, 1917, p. 2.
59. *Washington Star*, April 10, 1917, p. 2.
60. J. B. Bishop, p. 424.
61. *Washington Star*, April 10, 1917, p. 2.
62. Tumulty, p. 285.
63. *Washington Post*, April 11, 1917, p. 5; Leary, p. 95.
64. Pringle (*Roosevelt*), p. 595.
65. Leary, p. 100.
66. O'Toole, p. 311.
67. *New York Times*, May 11, 1917, p. 1.
68. *New York Times*, May 18, 1917, p. 2.
69. Pershing, p. 22; Pringle (*Roosevelt*), p. 598.
70. *New York Times*, May 8, 1917, p. 5.
71. Morison, p. 1185fn.
72. *Theodore Roosevelt Association Journal* (summer 1984), p. 18.
73. *Theodore Roosevelt Association Journal* (summer 1984), p. 16.
74. *Theodore Roosevelt Association Journal* (summer 1984), p. 18.
75. *Theodore Roosevelt Association Journal* (summer 1984), p. 18.
76. *Christian Science Monitor*, May 19, 1917, p. 7; *Outlook*, May 30, 1917, p. 176; J. B. Bishop, p. 425; Ellis, p. 337.
77. *New York Times*, May 20, 1917, p. 2.
78. *New York Times*, May 7, 1917, p. 3.
79. *New York Times*, May 20, 1917, p. 2.
80. Amos, pp. 65–66.
81. *New York Times*, May 20, 1917, p. 2.
82. Leary, p. 115.
83. O. K. Davis, p. 456.
84. Ellis, p. 337.
85. Downes, p. 247; Robenalt, p. 200.
86. F. Russell (*Shadow*), p. 279.
87. Downes, p. 247.
88. Roosevelt and Lodge, p. 523.
89. F. Russell (*Shadow*), p. 286.
90. Robenalt, pp. 240, 273.
91. Robenalt, pp. 240–41.
92. F. Russell (*Shadow*), p. 287.
93. *New York Times*, May 20, 1917, p. 2.
94. *New York Times*, May 20, 1917, p. 2.
95. *New York Times*, May 28, 1917, p. 1; *Outlook*, June 6, 1917, p. 211; J. B. Bishop, p. 428; Pringle (*Roosevelt*), pp. 597–98.
96. *New York Times*, May 7, 1917, p. 1.
97. *New York Times*, May 21, 1917, pp. 1–2.
98. Robenalt, pp. 239–40.

99. Shaff and Shaff, p. 160; Taliaferro, p. 163.

100. Bruns, pp. 258–59.

101. O'Toole, p. 311. Actually, Wilson appointed several Republicans or Progressives to prominent wartime posts, including Borglum, Taft, Bainbridge Colby, William Kent, Felix Frankfurter, Herbert Hoover, and even Charles Evans Hughes. Colby, Kent, and Frankfurter supported him in 1916. Hughes obviously did not.

102. O. K. Davis, p. 456.

"I WISH I COULD GET MY HANDS ON HIM!"

1. *New York Times*, April 7, 1917, p. 13.

2. *New York Times*, April 15, 1917, p. 17; *New York Sun*, April 15, 1917, p. 9; E. Morris (*Colonel*), pp. 485, 488.

3. *New York Times*, April 7, 1917, p. 13.

4. *Sea Power*, June 1916, p. 5.

5. *New York Times*, April 7, 1917, p. 13.

6. Hagedorn (*Sagamore*), p. 367.

7. *New York Sun*, April 15, 1917, p. 9.

8. *New York Times*, September 18, 1916, p. 5.

9. Hagedorn (*Sagamore*), pp. 366–67.

10. Morison, p. 1193.

11. Brands (*Letters*), pp. 626–27.

12. *New York Tribune*, January 3, 1918, p. 3.

13. Hagedorn (*Sagamore*), p. 371.

14. Dalton, p. 481.

15. *New York Tribune*, January 3, 1918, p. 3; Carroll, pp. 151–52; Brady, p. 81.

16. Brady, p. 82.

17. K. Roosevelt (*Quentin*), p. 32.

18. *New York Times*, July 11, 1917, p. 2.

19. *New York Times*, March 21, 1939, p. 29; Caroli, p. 270.

20. Reisner, p. 27.

21. Oliver, pp. 48–49.

22. Lewis, p. 564.

23. Morison, pp. 226–27.

24. *New York Times*, July 14, 1910, p. 5; Ramsaye, pp. 693–94.

25. Cobelle, pp. 64–66.

26. Lewis, p. 564.

27. *Journal of Negro History*, July 1962, p. 178.

28. Oliver, p. 41.

29. Gould, pp. 93, 149.

30. Rudwick, p. 8.

31. *Chicago Tribune*, November 4, 1916, p. 3.

32. *Chicago Tribune*, November 4, 1916, p. 3.

33. *Chicago Tribune*, November 4, 1916, p. 3.

34. *Chicago Tribune*, November 4, 1916, p. 3.
35. *Chicago Tribune*, November 6, 1916, p. 1.
36. *Chicago Tribune*, November 6, 1916, p. 1.
37. Rudwick, p. 13.
38. Rudwick, p. 14.
39. Rudwick, p. 133.
40. *New York Tribune*, July 7, 1917, p. 1.
41. *New York Tribune*, July 7, 1917, p. 1. TR's outrage was selective. May 1916 witnessed the barbaric, perhaps more horrifying, incredibly well-documented Waco, Texas, lynching of confessed murderer Jesse Washington. Like Wilson and just about everyone else (save the NAACP), Roosevelt said nothing.
42. *Brooklyn Daily Eagle*, July 7, 1917, p. 6.
43. *Brooklyn Daily Eagle*, July 7, 1917, p. 6.
44. *Brooklyn Daily Eagle*, July 7, 1917, p. 6.
45. *New York Tribune*, July 7, 1917, p. 1.
46. *New York Sun*, July 7, 1917, p. 2.
47. *New York Sun*, July 7, 1917, p. 2.
48. J. Greene, p. 36.
49. *New York Times*, July 7, 1917, p. 4.
50. *Chicago Tribune*, July 7, 1917, p. 4.
51. *New York Evening Telegram*, July 7, 1917, p. 3.
52. *Chicago Examiner*, July 7, 1917, p. 1.
53. *Chicago Tribune*, July 7, 1917, p. 4.
54. *New York Times*, July 7, 1917, p. 4.
55. *New York Sun*, July 7, 1917, p. 1.
56. *New York Evening Telegram*, July 7, 1917, p. 3.
57. *New York Sun*, July 7, 1917, p. 1.
58. *New York Sun*, July 7, 1917, p. 1.
59. Dalton, p. 493.
60. *New York Times*, October 26, 1917, p. 7.
61. Lewinson, pp. 83–86.
62. Cobelle, pp. 109–10.
63. *New York Sun*, July 23, 1917, p. 6.
64. Leary, p. 34.
65. Goodman, p. 18.
66. Swanberg, pp. 307–8; Lewinson, p. 83.
67. Clifford, p. 72.
68. Lewinson, p. 230.
69. *New York Sun*, November 4, 1917, p. 12.
70. Lewinson, p. 232.
71. *New York Herald*, October 30, 1917, p. 4.
72. *New York Herald*, October 30, 1917, p. 4.
73. *New York Times*, October 30, 1917, p. 5.

74. *New York Age*, November 1, 1917, p. 1. Another New York black newspaper, the *New York Amsterdam News*, observed, "It is a well-known fact that Hillquit has most of his strength among the Jews and the East Side Russian Bolshevitos and the discontented coloured population of Harlem. Hillquit's election would be followed by a wave of antisemitic feeling and additional strength to the anti-colored prejudiced" (*Amsterdam News*, November 7, 1917, page unknown).

75. *New York Times*, January 22, 1918, pp. 1–2.

76. *Ohio History Journal* (spring 1972), pp. 108–21.

77. *New York Sun*, November 2, 1917, p. 1.

78. *Providence (RI) Journal*, November 1, 1917, page unknown.

79. *Brooklyn Daily Eagle*, November 2, 1917, p. 2.

80. G. Watkins, p. 309; Mock, p. 195.

81. *New York Evening Post*, November 1, 1917, p. 9.

82. *New York Herald*, November 2, 1917, p. 10.

83. *Burlington (IA) Hawk-Eye*, November 2, 1917, p. 1.

84. *New York Herald*, November 2, 1917, p. 10.

85. *New York Tribune*, November 2, 1917, p. 14.

86. *New York Herald*, November 2, 1917, p. 10.

87. *New York Herald*, November 2, 1917, p. 10.

"EVERYBODY WORKS, BUT FATHER"

1. *New York Times*, October 25, 1917, p. 5; E. Morris (*Colonel*), p. 507.

2. Lewinson, p. 241.

3. Lewinson, pp. 232–33; Brown, p. 296.

4. Lewinson, p. 241; Nasaw, pp. 264–65.

5. Nasaw, p. 264.

6. *New York Times*, October 31, 1917, p. 6.

7. *New York Times*, January 12, 1936, p. 21.

8. Lewinson, p. 246; Brown, p. 296.

9. *Jewish Social Studies*, October 1970, p. 298.

10. *New York Sun*, July 23, 1917, p. 6.

11. O. K. Davis, p. 433. Mitchel lost despite significant fraud committed on his behalf (Brown, p. 295).

12. E. B. Roosevelt (*Yesterday*), pp. 76–77.

13. Teague, p. 162.

14. Teague, p. 162; Levin, p. 405.

15. Teague, p. 162.

16. Teague, p. 162; Levin, p. 406; Cook (Vol. 1), p. 223.

17. Renehan, p. 406.

18. Collier and Horowitz, p. 198.

19. S. J. Morris (*Edith*), p. 417.

20. Iglehart, p. 274.

21. Iglehart, p. 274.

22. Iglehart, p. 275.

23. Rinehart, p. 241.

24. K. Roosevelt (*Quentin*), p. 122.

25. Longworth, p. 258.

26. Hagedorn (*Sagamore*), p. 369.

27. Abbott, p. 305.

28. *Boston Post*, April 7, 1917, p. 2; Jeffers, pp. 76–77; Brady, pp. 52–53, 71.

29. K. Roosevelt (*Quentin*), p. 27; C. Bishop, pp. 85–86.

30. C. Bishop, pp. 108, 110–11; Collier and Horowitz, p. 203.

31. Brady, pp. 58–59.

32. C. Bishop, p. 132. His previous salary—with the *Outlook*—was but $12,000.

33. C. Bishop, p. 119.

34. C. Bishop, p. 121.

35. C. Bishop, p. 121.

36. C. Bishop, p. 121.

37. Jeffers, p. 88. TR referred to a 1905 hit song that went "Everybody works but Father and he sits around all day. . . . Everybody works at our house but my old man."

38. Morison, p. 1234.

39. *Topeka (KS) State Journal*, September 25, 1917, p. 7.

40. *Topeka (KS) State Journal*, September 25, 1917, p. 7.

41. *San Francisco Chronicle*, July 25, 1916, p. 4. For another, similar version of these remarks, see the *San Francisco Chronicle*, July 25, 1916, p. 3; Frost, pp. 84–85.

42. Hichborn, p. xxvii.

43. *San Francisco Chronicle*, November 18, 1917, p. 1.

44. Gentry, p. 235.

45. Morison, p. 1260; Ralston, p. 116; Frost, p. 264.

46. *Oakland Tribune*, December 4, 1917, p. 4.

47. *San Francisco Chronicle*, December 19, 1917, p. 2.

48. *Nomination of Felix Frankfurter*, p. 121.

49. Lash (*Frankfurter*), p. 23.

50. *Nomination of Felix Frankfurter*, p. 122.

51. Hirsch, p. 221.

52. Ralston, p. 30. TR was long aware of Older's attitude. See his February 4, 1916, letter to Lodge (Morison, p. 1013).

53. Frost, p. 292.

54. Morison, p. 1262; *Argonaut*, April 23, 1921, p. 259.

55. Morison, p. 1263; *Nomination of Felix Frankfurter*, p. 13; Gentry, p. 235.

56. The text of Frankfurter's report on the Bisbee deportations may be found at *Nomination of Felix Frankfurter*, pp. 118–21.

57. *Argonaut*, April 23, 1921, p. 259; Morison, p. 1264; *Nomination of Felix Frankfurter*, p. 13; J. B. Bishop, p. 264. In praising TR's laceration of Frankfurter, his friend Owen Wister describes the latter as "an Oriental," presumably a euphemism for Jew (Wister, p. 221).

58. *Nomination of Felix Frankfurter*, p. 14; Hirsch, pp. 57, 221.

59. Frost, p. 99.

60. Gentry, p. 280.
61. *San Francisco Chronicle*, November 25, 1918, p. 1; Wells, p. 329.
62. Wells, pp. 310–15.
63. *New York Times*, October 21, 1916, p. 8.
64. Grant, pp. 46–47.
65. Spiro, p. 158.
66. *Book Buyer*, January 1917, p. 7; *Atlantic Monthly*, February 1917, advertising section, p. 3; Spiro, p. 158. Did TR read Grant's whole book? Alvin Johnson, commenting on Roosevelt's effusive praise for Herbert Croly's *Promise of American Life*, states, "The natural inference was that Roosevelt had read the book cover to cover, something I doubted vehemently. Roosevelt had the habit of ennobling authors by reading specimen pages of their works" (A. Johnson, p. 233).

"I WOULD NOT HAVE IT OTHERWISE"

1. Smythe, p. 85.
2. *Chicago Tribune*, January 28, 1918, p. 1; *New York Times*, January 28, 1918, p. 1; *Current Opinion*, July 1918, pp. 3–4; J. C. Lane, pp. 220–21; Hagedorn (*Wood*, Vol. 2), pp. 259–60; Holme, p. 5.
3. Smythe, p. 86.
4. Hagedorn (*Wood*), p. 270; Smythe, p. 86; Villard, p. 158.
5. *New York Times*, March 26, 1920, p. 17; McCallum, pp. 223, 237–39; Hagedorn (*Wood*), p. 210; Palmer, p. 165.
6. Smythe, p. 2; McCallum, p. 267.
7. Smythe, p. 121.
8. Smythe, p. 122; Carroll, p. 181.
9. Smythe, pp. 123–24.
10. Hagedorn (*Wood*), p. 317.
11. J. C. Lane, p. 230.
12. Hagedorn (*Wood*), p. 317.
13. Hagedorn (*Wood*), p. 317.
14. *New York Times*, April 2, 1918, p. 13.
15. *New York Tribune*, July 18, 1918, p. 4; *New York Times*, July 21, 1918, p. 6; S. J. Morris (*Edith*), p. 419; Jeffers, p. 98; Brady, pp. 86–87; Brands (*T.R.*), p. xi.
16. K. Roosevelt (*Eden*), pp. 122–23; Jeffers, p. 99.
17. K. Roosevelt (*Eden*), pp. 201–4.
18. E. B. Roosevelt (*Day*), p. 78; E. Morris (*Colonel*), p. 501; Jeffers, p. 92.
19. Jeffers, p. 92.
20. E. B. Roosevelt (*Day*), p. 97.
21. Pearlman, p. 71.
22. N. Roosevelt, p. 188.
23. Rickenbacker, p. 193.
24. K. Roosevelt (*Quentin*), pp. 251–53.
25. K. Roosevelt (*Quentin*), pp. 27–28.
26. Renehan, p. 80.

27. K. Roosevelt (*Quentin*), pp. 14–21.
28. K. Roosevelt (*Quentin*), p. 27.
29. Renehan, p. 186; Carroll, p. 245.
30. Brands (*Letters*), pp. 630–31.
31. Brands (*T.R.*), p. 792.
32. O'Toole, p. 382.
33. K. Roosevelt (*Quentin*), pp. 136–37.
34. K. Roosevelt (*Quentin*), p. 133.
35. C. Bishop, p. 169.
36. Rickenbacker, p. 194.
37. E. B. Roosevelt (*Day*), p. 100.
38. E. B. Roosevelt (*Day*), p. 100.
39. *New York Times*, July 7, 1918, p. 1.
40. *New York Sun*, July 12, 1918, pp. 1, 4; Lewinson, p. 256.
41. Pearlman, p. 126.
42. Pearlman, p. 154.
43. Brady, p. 99.
44. Rickenbacker, p. 193.
45. C. Bishop, p. 179.
46. C. Bishop, pp. 179–85.
47. K. Roosevelt (*Quentin*), pp. 175–76.
48. Thwing, p. 212.
49. *McClure's*, November 1918, p. 11.
50. *McClure's*, November 1918, p. 11.
51. *New York Tribune*, July 18, 1918, p. 4.
52. *New York Sun*, January 7, 1919, p. 2.
53. *New England Magazine*, January 1904, p. 601; *New York Tribune*, July 18, 1918, p. 4; *New York Sun*, January 7, 1919, p. 2; Iglehart, p. 249; Amos, pp. 5–6; S. J. Morris (*Edith*), p. 266; E. Morris (*Colonel*), p. 538.
54. *New York Sun*, January 7, 1919, p. 2.
55. C. Bishop, p. 182.
56. C. Bishop, p. 182.
57. *New York Tribune*, July 19, 1918, p. 1.
58. *New York Times*, July 21, 1918, p. 6; Burns, p. 156.
59. *New York Times*, July 23, 1918, p. 6.
60. K. Roosevelt (*Quentin*), p. 160; Burns, p. 156.
61. Renehan, p. 199.
62. *New York Tribune*, July 19, 1918, p. 1; J. B. Bishop, pp. 453–54.
63. *New York Tribune*, July 19, 1918, p. 1; *New York Sun*, July 19, 1918, pp. 1, 8; J. B. Bishop, p. 454. Perkins, however, warned TR against running.
64. C. R. Robinson (*Brother*), p. 344.
65. Dalton, p. 503.
66. *New York Sun*, July 19, 1918, p. 8.
67. *Saratoga Springs (NY) Saratogian*, July 18, 1918, p. 1.

68. *New York Sun,* July 19, 1918, p. 8; *New York Tribune,* July 19, 1918, p. 6.
69. C. R. Robinson (*Brother*), p. 344. Corinne's words.
70. *Saratoga Springs (NY) Saratogian,* July 18, 1918, p. 1.
71. *New York Sun,* July 19, 1918, p. 8.
72. *New York Sun,* July 19, 1918, p. 8.
73. *New York Sun,* July 19, 1918, p. 8.
74. *New York Sun,* July 19, 1918, p. 8.
75. C. R. Robinson (*Brother*), p. 346. That TR would have a moment to spare and *not* read would have profoundly disturbed anyone personally familiar with him.
76. *New York World,* July 19, 1918, p. 6.
77. *New York World,* July 19, 1918, p. 6.
78. Hagedorn (*Sagamore*), p. 414.
79. *New York Times,* July 21, 1918, p. 1.
80. *New York Times,* July 21, 1918, pp. 1, 6.
81. Hagedorn (*Sagamore*), p. 414.
82. *New York Times,* July 21, 1918, p. 6; *New York Times,* July 24, 1918, p. 6; E. B. Roosevelt (*Day*), pp. 100–101.
83. *New York Times,* July 24, 1918, p. 6; E. B. Roosevelt (*Day*), p. 101.
84. E. B. Roosevelt (*Day*), pp. 101–2.
85. *New York Times,* July 21, 1918, p. 1; Brady, p. 87.
86. Wagenknecht, p. 287.
87. *New York Times,* 1934, April 11, 1934, p. 21; C. R. Robinson (*Brother*), p. 349.
88. Collier and Horowitz, p. 239.
89. C. Bishop, pp. 194–95; Renehan, p. 5.
90. N. Roosevelt, p. 20.
91. Morison, p. 1555; Dalton, p. 504.
92. J. B. Bishop, p. 455. TR exposed his grief most openly to women; he expressed essentially the same sentiments he expressed to Wharton to the historian and former British ambassador James Bryce (who also lost a nephew in the war) but omitted the thought that he "should break down if [he] tried" writing of Quentin (Bishop [*Roosevelt*], p. 455; Morison, p. 1358).
93. J. W. D. Seymour, pp. 166–67.
94. T. Roosevelt (*Adventure*), pp. 1–8.

"I HAVE KEPT MY PROMISE"

1. C. R. Robinson (*Brother*), pp. 362–63; Hays, p. 239; Collier and Horowitz, p. 243.
2. C. R. Robinson (*Brother*), pp. 346–47.
3. C. R. Robinson (*Brother*), p. 343.
4. *Delineator,* September 1919, p. 32; *New York Tribune,* October 5, 1919, pt. 7, p. 5; Hagedorn (*Sagamore*), p. 4.
5. *Washington (Washington Court House, OH) Herald,* September 30, 1918, p. 2; F. Russell (*Shadow*), p. 302.
6. Stoddard (*Knew*), p. 321.

7. C. R. Robinson (*Brother*), p. 319. Historian James O. Robertson observes, "Roosevelt had to be of two minds. He . . . wanted terribly to have Wilson defeated. [But], if Hughes won, Hughes would get the 1920 nomination, and Roosevelt, who was getting old, would never again be President. The strain of these two problems must have been enormous" (Robertson, p. 21).

8. Taliaferro, p. 145.

9. *McClure's*, August 1919, p. 57; Duffy, pp. 308–9; Manners, p. 305; O'Toole, pp. 366–67.

10. Morison, p. 1341.

11. Lurie, p. 185; Thompson, p. 80.

12. *Saturday Evening Post*, December 9, 1922, pp. 44, 46.

13. Wagenknecht, pp. 96–97; J. B. Bishop, p. 453.

14. Morison, p. 1306; Hagedorn (*Sagamore*), p. 4.

15. Thwing, p. 919.

16. *Washington Post*, March 29, 1918, p. 3.

17. Hagedorn (*Sagamore*), p. 397.

18. *Indiana Magazine of History*, September 1968, pp. 179–80, 188.

19. Robertson, pp. 32, 317.

20. Robertson, pp. 20, 316.

21. *Chicago Tribune*, February 12, 1918, p. 1.

22. *Chicago Tribune*, February 12, 1918, p. 1.

23. *Chicago Tribune*, February 14, 1918, p. 13.

24. *New York Times*, February 16, 1918, p. 20; Morison, p. 1282fn.

25. Morison, pp. 1282–83.

26. Morison, pp. 1283–84.

27. *Indiana Magazine of History*, September 1968, p. 189.

28. *New York Tribune*, February 17, 1918, p. 8; *Indianapolis News*, February 18, 1918, p. 18; *McClure's*, February 1920, p. 28.

29. *Portland Oregonian*, February 15, 1916, p. 1; *McClure's*, February 1920, p. 28.

30. Morison, p. 1281.

31. *Chicago Tribune*, February 14, 1918, p. 13.

32. *Portland Oregonian*, February 15, 1916, p. 1; *Bridgeport (CT) Telegram*, February 15, 1916, p. 20; *New York Sun*, February 16, 1918, p. 3.

33. *Indianapolis News*, February 18, 1918, p. 18.

34. Shaff and Shaff, pp. 157, 363.

35. Hagedorn (*Wood*), p. 332.

36. Harris, p. 9.

37. Watson, pp. 167–69.

38. *New York Sun*, January 7, 1919, p. 10.

39. *New York Times*, January 7, 1919, p. 2.

40. *New York Times*, June 17, 1916, p. 2.

41. Dalton, pp. 491, 644.

42. Edmund Morris Notes (p. 3), Theodore Roosevelt Collection Subject File: Health, Houghton Library, Harvard University.

43. E. Morris (*Colonel*), p. 508.
44. Dalton, p. 491.
45. Thompson, p. 208.
46. E. Morris (*Colonel*), pp. 508, 712.
47. E. Morris (*Colonel*), pp. 507, 712.
48. Leary, p. 20.
49. *New York Times*, October 23, 1917, p. 13; Leary, pp. 19–21.
50. Daniels (*Diaries*), p. 272.
51. Longworth, p. 269.
52. Longworth, p. 268.
53. Longworth, p. 269.
54. Morison, pp. 1282–84; Dalton, p. 496.
55. *New York Tribune*, October 5, 1919, pt. 7, p. 5.
56. *Delineator*, September 1919, p. 31.
57. Dalton, p. 496.
58. *New York Times*, January 7, 1919, p. 2.
59. *New York Times*, February 7, 1918, p. 22.
60. *New York Times*, February 7, 1918, p. 22.
61. *New York Times*, February 7, 1918, p. 22; *New York Tribune*, January 7, 1919, p. 5; *New York Sun*, February 8, 1918, p. 8; Dalton, p. 496.
62. *New York Times*, February 7, 1918, p. 22; *New York Tribune*, January 7, 1919, p. 5.
63. Dalton, p. 496.
64. *New York Tribune*, February 9, 1918, p. 1; Hagedorn (*Boy's*), pp. 379; Dalton, p. 497.
65. *New York Tribune*, February 8, 1918, p. 8.
66. C. R. Robinson (*Brother*), p. 338.
67. *New York Tribune*, January 9, 1919, p. 1.
68. Morison, p. 1286.
69. *Brooklyn Daily Eagle*, March 4, 1918, p. 20. TR's mother also suffered from deafness, as would his sister "Bye" (Caroli, pp. 74, 130).
70. *New York Tribune*, January 7, 1919, p. 2.
71. *Brooklyn Daily Eagle*, March 4, 1918, p. 20.
72. Pringle (*Roosevelt*), p. 600.
73. E. Morris (*Colonel*), pp. 720, 724; Edmund Morris Notes (p. 3), Theodore Roosevelt Collection Subject File: Health, Houghton Library, Harvard University.
74. *New York Times*, January 7, 1919, p. 2; *Washington Star*, January 6, 1919, p. 1; *Washington Herald*, January 7, 1919, p. 1; Leary, pp. 180–81; Hagedorn (*Sagamore*), p. 211; Busch, p. 824; Edmund Morris Notes (p. 3), Theodore Roosevelt Collection Subject File: Health, Houghton Library, Harvard University. Cecil Spring-Rice also suffered from facial erysipelas and grew a beard to hide his disfigurement (S. J. Morris [*Edith*], p. 396).
75. *New York Times*, January 7, 1919, p. 2.
76. Wister, p. 369.
77. Amos, p. 160.
78. Pringle (*Roosevelt*), p. 601.
79. S. J. Morris (*Edith*), pp. 428, 554.

80. *New York Evening Telegram*, October 24, 1918, p. 2. Eventually, the axle from Quentin's plane reached Sagamore Hill, and Edith displayed it above the North Room's fireplace.

81. *New York Herald*, January 7, 1919, p. 2. TR reiterated his request in a November 3, 1918, letter to Lt. Col. Charles C. Pierce ("Letter from Theodore Roosevelt to Lieutenant Colonel Charles C. Pierce," National Archives Catalog, https://catalog.archives .gov/id/6706623).

82. Hagedorn (*Sagamore*), p. 398.

83. Roosevelt (*Star*), p. xxxiv.

84. Daniels (*Diaries*), p. 216.

85. *New York Times*, January 27, 1918, p. 5.

86. *The Nation*, November 9, 1918, p. 546.

87. Link (*Papers*, Vol. 45), p. 320.

88. Sullivan (Vol. 5), p. 203.

89. Roosevelt (*Star*), pp. 134–35.

90. *New York Times*, May 11, 1918, p. 1.

91. *New York Times*, May 11, 1918, p. 1.

92. *New York Times*, May 26, 1918, p. 19.

93. *Metropolitan Magazine*, October 1918, p. 69.

94. *Outlook*, September 18, 1918, p. 93.

95. Lorant, p. 620.

96. Hagedorn (*Sagamore*), p. 330.

97. *The Nation*, October 12, 1918, p. 405.

98. *The Writer*, June 1918, p. 81.

99. *New York Times*, March 27, 1918, p. 11.

100. Fleming, p. 291.

101. O'Toole, p. 400.

102. *Pittsburgh Post-Gazette*, October 26, 1918, p. 5.

103. *New York Times*, October 25, 1918, p. 2.

104. *New York Times*, October 29, 1918, p. 7.

105. *New York Sun*, November 2, 1918, p. 3; Morison, pp. 1383–84.

106. Morison, p. 1384fn.

107. *New York Times*, October 29, 1918, p. 7; Gardner, p. 393.

108. Morison, p. 1388.

109. Morison, pp. 1371–72, 1376, 1384.

110. Livermore, pp. 197–98.

111. Fuess, p. 156.

112. *Boston Globe*, October 28, 1916, p. 5.

113. *New York Times*, October 29, 1918, p. 7.

114. *New York Times*, October 29, 1918, p. 7.

115. *New York Times*, October 29, 1918, p. 7.

116. *New York Sun*, November 1, 1918, p. 4.

117. *New York Tribune*, January 7, 1919, p. 2; *New York Times*, January 7, 1919, p. 2; Morison, p. 1417; T. H. Russell, p. 374; Gardner, pp. 397–98.

118. Renehan, pp. 242, 264; Brands (*T.R.*), p. 810.
119. Renehan, pp. 212–13.
120. *New York Sun*, November 2, 1918, p. 7.
121. *New York Age*, November 9, 1918, p. 1.
122. *Scribner's Magazine*, April 1899, pp. 435–36.
123. Griffith, pp. 1036–37.
124. Dalton, p. 510.
125. S. J. Morris (*Edith*), p. 429; E. Morris (*Colonel*), p. 544; Edmund Morris Notes (p. 4), Theodore Roosevelt Collection Subject File: Health, Houghton Library, Harvard University.
126. S. J. Morris (*Edith*), p. 429.
127. S. J. Morris (*Edith*), p. 429; Edmund Morris Notes (p. 4), Theodore Roosevelt Collection Subject File: Health, Houghton Library, Harvard University. The physician was Dr. George W. Faller.
128. N. Roosevelt, p. 108. Some say TR walked more than a mile to the polls. In view of his dicey physical condition and Nicholas's personal testimony to the contrary, this assertion seems highly unlikely—but not as unlikely as walking *back* a mile *uphill*.
129. Morison, p. 1392. To Lodge.
130. Roosevelt (*Star*), p. 270; Creel, p. 160.
131. Livermore, p. 55; Weed, p. 42.
132. *New York Sun*, June 8, 1918, p. 6; Kennedy (*Over Here*), p. 108; Weed, p. 39.
133. *Asheboro (NC) Courier*, December 19, 1918, p. 4.
134. *New York Times*, November 12, 1918, p. 15.
135. *New York Times*, November 12, 1918, p. 15.
136. *New York Times*, December 25, 1918, p. 7.
137. Wagenknecht, p. 32.
138. E. Morris (*Colonel*), p. 346. Some say it was arthritis (Caroli, pp. 120, 163).
139. *Saturday Evening Post*, December 9, 1922, p. 46.
140. Brands (*T.R.*), p. 810; Thompson, p. 286.
141. *Saturday Evening Post*, December 9, 1922, p. 44.
142. Straus, p. 432; E. Morris (*Colonel*), p. 548; Edmund Morris Notes (p. 4), Theodore Roosevelt Collection Subject File: Health, Houghton Library, Harvard University.
143. C. R. Robinson (*Brother*), p. 361.
144. Dalton, p. 512.
145. *Jamestown Journal*, January 6, 1919, p. 6.
146. *New York Times*, December 21, 1917, p. 6; *New York Tribune*, December 21, 1917, p. 3; *New York Sun*, December 21, 1917, p. 5.
147. C. R. Robinson (*Brother*), p. 361.
148. Straus, p. 432.
149. Garland, p. 202.
150. Garland, p. 203.
151. Garland, pp. 204–5.
152. Nevins, pp. 351–52; Dos Passos, p. 432.

153. C. R. Robinson (*Brother*), pp. 361–62; S. J. Morris (*Edith*), p. 430; Gardner, p. 395; Dalton, pp. 511, 650; Schriftgiesser, pp. 304–5.

154. C. R. Robinson (*Brother*), pp. 361–62.

155. *La Grande (OR) Observer*, January 9, 1919, p. 1.

156. White (*Autobiography*), p. 548.

157. W. Johnson, p. 195.

158. White (*Autobiography*), p. 548.

159. Stoddard, p. 321.

160. Morison, p. 1414.

161. Sullivan (Vol. 5), p. 502. He had said earlier that year, "If the Republican Party wants me . . . and I can advance the ideals for which I stand, I will be a candidate. But I will not lift a finger for the nomination" (*Delineator*, September 1919, p. 32).

162. Wagenknecht, p. 233.

163. Amos, p. 146.

164. Collier and Horowitz, pp. 240–41.

165. *Saturday Evening Post*, December 9, 1919, p. 44. "The complete degeneration of his mental organs" was Dr. Richards's recollection of the article's contents.

166. E. Morris (*Colonel*), p. 549.

167. *New York Tribune*, January 7, 1919, p. 2.

168. C. R. Robinson, p. 362.

169. Corinne's other grandchildren included the future syndicated columnists Joseph and Stewart Alsop.

170. *New York Times*, October 4, 1996, p. B16.

171. C. R. Robinson, p. 1382; Gardner, p. 395; Brands (*T.R.*), p. 810. Owen Wister, TR's houseguest just before that sixtieth birthday, composed a poem marking the occasion. Wister noted, "I have his letter about those verses; short, in his own hand; and of great sadness" (Wister, p. 372).

172. Teague, p. 155.

173. C. R. Robinson (*Brother*), pp. 362–63.

174. *Saturday Evening Post*, December 9, 1922, p. 42.

175. *Saturday Evening Post*, December 9, 1922, p. 44.

176. *New York Sun*, January 7, 1919, p. 10.

177. Leary, pp. 260–61.

178. *New York Sun*, January 7, 1919, p. 10.

179. *Saturday Evening Post*, December 9, 1922, p. 46.

180. S. J. Morris (*Edith*), p. 431.

181. *Chicago Tribune*, December 25, 1918, p. 3.

182. S. J. Morris (*Edith*), p. 430.

183. O'Toole, p. 402.

184. T. H. Russell, p. 374.

185. *New York Tribune*, January 7, 1919, p. 2.

186. T. Roosevelt (*Cowles*), pp. 317–18.

187. Thompson, p. 287.

188. S. J. Morris (*Edith*), p. 431.
189. Dalton, p. 651.
190. *Saturday Evening Post*, December 9, 1922, p. 46.
191. Morison, p. 1419.
192. *New York Sun*, January 8, 1919, p. 5; J. B. Bishop, pp. 469–70.
193. Morison, p. 1420; J. B. Bishop, p. 470.
194. *Commercial and Financial Chronicle*, January 18, 1919, p. 232.
195. Morison, p. 1411.
196. *New York Sun*, January 7, 1919, pp. 2, 10.
197. *New York Sun*, January 7, 1919, p. 2; T. H. Russell, p. 367.
198. J. B. Bishop, p. 474.
199. Morison, p. 6436. Most likely the last words he ever physically wrote.
200. *New York Sun*, January 7, 1919, p. 2.
201. *Jamestown Journal*, January 6, 1919, p. 6.
202. Hagedorn (*Sagamore*), p. 392.
203. Hobbs, p. 204.
204. *New York Sun*, January 7, 1919, p. 2; S. J. Morris (*Edith*), p. 431.
205. O'Toole, p. 403; E. Morris (*Colonel*), p. 550; Edmund Morris Notes (p. 4), Theodore Roosevelt Collection Subject File: Health, Houghton Library, Harvard University.
206. *Brooklyn Daily Eagle*, January 6, 1919, p. 1; *Harrisburg Telegraph*, January 6, 1919, p. 1.
207. *Harrisburg Telegraph*, January 6, 1919, p. 1; S. J. Morris (*Edith*), p. 431. Newspaper reports incorrectly reported her name as "Thoms." A biographer describes her as Scottish born, though this may not be the case. Eerily, among the three pilots claiming credit for the combat "kill" of Quentin Roosevelt was a Lieutenant Karl Thom.
208. *New York World*, January 7, 1919, p. 2.
209. Renehan, p. 220.
210. Edmund Morris Notes (p. 5), Theodore Roosevelt Collection Subject File: Health, Houghton Library, Harvard University.
211. *New York Tribune*, January 7, 1919, p. 2.
212. *New York Sun*, January 7, 1919, p. 2; *Chicago Tribune*, January 7, 1916, p. 5; T. H. Russell, p. 367.
213. Gardner, p. 398.
214. Dalton, p. 512.
215. Roosevelt (*Day*), p. 128.
216. Amos, p. 154.
217. *Brooklyn Daily Eagle*, January 6, 1919, p. 1; *Washington Star*, January 6, 1919, p. 1; *Harrisburg Telegraph*, January 6, 1919, p. 1.
218. Amos, pp. 154–55.
219. *New York Sun*, January 7, 1919, p. 2.
220. Leary, p. 323.
221. *New York Times*, January 9, 1919, p. 4.
222. Brands (*T.R.*), p. 810.
223. S. J. Morris (*Edith*), p. 433; Renehan, p. 220.

224. *New York World*, January 7, 1919, p. 2; S. J. Morris (*Edith*), p. 433.
225. O'Toole, p. 403.
226. Noyes, p. 112.
227. Noyes, p. 112.
228. *New York Sun*, January 7, 1919, p. 2; *New York Times*, January 7, 1919, p. 2.
229. *New York World*, January 7, 1919, p. 2.
230. *New York Tribune*, January 7, 1919, p. 2.
231. S. J. Morris (*Edith*), p. 433.
232. Hagedorn (*Sagamore*), p. 424; Morris (*Colonel*), p. 551.
233. Hagedorn (*Sagamore*), p. 424.
234. *New York Times*, January 7, 1919, p. 2.
235. *Saturday Evening Post*, December 9, 1922, p. 46.
236. S. J. Morris (*Edith*), p. 433.
237. S. J. Morris (*Edith*), p. 433; Renehan, p. 224.
238. *New York World*, January 7, 1919, p. 2.
239. *New York Sun*, January 7, 1919, p. 2; *Washington Herald*, January 7, 1919, p. 2.
240. *New York Times*, January 7, 1919, p. 2. According to the Greek-born Manhattan porter George Syran (quoting Clara L. Lee, the wife of TR's chauffeur Charles H. Lee), Dr. Faller administered "a light stimulant" to TR before nurse Thom administered the morphine, leading one to believe that she administered it sometime after Faller departed, say, as TR prepared for bed (Edmund Morris Notes [p. 5], Theodore Roosevelt Collection Subject File: Health, Houghton Library, Harvard University).
241. TR to Kermit, June 7, 1912 ("Letter from Theodore Roosevelt to Kermit Roosevelt," Theodore Roosevelt Center, http://www.theodorerooseveltcenter.org/Research /Digital-Library/Record/ImageViewer.aspx?libID=o281562&imageNo=1); Dalton, p. 377. Theodore and Edith both suffered from erysipelas. Both experienced painful horse falls—TR in 1915, Edith in September 1911. Her tumble triggered a thirty-six-hour coma, followed by blinding headaches, a temporary deprivation of her sense of taste, and the permanent loss of her sense of smell (S. J. Morris [*Edith*], pp. 373–74; Gould, pp. 122–23).
242. Dalton, p. 651; Edmund Morris Notes (p. 5), Theodore Roosevelt Collection Subject File: Health, Houghton Library, Harvard University.
243. S. J. Morris (*Edith*), p. 433; E. Morris (*Colonel*), pp. 551, 724; Renehan, p. 224; Dalton, p. 513; Jeffers, p. 118.
244. *New York Sun*, January 7, 1919, p. 2.
245. Amos, p. 155.
246. Amos, p. 156. Edith checked on TR twice, at 12:30 a.m. ("lying on side, sleeping so comfortably") and 2:00 a.m. (condition unchanged) (S. J. Morris [*Edith*], p. 433; E. Morris [*Colonel*], p. 552; Edmund Morris Notes [p. 5], Theodore Roosevelt Collection Subject File: Health, Houghton Library, Harvard University).
247. *New York World*, January 7, 1919, p. 2. Amos informed George Syran that he found TR's "breathing different—a kind of roughling [*sic*]—forehead warm" (Edmund Morris Notes [p. 5], Theodore Roosevelt Collection Subject File: Health, Houghton Library, Harvard University).

248. Amos, p. 156.

249. Amos, p. 158.

250. *New York Sun*, January 7, 1919, p. 2.

251. C. R. Robinson (*Brother*), pp. 364–65.

252. *New York Tribune*, January 7, 1919, p. 2; *New York Times*, January 7, 1919, p. 2.

253. *Harrisburg Telegraph*, January 6, 1919, p. 1.

254. Amos, p. 158.

255. *Natural History*, December 1919, pp. 546, 758.

256. *Natural History*, December 1919, pp. 510; J. B. Bishop, facing p. 472; Lorant, p. 627; E. Morris (*Colonel*), p. 726.

257. *New York World*, January 7, 1919, p. 2; *Fort Scott (KS) Tribune*, January 6, 1919, p. 1.

258. Renehan, pp. 222, 265.

259. Scott, p. 430.

260. S. J. Morris (*Edith*), p. 435.

261. McCallum, pp. 278, 303.

262. *Philadelphia Evening Public Ledger*, January 7, 1919, p. 1.

263. Manners, pp. 310–11.

264. Krock, p. 110.

265. Pringle (*Roosevelt*), p. 602.

266. Ross, p. 150.

267. Manners, p. 310.

268. Berg, p. 522. The family responded with equivalent reserve (*New York Sun*, January 8, 1919, p. 5).

269. Lloyd George, p. 147.

270. Manners, p. 309.

271. White (*Autobiography*), p. 551.

272. White (*Autobiography*), p. 551.

273. W. Johnson, p. 195.

274. Garland, pp. 214–15.

275. *Review of Reviews*, July 1919, p. 79.

276. *New York Tribune*, January 7, 1919, p. 5.

277. *New York Times*, February 10, 1919, p. 6.

278. Morgan, p. 212.

279. *Chicago Tribune*, January 7, 1919, p. 5.

280. Taliaferro, p. 174.

281. *Boston Globe*, January 8, 1919, p. 4; *New York Herald*, January 8, 1916, p. 6.

282. C. R. Robinson (*Brother*), p. 365.

283. *New York Times*, January 7, 1919, p. 2; *New York Sun*, January 7, 1919, p. 2.

284. *New York Sun*, January 7, 1919, p. 2.

285. *New York Sun*, January 8, 1919, p. 5.

286. *New York Times*, January 8, 1919, p. 4. Though TR often attended Christ Church, he was actually Dutch Reformed. Edith was the Episcopalian. As a child, he attended the Madison Square Presbyterian Church. At age sixteen, he joined St. Nicholas Collegiate Reformed Protestant Dutch Church at Fifth Avenue and 48th Street, and this

remained his Manhattan church of choice. He married Alice Lee in a Unitarian service and Edith at St. George's, Hanover Square, a London Anglican parish. Alice Lee Roosevelt and Martha Bulloch Roosevelt's joint funeral was at Manhattan's Fifth Avenue Presbyterian Church (S. J. Morris [*Edith*], p. 74). As governor, he frequented another Dutch Reformed congregation, Albany's First Reformed Church. During his vice presidency and presidency, he first attended an Episcopal church before faithfully attending Washington's Grace Reformed Church, a German, rather than Dutch, Calvinist denomination. At Syracuse in 1915, he attended the city's First Reformed Church. In 1900, he declared that he "should be opposed to founding" a Dutch Reformed church at Oyster Bay, "as it would be an injury to the other churches already established." He did, however, financially assist in construction of the local Catholic parish, St. Dominic's (*Outlook*, November 24, 1900, p. 724).

287. Cheney, p. 126.
288. Cheney, p. 125.
289. *Outlook*, January 22, 1919, p. 133.
290. *New York Sun*, January 8, 1919, p. 5.
291. *New York Times*, January 8, 1919, p. 4; *New York World*, January 8, 1919, p. 2; *New York Sun*, January 8, 1919, pp. 1, 5.
292. Drinker and Mowbray, p. 461.
293. Manners, p. 312.
294. *New York Herald*, January 8, 1919, p. 6.
295. *New York Herald*, January 8, 1919, p. 6.
296. *New York Herald*, January 8, 1919, p. 6; *New York Tribune*, January 18, 1919, p. 5.
297. *New York Times*, January 9, 1919, p. 4.
298. *Pittsburgh Daily Post*, March 14, 1921, p. 2. Mysteriously, the author is unable to locate a citation for this famous quotation earlier than this date.

EPILOGUE: "DEATH WAS THE ONLY RELIEF"

1. A. Smith, pp. 271–72; Cordery (*Alice*), p. 323; Peyser and Dwyer, p. 120.
2. *Chicago Tribune*, August 7, 1942, p. 1. Pinchot's daughter, actress Rosamond Pinchot, committed suicide by carbon monoxide asphyxiation in January 1938.
3. Renehan, pp. 229–32; Peyser and Dwyer, p. 220. Fourteen Rough Rider enlisted men committed suicide; just twenty-four died from combat. A number of Rough Riders also committed suicide almost immediately after the war ("Rough Riders," Wikipedia, https://en.wikipedia.org/wiki/Rough_Riders; June 4, 2014, post to the Theodore Roosevelt Association Facebook page at https://www.facebook.com/permalink.php?story_fbid=10152080080066879&id=41852696878).
4. *New York Times*, August 18, 1891, p. 8; Cook (Vol. 1), pp. 63–88; Peyser and Dwyer, pp. 16, 23–24. Elliott's daughter Eleanor "confronted depression [and] rejected suicide" following her 1918 discovery of her husband's affair with Lucy Mercer, daughter of Rough Rider Major Carroll Mercer (Cook [Vol. 3], p. 3). For solace, while in Washington, Eleanor often visited the Rock Creek Cemetery grave of Henry Adams's wife "Clover," who ingested potassium cyanide upon discovering her own husband's involvement with

the wife of U.S. senator J. Donald Cameron (Cook [Vol. 1], pp. 245–48). Eleanor's aunt, Edith Hall "Pussie" Morgan, "frequently threatened suicide" (Persico, p. 134). Howard Cary, Eleanor's early and ardent suitor, Franklin's Harvard classmate, and an usher at their March 1905 wedding—while still attired in his evening clothes—shot himself through the right temple while visiting London in May 1906 (*Pittsburgh Press*, March 19, 1905, p. 5; *Baltimore Sun*, May 8, 1906, p. 1; Cook [Vol. 1], pp. 152–53). FDR's personal secretary and confidant, Marguerite "Missy" LeHand, became suicidal in mid-1927. During the 1941–1942 Christmas holidays she attempted suicide by swallowing chicken bones (Asbell, p. 402; Persico, p. 170; Goodwin [*Ordinary*], pp. 117, 307; K. Smith, pp. 76–78, 255, 311). Franklin's longtime close friend Livingston "Livy" Davis inexplicably shot himself in the head in January 1932 (*Brooklyn Daily Eagle*, January 12, 1932, p. 17; Persico, p. 196); his twenty-two-year-old second cousin, Robert Burnett "Bobby" Delano, jilted by his fiancée, shot himself through the mouth in northern Argentina in May 1936 (*Fort Hamilton [OH] News*, June 2, 1936, p. 1; *Chicago Tribune*, June 2, 1936, p. 3; *Brooklyn Daily Eagle*, June 2, 1936, p. 7). In November 1947, Lucy Mercer's older sister Violetta, threatened by divorce, shot herself in the head at her sister's South Carolina estate (Persico, pp. 354–55). Franklin and Eleanor's son-in-law, journalist John Boettiger, after overdosing on sleeping pills, jumped from the seventh-story window of his Manhattan apartment hotel in October 1950 (*Detroit News*, November 1, 1950, p. 1; Goodwin [*Ordinary*], p. 635). In April 1934, *Time* falsely reported that Anna's first husband, Curtis B. Dall, had attempted suicide in the White House. He sued and collected $20,000 (*New York Times*, May 6, 1937, p. 1; *New York Times*, May 5, 1937, p. 17; *Chicago Tribune*, October 2, 1941, p. 2).

5. *Pittston (PA) Gazette*, February 22, 1909, p. 1; *Asbury Park (NJ) Evening Press*, February 22, 1909, p. 5. Authors Sylvia Jukes Morris (p. 339), Carol Felsenthal (p. 152), and Peter Collier and David Horowitz (p. 254) accept the idea of drunken accidental death.

6. *Time*, April 25, 1938, p. 22; Lemanski, p. 176. The 1910s marked the highest U.S. rate of suicide by poisoning (i.e., drugs); the decade's rate of both male and female suicides fell barely short of the record set in the Great Depression–wracked 1930s (*Forensic Pathology Reviews* 3, p. 311). The war must have played and immense role in that. The year 1919 witnessed a wave of suicides by military veterans in Canada (and, presumably elsewhere): 40 percent of all Canadian suicides that year were of veterans; the figure rose to 80 percent for all male suicides age eighteen to thirty-nine (Jonathan Scotland, "Soldier Suicide after the Great War: A First Look," ActiveHistory.ca, March 24, 2014, http://activehistory.ca/2014/03/soldier-suicide-after-the-great-war-a-first -look).

7. Collier and Horowitz, p. 444; Lemanski, p. 176.

8. *Brooklyn Daily Eagle*, January 7, 1953, p. 13.

9. Felsenthal, pp. 203, 231–35; Peyser and Dwyer, pp. 257–59; Caroli, p. 429; Cordery (*Alice*), p. 447; Collier and Horowitz, p. 474; Teichmann, p. 198. Alice's biographer Howard Teichmann contends that Paulina "lost count." Stacy Cordery seems ambivalent regarding a suicide verdict.

10. Caroli, pp. 351–52. TR's mother, Martha Bulloch Roosevelt, suffered from postpartum depression (W. E. Wilson, p. 101). As mentioned earlier, Ted Jr. may have suffered

a nervous breakdown at age eleven (Pearlman, p. 68; Collier and Horowitz, p. 125; Jeffers, p. 62).

11. K. Roosevelt (*Quentin*), pp. 19–21. Quentin's uncle Elliott had also penned a short story concerning suicide (*Hudson Valley Regional Review*, March 1988, p. 26).

12. Millard, p. 267.

13. O. K. Davis, p. 434. William Roscoe Thayer contends that Roosevelt "secretly determined to shoot himself" in Brazil (Thayer, p. 393). O. K. Davis specifically contradicts his account, conveying the morphine-related account. Responding to the author's query, staff at Sagamore Hill reported, "Although we do have TR's medical kit, the glass vials in it are not marked in any way and they are all empty. There are two pill boxes. One contains Chlorate of Potash tablets, used for hoarseness and huskiness. The other contains packets of an unknown substance" (email to author, July 18, 2017).

14. Collins, p. 3.

15. S. J. Morris (*Edith*), p. 530.

16. Renehan, p. 429.

17. Pringle (*Taft*), p. 748.

18. Renehan, pp. 50, 251.

19. Wagenknecht, p. 194.

20. Before Franklin Roosevelt famously pronounced Alfred E. Smith "the Happy Warrior," Bradley Gilman penned the TR biography *Roosevelt: The Happy Warrior*.

21. O. K. Davis, p. 447.

22. Ickes, p. 176.

23. Amos, p. 65.

24. E. Morris (*Colonel*), p. 452.

25. *Outlook*, August 12, 1905, pp. 913–14.

26. E. Morris (*Colonel*), p. 451.

27. E. A. Robinson, p. 35. In the *Outlook*, TR wrote, "'Richard Cory' illustrates a very ancient but very profound philosophy of life with a curiously local touch which points its keen insight." He again specifically praised the poem in a July 1908 letter to playwright David Gray (Wagenknecht, p. 70fn).

28. Wagenknecht, p. 192.

29. T. Roosevelt (*Ranch*), p. 59. "It caught up with him between 1909 . . . and 1919," contends historian Lewis Gould (Chris Lehmann, "A Historian's Pivotal Take on Theodore Roosevelt," NPR, June 23, 2006, http://www.npr.org/templates/story/story.php?storyId=5504102).

30. Roosevelt and Lodge, p. 61; Wagenknecht, p. 192.

31. Einstein, pp. 39, 59–60. Einstein served in TR's consular service. Roosevelt later provided an introduction to his *A Prophecy of the War: 1913–1914*.

32. Wister, p. 68; Wagenknecht, p. 192.

33. Abbott, p. 285.

34. E. Morris (*Rise*), p. 831.

35. Howe, p. 140; Chessman, p. 45; E. Morris (*Rise*), p. 705. TR, however, endured a similar tongue-lashing the following evening "with a courtesy, deference, and self-control that were absolutely marvellous" (Howe, p. 143).

36. Roosevelt and Lodge, p. 349; Chessman, pp. 46–47; N. Miller (*Life*), p. 315.
37. Morison, p. 1555; Dalton, p. 504.
38. Garland, p. 203. Thought Garland, "For the first time . . . I had sensed a mood of resignation, of renunciation in his voice" (Garland, p. 214).
39. Lizzi, pp. 97–98.
40. Amos, p. 156.
41. *New York World*, January 7, 1919, p. 2.
42. "Morphine Overdose—Amount, Symptoms, Treatment," Overdose Info, https://overdoseinfo.com/morphine-overdose-amount-symptoms-signs-treatment.
43. E. Morris (*Colonel*), p. 725. The doctors' confusing diagnosis of TR's conditions continued even after death. The insurance policy death claim lists "Apoplexy—Thrombosis of Brain" as the cause of death. Edmund Morris Notes (p. 6), Theodore Roosevelt Collection Subject File: Health, Houghton Library, Harvard University.
44. E. Morris (*Colonel*), p. 725. Edmund Morris's personal chronology regarding TR's health records that an "overdose of morphine" or "too much of the drug" "can cause asphyxia or respiratory depression" (the later phrase is used twice) (Edmund Morris Notes [pp. 5, 7], Theodore Roosevelt Collection Subject File: Health, Houghton Library, Harvard University).

BIBLIOGRAPHY

BOOKS

Abbott, Lawrence F. *Impressions of Theodore Roosevelt*. Garden City, NY: Doubleday, Page & Company, 1919.

Alexander, Bevin. *How America Got It Right: The U.S. March to Military and Political Supremacy*. New York: Three Rivers Press, 2005.

American Civil Liberties Union. *The Story of Mooney and Billings*. New York: American Civil Liberties Union, 1928.

Amos, James E. *Theodore Roosevelt: Hero to His Valet*. New York: John Day, 1927.

Annin, Robert Edwards. *Woodrow Wilson: A Character Study*. New York: Dodd, Mead and Company, 1924.

Anthony, Carl Sferrazza. *Florence Harding: The First Lady, the Jazz Age and the Death of America's Most Scandalous President*. New York: Morrow, 1998.

Asbell, Bernard. *The F. D. R. Memoirs: A Speculation on History*. New York: Doubleday, 1973.

Auchincloss, Louis. *Theodore Roosevelt*. New York: Times Books, 2001.

Axelrod, Alan. *Patton: A Biography*. Basingstoke, UK: Palgrave Macmillan, 2009.

Axson, Stockton. *"Brother Woodrow": A Memoir of Woodrow Wilson*. Princeton, NJ: Princeton University Press, 1993.

Bailey, Frankie Y., and Alice P. Green. *Wicked Albany: Lawlessness and Liquor in the Prohibition Era*. Charleston, SC: History Press, 2009.

Baker, Ray Stannard, ed. *Woodrow Wilson: Life and Letters: Facing War, 1915–1917*. Garden City, NY: Doubleday, Doran & Company, Inc., 1937.

———. *Woodrow Wilson: Life and Letters: Governor, 1913–1915*. Garden City, NY: Doubleday, Doran & Company, Inc., 1931.

———. *Woodrow Wilson: Life and Letters: Princeton, 1890–1913*. Garden City, NY: Doubleday, Doran & Company, Inc., 1927.

Beasley, Maurine H., Holly C. Shulman, and Henry R. Beasley, eds. *The Eleanor Roosevelt Encyclopedia*. Westport, CT: Greenwood Press, 2001.

Beers, Paul B. *Pennsylvania Politics Today and Yesterday: The Tolerable Accommodation*. University Park: Pennsylvania State University Press, 1980.

Bell, H. C. F. *Woodrow Wilson and the People*. Garden City, NY: Doubleday, Doran & Company, Inc., 1945.

Berg, A. Scott. *Wilson*. New York: G. P. Putnam's Sons, 2014.

Bernstorff, Count. *My Three Years in America*. New York: Charles Scribner's Sons, 1920.

Bishop, Chip. *Quentin and Flora: A Roosevelt and a Vanderbilt in Love during the Great War*. Charleston, SC: CreateSpace, 2014.

Bishop, Joseph Bucklin. *Theodore Roosevelt and His Time: Shown in His Own Letters*. Vol. 2. New York: Charles Scribner's Sons, 1920.

Blackton, J. Stuart. *The Battle Cry of Peace: A Call to Arms against War*. Brooklyn, NY: M. P. [Motion Picture] Publishing Company, 1915.

Blum, Howard. *Dark Invasion: 1915: Germany's Secret War and the Hunt for the First Terrorist Cell in America*. New York: Harper, 2014.

Blum, John M. *Joe Tumulty and the Wilson Era*. Boston: Houghton Mifflin Co., 1951.

Blum, John Morton. *Woodrow Wilson and the Politics of Morality*. Boston: Little, Brown & Co., 1956.

Brady, Tim. *His Father's Son: The Life of Gen. Theodore Roosevelt, Jr.* New York: Berkley, 2017.

Braeman, John. *Albert J. Beveridge: American Nationalist*. Chicago: University of Chicago Press, 1971.

Bragdon, Henry Wilkinson. *Woodrow Wilson: The Academic Years*. Cambridge, MA: Belknap Press of Harvard University Press, 1967.

Brands, H. W., ed. *The Selected Letters of Theodore Roosevelt*. Lanham, MD: Rowman & Littlefield, 2007.

———. *T.R.: The Last Romantic*. New York: Basic Books, 1997.

———. *Traitor to His Class: The Privileged Life and Radical Presidency of Franklin Delano Roosevelt*. New York: Doubleday, 2008.

Broderick, Francis L. *Progressivism at Risk: Electing a President in 1912*. New York: Greenwood Press, 1989.

Brown, Roscoe C. E. *History of the State of New York Political and Governmental*. Vol. 4: *1896–1920*. Syracuse, NY: Syracuse Press, Inc., 1922.

Brownlow, Kevin, and John Kobal. *Hollywood: The Pioneers*. New York: Knopf, 1979.

Bruns, Roger A. *Preacher Billy Sunday and Big-Time American Evangelism*. Urbana: University of Illinois Press, 2002.

Burns, Eric. *The Golden Lad: The Haunting Story of Quentin and Theodore Roosevelt*. New York: Pegasus, 2016.

Burton, David H. *Cecil Spring-Rice: A Diplomat's Life*. Rutherford, NJ: Fairleigh Dickinson University Press, 1990.

Busch, Noel F. *T.R.: The Story of Theodore Roosevelt and His Influence on Our Times*. New York: Reynal & Company, 1963.

Butler, Nicholas Murray. *Across the Busy Years*. New York: Charles Scribner's Sons, 1940.

Carlisle, Rodney P., and Joe H. Kirchberger. *World War I*. New York: Facts on File, Inc., 2007.

Caroli, Betty Boyd. *The Roosevelt Women*. New York: Basic Books, 1998.

Carroll, Andrew. *My Fellow Soldiers: General John Pershing and the Americans Who Helped Win the Great War*. New York: Penguin Press, 2017.

Chace, James. *1912: Wilson, Roosevelt, Taft and Debs—the Election That Changed the Country*. New York: Simon & Schuster, 2004.

Chamberlain, John. *Farewell to Reform: The Rise, Life and Decay of the Progressive Mind in America.* Chicago: Quadrangle Books, 1965.

Cheney, Albert Loren. *Personal Memoirs of the Home Life of the Late Theodore Roosevelt as Soldier, Governor, Vice-President, President, in Relation to Oyster Bay.* Washington, DC: Cheney Publishing Company, 1919.

Cherny, Robert W. *A Righteous Cause: The Life of William Jennings Bryan.* Norman: University of Oklahoma Press, 1994.

Chessman, G. Wallace. *Governor Theodore Roosevelt: The Albany Apprenticeship, 1898–1900.* Cambridge, MA: Harvard University Press, 1965.

Clifford, John Garry. *The Citizen Soldiers: The Plattsburg Training Camp Movement, 1913–1920.* Lexington: University Press of Kentucky, 2015.

Cohen, Julius Henry. *They Builded Better Than They Knew.* New York: Julian Messner, Inc., 1946.

Colby, Frank Moore, ed. *The New International Year Book: A Compendium of the World's Progress for the Year 1916.* New York: Dodd, Mead and Company, 1917.

Collier, Peter, and David Horowitz. *The Roosevelts: An American Saga.* New York: Simon & Schuster, 1994.

Collins, Michael L. *That Damned Cowboy: Theodore Roosevelt and the American West, 1883–1898.* New York: Peter Lang, 1991.

Cook, Blanche Wiesen. *Eleanor Roosevelt.* Vol. 1: *1884–1933.* New York: Penguin Books, 1992.

———. *Eleanor Roosevelt.* Vol. 2: *The Defining Years, 1933–1938.* New York: Viking, 1999.

———. *Eleanor Roosevelt.* Vol. 3: *The War Years and After, 1939–1962.* New York: Penguin Publishing Group, 2016.

Cooper, John Milton. *The Warrior and the Priest.* Cambridge, MA: Harvard University Press, 1983.

———. *Woodrow Wilson: A Biography.* New York: Alfred A. Knopf, 2009.

Cordery, Stacy A. *Alice: Alice Roosevelt Longworth, from White House Princess to Washington Power Broker.* New York: Penguin Books, 2007.

———. *Theodore Roosevelt: In the Vanguard of the Modern.* Belmont, CA: Thomson/Wadsworth, 2003.

Craig, Douglas B. *Progressives at War: William G. McAdoo and Newton D. Baker, 1863–1941.* Baltimore: Johns Hopkins University Press, 2013.

Cramer, C. H. *Newton D. Baker: A Biography.* Cleveland, OH: World Publishing Company, 1961.

Cranston, Alan. *The Killing of the Peace.* New York: Viking Press, 1945.

Creel, George. *The War, the World and Wilson.* New York: Harper & Brothers, 1920.

Dall, Curtis Bean. *FDR: My Exploited Father-in-Law.* Washington, DC: Liberty Lobby, 1967.

Dalton, Kathleen. *Theodore Roosevelt: A Strenuous Life.* New York: Vintage, 2004.

Daniels, Josephus. *The Cabinet Diaries of Josephus Daniels, 1913–1921.* Lincoln: University of Nebraska Press, 1963.

———. *Editor in Politics.* Chapel Hill: University of North Carolina Press, 1941.

———. *The Life of Woodrow Wilson*. Chicago: John C. Winston Co., 1924.

———. *The Wilson Era: Years of Peace—1910–1917*. Chapel Hill: University of North Carolina Press, 1944.

———. *The Wilson Era: Years of Peace—1913–1917*. Chapel Hill: University of North Carolina Press, 1944.

———. *The Wilson Era: Years of War and After—1917–1923*. Chapel Hill: University of North Carolina Press, 1946.

Davenport, Walter. *Power and Glory: The Life of Boies Penrose*. New York: G. P. Putnam's Sons, 1931.

Davis, Kenneth S. *FDR: The Beckoning of Destiny, 1882–1928*. New York: History Book Club, 2004.

Davis, Oscar King. *Released for Publication: Some Inside Political History of Theodore Roosevelt and His Times, 1898–1918*. Boston: Houghton Mifflin, 1925.

Democratic National Committee. *The Democratic Text Book, 1916*. New York: Democratic National Committee, 1916.

Devlin, Patrick. *Too Proud to Fight: Woodrow Wilson's Neutrality*. New York: Oxford University Press, 1975.

Dewey, Donald. *Buccaneer: James Stuart Blackton and the Birth of American Movies*. Lanham, MD: Rowman & Littlefield, 2016.

Doenecke, Justus D. *Nothing Less Than War: A New History of America's Entry into World War I*. Lexington: University of Kentucky Press, 2011.

Donn, Linda. *The Roosevelt Cousins: Growing Up Together*. New York: Alfred A. Knopf, 2001.

Dorsey, Leroy G. *We Are All Americans, Pure and Simple: Theodore Roosevelt and the Myth of Americanism*. Tuscaloosa: University of Alabama Press, 2007.

Dos Passos, John. *Mr. Wilson's War*. Garden City, NY: Doubleday, 1962.

Downes, Randolph C. *The Rise of Warren Gamaliel Harding, 1865–1920*. Columbus: Ohio State University Press, 1970.

Drinker, Frederick E., and Jay Henry Mowbray. *Theodore Roosevelt: His Life and Work*. Philadelphia: National Publishing Company, 1919.

Du Bois, W. E. B. *The Autobiography of W. E. B. Du Bois: A Soliloquy on Viewing My Life from the Last Decade of Its First Century*. New York: Oxford University Press, 2007.

Dubofsky, Melvyn. *The State and Labor in Modern America*. Chapel Hill: University of North Carolina Press, 1994.

Duffy, Herbert Smith. *William Howard Taft*. New York: Minton, Balch, 1930.

Ealy, Lawrence O. *Yanqui Politics and the Isthmian Canal*. University Park: Pennsylvania State University Press, 1971.

Eaton, Herbert. *Presidential Timber: A History of Presidential Nominating Conventions, 1868–1960*. New York: Free Press of Glencoe, 1964.

Editors of the *New Republic* and Dorothy Whitney Straight. *The New Republic Book: Selections from the First-Hundred Issues*. New York: Republic Publishing Company, Inc., 1916.

Einstein, Lewis D. *Theodore Roosevelt, His Mind in Action*. Boston: Houghton, Mifflin Company, 1930.

Eisenhower, John S. D. *Teddy Roosevelt and Leonard Wood: Partners in Command.* Columbia: University of Missouri Press, 2014.

Elletson, E. H. *Roosevelt and Wilson: A Comparative Study.* London: John Murray, 1965.

Ellis, Walter Robb. *Echoes of Distant Thunder: Life in the United States, 1914–1918.* New York: Coward, McCann & Geoghegan, 1975.

Executive Committee of the Progressive National Committee. *The Progressive Party: Its Record from January to July 1916.* New York: Mail and Express Job Print, 1916.

Farley, John W. *Statistics and Politics.* 2nd ed. Memphis: Saxland Publishing Company, 1920.

Fausold, Martin L. *Gifford Pinchot: Bull Moose Progressive.* Syracuse, NY: Syracuse University Press, 1961.

———. *James W. Wadsworth, Jr.: The Gentleman from New York.* Syracuse, NY: Syracuse University Press, 1975.

Felsenthal, Carol. *Alice Roosevelt Longworth.* New York: G. P. Putnam's Sons, 1988 (reissued by St. Martin's Press as *Princess Alice: The Life and Times of Alice Roosevelt Longworth*).

Finnegan, John Patrick. *Against the Specter of a Dragon: The Campaign for American Military Preparedness, 1914–1917.* Westport, CT: Greenwood Press, 1974.

Fleming, Thomas. *The Illusion of Victory: Americans in World War I.* New York: Basic Books, 2003.

Frankenberg, Theodore Thomas. *Billy Sunday, His Tabernacles and Sawdust Trails: A Biographical Sketch of the Famous Baseball Evangelist.* Columbus, OH: F. J. Heer Printing Co., 1917.

Frost, Richard H. *The Mooney Case.* Stanford, CA: Stanford University Press, 1974.

Fuess, Claude M. *Calvin Coolidge: The Man from Vermont.* Boston: Little, Brown and Company, 1940.

Gable, John Allen. *The Bull Moose Years: Theodore Roosevelt and the Progressive Party.* Port Washington, NY: Kennikat Press, 1978.

Gardner, Joseph L. *Departing Glory: Theodore Roosevelt as Ex-president.* New York: Charles Scribner's Sons, 1973.

Garland, Hamlin. *My Friendly Contemporaries: A Literary Log.* New York: Macmillan, 1932.

Garraty, John A. *Henry Cabot Lodge: A Biography.* New York: Alfred A. Knopf, 1968.

———. *Right-Hand Man: The Life of George W. Perkins.* New York: Harper & Brothers, 1960.

Gentry, Curt. *Frame-up: The Incredible Case of Tom Mooney and Warren Billings.* New York: W. W. Norton & Co., 1967.

George, Alexander L., and Juliette L. George. *Woodrow Wilson and Colonel House: A Personality Study.* New York: John Day Co., 1956.

Gerard, James W. *Face to Face with Kaiserism.* New York: George H. Doran Company, 1917.

Gertz, Elmer. *Odyssey of a Barbarian: The Biography of George Sylvester Viereck.* Buffalo, NY: Prometheus Books, 1978.

Gilbert, Clinton W. *The Mirrors of Washington.* New York: G. P. Putnam's Sons, 1921.

Gilman, Bradley. *Roosevelt: The Happy Warrior*. Boston: Little, Brown and Company, 1921.

Ginger, Ray. *The Bending Cross: Biography of Eugene Victor Debs*. New Brunswick, NJ: Rutgers University Press, 1949.

Glad, Betty. *Charles Evans Hughes and the Illusions of Innocence: A Study in American Diplomacy*. Urbana: University of Illinois Press, 1966.

Goodman, Fred. *The Secret City: Woodlawn Cemetery and the Buried History of New York*. New York: Broadway Books, 2004.

Goodwin, Doris Kearns. *The Bully Pulpit: Theodore Roosevelt, William Howard Taft, and the Golden Age of Journalism*. New York: Simon & Schuster, 2013.

——. *No Ordinary Time: Franklin and Eleanor Roosevelt: The Home Front in World War II*. New York: Simon & Schuster, 1994.

Gould, Lewis L. *Edith Kermit Roosevelt: Creating the Modern First Lady*. Lawrence: University of Kansas Press, 2013.

Grant, Madison. *The Passing of the Great Race: Or, The Racial Basis of European History*. New York: Charles Scribner's Sons, 1916.

Gratten, C. Hartley. *Why We Fought*. New York: Vanguard Press, 1929.

Greene, Francis Vinton. *The Present Military Situation in the United States*. New York: Charles Scribner's Sons, 1915.

Greene, Julie. *Pure and Simple Politics: The American Federation of Labor and Political Activism, 1881–1917*. Cambridge, MA: Cambridge University Press, 1998.

Griffith, William, ed. *Roosevelt, His Life, Meaning and Messages: Newer Roosevelt Messages*. New York: Current Literature Publishing Company, 1919.

Gunther, Gilbert. *Learned Hand: The Man and the Judge*. New York: Knopf, 1994.

Hagedorn, Hermann. *The Boy's Life of Theodore Roosevelt*. New York: Harper & Brothers Publishers, 1918.

——. *The Bugle That Woke America: The Saga of Theodore Roosevelt's Last Battle for His Country*. New York: John Day Co., 1940.

——. *Leonard Wood: A Biography*. New York: Harper & Bros., 1931.

——. *The Roosevelt Family of Sagamore Hill*. New York: Macmillan Company, 1954.

Hale, William Bayard. *The Story of a Style*. New York: B. W. Huebsch, Inc., 1920.

——. *Woodrow Wilson: The Story of His Life*. Garden City, NY: Doubleday, Page, 1912.

Harbaugh, William H. *The Life and Times of Theodore Roosevelt*. New York: Oxford University Press, 1975.

Harris, Ray Baker. *Warren G. Harding: An Account of His Nomination for the Presidency by the Republican Convention of 1920*. Washington: Privately printed, 1957.

Hart, Albert Bushnell, and Herbert Ronald Ferleger, eds. *Theodore Roosevelt Cyclopedia*. New York: Roosevelt Memorial Association, 1941.

Hart, George L. *Official Report of the Proceedings of the Sixteenth Republican National Convention, Held in Chicago, Illinois, June 7, 8, 9 and 10, 1916: Resulting in the Nomination of Charles Evans Hughes, of New York, for President and the Nomination of Charles Warren Fairbanks, of Indiana, for Vice-President*. New York: Tenny Press, 1916.

Hart, James, ed. *The Man Who Invented Hollywood: The Autobiography of D. W. Griffith*. Louisville, KY: Touchstone Publishing Company, 1972.

Hart, Peter. *The Somme: The Darkest Hour of the Western Front.* New York: Pegasus Books, 2008.

Hart, W. O. *The Democratic Conventions of 1908, 1912, 1916: Republican Conventions of 1912, 1916, and Progressive Convention of 1912, with Other Political and Historical Observations.* New Orleans: Privately printed for the author, 1916.

Hays, Will H. *The Memoirs of Will H. Hays.* Garden City, NY: Doubleday, 1955.

Henderson, Robert M. *D. W. Griffith: His Life and Work.* New York: Oxford University Press, 1972.

Herman, Gerald. *The Pivotal Conflict: A Comprehensive Chronology of the First World War, 1914–1919.* New York: Greenwood Press, 1992.

Hernon, Joseph Martin. *Profiles in Character: Hubris and Heroism in the U.S. Senate, 1789–1990.* Armonk, NY: M. E. Sharpe, 1997.

Hichborn, Franklin. *"The System": As Uncovered by the San Francisco Graft Prosecution.* San Francisco: Press of the James H. Barry Company, 1915.

Hirsch, H. N. *The Enigma of Felix Frankfurter.* New York: Basic Books, 1981.

Hobbs, William H. *Leonard Wood: Soldier, Administrator, and Citizen.* New York: G. P. Putnam's Sons, 1920.

Hodgson, Godfrey. *Woodrow Wilson's Right Hand: The Life of Colonel Edward M. House.* New Haven, CT: Yale University Press, 2006.

Hollander, Neil. *Elusive Dove: The Search for Peace during World War I.* Jefferson, NC: McFarland, 2013.

Holme, John G. *The Life of Leonard Wood.* Garden City, NY: Doubleday Page & Company, 1920.

Hoover, Herbert. *The Memoirs of Herbert Hoover: Years of Adventure, 1874–1920.* New York: Macmillan, 1951.

Houston, David F. *Eight Years with Wilson's Cabinet: 1930 to 1920.* Vol. 1. Garden City, NY: Doubleday, Page & Company, 1926.

Howe, M. A. De Wolfe Howe. *John Jay Chapman and His Letters.* Boston: Houghton Mifflin Company, 1937.

Howland, Harold. *Theodore Roosevelt and His Times: A Chronicle of the Progressive Movement.* New Haven, CT: Yale University Press, 1921.

Hughes, Charles Evans. *The Autobiographical Notes of Charles Evans Hughes.* Cambridge, MA: Harvard University Press, 1973.

Hull, Isabel V. *A Scrap of Paper: Breaking and Making International Law during the Great War.* Ithaca, NY: Cornell University Press, 2014.

Hurst, James W. *Pancho Villa and Black Jack Pershing: The Punitive Expedition in Mexico.* Westport, CT: Praeger, 2008.

Ickes, Harold. *The Autobiography of a Curmudgeon.* New York: Reynal & Hitchcock, 1943.

Iglehart, Ferdinand Cowle. *Theodore Roosevelt: The Man as I Knew Him.* New York: Christian Herald, 1919.

Isenberg, Michael T. *War on Film: The American Cinema and World War I, 1914–1941.* Rutherford, NJ: Farleigh Dickinson University Press, 1981.

Jeffers, Harry Paul. *Theodore Roosevelt Jr.: The Life of a War Hero.* Novato, CA: Presidio, 2002.

Jessup, Philip C. *Elihu Root*. New York: Dodd, Mead & Company, 1938.

Johnson, Alvin. *Pioneer's Progress: An Autobiography*. New York: Viking Press, 1952.

Johnson, Neil M. *George Sylvester Viereck: German-American Propagandist*. Urbana: University of Illinois Press, 1972.

Johnson, Walter, ed. *Selected Letters of William Allen White, 1899–1943*. New York: Henry Holt and Company, 1947.

Jones, John Price. *The German Secret Service in America: 1914–1918*. Boston: Small, Maynard and Company, 1919.

Karsten, Peter, ed. *Encyclopedia of War and American Society*. Vol. 1. Thousand Oaks, CA: Sage Publications, 2006.

Katz, Friedrich. *The Life and Times of Pancho Villa*. Stanford, CA: Stanford University Press, 1998.

Kazin, Michael. *A Godly Hero: The Life of William Jennings Bryan*. New York: Alfred A. Knopf, 2006.

———. *War against War: The Fight for American Peace, 1914–1918*. New York: Simon & Schuster, 2017.

Keane, Michael. *George S. Patton: Blood, Guts, and Prayer*. Washington, DC: Regnery Publishing, 2014.

Kennedy, David M. *Over Here: The First World War and American Society*. New York: Oxford University Press, 1980.

Knock, Thomas J. *To End All Wars: Woodrow Wilson and the Quest for a New World Order*. New York: Oxford University Press, 1992.

Kohlsaat, H. H. *From McKinley to Harding: Personal Recollections of Our Presidents*. New York: Charles Scribner's Sons, 1923.

Kolko, Gabriel. *The Triumph of Conservatism: A Reinterpretation of American History, 1900–1916*. New York: Free Press, 1963.

Kremer, J. Bruce, comp. *Official Report of the Proceedings of the Democratic National Convention, Held in Saint Louis, Missouri, June 14, 15 and 16th, 1916: Resulting in the Nomination of Hon. Woodrow Wilson (of New Jersey) for President and Hon. Thomas Riley Marshall (of Indiana) for Vice-President*. Chicago: [No publisher], 1916.

Krock, Arthur. *Memoirs: Sixty Years on the Firing Line*. New York: Funk & Wagnalls, 1968.

Lane, Franklin K. *The Letters of Franklin K. Lane, Personal and Political*. Boston: Houghton Mifflin Company, 1922.

Lane, Jack C. *Armed Progressive: General Leonard Wood*. San Rafael, CA: Presidio Press, 1978.

Langdale, Alan, ed. *Hugo Munsterberg on Film: The Photoplay: A Psychological Study and Other Writings*. New York: Routledge, 2012.

Langland, James, M. A., ed. *The Chicago Daily News Almanac and Year Book for 1917*. Chicago: Chicago Daily News Company, 1916.

Lansing, Robert. *War Memories of Robert Lansing, Secretary of State*. Indianapolis: Bobbs-Merrill Company, 1935.

Largey, Michael D. *Vodou Nation: Haitian Art Music and Cultural Nationalism*. Chicago: University of Chicago Press, 2006.

Lash, Joseph P. *Eleanor and Franklin: The Story of Their Relationship Based on Eleanor Roosevelt's Private Papers*. New York: W. W. Norton, 1971.

———, ed. *From the Diaries of Felix Frankfurter: With a Biographical Essay and Notes by Joseph P. Lash*. New York: Norton, 1975.

Leary, John J., Jr. *Talks with T.R.* Boston: Houghton Mifflin Company, 1919.

Lelyveld, Joseph. *His Final Battle: The Last Months of Franklin Roosevelt*. New York: Alfred A. Knopf, 2016.

Lemanski, William E. *Lost in the Shadow of Fame: The Neglected Story of Kermit Roosevelt, a Gallant and Tragic American*. Camp Hill, PA: Sunbury Press, Inc., 2012.

Levin, Phyllis Lee. *Edith and Woodrow: The Wilson White House*. New York: Scribner, 2001.

Lewinson, Edwin R. *John Purroy Mitchel: The Boy Mayor of New York*. New York: Astra Books, 1965.

Lewis, Alfred Henry. *A Compilation of the Messages and Speeches of Theodore Roosevelt, 1901–1905*. Vol. 1. New York: Bureau of Literature and Art, 1906.

Link, Arthur S., ed. *The Papers of Woodrow Wilson*. Vol. 5. Princeton, NJ: Princeton University Press, 1968.

———, ed. *The Papers of Woodrow Wilson*. Vol. 11. Princeton, NJ: Princeton University Press, 1971.

———, ed. *The Papers of Woodrow Wilson*. Vol. 12. Princeton, NJ: Princeton University Press, 1972.

———, ed. *The Papers of Woodrow Wilson*. Vol. 18. Princeton, NJ: Princeton University Press, 1975.

———, ed. *The Papers of Woodrow Wilson*. Vol. 31. Princeton, NJ: Princeton University Press, 1979.

———, ed. *The Papers of Woodrow Wilson*. Vol. 33. Princeton, NJ: Princeton University Press, 1980.

———, ed. *The Papers of Woodrow Wilson*. Vol. 37. Princeton, NJ: Princeton University Press, 1981.

———, ed. *The Papers of Woodrow Wilson*. Vol. 42. Princeton, NJ: Princeton University Press, 1983.

———, ed. *The Papers of Woodrow Wilson*. Vol. 45. Princeton, NJ: Princeton University Press, 1984.

———, ed. *The Papers of Woodrow Wilson*. Vol. 50. Princeton, NJ: Princeton University Press, 1985.

———, ed. *Wilson: Campaigns for Progressivism and Peace, 1916–1917*. Princeton, NJ: Princeton University Press, 1965.

———. *Woodrow Wilson and the Progressive Era, 1910–1917*. New York: Harper Torchbooks, 1963.

Livermore, Seward W. *Politics Is Adjourned: Woodrow Wilson and the War Congress, 1916–1918*. Seattle: University of Washington Press, 1968.

Lizzi, Dominick C. *Governor Martin H. Glynn: Forgotten Hero*. Valatie, NY: Valatie Press, 1994.

Lloyd George, David. *Memoirs of the Peace Conference*. New Haven, CT: Yale University Press, 1939.

Logan, Rayford W. *The Betrayal of the Negro: From Rutherford B. Hayes to Woodrow Wilson*. New York: Collier Books, 1965.

Loizillon, Gabriel J. *The Bunau-Varilla Brothers and the Panama Canal*. Morrisville, NC: Lulu Press, 2016.

Longworth, Alice Roosevelt. *Crowded Hours: Reminiscences of Alice Roosevelt Longworth*. New York: Charles Scribner's Sons, 1933.

Lorant, Stefan. *The Glorious Burden: The History of the Presidency and Presidential Elections from George Washington to James Earl Carter, Jr.* Lenox, MA: Authors Edition, 1976.

Lovell, S. D. *The Presidential Election of 1916*. Carbondale: Southern Illinois University Press, 1980.

Lurie, Jonathan. *William Howard Taft: The Travails of a Progressive Conservative*. New York: Cambridge University Press, 2012.

MacMillan, Neil. *Wicked Syracuse: A History of Sin in Salt City*. Charleston, SC: History Press, 2013.

Manners, William. *TR and Will: A Friendship That Split the Republican Party*. New York: Harcourt, Brace & World, Inc., 1969.

Martin, Ralph G. *Ballots and Bandwagons*. Chicago: Rand, McNally & Company, 1964.

Mayer, George H. *The Republican Party, 1854–1964*. New York: Oxford University Press, 1964.

McAdoo, William Gibbs. *Crowded Years: The Reminiscences of William G. McAdoo*. Boston: Houghton-Mifflin Co., 1931.

McCaleb, Walter Flavius. *Theodore Roosevelt*. New York: A. & C. Boni, 1931.

McCallum, Jack. *Leonard Wood: Rough Rider, Surgeon, Architect of American Imperialism*. New York: New York University Press, 2006.

McCombs, William F. *Making Woodrow Wilson President*. New York: Fairview Publishing Company, 1921.

McCullough, David. *Mornings on Horseback: The Story of an Extraordinary Family, a Vanished Way of Life and the Unique Child Who Became Theodore Roosevelt*. New York: Simon & Schuster, 1981.

McGeary, M. Nelson. *Gifford Pinchot, Forester-Politician*. Princeton, NJ: Princeton University Press, 1960.

McInerney, Thomas J., and Fred L. Israel, eds. *Presidential Documents: Words That Shaped a Nation from Washington to Obama*. New York: Routledge, 2013.

McKenna, Marian C. *Borah*. Ann Arbor: University of Michigan Press, 1961.

Millard, Candice. *The River of Doubt: Theodore Roosevelt's Darkest Journey*. New York: Random House, 2005.

Miller, Nathan. *F.D.R.: An Intimate History*. Garden City, NY: Doubleday, 1983.

———. *The Roosevelt Chronicles: The Story of a Great American Family*. Garden City, NY: Doubleday, 1979.

———. *Theodore Roosevelt: A Life*. New York: William Morrow and Company, 1992.

Miller, William J. *Henry Cabot Lodge: A Biography*. New York: Heineman, 1967.

Millis, Walter. *Road to War: America, 1914–1917*. Boston: Houghton Mifflin Co., 1935.

Millman, Chad. *The Detonators: The Secret Plot to Destroy America and an Epic Hunt for Justice*. Boston: Little, Brown and Company, 2006.

Mitgang, Herbert. *The Man Who Rode the Tiger: The Life and Times of Judge Samuel Seabury*. Philadelphia: J. P. Lippincott, 1973.

Mock, James R. *Censorship, 1917*. Princeton, NJ: Princeton University Press, 1941.

Morais, Herbert M., and William Cahn. *Gene Debs: The Story of a Fighting American*. New York: International Publishers, 1948.

Morehead, Alan. *The Russian Revolution*. New York: Harper & Brothers, 1958.

Morgan, Ted. *FDR: A Biography*. New York: Simon & Schuster, 1985.

Morison, Elting E., ed. *The Letters of Theodore Roosevelt*. 8 vols. Cambridge, MA: Harvard University Press, 1954.

Morris, Edmund. *Colonel Roosevelt*. New York: Random House, 2011.

———. *The Rise of Theodore Roosevelt*. New York: Random House, 1979.

———. *Theodore Rex*. New York: Random House, 2001.

Morris, Sylvia Jukes. *Edith Kermit Roosevelt: Portrait of a First Lady*. New York: Modern Library, 2001.

Morrissey, Alice M. *The American Defense of Neutral Rights, 1914–1917*. Cambridge, MA: Harvard University Press, 1939.

Mowry, George E. *Theodore E. Roosevelt and the Progressive Movement*. Madison: University of Wisconsin Press, 1946.

Moynahan, Brian. *Rasputin: The Saint Who Sinned*. New York: Random House, 1997.

Münsterberg, Hugo. *The Americans*. New York: D. Appleton and Company, 1914.

Münsterberg, Margaret. *Hugo Münsterberg: His Life and Work*. New York: D. Appleton and Company, 1922.

Nasaw, David. *The Chief: The Life of William Randolph Hearst*. Boston: Houghton Mifflin, 2000.

Nevins, Allen. *Henry White: Thirty Years of American Diplomacy*. New York: Harper & Brothers, 1930.

New England Branch of the National German-American Alliance. *The German Element in the United States*. Boston: New England Branch of the National German-American Alliance, 1912.

New York Evening Mail. *The Gravest 366 Days: Editorials Reprinted from the Evening Mail of New York City*. New York: New York Evening Mail, 1916.

Nordholt, Jan Willem Schulte. *Woodrow Wilson: A Life for World Peace*. Berkeley: University of California Press, 1991.

Noyes, Alfred. *Two Worlds for Memory*. Philadelphia: J. P. Lippincott, 1953.

O'Leary, Jeremiah A. *My Political Trials and Experiences*. New York: Jefferson Publishing Co., Inc., 1919.

Oliver, Lawrence J. *Brander Matthews, Theodore Roosevelt and the Politics of American Literature, 1880–1920*. Knoxville: University of Tennessee Press, 1992.

O'Toole, Patricia. *When Trumpets Call: Theodore Roosevelt after the White House*. New York: Simon & Schuster, 2005.

Page, Walter Hines. *The Life and Letters of Walter H. Page*. Vol. 1. Garden City, NY: Doubleday, Page & Company, 1923.

Palmer, Frederick. *Newton D. Baker: America at War.* Vol. 1. New York: Dodd, Mead & Company, 1931.

Patton, Robert H. *The Pattons: A Personal History of an American Family.* New York: Crown Publishers, Inc., 1994.

Pearlman, Michael. *To Make Democracy Safe for America: Patricians and Preparedness in the Progressive Era.* Urbana: University of Illinois Press, 1984.

Perkins, Dexter. *Charles Evans Hughes and American Democratic Statesmanship.* Boston: Little, Brown & Co., 1956.

Pershing, John J. *My Experiences in the World War.* New York: Frederick A. Stokes Company, 1931.

Persico, Joseph E. *Franklin and Lucy: President Roosevelt, Mrs. Rutherfurd, and the Other Remarkable Women in His Life.* New York: Random House, 2008.

Peterson, H. C. *Propaganda for War: The Campaign against American Neutrality, 1914–1917.* Norman: University of Oklahoma Press, 1939.

Peyser, Marc, and Timothy Dwyer. *Hissing Cousins: The Untold Story of Eleanor Roosevelt and Alice Roosevelt Longworth.* New York: Knopf, Doubleday, 2015.

Pietrusza, David. *Rothstein: The Life, Times, and Murder of the Criminal Genius Who Fixed the 1919 World Series.* New York: Carroll & Graf, 2003.

Pinchot, Amos R. E. *History of the Progressive Party, 1912–1916.* Edited by Helene Maxwell Hooker. New York: New York University Press, 1958.

Pines, Burton Yale. *America's Greatest Blunder: The Fateful Decision to Enter World War One.* New York: RSD Press, 2013.

Pizzitola, Louis. *Hearst over Hollywood: Power, Passion, and Propaganda in the Movies.* New York: Columbia University Press, 2002.

Pringle, Henry F. *The Life and Times of William Howard Taft.* Vol. 2. New York: Farrar & Rinehart, Inc., 1939.

———. *Theodore Roosevelt: A Biography.* New York: Harcourt Brace & Co., 1956.

Procter, Ben. *William Randolph Hearst: The Later Years, 1911–1951.* New York: Oxford University Press, 2007.

Pusey, Merlo J. *Charles Evans Hughes.* New York: Macmillan Company, 1951.

Ralston, John C. *Fremont Older and the 1916 San Francisco Bombing: A Tireless Crusade for Justice.* Charleston, SC: History Press, 2013.

Ramsaye, Terry. *A Million and One Nights: A History of the Motion Picture through 1925.* New York: Simon & Schuster, 1986.

Record of the Constitutional Convention of the State of New York 1915: Begun and Held at the Capitol in the City of Albany on Tuesday the Sixth Day of April. Albany: J. B. Lyon Company, Printers, 1915.

Reisner, Christian Fichthorne. *Roosevelt's Religion.* New York: Abingdon Press, 1922.

Renehan, Edward J., Jr. *The Lion's Pride: Theodore Roosevelt and His Family in Peace and War.* New York: Oxford University Press, 1998.

Republican National Committee. *Republican Campaign Text-Book 1916.* Washington, DC: Republican National Committee, 1916.

Richardson, James D., ed. *A Compilation of the Messages and Papers of the Presidents.* Vol. 16. New York: Bureau of National Literature, 1918.

Richberg, Donald R. *My Hero: The Indiscreet Memoirs of an Eventful but Unheroic Life.* New York: G. P. Putnam's Sons, 1954.

———. *Tents of the Mighty.* Chicago: Willett, Clark & Colby, 1930.

Rickenbacker, Eddie. *Fighting the Flying Circus.* New York: Frederick A. Stokes Co., 1919.

Rinehart, Mary Roberts. *My Story.* New York: Farrar & Rinehart, 1931.

Robenalt, James D. *The Harding Affair: Love and Espionage during the Great War.* New York: Palgrave Macmillan, 2009.

Robertson, James Oliver. *No Third Choice: Progressives in Republican Politics, 1916–1921.* New York: Garland Publishing, 1983.

Robinson, Corinne Roosevelt. *My Brother, Theodore Roosevelt.* New York: Charles Scribner's Sons, 1921.

———. *Service and Sacrifice: Poems.* New York: Charles Scribner's Sons, 1919.

Robinson, Edwin Arlington. *The. Children of the Night: A Book of Poems.* New York: Charles Scribner's Sons, 1897.

Roosevelt, Eleanor B. (Mrs. Theodore Roosevelt, Jr.). *Day before Yesterday: The Reminiscences of Mrs. Theodore Roosevelt, Jr.* Garden City, NY: Doubleday & Company, Inc., 1959.

Roosevelt, Kermit, ed. *Quentin Roosevelt: A Sketch with Letters.* New York: Charles Scribner's Sons, 1921.

———. *War in the Garden of Eden.* New York: Charles Scribner's Sons, 1919.

Roosevelt, Nicholas. *Theodore Roosevelt: The Man as I Knew Him.* New York: Dodd, Mead, 1967.

Roosevelt, Theodore. *America and the World War.* New York: Charles Scribner's Sons, 1915.

———. *Americanism and Preparedness: Speeches of Theodore Roosevelt: July to November, 1916.* New York: Mail and Express Job Print, 1917.

———. *Fear God and Take Your Own Part.* New York: George H. Doran Company, 1916.

———. *The Foes of Our Own Household.* New York: George H. Doran Company, 1917.

———. *The Great Adventure: Present-Day Studies in American Nationalism.* New York: Charles Scribner's Sons, 1918.

———. *Letters from Theodore Roosevelt to Anna Roosevelt Cowles, 1870–1918.* New York: C. Scribner's Sons, 1924.

———. *Ranch Life and the Hunting-Trail.* New York: Century Co., 1899.

———. *Theodore Roosevelt: An Autobiography.* New York: Macmillan Co., 1913.

———. *Theodore Roosevelt in the Kansas City Star: War Time Editorials by Theodore Roosevelt.* Boston: Houghton Mifflin Company, 1921.

Roosevelt, Theodore, and Henry Cabot Lodge. *Selections from the Correspondence of Theodore Roosevelt and Henry Cabot Lodge, 1884–1918.* New York: Charles Scribner's Sons, 1925.

Roosevelt, W. Emlen. *Roosevelt vs. Newett: A Transcript of the Testimony Taken and Depositions Read at Marquette, Mich.* [No place]: Privately printed, 1914.

Rosenthal, Michael. *Nicholas Miraculous: The Amazing Career of the Redoubtable Dr. Nicholas Murray Butler.* New York: Farrar, Straus, and Giroux, 2006.

Ross, Ishbel. *Power with Grace: The Life Story of Mrs. Woodrow Wilson.* New York: G. P. Putnam, 1975.

Rudwick, Elliott M. *Race Riot at East St. Louis: July 2, 1917.* Carbondale: Southern Illinois University Press, 1964.

Russell, Francis. *The President Makers: From Mark Hanna to Joseph P. Kennedy.* Boston: Little, Brown and Company, 1976.

———. *The Shadow of Blooming Grove: Warren G. Harding in His Times.* New York: McGraw-Hill, 1968.

Russell, Thomas Herbert. *Life and Work of Theodore Roosevelt: Typical American: Patriot, Orator, Historian, Sportsman, Soldier, Statesman and President.* Chicago: Homewood Press, 1919.

Sarasohn, David. *The Party of Reform: Democrats in the Progressive Era.* Jackson: University Press of Mississippi, 1989.

Schickel, Richard. *D. W. Griffith: An American Life.* New York: Limelight Editions, 1996.

Schriftgiesser, Karl. *The Gentleman from Massachusetts: Henry Cabot Lodge.* Boston: Little, Brown and Company, 1944.

Scott, James Brown. *Robert Bacon: Life and Letters.* Garden City, NY: Doubleday, Page & Co., 1923.

Selections from the Correspondence of Theodore Roosevelt and Henry Cabot Lodge, 1884–1918. Vol. 2. New York: Charles Scribner's Sons, 1925.

Seymour, Charles, ed. *The Intimate Papers of Colonel House.* 4 vols. Boston: Houghton Mifflin Co., 1926.

Seymour, James William Davenport. *Memorial Volume of the American Field Service in France, "Friends of France," 1914–1917.* Boston: Houghton Mifflin Company, 1920.

Shachtman, Tom. *Edith and Woodrow: A Presidential Romance.* New York: Putnam, 1981.

Shaff, Howard, and Audrey Karl Shaff. *Six Wars at a Time: The Life and Times of Gutzon Borglum, Sculptor of Mount Rushmore.* Sioux Falls, SD: Center for Western Studies, 1985.

Sherman, Richard B. *The Republican Party and Black America: From McKinley to Hoover: 1896–1933.* Charlottesville: University Press of Virginia, 1973.

Sinclair, Andrew. *The Available Man: The Life behind the Masks of Warren G. Harding.* New York: Macmillan Company, 1965.

Slide, Anthony American. *Racist: The Life and Films of Thomas Dixon.* Louisville: University of Kentucky Press, 2004.

Smith, Amanda. *Newspaper Titan: The Infamous Life and Monumental Times of Cissy Patterson.* New York: Alfred A. Knopf, 2011.

Smith, Kathryn. *The Gatekeeper: Missy LeHand, FDR, and the Untold Story of the Partnership That Defined a Presidency.* New York: Touchstone, 2016.

Smythe, Donald. *Pershing: General of the Armies.* Bloomington: Indiana University Press, 1986.

Soister, John T., and Henry Nicolella. *American Silent Horror, Science Fiction and Fantasy Feature Films, 1913–1929.* Jefferson, NC: McFarland, 2012.

Spiro, Jonathan Peter. *Defending the Master Race: Conservation, Eugenics, and the Legacy of Madison Grant*. Burlington: University of Vermont Press, 2009.

Startt, James D. *Woodrow Wilson and the Press: Prelude to the Presidency*. New York: Palgrave Macmillan, 2004.

Steel, Ronald. *Walter Lippmann and the American Century*. Boston: Atlantic–Little, Brown, 1980.

Stimson, Henry L., and McGeorge Bundy. *On Active Service in Peace and War*. New York: Harper & Brothers, 1947.

Stoddard, Henry L. *As I Knew Them: Presidents and Politics from Grant to Coolidge*. New York: Harper & Brothers, 1927.

———. *It Costs to Be President*. New York: Harper & Brothers, 1938.

———. *Theodore Roosevelt the Man: Some Memories of the Greatest American of His Time*. New York: New York Evening Mail, 1919.

Straus, Oscar S. *Under Four Administrations: From Cleveland to Taft*. New York: Houghton Mifflin Company, 1922.

Sullivan, Mark. *Our Times*. Vol. 3: *Pre-war America*. New York: Charles Scribner's Sons, 1939.

———. *Our Times*. Vol. 4: *The War Begins, 1909–1914*. New York: Charles Scribner's Sons, 1939.

———. *Our Times*. Vol. 5: *Over Here, 1914–1918*. New York: Charles Scribner's Sons, 1939.

Swanberg, W. A. *Citizen Hearst*. New York: Scribner's, 1961.

Taft, Horace Dutton. *Memories and Opinions*. New York: Macmillan & Co., 1942.

Taliaferro, John. *Great White Fathers: The Story of the Obsessive Quest to Create Mount Rushmore*. New York: PublicAffairs, 2002.

Teague, Michael. *Mrs. L: Conversations with Alice Roosevelt Longworth*. Garden City, NY: Doubleday, 1981.

Teichmann, Howard. *Alice: The Life and Times of Alice Roosevelt Longworth*. Englewood Cliffs, NJ: Prentice-Hall, 1979.

Teitelbaum, Louis M. *Woodrow Wilson and the Mexican Revolution, 1913–1916: A History of United States–Mexican Relations: From the Murder of Madero until Villa's Provocation across the Border*. New York: Exposition Press, 1967.

Thayer, William Roscoe. *Theodore Roosevelt: An Intimate Biography*. Boston: Houghton Mifflin Company, 1919.

Thelen, David P. *Robert La Follette and the Insurgent Spirit*. Boston: Little, Brown and Company, 1976.

Thomas, Charles T. *Culture at Twilight: The National German-American Alliance, 1901–1918*. New York: Peter Lang, 1999.

Thomas, G. Scott. *Counting the Votes: A New Way to Analyze America's Presidential Elections*. Santa Barbara, CA: Praeger, 2015.

Thompson, J. Lee. *Never Call Retreat: Theodore Roosevelt and the Great War*. Basingstoke, UK: Palgrave Macmillan, 2014.

Thwing, Eugene. *The Life and Meaning of Theodore Roosevelt*. New York: Current Literature Publishing Company, 1919.

Tilchin, William N., and Charles E. Neu, eds. *Artists of Power: Theodore Roosevelt, Woodrow Wilson, and Their Enduring Impact on U.S. Foreign Policy.* Westport, CT: Praeger Security International, 2006.

Tobin, Eugene M. *Organize or Perish: America's Independent Progressives, 1913–1933.* New York: Greenwood Press, 1986.

Todd, Frank Morton. *The Story of the Exposition: Being the Official History of the International Celebration Held at San Francisco in 1915 to Commemorate the Discovery of the Pacific Ocean and the Construction of the Panama Canal.* Vol. 3. New York: G. P. Putnam's Sons, 1921.

Traxel, David. *1898: The Birth of the American Century.* New York: Vintage Books, 1998.

Tribble, Edward. *A President in Love: The Courtship Letters of Woodrow Wilson and Edith Bolling Galt.* Boston: Houghton Mifflin, 1981.

Trimble, Marian Blackton. *J. Stuart Blackton: A Personal Biography by His Daughter.* Metuchen, NJ: Scarecrow Press, 1985.

Tumulty, Joseph P. *Woodrow Wilson as I Knew Him.* Garden City, NY: Doubleday, Page & Co., 1921.

Van Winkle, Marshall. *Sixty Famous Cases: 29 English Cases—31 American Cases, from 1778 to the Present: Trials Selected and Accounts Narrated.* Vol. 7. Long Branch, NJ: W. S. Ayres, 1956.

Viereck, George Sylvester. *Roosevelt: A Study in Ambivalence.* New York: Jackson Press, 1919.

———. *Songs of Armageddon, and Other Poems.* New York: Mitchell Kennerley, 1916.

———. *Spreading Germs of Hate.* London: Duckworth, 1931.

———. *The Strangest Friendship in History: Woodrow Wilson and Colonel House.* New York: Liveright Co., 1932.

Villard, Oswald Garrison. *Fighting Years: Memoirs of a Liberal Editor.* New York: Harcourt, Brace and Company, 1939.

von Mach, Edmund. *What Germany Wants.* Boston: Little, Brown, 1914.

von Papen, Franz. *Memoirs.* New York: E. P. Dutton, 1953.

von Weigand, Karl H. *Misconceptions about the Great War.* New York: Fatherland Corporation, Inc., 1915.

Wagenknecht, Edward. *The Seven Worlds of Theodore Roosevelt.* Guilford, CT: Lyons Press, 2009.

Walworth, Arthur. *Woodrow Wilson.* Vol. 1. New York: Longmans, Green, 1958.

Watkins, Glenn. *Proof through the Night: Music and the Great War.* Vol. 1. Berkeley: University of California Press, 2003.

Watkins, T. H. *Righteous Pilgrim: The Life and Times of Harold L. Ickes, 1874–1952.* New York: Henry Holt, 1990.

Watson, James E. *As I Knew Them.* Indianapolis: Bobbs-Merrill, 1936.

Weed, Clyde P. *The Transformation of the Republican Party, 1912–1936: From Reform to Resistance.* Boulder, CO: First Forum Press, 2012.

Wells, Evelyn. *Fremont Older.* New York: D. Appleton–Century Company Inc., 1936.

Wesser, Robert. *Charles Evans Hughes: Politics and Reform in New York, 1905–1910.* Ithaca, NY: Cornell University Press, 1967.

Whalen, William Joseph. *The Latter-Day Saints in the Modern Day World: An Account of Contemporary Mormonism.* Notre Dame, IN: University of Notre Dame Press, 1967.
White, William Allen. *The Autobiography of William Allen White.* New York: Macmillan Company, 1946.
———. *A Puritan in Babylon: The Story of Calvin Coolidge.* New York: Macmillan Company, 1937.
Wickware, Francis G. *The American Year Book: A Record of Events and Progress: 1915.* New York: D. Appleton & Co., 1916.
———. *The American Year Book: A Record of Events and Progress: 1916.* New York: D. Appleton & Co., 1917.
Wiggins, Robert Peyton. *The Federal League of Base Ball Clubs: The History of an Outlaw Major League, 1914–1915.* Jefferson, NC: McFarland, 2009.
Wilson, Edith Bolling Galt. *My Memoir.* Indianapolis: Bobbs-Merrill, 1939.
Wilson, Walter E. *The Bulloch Belles: Three First Ladies, a Spy, a President's Mother and Other Women of a 19th Century Georgia Family.* Jefferson, NC: McFarland, 2015.
Wilson, Woodrow, and Ellen Axson Wilson. *The Priceless Gift: The Love Letters of Woodrow Wilson and Ellen Axson Wilson.* New York: McGraw-Hill, 1962.
Wister, Owen. *Roosevelt: The Story of a Friendship, 1880–1919.* New York: Macmillan Company, 1930.
Wolraich, Michael. *Unreasonable Men: Theodore Roosevelt and the Republican Rebels Who Created Progressive Politics.* New York: St. Martin's Press, 2014.
The World Almanac and Encyclopedia: 1917. New York: Press Publishing Co., 1917.
Young, Ernest William. *The Wilson Administration and the Great War.* Boston: R. G. Badger, 1962.

Congressional Hearings
Nomination of Felix Frankfurter: Hearings before a Subcommittee of the Committee on the Judiciary, United States Senate, Seventy-Sixth Congress, First Session on the Nomination of Felix Frankfurter to Be an Associate Justice of the Supreme Court: January 11 and 12, 1939. Washington, DC: U.S. Government Printing Office, 1939.

Special Collections
Theodore Roosevelt Collection, Houghton Library, Harvard University.

Court Decisions
Barnes v. Roosevelt, 87 Misc. 55 (N.Y. Misc. 1914).

Theses
Alexander, John D., SJ. "The Issues of the Election of 1916: A Thesis Submitted in Partial Fulfillment of the Requirements for the Degree of Master of Arts in Loyola University," June 1949.

Cobelle, Pete W. "George Perkins and the Progressive Party: A Study of Divergent
    Goals Presented to the Graduate Council of the North Texas State University
    in Partial Fulfillment of the Requirements for the Degree of Master of Science,"
    January 1969.

PERIODICALS

American Heritage
American Legion Monthly
American Monthly Review of Reviews
Argonaut
Atlantic Monthly
Book Buyer
Christian Advocate
Collier's Weekly
Commercial and Financial Chronicle
Congressional Record
The Cosmopolitan
Current Literature
Current Opinion
Delineator
The Dial
Everybody's
The Fatherland
Forensic Pathology Reviews
The Forum
Fourth Estate
The Freeman
Friends' Intelligenser
Garment Worker
Harper's Weekly
Hudson Valley Regional Review
Independent
Indiana Magazine of History
The International
Jewish Social Studies
Journal of Negro History
Life
Literary Digest

McClure's
Metropolitan Magazine
Motion Picture News
Motion Picture World
Moving Picture World
Munsey's Magazine
The Nation
Natural History
New England Magazine
New Outlook
New Republic
New York History
New York Times Current History
North American Review
Ohio History Journal
The Outlook
Pan-American Magazine
Presidential Studies Quarterly
Printer's Ink
The Public
Review of Reviews
Saturday Evening Post
Saturday Review
Scribner's Magazine
Sea Power
Theodore Roosevelt Association Journal
Time
Trusts & Estates
Variety
Women's Home Companion
The Writer

NEWSPAPERS

Ardmore (OK) Daily Ardmorite
Arizona Republic
Asbury Park (NJ) Evening Press

Asheboro (NC) Courier
Atlanta Constitution
Baltimore Sun

Boston Evening Post
Boston Globe
Boston Post
Bridgeport (CT) Telegram
Brooklyn Daily Eagle
Brooklyn Standard Union
Buffalo Express
Buffalo News
Burlington (IA) Hawk-Eye
Cedar Rapids (IA) Gazette
Chicago Examiner
Chicago Tribune
Christian Science Monitor
Cincinnati Enquirer
Cumberland (MD) Times
Columbus Dispatch
The Day (New London, CT)
Decatur (IL) Daily Review
Denton (MD) Journal
Detroit Free Press
Detroit News
Duluth (MN) Herald
Elyria (OH) Chronicle-Telegram
Escabana (MI) Daily Press
Fort Hamilton (OH) News
Fort Scott (KS) Tribune
Fort Wayne (IN) Daily News
Harrisburg Telegraph
Helena (MT) Independent
Indianapolis News
Jamestown Journal
Keokuk (IA) Gate City
La Grande (OR) Observer
Logansport (IN) Journal-Tribune
Los Angeles Herald
Los Angeles Times
Marion (OH) Star
New York Age
New York Amsterdam News
New York Clipper
New York Dramatic Mirror
New York Evening Mail
New York Evening Post
New York Evening Telegram

New York Herald
New York Press
New York Sun
New York Times
New York Tribune
New York World
Norwalk (OH) Reflector-Herald
Oakland Tribune
Oshkosh Northwestern
Oswego Palladium-Times
Philadelphia Evening Public Ledger
Philadelphia Inquirer
Philadelphia Record
Pittsburgh Daily Post
Pittsburgh Post-Gazette
Pittsburgh Press
Pittston (PA) Gazette
Portland Oregonian
Portsmouth (OH) Daily Times
Providence (RI) Journal
Rochester Democrat & Chronicle
San Francisco Chronicle
Saratoga Springs (NY) Saratogian
Spokane Spokesman-Review
St. Johnsbury (VT) Caledonian
St. Louis Post-Dispatch
Syracuse Herald
Syracuse Journal
Topeka (KS) State Journal
Trenton Evening Times
Uniontown (PA) Morning Herald
Utica (NY) Herald-Dispatch
Wadesboro (NC) Messenger and
    Intelligencer
Washington (Washington Court House, OH)
    Herald
Washington Herald
Washington Post
Washington Star
Washington Times
Wilmington (DE) News Journal
Woodland (CA) Daily Democrat
Xenia (OH) Gazette
York (PA) Daily

INDEX

Abbott, Lawrence F., 33, 220, 291
Abbott, Lyman, 8, 33, 76, 205
Adams, Brooks, 139
Adams, Henry, 8
Adams, John T., 250
Adamson Act, 170
Addams, Jane, 48, 93–94
AEF. *See* American Expeditionary Force
African-Americans, 207, 213, 263
Albert, Heinrich, 85
Aldrich, Nelson, 21
Alexander, Eleanor Butler. *See*
    Roosevelt, Eleanor Butler
    Alexander
Allen, Henry J., 48, 101, 254
Allies, 47, 168, 170, 182, 223, 225
Amazon expedition, 53, 218, 288;
    aftereffects of, 252, 267
American Air Service, 237
American Defense Society, 272
American Expeditionary Force (AEF),
    199, 234
American Federation of Labor, 62
Americanism, 81, 118, 198, 272–73
American Labor Council, 258
American Legion, 60
American Red Cross, 240
Amos, James, 3, 274, 289; on TR's
    breathing, 278–79, 293; on TR's
    depression, 196

The Anarchians (Aristophanes), 16
Andrews, William Shankland, 10
antiwar songs, 51
Arabic, SS (British White Star liner), 91
Aristophanes, 16
Armour, J. Ogden, 119
Armour & Company, 166
Army League, 194–95
Army-Navy Game, 31
Arnold, George Stanleigh, 226
arsenic, 278
assassination attempt, against TR, 26
Atlantic war zones, 12–13
Axson, Margaret, 31–32

Bachman, Gustav, 91
Bacon, Robert, 62, 167–68, 202, 280;
    National Security League of, 92;
    as TR's chief friend, 100–101
Baker, Julian, 186
Baker, Newton D., 55, 194, 231; as
    secretary of war, 88, 186; troops
    dispatched by, 89
Baker, Ray Stannard, 170, 282
Ballinger, Richard, 21
Baltimore Music Hall, 29
Bannwart, Alexander W., 189, 190,
    195
Baralong, HMS (merchant ship), 91
Barnes, Thurlow Weed, 9–10

Barnes, William F. ("Billy"), 58, 102, 132, 241; allied with TR, 9–10; TR sued by, 8–16, 17

Barnes v. Roosevelt, 8–9, 10–11, 14, 17, 47, 53, 98–99, 125

Baruch, Bernard, 166, 218

Bass, Robert P., 49, 148

The Battle Cry of Peace (film), 77, 78–79

Battle of Jutland, 181

Battle of Manila Bay (film), 75

Battle of Santiago (film), 75

Beck, James M., 266

Beebe, William, 275

Belgium, 38–39, 43

Belmont, August, 10

Bennet, William S., 198

Berger, Victor, 211

Berlin, Irving, 51

Beveridge, Albert, 49, 93, 172

Bigelow, Herbert S., 213

Bigelow, Thomas Sturgis, 178

Billings, Warren, 223–24

birding, 275–76

The Birth of a Nation (film), 74, 78, 87

Bishop, Joseph Bucklin, 266

Black, Frank, 28

Blackton, J. Stuart, 75–79, 81

Bliss, Tasker, 54, 194

Bolsheviks, 260

Bonaparte, Charles J., 20

Borah, William E., 93, 100, 113, 135, 261; nomination offered to, 25; personal habits of, 146–47; Progressive Party and, 146

Borglum, Gutzon, 48–49, 113, 137–38, 248

Bowers, John M., 11

Boy Scouts of America, 285

Brandeis, Louis, 173

Breckinridge, Henry, 54, 65

Bright's disease, 27, 36

Brisbane, Arthur, 133

Bristow, George L., 49

British Military Cross, 233

Brooklyn Eagle, 105

Broun, Heywood, 130, 164

Brown, Mary L., 245

Bryan, Alfred, 51

Bryan, William Jennings, 27, 55, 77, 121; convention address and, 154–55; on Democratic convention, 24; foreign policy experience of, 35; *Lusitania* sinking and, 42; paid speeches by, 35; at Progressive convention, 134; as secretary of state, 34

Bryce, James, 163

Buckner, Emory, 225

Bull Moose Party, 53, 97, 108, 127, 249; celebrities following, 48; gubernatorial candidates of, 50; Perkins and delegates of, 141–42; platform, 129–30; suicide and, 26; TR creating party name, 25; White, W., comments on, 50

Burke, Frank, 85–86

Burkett, Elmer E., 155

Burleson, Albert, 258–59

Burnham, Charles E., 283

Burns, Edward, 17

Burns, William J., 274

Burr, Aaron, 131

Burton, Theodore, 114, 128

Butler, Nicholas Murray, 114, 117, 132, 135, 160; Lodge despised by, 146; TR candidacy retort of, 140; TR's rocky history with, 144–45; Wood, L., thoughts on, 145

Calder, William M., 167
Calero y Sierra, Manuel, 67
California Exposition Commission, 95
candidates, 50, 144; Hughes as dismal, 166; Root as, 89–90, 104; third-party, 48, 114, 161; TR as Republican, 252, 267; TR supporting Hughes as, 123–24
Cannon, Joseph ("Uncle Joe"), 8, 21, 137
Cardenas, Julio, 89
Caribbean tour, 104–5, 205
Carnegie, Andrew, 28
Carnegie Hall, 262–63
Carow, Emily Tyler, 203
Carranza, Venustiano, 67–68, 70, 167
Castle, Irene, 73
Catt, Carrie Chapman, 129
Chalmers, Hugh, 119
Chamberlain, John, 22
Chanler, Winthrop Astor ("Wintry"), 260
Chesapeake (war ship), 192
Chicago, 136–37
Childs, William Hamlin, 48
China, 16
Choate, Joseph H. ("Joe"), 27, 118
Circle for Negro War Relief, 262
City of Memphis (merchant steamships), 185
Civilization: An Epic of Humanity (film), 74
Clayton Antitrust Act, 34
Clemenceau, Georges, 198
Cleveland, Grover, 30–31, 61
Cobb, Zack Lamar, 138
Colby, Bainbridge, 49, 152
Coles, Russell J., 187–88, 271, 284
colonization scheme, 206

Congress: of Forums, 183; Panama Canal debate of, 17–18; Republicans winning control of, 263; war declared by, 190; Wilson, W., and special session of, 187
conscription system, 193
Continental Army Plan, 87–88
Coolidge, Calvin, 261–62
Coolidge, Hamilton, 240, 244
Cooper, Jack, 253
copper strike, 227
Cortelyou, George B., 20, 144
Cosgriff, Harry H., 95
counterespionage, 218
Court of Appeals, 168
Court of the Universe, 95
Cowles, Anna Roosevelt ("Bye"), 60, 103, 162, 264, 271
Crane, W. Murray, 114, 117, 135
Creel, George, 46
Crêteà-Pierrot (armed cruiser), 45
Croly, Herbert, 22, 48, 94
Crowley, Aleister, 83
Crowninshield, Frank, 62
Cummins, Albert, 49, 100, 113
Cushing, USS, 12
cyanide, 283

Dailey, Frank C., 206
Daniels, Josephus, 34, 47, 181, 258, 283; war's edge and, 55–57; Wilson, W., and criticism of, 58
Daugherty, Harry M., 247
Davenport, Frederick, 50
Davis, Jefferson, 26, 64
Davis, Katherine Bement, 175
Davis, Oscar King ("O. K."), 135; Hughes as dismal candidate from, 166; Progressive Party and, 113,

161; on TR's bitterness, 199; TR
  telegram read by, 151
Davis, Richard Harding, 62
Davison, Trubee, 243
Dawson, Warrington, 205
death, 279, 281–85; on battlefield,
  184, 289; of Coolidge, H., 244;
  fearlessly facing, 245–46; fighting,
  294–95; mask, 280, 294; of
  Mitchel, 237–38; of Robinson,
  D., 267; of Robinson, S., 287;
  of Roosevelt, Q., 1, 238, 243;
  TR and heroic, 268–69; TR and
  thoughts on afterlife, 289; watch,
  255–56
Debs, Eugene V., 179, 211
Defenseless America (Maxim), 75–76
delegate-selection process, 114, 141–42
democracy, Russia and, 206
Democratic Party, 24, 33
Depew, Chauncey, 26, 133
depression, 196, 262, 289–91
Derby, Ethel Roosevelt, 175, 210–11,
  241, 284; children of, 202, 271
Derby, Richard, 1, 62, 202, 203, 240,
  244, 281
Dernberg, Bernhard, 83
devilfish, 187–88, 267
Dewey, George, 76, 77
Díaz, Porfirio, 45, 67
Dixon, Joseph M., 49
Dixon, Thomas, Jr., 74, 87
Dolliver, Jonathan P., 21
Dolphin, USS (naval gunboat), 67
Dos Passos, John, 90
draft dodger, 61
Dresden (light cruiser), 44
drunkenness, 8
Du Bois, W. E. B., 262

Duncan, George B., 234
Dunne, Finley Peter, 35
du Pont, Alfred I., 119

Edison, Charles, 48
Edison, Thomas Alva, 119
Einstein, Lewis, 291
Emanuel, Alfred, 10
Emergency Peace Federation, 190
Emerson, Guy, 118
enlistment, of Roosevelt sons, 203
Erskine, Albert R., 119, 287
exports, U.S., 90–91

Fairbanks, Charles W., 100, 114, 128,
  144; Hughes on ticket with, 163;
  vice president nomination of,
  155
Falaba (British liner), 12
Fall, Albert B., 133, 261
Faller, George W., 273, 276–78
The Fall of a Nation (Dixon, T.), 74, 87
Fassett, J. Stoat, 241
*The Fatherland: Fair Play for Germany
  and Austria-Hungary* (Viereck,
  G.), 46, 83
Federal Reserve Act, 34
Fiala, Anthony, 280
Fickert, Charles M. ("Legs"), 223–27
film industry, 74–76
films: *The Battle Cry of Peace*, 77, 78–79;
  Battle of Manila Bay, 75; *Battle of
  Santiago*, 75; *The Birth of a Nation*,
  74, 78, 87; *Civilization: An Epic
  of Humanity*, 74; *Intolerance*, 74;
  Patria, 73; *Pearl of the Army*, 75;
  War Brides, 74
Fish, Hamilton ("Ham"), Jr., 49, 63,
  169, 202

Fitzgerald, John ("Honey Fitz"), 173
Florida (battleship), 68
Ford, Henry, 79, 114, 119–20
foreign policy: Bryan, W., experience in, 35; of Wilson, W., 89, 176
Fourth Liberty Loan Drive, 1–3
Frankfurter, Felix, 94, 225–28
Fraser, James Earle, 280
free speech, 213
free trade, 20
Frohman, Charles, 13
funeral, of TR, 283–85, 294
Funk, Albert, 26

Galt, Edith Bolling. *See* Wilson, Edith Bolling Galt
Gardner, Augustus P. ("Gussie"), 45, 57, 114, 201, 231
Gardner, Halbert P., 153
Garfield, James R., 20, 50, 103, 148
Garfield, Lucretia, 163
Garland, Hamlin, 265, 282, 292
Garrison, Lindley M., 34, 42, 76, 77; buffoonery of, 65; Continental Army Plan advocated by, 56; resignation of, 87–88
Gary, Elbert H., 96
George, David Lloyd, 282
Gerard, James W., 182
Gerardi, Giovanni Michael, 276–77
German-American Alliance, 122
German-American Newspaper Publishers Association, 136
German-Americans, 46, 83–84
Germany: Belgium actions of, 38–39; British warships and, 44; Haitian affairs involvement of, 44–45, 66; *Lusitania* sinking regrets of, 14–15; Mexican commercial interests of, 45; North Sea blockade of, 91; Roosevelt, Q., shot down by, 239–40; Royal Navy blockading ports of, 40; SMS *Panther* gunboat of, 44–45; *Sussex* Pledge of, 181–82; TR comments on, 83–84; TR's invasion warnings about, 222–23; U-boat policy of, 58, 91, 95; U.S. invasion by, 121; White, W., fearing invasion by, 45–46; Wilhelm II of, 37, 45
Geronimo, 61
Gillette, William, 48
"Glory, Glory Hallelujah," 120
Glynn, Martin, 164, 292–93
Gompers, Samuel, 62, 206, 207–10
Gooding, Frank, 261
Granados, Enrique, 92
Grand Old Party (GOP). *See* Republican Party
Grant, Madison, 228–29, 271
Great Britain, 40, 233–34; Germany and warships of, 44; liners of, 12; North Sea blockade by, 91
Greeley, Horace, 64
Greenway, Isabella, 227
Greenway, John C. ("Jack"), 184, 202, 227
Greer, David, 283
Gregory, Thomas W., 206
Grey, Edward, 40
Griffith, D. W., 74, 87
Grimshaw, Charles B., 269–70
Gronna, Asle, 93
gubernatorial candidates: Bull Moose, 50; Hughes as, 123–24
Guiana (steamer), 104
Gulflight (oil tank steamer), 12

Hadley, Herbert S., 25
Haggard, H. Rider, 266
Haiti, 44–45, 66
Hale, Matthew, 114
Hamilton, Allan McLane, 7–8
Hammond, Percy, 133
Hand, Learned, 22
Hanna, Mark, 7
Harding, Warren Gamaliel, 148, 247;
    Hughes nomination and, 163–64;
    keynote address of, 130–31, 132;
    TR complimenting, 198; TR's
    relationship with, 197–98; vote
    ordered by, 149
Harlem Hellfighters, 202
Harpalyce, relief supplies fetched by, 11
Harris, Frank, 83
Hartwell, John A. ("Josh"), 274
Harvard Club, 196
Harvey, George, 29, 125
Haughton, Percy Duncan, 62
Hausmann, John E., 60
Hayes, Walter J., 159
Hays, William ("Will"), Sr., 243, 254,
    264, 273
health issues, of TR: abscesses in ears,
    255, 256; arteriosclerosis, 254;
    arthritic pain, 261; chest pains,
    162–63; death watch, 255–56;
    erysipelas, 256; hospital stay
    for, 269–70; jungle fever, 253;
    medications for, 278; myocardial
    infarction, 294; nervous
    breakdown, 59; pleurisy, 253;
    ptomaine poisoning and, 256;
    pulmonary embolism, 264, 293;
    recovery from, 273–74; rectal
    abscess surgery, 254; rheumatism,

264, 273, 275, 277; sciatica, 271;
    tooth extractions, 265
Hearst, William Randolph, 138;
    Lusitania sinking denounced by,
    41; political support of, 211–12;
    Villa confiscating property of,
    70–71
Heney, Francis J., 49, 223
Henning, Arthur Sears, 137
Herman, David B., 189
Hibben, John Grier, 28
Hilles, Charles D., 136
Hillquit, Morris, 211, 212, 217
Hinman, Harvey D., 9
Hippodrome Theatre, 272–73
Hitchcock, Frank, 125
Hitchcock, Thomas, 274
Holmes, Christian, 2–3
Hoover, Herbert, 39, 48
Hoover, Irwin ("Ike"), 189
Hopkins, J. A. H., 163
House, Edward Mandell, 29, 36, 55,
    86, 91
Hubbard, Elbert, 13
Huerta, Victoriano, 67–70
Hughes, Charles Evans, 9, 102, 114; as
    bearded iceberg, 123; campaign
    ads for, 176–77; campaign fiasco
    of, 167–68; as dismal candidate,
    166; as governor, 124; Fairbanks
    on ticket with, 163; Harding
    and nomination of, 163–64; lead
    taken by, 178; nomination of,
    125–26, 141–42, 149–50, 155–56;
    Stoddard comments on, 124–26;
    Taft, W., and nomination of,
    100; TR endorsing, 163; TR
    hating, 122–24; TR sabotaging

1908 presidential bid of, 124; TR supporting gubernatorial bid of, 123–24; Whitman nominating, 132; women supporters of, 166–67
Hylan, John Francis ("Red Mike"), 212, 217
"The Hymn of Armageddon" (Viereck, G.), 82

Ickes, Harold, 8, 93, 113, 202, 289
"I Didn't Raise My Boy to Be a Soldier" (song), 51
Iglehart, Ferdinand Cowle, 219
Illinois (merchant steamship), 185
immigration, 74
Ince, Thomas, 74
Independent Citizens Committee on Welcoming Returning Soldiers, 275
Independent Party, 27
industrial coercion, 207
Industrial Workers of the World (IWW), 226–27
Intolerance (film), 74
The Iron Ore, 8
Italian immigrants, 152
Ivins, William N., Sr., 10, 98–99
IWW. *See* Industrial Workers of the World

Jackson, William P. ("Young Bill"), 135
Japan, 73
Jeffries, James J. ("The Great White Hope"), 204
Johnson, Adna R., 135
Johnson, Hiram, 49, 93, 113, 139; McGrath comments on, 94–96; TR conferring with, 156

Johnson, James Weldon, 204
Joy, Henry B., 119
Jusserand, Jean Jules, 187, 194
Jutland, Battle of, 181

Karb, George, 3
Kelsey, Otto, 124
Kent, William, 224
Kenyon, William S., 93
Kern, Jerome, 13
Khaki Club, 3–5
King, John T., 251–52, 272
Kirby, E. N., 258
Knox, Frank, 48, 201
Knox, Philander, 144
Krock, Arthur, 281
Ku Klux Klan, 205

Ladenburg, Eugenie Mary ("May"), 218
La Follette, Robert ("Fighting Bob"), 21, 25, 93, 113–14, 222
La Guardia, Fiorello, 201
Lane, Franklin K., 42, 125
Lansing, Robert, 77, 95, 177
Lauzanne, Stéphane, 266
Lawrence, T. E., 234
Lawson, Thomas W., 48
League of Nations, 248, 265, 266, 272, 285
Leary, John J. ("Jack"): TR's arteriosclerosis comments to, 254; TR's comments to, 59, 125, 179, 181, 193; on TR's depression, 196
Lee, Arthur Hamilton, 39, 43, 52, 53
Lee, Charles H., 273, 279
Leiter, Joseph, 194–95
Leopard (war ship), 192
Levien, Sonya, 120

Lewis, Edwin N., 248
Lewis, William Draper, 50
Liberal Party, 49
"Lift Every Voice and Sing" (Johnson, J.), 204
Lighte, Charles, Jr., 108–9, 111
Lighte, Emma, 108–9, 111
Lippmann, A. Jonas, 174
Lippmann, Walter, 48, 94, 128, 139, 166
Lockwood, Grace Stackpole. *See* Roosevelt, Grace Stackpole Lockwood
Lockwood, Thomas S., 274
Lodge, Henry Cabot, 39, 60, 146; party platforms crafted by, 129–30; Progressive Party and, 149; Roosevelt, Edith, sympathies from, 282–83; TR suggesting nomination of, 148, 160; on wild justice, 152; Wilson, W., allegations from, 174
Loeb, Usher William, 285
Logan Act, 39
London, Meyer, 217
Longworth, Alice Roosevelt, 31, 58, 82, 133, 254, 271, 274; at TR's funeral, 284; daughter of, 288; and departure of Roosevelt, Q., 220; during election of 1916, 175, 178, 179; marriage of, 27; and suffrage, 129; as wartime volunteer, 218; on Wilson, W., 191; on Wood, L., 232
Longworth, Nicholas, 27, 178, 179, 191, 284
Luke, Gospel of, 292
Lusitania, RMS (luxury passenger ship): Hearst denouncing sinking of, 41; House traveling on, 91; infants lost on, 173; sinking of, 12–13, 40; TR's thoughts on, 14–15; U.S. response to sinking of, 42; Wilson, W., and sinking of, 41–42

Mackay, Charles, 119
Madero, Francisco, 67
Madison Square Garden, 214–15
Maine Republican Convention, 249
March, Peyton C., 257
Marks, Andrew R., 293
Marks, Paul, 293
Marshall, George C., 234
Marshall, Thomas R., 154, 177, 260–61, 285
Martin, Walton, 254–55
Matthews, Brander, 205
Mattinecock Lodge, 273, 283
Maxim, Hudson, 75, 79
McAdams, Clark, 148
McAdoo, William Gibbs, 27, 35, 86, 138
McConnell, William J., 147
McCormick, Joseph Medill, 48, 50, 97, 101, 149; suicide of, 287; TR endorsing, 261
McGee, James E., 238
McGrath, John W. ("Mac"), 84, 94–96, 104, 144; to Chicago, 126; guilty verdict and appeal of, 110–11; Lighte, C., assault charges against, 107–10
McKinley, William, 7, 26, 30, 61
merchant steamships, 91, 185
Metropolitan Magazine, 14, 120–21, 245–46
Mexico, 45, 66–71, 165
Meyer, George von L., 117, 119, 132, 138

military honors, for Roosevelt, Q., 239
military training, 57, 62, 122, 193, 201, 203
Miller, J. Martin, 8
Milwaukee, Wisconsin, 26, 109–10
Mitchel, John Purroy, 62, 76, 201, 208, 210; death of, 237–38; farewell dinner for, 254; Hillquit crushing, 217; and running for reelection, 211–12, 214, 217
A Monograph of the Pheasants (Beebe), 275
Mooney, Tom, 223–24
Moore, Alexander, 48, 223
Mormons, attack on, 88
morphine, 264, 278, 293–94
Morris, Sylvia Jukes, 289
Mowry, George E., 165
Muck, Karl, 213–14
Munsey, Frank A., 48–49, 98, 282
Münsterberg, Hugo, 85
murders, Mexico and, 69–70
"Murder on the High Seas," 14–15
Murdock, Victor, 49, 134, 153–54, 163
Murphy, Charles Francis, 9
"My Country 'Tis of Thee," 133

The Nation, 260
National American Woman Suffrage Association, 129
National Forest Service, 18
National Guard, 195
national honors, for TR, 285
National Park Service, 170
national political conventions, 127, 130–32, 132, 133–34, 137–38
National Press Club, 254
National Security League, 92, 101
National Theatre, 174

"The Navy as Peacemaker," 58
Nazimova, Alla, 74
Neandross, Sigurd, 280
The Negro in the United States (Le Negro aux États-Unis) (Warrington), 205
"Negro Problem" (speech), 204
negro voters, 207
Nelson, W. R., 48
neutrality, 165, 181; armed, 185; tradition of, 36; TR on, 15, 36, 38, 64; Wilson, W., and, 36, 46, 47, 89
Newberry, Truman H., 20, 119, 261
Newett, George A., 8, 12
New Freedom, 34
New Hampshire (battleship), 68
Newlands Labor Act, 34
New Nationalism, 22
New York American, 176
New York Dramatic Mirror, 77
New York Evening Mail, 48, 101, 103–5
New York Times, 164, 283, 285
New York World, 105
"Ninevah" (Viereck, G.), 82
Nobel Peace Prize, 20, 52
nomination process, 25, 100, 122; Fairbanks as vice president in, 155; gubernatorial, 291–92; Harding and, 163–64; of Hughes, 155–56; Hughes and, 125–26, 141–42, 149–50, 155–56; Murdock and TR in, 153–54; of national political convention, 133–34; Pinchot, G., and, 143; Republicans first-ballot, 140; Republicans second-ballot, 141; TR not accepting Progressive, 156–57; TR's chance in, 102, 113;

TR suggesting Lodge for, 148, 160; of Weeks, 138; Wilson, W., victory and, 144, 164
Norris, George, 93
Nortoni, Albert D., 49
Noyes, Alfred, 276
Nugent, James R., 29

Oland, Werner, 73
Olander, Victor, 208
O'Laughlin, John Callan ("Cal"), 12, 191–92, 201
Older, Fremont, 223–24, 226–27
Old Guard Republicans, 8, 144, 172; Taft, W., and, 21, 25; Progressives and, 128, 169; Smoot and, 148; TR drawing closer to, 210
O'Leary, James Patrick, 128
O'Leary, Jeremiah A., 171, 173
"Open Shop" movement, 223
Orozco, Pascual, 67
The Outlook, 37–38, 220

pacifism, 35, 154, 164, 188
Page, Walter Hines, 40, 42
Panama Canal: Congress debating, 17–18; profiteering from, 7, 36; TR's pride in, 35–36
Panther, SMS (German gunboat), 44–45
Parker, Alton B., 77
Parker, John M., 139, 148, 151–52, 195
Parker, R. Wayne, 95
Partridge, Bellamy, 281
The Passing of the Great Race: Or, The Racial Basis of European History (Grant), 228
Patria (silent film), 73
patriotism, 191, 214

Patterson, Joseph Medill, 43
Patton, George S., Jr., 40–41
Patton, George S., Sr., 40–41, 89, 179
Payne, Oliver Hazard, 221
Payne-Aldrich Tariff, 20
Peabody, Anna May, 189
Pearl of the Army (film), 75
Peck, Mary Allen, 173
Penrose, Boies, 21, 117, 252–53
Perkins, George W., 48, 97–98, 109, 110, 115; Bull Moose delegates and, 141–42; campaign tour ending and, 179; Pinchot, G., skewered by, 249; as Progressive, 128; Republican negotiations of, 151; TR boosted by, 118; TR influenced by, 251; TR reassuring, 159; TR's conversation with, 147; White, E., missive to, 249–50
Perry, James DeWolf, 62–63, 202
Pershing, John J. ("Black Jack"), 89, 138, 195, 199, 231–33
Phillips, Carrie Fulton, 131–32, 190
Pinchot, Amos, 97–98; angry Progressives and, 157; crowd surge noted by, 151; missive penned by, 169; suicide attempt of, 287; TR constantly sniped by, 174; war party observed by, 201
Pinchot, Gifford, 21, 49, 93, 128; Perkins skewering, 249; pledge of, 155; TR nomination and, 143
Platt, Thomas ("The Easy Boss"), 27, 102
Plattsburgh camp, 62–63
poetry: by Robinson, C., 19–20; by Robinson, E., 290; by Wharton, 282
political party platforms, 129–30

Postkuchen, Herbert, 91
Powell, Adam Clayton, Sr., 212
Powers, William, 107–11
predatory capitalists, 211
Preparedness, 2, 46, 56, 167–68; armed
    forces, 183; citizens demanding,
    92; conscription system and,
    193; national defense and, 65;
    "Open Shop" movement and, 223;
    Sagamore Hill event for, 92–93;
    sentiments against, 226; U.S.,
    78–79; Wilson, W., words of, 171;
    Wood, L., worldview of, 62
Preparedness Day Parade, 223
president, 155; campaign for, 179,
    247–48; general election and,
    211; Hughes presidential bid for,
    124; Root candidate for, 89–90,
    104; standing by, 64; Taft, W.,
    commenting on permanent,
    23–24; TR successful as, 17–18;
    Wilson, W., as Princeton, 30–31
presidential primaries (1912), 24–25
Princeton University, 30–31
Pringle, Henry F., 256, 281
Prinz Eitel Friedrich (merchant cruiser),
    44
Progressive National Committee, 127,
    160, 163
Progressive Party, 9, 97; ally meeting of,
    101; Borah and, 146; Bryan, W.,
    at convention of, 134; convention
    rage and, 157–58; Davis, O., and,
    113, 161; dead party walking,
    249; deep divisions in, 134–35;
    five man committee of, 134;
    generosity of, 155; Lippmann,
    W., comments on loyalty in, 139;
    Lodge and, 149; McGrath verdict

and, 110–11; movement, 22–23;
    national political convention and,
    127; Parker, P., ambassador of,
    151–52; in Pennsylvania, 117;
    Perkins as moderate in, 128;
    Pinchot, A., and angry, 157;
    Republican conference committee
    and, 141–42, 144; TR not
    accepting nomination in, 156–57;
    TR's letter to, 147–48; TR
    supporters launching, 25; women
    of, 162
Prohibition, 154, 249
Pulitzer, Joseph, 7

Quigg, Lemuel, 27, 102

race relations, 205–6
race suicide, 228
racial issues, 203–6
railroad strike, 170
Reid, Ogden Mills, 271–72
Renehan, Edward J., 235
Renick, Edward I., 29
reporters, TR liked by, 18
Republican Party, 117; challenges
    facing, 165–66; Congress control
    won by, 263; delegate-selection
    process of, 114; first-ballot
    nominations of, 140; gubernatorial
    nomination of, 291–92; Hughes
    nomination for, 125–26, 141–42,
    149–50, 155–56; Murdock and,
    134; national chairman for, 250;
    national political convention
    and, 127; Perkins negotiations
    with, 151; platform, 129–30;
    Root backed by, 99–100; Root
    nomination and, 122; second-

ballot nominations of, 141;
Stimson gubernatorial nod from,
9–10; third-party candidacy
and, 161; TR as candidate for,
252, 267; TR as nominee for,
128, 176–79; TR meeting with,
115–16; TR returning to, 175,
197; TR's chance of nomination
for, 102, 113
Republican-Progressive conference
committee, 141–42, 144
Republican State Convention (Saratoga,
New York), 241–42
restrictionist immigration, 74
Revell, Alexander Hamilton, 48, 287
Rhinelander, Philip Newbold, 245
Richards, John H., 264, 271, 274
Rickenbacker, Eddie, 234, 237–38
Riis, Jacob, 8
Rinehart, Mary Roberts, 219–20
rioting, U.S., 203–4
"River of Doubt." See Amazon
expedition
Robins, Raymond, 150–51, 152,
154–55, 257
Robinson, Corinne Roosevelt:
grandchildren of, 268; poem by,
19–20; TR health issues and,
255–56; TR meetings arranged
by, 266; TR's funeral attended by,
283, 284; TR's "only one fight
left" comment to, 247
Robinson, Douglas, 31–32, 36, 267
Robinson, Douglas, Jr., 7
Robinson, Edwin Arlington, 290
Robinson, Monroe, 203
Robinson, Stewart Douglas, 241, 287
Robinson, Theodore Douglas, 241–42,
244

Rockefeller, John D., 262
Rodenberg, William, 206
Roosevelt, Alice Hathaway Lee, 27, 289
Roosevelt, Anna Eleanor, 56, 60, 179,
227, 283
Roosevelt, Archibald, 47–48, 53,
220, 274; depression of, 262;
enlistment of, 202–3; France
service of, 218; injuries of, 1, 233,
237; marriage, 201, 221; playing
Santa, 264; surgery for, 237; at
TR's funeral, 284, 285
Roosevelt, Belle Willard, 202
Roosevelt, Dirck, 288
Roosevelt, Edith Kermit, 11, 25, 92,
240; answering invitations for
TR, 275; comments on TR, 277;
Lodge wiring sympathies to, 282–
83; race relations study of, 205–6;
Taft, W., cabling, 281; and TR
complaint about breathing, 278;
TR's too substantial form and,
253–54; Wilson, W., sympathies
to, 256
Roosevelt, Eleanor Butler Alexander,
218, 237, 274, 284; Roosevelt,
Theodore, injuries described by,
234, 244; Roosevelt, Theodore,
marrying, 221; women marchers
organized by, 92
Roosevelt, Elliott, 287
Roosevelt, Franklin Delano, 56, 58,
218; appendectomy of, 63;
gubernatorial race pondered by,
10–11; on reelection of Wilson,
W., 179; TR's death and, 283
Roosevelt, Grace Stackpole Lockwood,
201
Roosevelt, James, 35

Roosevelt, Kermit, 1, 162–63, 220; alcoholism of, 218, 287; during Amazon expedition, 288; enlistment of, 203; marriage, 221; military service of, 219, 233–34; suicide of, 287; TR praising writing of, 290; TR's death and, 280–81; TR writing to, 50, 260, 262, 268

Roosevelt, Nicholas, 137, 145, 244

Roosevelt, Quentin: death of, 1, 238–41, 243; flight lessons of, 237; Germany shooting down, 239–40; last letters of, 240–41; military honors for, 239; not ready for combat, 234–35; proposed reburial of, 257–58; rubber boots issued and, 235; suicidal tales penned by, 235–36, 288; TR's broken heart from, 3–4, 243, 245, 257; TR speaking of, 241, 243; TR worried about, 220–21; TR writing about, 245–46, 257–58; TR writing to, 222, 236; twenty-first birthday of, 269

Roosevelt, Sara Delano ("Sally"), 57

Roosevelt, Theodore, Sr. ("Thee"), 61

Roosevelt, Theodore (TR). *See specific topic*

Roosevelt, Theodore, III ("Ted Jr."), 1–2, 220; as American Legion founding member, 60; appointed commander, 234; enlistment of, 202–3; France service of, 218; injuries of, 233, 234, 243–44; nervous breakdown of, 59; operation saving leg of, 244; Roosevelt, Eleanor, marrying, 221; TR's death and, 280–81

Roosevelt, William Emlen, 159, 255, 276

Roosevelt: His Mind in Action (Einstein), 291

Roosevelt Non-Partisan League: A Union of Patriotic Citizens of All Parties, 118–20

Roosevelt Republican Committee, 119

Root, Elihu: description of TR as fighter, 23; as presidential candidate, 89–90, 104; Republican nomination and, 122; Republicans backing, 99–100; retirement of, 174; TR gushing about, 28; TR not supporting, 90; on TR's enemy list, 10; visiting TR, 265; Wilson, W., foreign policy and, 89

Rosenwald, Julius, 133

Rossè, James, 292–93

Rousseau, Theodore, 210

Rowell, Chester H., 48, 224–25

Royal Navy, 40

Russell, Lillian, 48

Russia, 206, 208

Sagamore Hill, 17, 83, 120; grandchildren at, 202, 271; Hoover, H., visiting, 39; Noyes visiting, 276; as poor place to winter, 273; Preparedness event at, 92–93; private family gathering at, 283–84; reporters at, 159; stables of, 240; surgery performed at, 254; TR's love for, 277; Wilson, W., visiting, 30

Sanders, Archie, 124

Saratoga Convention Hall, 241–42

Sargent, John Singer, 291

Satō, Aimaro, 194

Satterlee, Herbert Livingston, 98
Schrank, John Flammang, 26
Schwieger, Walther, 13
Scobey, Ed, 197–98
Scott, Hugh L., 88
Seabury, Samuel, 168–70, 195
The Secret of the Submarine, 74
Selective Service Act, 196, 198
Selznick, Lewis J., 74
Sheehan, William ("Blue-Eyed Billy"),
    11
Sherman, Lawrence Yates, 100, 114
Smith, Jess W., 247
Smith, Jim, 28
Smith, William Alden, 114
Smoot, Reed, 135, 148
Socialists, 211, 212, 217
songs, antiwar, 51
speeches, 213; Bryan, W., giving paid,
    35; at Carnegie Hall, 262–63;
    Harding, keynote address of,
    130–31, 132; at Khaki Club, 3–5;
    at Milwaukee, Wisconsin, 26,
    109–10; "Negro Problem," 204;
    at Saratoga Convention Hall,
    241–42; weasel words in, 171, 194
Spreckels, Rudolph, 223–24
Spring-Rice, Cecil, 39–40, 60, 93, 187,
    260
Square Deal, 22
St. Louis, East, 207
"The Star-Spangled Banner," 75,
    213–14
"Stay Down Here Where You Belong"
    (Berlin), 51
Stearns, Frank W., 261
Steel Corporation, 98
Steel Trust, 97
Stimson, Henry L., 7, 9–10, 45, 77, 201

Stoddard, Henry L., 179, 266; Hughes
    comments by, 124–26; *New York
    Evening Mail*, 48, 101, 103–5
Stone, William J. ("Gumshoe Bill"),
    195, 213
Stoney, Gaillard ("Gailly"), 96, 110
Stout, Ralph, 281
Straight, Willard, 65, 221
Strange, Robert, 204
Straus, Oscar S., 20, 50, 175, 265
Stricker, Josephine M., 239, 251, 255,
    272, 274
Sturm, Paulina Longworth, 288
submarine warfare, 91–92, 182, 185
suicide, 228; Bull Moose Party and, 26;
    of Erskine, 287; of McCormick,
    287; morphine overdose and,
    293–94; Pinchot, A., attempting,
    287; of Revell, 287; of Robinson,
    S., 241; Roosevelt, Q, penning
    tale about, 288; of Roosevelt, D.,
    288; of Roosevelt, K., 287; of
    Sturm, 288; TR's leaning toward,
    288
Sullivan, John L., 131
Sullivan, Mark, 21, 90, 124, 259
Sunday, William ("Billy"), 121, 190–91
Sussex (passenger ferry), 92
Sussex Pledge, 92, 181–82

Taft, Nellie, 172, 248
Taft, William Howard, 7, 77, 289;
    Dollar Diplomacy of, 145;
    Hughes nomination and, 100;
    Mexican embargo from, 66–67;
    Old Guard alliance of, 21;
    permanent TR presidency and,
    23–24; presidential primaries
    (1912) and, 25; protectionism and,

20; rapprochement with TR, 172, 248; Roosevelt, Edith, cabled by, 281; TR friendship with, 21, 285; war avoidance view of, 93; Wood, L., appointed by, 61–62

Talmadge, George E., 284

Tarbell, Ida, 157–58

Teddycide, 26

"Theodore Roosevelt Day," 94–95

third-party candidacy, 48, 114, 161

Thom, Alice F., 274

Thomashefsky, Boris, 174

Thompson, Philip, 239

"too proud to fight" dictum, 43, 138

Treasury Department, 85–86

Treaty of Bogotá, 36

The Triumphant Life of Theodore Roosevelt (Miller), 8

Trotsky, Leon, 77–78

Tumulty, Joseph, 68, 87, 191–93, 258

U.S. Steel, 165–66

U-boat policy, 58, 91, 95

Union League Club, 172, 184

union members, 172–73, 203–4

Union Station, 121

United States (U.S.), 165–66; exports of, 90–91; German invasion of, 121; *Lusitania* sinking and response of, 42; Mexican feelings against, 68–69; Preparedness in, 78–79; rioting in, 203–4

universal military training, 57, 122, 193

Untermyer, Samuel, 126

Utah (battleship), 68

Vanderbilt, Alfred Gwynne, 13

Vanderbilt, Cornelius ("Neily"), III, 76

Van Valkenburg, E. A., 48

Vardaman, James K., 7

Variety magazine, 77

Viereck, George Sylvester, 37, 81–82; cross-ocean invasion and, 85; *The Fatherland* by, 46, 83; TR's Germany comments upsetting, 83–84; TR's trust lost by, 85–86

Viereck, Louis, 81–82

Vigilancia (merchant steamships), 185

Villa, Francisco ("Pancho"), 67, 69; Hearst property confiscated by, 70–71; Mormon settlement attacked by, 88; Pershing chasing, 138

Villard, Oswald Garrison, 18, 61, 96, 124

Villistas, 70–71, 88–89

violence, in Mexico, 69

von Bernstorff, Johann Heinrich, 90, 173

von Bethmann-Hollweg, Theobald, 90

von Terpitz, Alfred, 91

Wadsworth, James W., Jr., 168

Wadsworth, James W., Sr., 124

Wagenknecht, Edward, 290–91

Wall Street, 285

Wanamaker, John, 175

war bonds, 1–2

War Brides (film), 74

War College, 54–55

warfare: Congress declaring, 190; Daniels and edge of, 55–57; European, 54; Socialists against, 217; sons training for, 59; submarine, 91–92, 182, 185; Taft, W., view on avoidance of, 93; triumphs of, 60; Wilson, W., demanding, 188–89

wartime industries, 90–91
war zones, Atlantic, 12–13
Washburn, Charles G., 117
Washington, Booker T., 7, 204
Watson, James ("Sunny Jim"), 252
Weeks, John W., 100, 117, 128, 261;
    delegate-selection process and,
    114; nomination of, 138
Welliver, Judson, 139
"We Stand for Peace While Others
    War" (Williams), 51
Weyl, Nathaniel, 94
Wharton, Edith, 203, 245, 282
wheat prices, 90, 166, 263
Whigham, Henry J., 14
White, Edward D., 125, 184, 249–50
White, Henry, 265
White, Pearl, 75
White, William Allen, 50, 93, 115, 135,
    148; on Bull Moose Party, 50;
    convention rage noted, 157, 158;
    emotional call by, 162; German
    invasion fear of, 45–46; on
    Harding, 131; on TR, 18, 24, 139;
    TR and letter from, 163; TR's
    comments to, 249; TR's death
    and, 282; visiting TR, 266
White House, 20, 30–32, 189, 193, 240
Whitman, Charles Seymour, 8, 125,
    195, 211; Hughes nominated
    by, 132; Seabury swamped by,
    169–70; TR backing, 168–69
Whitney, Dorothy Payne, 221
Whitney, Flora Payne ("Foufie"), 221,
    222, 236, 276
Whitney, Gertrude Vanderbilt, 221
Whitney, William C., 221
Wilhelm II (kaiser), 37, 45
Wilkinson, Horace S., 13, 48, 101

Willard, Belle Wyatt. See Roosevelt,
    Belle Willard
Willcox, William, 207
Williams, W. W., 51
Wilson, Edith Bolling Galt, 40–42
Wilson, Ellen Axson, 27, 31, 36
Wilson, Henry Lane, 67
Wilson, Woodrow: Adamson Act and,
    170; alleged infidelities of, 173;
    Allies favored by, 47; Baker, N.,
    working for, 194; campaign ads
    for, 176–77; Congress special
    session by, 187; Daniels criticism
    and, 58; European war and,
    54; foreign policy of, 89, 176;
    inaugural address of, 31; industrial
    coercion warning from, 207;
    League of Nations and, 285;
    Lodge allegations about, 174;
    Lusitania sinking and, 41–42;
    Mexican chaos and, 67; Mexican
    policy of, 70–71; New Freedom
    from, 34; nominations and
    victory of, 144, 164; Parker, J.,
    defying, 195; Plattsburgh camp
    endorsed by, 62–63; politics
    adjourned by, 260–61; popular
    vote received by, 34; Preparedness
    words of, 171; Roosevelt,
    Edith, sympathies from, 256;
    Roosevelt, F., comments on,
    179; schoolchildren's petition to,
    96; Selective Service Act signed
    by, 196; South and West swept
    by, 178–79; too proud to fight
    dictum from, 43; TR excoriating,
    2, 36, 122; TR hating, 16, 116;
    TR meetings with, 29–30, 189,
    191–93; TR's death and, 281–82;

TR's praise for, 189–90; TR's similarities with, 26–27; TR's verbal missiles against, 175–76; turning on TR, 33; universal military training and, 57; war demanded by, 188–89; weasel words of, 171, 194; White, E., swearing in, 184; Wilson, Edith, on mind of, 41; women's vote and, 179; Wood meeting with, 232; as Princeton University president, 30–31

Wise, Stephen, 114, 212

Wister, Owen ("Dan"), 42–43, 204, 257

women: as Hughes supporters, 166–67; marching, 92; of Progressive Party, 162; suffrage, 129, 249; Wilson, W., and vote of, 179

Women's Peace Party, 93

Wood, Leonard, 8, 45; background of, 61–62; brain surgery on, 232; Butler's thoughts on, 145; field mortar exploding injuring, 231; National Security League cofounder, 101; Pershing stripping command of, 231–33; Plattsburgh volunteers behind, 65; Preparedness worldview of, 62; summer camps established by, 62; Sunday honored by, 190–91; Taft, W., appointing, 61–62; on TR's death, 281; TR support of, 136–37; Wilson, W., meeting with, 232

Woods, Arthur, 62, 201

Wright, Luke, 20

Yale University, 30

The Yellow Menace, 74

Ypiranga, SS (tank steamer), 68

Zapata, Emiliano, 67

Zimmermann Telegram, 182–83

About the Author

David Pietrusza has appeared on *Morning Joe*, the Voice of America, the History Channel, the American Heroes Channel, C-SPAN, NPR, AMC, and ESPN. He has spoken at the John F. Kennedy Presidential Library, the Franklin D. Roosevelt Presidential Library and Museum, the Harry S. Truman Library and Museum, the Library and Museum of the National Baseball Hall of Fame, and various universities and festivals. His books include *1932: The Rise of Hitler and FDR—Two Tales of Politics, Betrayal, and Unlikely Destiny*; *1920: The Year of the Six Presidents*; *Rothstein: The Life, Times, and Murder of the Criminal Genius Who Fixed the 1919 World Series* (an Edgar Award finalist); *1948: Harry Truman's Improbable Victory and the Year That Transformed America*; and *1960: LBJ vs. JFK vs. Nixon: The Epic Campaign That Forged Three Presidencies*. He lives in upstate New York. Visit www.davidpietrusza com.